Managing Supply Chains

Concepts, Tools, and Applications

Ananth V. Iyer
Krannert School of Management
Purdue University

HERCHER Publishing Incorporated
Naperville, Illinois

HERCHER Publishing Incorporated
Naperville, Illinois 60564

Richard T. Hercher, Jr., Publisher
Elizabeth Hercher, Editorial Assistant
Carol Rose, Managing Editor
Jennifer Murtoff, Editor
Laurie Entringer, Designer
Precision Graphics, Composition
Tributary Sales Resources, Marketing
Courier Companies, Inc., Printing
Fotofolio, Cover Photos

Printed in the United States of America

ISBN: 978-1-939297-01-3

This book is dedicated to my family—Rani, Apsara, and Vidhya—
and to the memory of my parents.

Ananth Iyer

Preface

Why are there pictures of coffee, chocolate, cake, and coupons on the cover of this book? They were gifts from German students who had just finished my class on supply chain management and were intended to represent the 4C framework that underlies this book's content. In this book, however, the 4Cs are *Chain structure and ownership, Capacity, Coordination,* and *Competitiveness.* If you visualize the set of ordinary items on the cover of this book, you can use them as a mnemonic to remember the 4Cs of supply chain management—and we have accomplished a key goal of this book in this very first paragraph.

This book has been several years in the making. My goal is to bridge the gap between applications, tools, and concepts, linking ideas generated by researchers, practices described in the press, and tools that can be used to generate insights. Connecting these worlds, each of which has been developed by people passionate about supply chain management, will make for a smoother transition between theory and practice. This textbook is a static object that can serve as the start of conversations between you, your professor, your fellow students, your current or future work colleagues, and me, albeit remotely, engaging your heart and mind in understanding, managing, and enabling supply chain systems—leading to growth and commerce, while promoting sustainability. In order to support those conversations, I write a daily blog (http://aviyer2010.wordpress.com/) to cover current ideas linked to global supply chain management.

Supply chain management is primarily about a collection or a chain of companies that coordinate their activities and choose the appropriate capacities and some metric of competition to deliver a valuable product or service to customers. This activity is inherently global in many industries and is thus subject to the vagaries of economic shocks, political upheavals, weather-related disruptions, and many other factors. Ensuring that the supply chain keeps its commitment to customers requires planning, contracting to share risk, and adapting to changes in all functions and transactions. Ensuring that transportation capacity is available and deliveries take place as scheduled, suppliers invest effort, people, and resources to keep component designs competitive, and warehouses and associated inventories are deployed to optimize performance. These are a few examples of topics we will discuss in detail.

Information systems now have a ubiquitous presence, enabling customers to access data regarding products and schedules from product genesis to final delivery, and judge whether they approve. Virtually, the supply chain sits in a glass box, with every decision or choice documented and rated, thus impacting customer purchase decisions, the top-line revenue of the firm, and, finally, the bottom-line profits. Customers care about sustainable choices, and firms who recycle and reuse both reduce costs and attract customers. Matching information and material flows is key to effective supply chain management and sustainability.

This book is written to make you aware of the choices made by existing supply chain managers and to provide you with suggestions for alternate solutions as well as the tools to analyze their impacts. Vigilance about the competitiveness of current choices ensures that managerial interventions can be made when necessary to make course corrections.

Circumstances may require a shift to outsourcing from local sourcing, which may involve higher costs but also higher profits, if the resulting decisions are made quickly and adapt to current trends. For example, moving from a promotion-intensive retail environment to an every-day-low-price format may improve or decrease profits, depending on the context. The models and tools we will discuss will enable these decisions.

The concepts in this book have been tested on over a thousand students, and the book includes new cases developed to illustrate contexts based on my consulting and research experience. Several of the chapters are motivated by the content of research papers, which

I have adapted to be accessible to students in a business school or an industrial engineering course. The problem sets provide many contexts to test your ability to apply the tools we will learn. The applications are highlighted with specific case studies, references to websites that provide updated content, and trade and government publications to let you gauge the financial impact of choices. Through this work, I hope you will be convinced and understand that supply chains can and do have a significant impact.

This book is built on the shoulders of insight generated by practitioners in industry, as well as by researchers and students in universities. But it would not have been possible without the support of my family, to whom I am eternally grateful. I am also grateful for the environment in the operations management group, and all the faculty colleagues and graduate and doctoral students at the Krannert School of Management here at Purdue, where I have been fortunate to try out many of these concepts on students. I take responsibility for any errors and have endeavored to acknowledge all sources for their input.

I would like to acknowledge the many coauthors and students over the years who have made the journey to write this book memorable. My students and now faculty include professors Apurva Jain at the University of Washington at Seattle; Jinghua Wu at Renmin University; Zhengping Wu at Singapore Management University; Mohammad Saoud at Kuwait University; Hung Do Tuan at the University of Vermont; Asima Mishra at Intel Labs; and Kyoungsun Lee, now in South Korea. Other collaborating faculty whose insights and research influenced and are represented in this book include Professors Sridhar Seshadri at the University of Texas at Austin, Arnd Huchzermeier at WHU-Koblenz, Vinayak Deshpande at the University of Texas at Austin, Svenja Sommer at HEC Paris, and Lee Schwarz at Purdue University. I deeply appreciate the opportunity to work with each of them.

The following colleagues provided detailed reviews and hundreds of very thoughtful and valuable suggestions for improvement to this text. I am very grateful to each and hope each will be pleased with how it has turned out.

Sridhar Seshadri, University of Texas, Austin
Apurva Jain, University of Washington, Seattle
Mark Ferguson, Clemson University
Vijay Kannan, Utah State University
Corrington Hwong, Baruch College, The City University of New York
Adam Rapp, Kent State University
Howard Kreye, University of New Mexico
Paul Hong, University of Toledo

My publisher, Dick Hercher, has been a staunch advocate of this book through its many manifestations—I hope you enjoy his efforts and enable his fledgling company to soar. Jennifer Murtoff, the copyeditor, has been a diligent and effective advisor, turning notes into precise text and reminding me time and again of the reader's perspective. My daughters Apsara and Rani have suffered through many years of hearing about the 4Cs (which I tried out on them during their elementary school years), and my wife Vidhya has endured the long journey of this book from start to finish—I thank them for their patience and support on this journey.

So please enjoy this book, and, if you can, drop me an email so that I can learn of your experience with it. If you decide to make a career in managing supply chains, you will find a large global community ready to welcome your ideas. Enjoy the ride and remember the 4Cs described in this book.

Ananth Iyer
Aviyer2009@gmail.com
Purdue University
West Lafayette, Indiana

Brief Contents

Contents

Chapter 1

Introduction to Supply Chains

The supply chain of a firm consists of the business entities from raw material supplier to customer. The supply chain is the firm's lifeblood—delivering product to customers to generate revenue, procuring components or services at globally competitive prices, and shepherding new ideas from design to delivery to enable sustained competitiveness. This book provides concepts, tools, and applications to understand how to manage supply chains effectively. Understanding supply chains is important because of their large economic footprint. The Twenty-Second Annual State of Logistics report ([12]), published in June 2011, estimated that supply chain costs were 8.3% of the overall US gross domestic product: an estimated $1.25 trillion. This supply chain cost estimate was based on $2.1 trillion of US inventory carried across the economy.

But how is supply chain management (SCM) defined by professional organizations? The Council of Supply Chain Management Professionals (CSCMP), a professional society, states on its website ([22]) that

> Supply chain management encompasses the planning and management of all activities involved in sourcing and procurement, conversion, and all logistics management activities. Importantly, it also includes coordination and collaboration with channel partners, which can be suppliers, intermediaries, third-party service providers, and customers. In essence, supply chain management integrates supply and demand management within and across companies.

In this book, we will use a 4C framework focused on chain structure, capacity, coordination, and competitiveness to understand effective management of these steps.

1.1 SUPPLY CHAIN ARCHITECTURE

To present the different perspectives of this book, imagine the choices made by the architect of a building. If you step far enough away from the building, you observe the architect's choices of shape of the building and how it fits in with its neighbors: its curb appeal, its contribution to the skyline, the type of architectural style, and so on. As you step closer to the building, you observe more details: layouts of various functional components such as access, elevators, information desks, and lobby; the number of different companies that share the building and their distribution; and so on. Finally, if you are one of the people using the building, you observe how traffic flows through the building: congestion and delays for elevators, flows of freight and postal deliveries, how special visitors are handled, how security is managed, the heating and cooling, building noise, and so on. Now transfer the same set of choices and vantage points to a supply chain. This book is about understanding and improving choices made in the operation of a supply chain, at all of these viewing distances.

The first goal of this book is to focus on supply chain architecture by focusing on four specific concepts, i.e., the **4Cs of supply chain management**. These four Cs are **chain** structure and ownership, **capacity**—its type and location across the supply chain, **coordination** mechanisms, and **competitiveness**—the metrics of competition and the competitive pressures faced by the supply chain. Choices made regarding each of these 4Cs generate possible supply chain architectures.

The next goal of this book is to focus on **applications** of these concepts to manage transactions within the supply chain architecture. Consider the functional transactions within a supply chain. Functional transactions refer to flows due to transportation, purchasing, warehousing, spare-parts management, recycling flows, and so on. Sector-specific applications will focus on details of transactions for industry-specific supply chains such as the grocery, apparel industry, humanitarian logistics, and developing country supply chains. For each of these flows, use of the 4C concept will enable us to understand how these transactions can be managed and performance improved or optimized.

The third and final goal of the book is to provide **tools** that can be used to manage and improve performance of a supply chain. These tools include simulation models, linear programming models, and calculus-based models. By permitting a quantitative estimate of the impact of improvements to the supply chain, these tools will enable management to get a forecast of the relative quantitative impact of alternate choices in managing the supply chain.

Thus there are three goals for this book: (1) an emphasis on concepts embodied by the 4Cs, (2) a focus on applications through consideration of transactions, and (3) a use of tools to estimate the impact of changes. Our pedagogical device will thus be a focus on concepts, applications, and tools to develop your capability in the field of supply chain management.

1.1.1 Chain Structure

The chain structure of a supply chain for a product or service is the collection of entities and paths through which material and information flow. Its description includes the ownership of the associated entities. Both information and material flows affect costs in a supply chain, so altering either of these can impact performance. Intuitively, longer chains might suffer from longer lead times and thus higher variability as one moves upstream. Similarly, chain structures that combine several parts into an assembled kit will suffer if their performance is constrained by a weak supplier. The inventory policies and capacities of a warehouse affect the retail outlets that share the space. In more general contexts, the network that governs the chain of flows may have systematic effects on performance through its ability to redeploy flows as conditions change. Country boundaries that a chain crosses are also of concern because they affect duties, taxation, and so on. In short, supply chain structure, the first C, affects supply chain performance.

1.1.2 Capacity

Capacity at any given stage in a supply chain is defined as the designed quantity of resources available to handle transactions that flow through that stage. Capacity decisions may require both long- and short-term considerations. Long-term contracts relate to plant sizing, infrastructure investments, and so on. Tactical decisions regarding capacity include short-term adjustments in workforce, scheduling considerations, and other factors. Capacity decisions often require a forecast of possible transaction flows. For example, given the long lead times for start-up of a supply chain, capacity decisions require demand forecasts with the possible consequence of large errors. This necessitates capacity buffers or contingency arrangements to deal with demand surges. Aligning capacity to impending demand is thus a key factor in determining supply chain performance, hence the importance of the second C, capacity.

1.1.3 Coordination

Coordination deals with the rules of engagement or contracts between separate entities in the supply chain. Many supply chains involve different owners, both locally and globally. As ownership of a supply chain gets fragmented, coordination becomes essential to guarantee performance. In addition, legally acceptable rules of engagement may change with country boundaries and must be observed. These rules of operation may impact the amount that can be ordered during a period, the prices that will be charged, the committed quantities over a period of time, the guaranteed delivery time, the agreed-upon efforts and rewards, and so on. In this book we will provide a number of possible coordination mechanisms, discuss their impact on supply chain performance, and provide applications to practice. Thus, coordination represents the third C in our list of concepts.

1.1.4 Competitiveness

Competitiveness is the fourth C in our list of concepts. Managing the competitiveness of a supply chain requires two sets of choices—the choice of the metrics of competition as well as responses to competitors' choices. Typical metrics used include lead time, cost, profit, product variety, consistency, service level, fill rate, and others. For a monopolist, it is important to identify appropriate metrics to coordinate optimal choices across the supply chain. However, competition has an impact on the feasible choices for a supply chain manager. In general, competition forces the supply chain manager to think about how best to compete, given other competitors' actions, also known as an *equilibrium view* (Nash equilibrium) of required performance. In some cases, intense competition may force choices that significantly decrease profits but that are a necessary component to participate. Thus both the choice of metrics of competition as well as the level of competitive intensity affect supply chain choices and performance.

The next section will provide examples from sector-specific supply chains to illustrate the 4C concepts.

1.2 THE BOOK SUPPLY CHAIN

The printing industry has annual revenues of over $210 billion. In the book supply chain, book printing is a $5 billion industry. The typical book supply chain operates as follows ([76]): Authors work with publishers to create content, who in turn place orders with printers. Printers print the physical books and ship them to wholesalers in full truckload quantities. These larger loads received at wholesalers undergo break bulk (i.e., they are broken down into smaller shipments) at their fulfillment centers. Bookstores order books from the wholesalers and then manage retail sales. As an example, Ingram Book Company, a wholesaler, processed over 115 million books through eleven fulfillment centers to serve 32,000 outlets and accounts for one-third of all units shipped through wholesalers ([76]).

The top five printers constitute over 40% of the printing market volume. Printing economics dictate the use of large presses that can print 10,000 copies of a 250-page book in two hours with about one hour to set up the press. An average of 1 billion trade books is purchased in the United States. Of these, 50% are backlist books (i.e., published in previous years). The other 50% of the demand consists of orders for the 51,000 current titles, i.e., released that year. The average new title sells fewer than 10,000 copies over its lifetime. With 25,000 publishers and 51,000 new titles per year, the average publisher releases two titles a year. The largest, Random House, released 11,000 titles in 2011. The top ten publishers account for 20% of new titles. The largest publishers have a backlist of 30,000 titles. (For details see [76].)

In the retail environment, bestsellers account for only 3% of sales. The number of bookstores, or retail outlets, went up from 6,500 in 1991 to 10,600 in 2007. In 2008, retail returns of books to the publisher were estimated to be 25% ([91]). An efficient supply network could save over $2 billion—the profit from sale of 1 billion trade books is about $4 billion.

1.2.1 The Book Supply Chain Architecture

The book supply chain involves the printer, the wholesaler, the retail store, and the customer. Ownership of this supply chain is fragmented, with each entity's success based on different metrics. For printers to be competitive, they must have large-volume press runs that economize printing costs. Capacity decisions are made by retailer and wholesaler and determine the level of inventory and lead time to satisfy demand. Coordination between wholesaler and retailer depends on the flexibility offered for books to be returned from the retailer to the wholesaler. At the store level, competitiveness requires a large variety of books to be in stock, the flexibility for the customer to browse books before purchase, accessible locations, and other factors. The wholesaler has to be flexible to accommodate bookstore returns. The flexibility to return books provides the incentive for the bookstore to order efficient quantities from the supply chain.

1.3 THE DIAPER SUPPLY CHAIN

Diapers are a steady-selling item at the retail store. Yet, in the past, Procter and Gamble (P&G) faced large demand swings that percolated through the supply chain. These demand swings, termed the *bullwhip effect*, caused increased order volatility to suppliers and plants. One reason for such volatility was the different price brackets that were offered to retailers every day. Every retailer adjusted orders to attain the lowest cost procurement price for products. In addition, they offered products with volume discounts, discounts for joint purchases, customer backhaul discounts, and so on. The net effect was that the orders, i.e., demand seen by P&G, was unpredictable, even if retail demands were reasonably stable. The impact of these demand fluctuations was substantial. Additional plant capacity, premium transportation payments, large finished goods inventories, warehouse space, raw material inventories—all added to the total cost to produce and distribute products ([38],[49]). Choices across supply chain participants were thus impacting performance.

The stimulus for change came from the increasing brand premium that customers were being forced to pay. P&G customers paid a brand premium of over $105 compared to a basket of generic products (a consumer's typical mix of product purchased over a year). But the quality of generics was improving, and more and more customers seemed unwilling to pay the brand premium. Demand was declining, and P&G had to make significant changes to lower supply costs.

P&G evolved a new supply chain strategy. A new pricing plan was offered with a clearly stated, stable price that would remain in place except for known price adjustments due to backhaul, annual volume discounts, and so on. The new pricing scheme resulted in a dramatically lower order variability and correspondingly lower asset requirements. P&G closed over thirty plants and reduced supply chain assets such as warehouses and associated material handling equipment. Inventory turns increased significantly from sixteen to twenty-seven per year and in some cases up to seventy turns. But significant management attention was required: sales had new roles, customers had to get used to fewer price changes and hence lower order volatility, merchandising and product variety had to be tended to garner sales growth. Would such a system last? Would it be appropriate for new products? How would it affect P&G's competitiveness in the industry?

1.3.1 P&G's Supply Chain Architecture

The diaper supply chain consists of flow from manufacturer to distributor to retail store to customer. The supply chain for diapers generated large volume fluctuations at the manufacturer. Coordination with wholesalers was based on pricing. But the price variation used to attract retail purchases generated volume fluctuations for the manufacturing plants. Retailer competitiveness demanded that their buyers minimize the cost of goods sold, thus generating large order fluctuations. Manufacturer plant capacity, warehouse capacity at manufacturers and retailers, and transport capacity are all affected by the demand fluctuations. Coordination agreements in this industry include vendor-managed inventory (P&G manages the inventory at the Walmart warehouses), scanner-based promotions (where the manufacturer pays the retailer based on units sold during a particular period). Changes in the coordination agreements impact the entire supply chain.

1.4 CEMEX: A NEW APPROACH TO DISTRIBUTING CEMENT

Cemex is a Mexican cement manufacturer with worldwide operations ([10],[98]). One of the company's main operations focuses on delivering mixed cement (i.e., concrete) to builders. Once mixed, concrete has to be used within a few hours. However, it is common for contractors to order the cement and try to cancel at the last minute to accommodate schedule delays in other steps. The industry service level was poor and flexibility to reschedule shipments in transit was minimal.

Cemex decided to leverage technology for concrete delivery the way Federal Express uses global positioning system (GPS) technology to track packages. Cemex invested over $200 million in a state-of-the-art information system that permitted GPS tracking of all of its delivery trucks ([10]). This close link between customer information, truck locations, and mixing centers enabled deliveries to be committed within a fifteen-minute window while permitting reschedules up to thirty minutes before delivery at no extra charge. Such flexibility has resulted in rapid growth in a mature industry.

But the next step was for Cemex to target the poorest segment of the population in Mexico. This segment was large and required special distribution and credit management capabilities. A key feature was the management of savings in poor households that could lead to tangible improvements in the housing, such as the addition of a room. Cemex created a savings plan whereby groups of families jointly worked to save to finance home improvements. The initiative, termed *Patrimonio Hoy* ([108]), rewarded families who saved consistently with construction material provided in advance by Cemex. Customers also had the flexibility to store material at Cemex or store it themselves. A new feature allowed US-based family members to deposit funds with Cemex's financial representative in the United States, in return for either funds provision or material provision to their family in Mexico. The impact of these customer commitments increased the participation of Cemex further downstream and the complexity of the associated logistics system but potentially generated a more stable source of demand.

1.4.1 The Cemex Supply Chain Architecture

The supply chain involves flows from the cement manufacturer to the concrete mixer to the construction site. Cemex modified these flows through the intensive use of technology. Dynamic routing enabled last-minute cancellations to be accommodated. This coordination between Cemex and the user provided significant value for the user but depended on Cemex's ability to accommodate such requests efficiently. The result was a more competitive supply chain that was responsive to customer demand and thus enabled significant market share growth. Having the right level of ability to accommodate change requests played a key role in this system. Coordinating incentives also included having visibility regarding future demands through the use of credit terms to enable management of the financing of construction materials, further increasing the success of the supply chain.

1.5 ZARA AND THE APPAREL SUPPLY CHAIN

Zara is a multibillion dollar Spanish company with stores all over the world. Zara owns large sections of the apparel supply chain and manages the entire chain to speed up innovation and product availability. One secret to Zara's success is the constant flow of customer requests and information from stores to the design studios. In turn, Zara generates a constant flow of product from plants to stores, even at the expense of retiring products for which there is demand.

Zara represents a new generation of supply chains in the apparel industry. The following anecdote regarding Zara says it all:

> When Madonna went on tour in Spain in early 2001, she started in Madrid and ended in Barcelona ten days later. The fashion that teenagers picked up from Madonna's outfits was developed, manufactured, and available in stores in Barcelona by the time the tour ended. A remarkable ten days from design, development, manufacturing to store availability ([10],[74]).

Zara sources the fabric from all over the world (Italy, China, Japan, India). Zara owns its own cutting machines that cut the fabric in batches, using laser-cutting devices, and optimize layouts within each roll to minimize scrap. Independent sewing shops in Europe do all of the stitching. The apparel comes back to Zara, where it is ironed, packaged, and grouped by store. Zara contracts with independent trucking companies to distribute the products to stores that are solely owned by Zara.

Customers expect fresh assortments every time they visit the store and do not expect products to be in stock for a long time. By controlling most steps in the supply chain, Zara is able to respond faster to market trends. This also decreases the cost of errors in the forecast. But Zara may also have identified that having a fast supply chain enables it to charge a price premium for the market segment it targets. Is such a high degree of supply chain ownership necessary for Zara? How can competitors respond in the apparel market?

1.5.1 Zara's Supply Chain Architecture

Zara has a vertically integrated supply chain with intense coordination between levels. Store managers pass along customer requests to designers, who then incorporate customer suggestions into new designs that are manufactured and delivered frequently to stores. This coordination enables faster cycle times, under two weeks from start to finish. Capacity for cutting, packing, delivery, and so on are owned and deployed by Zara to maximize flexibility. The sewing capacity is subcontracted but managed by Zara. Is the Zara supply chain competitive? The company has a market value that is significantly larger than most firms in the apparel industry. Success has come from significant control of assets as well as an intense coordination of information flows throughout the supply chain.

1.6 GLOBAL APPAREL SUPPLY CHAIN MANAGEMENT

Li & Fung is a Hong Kong–based company that specializes in supply chain management ([82]). The origins of the firm can be traced to Victor Fung's grandfather, who worked as a translator of business documents from Chinese to English. The firm had a fee of 15% of sales, which rapidly reduced to under 1% of sales and became nonexistent. The company then moved to serve as a broker or agent for manufacturers in Taiwan and China, thus providing regional sourcing capability. The next step was a move to assortment packing: an order for a product might involve making components in different places, creating a kit sent for assembly, and then packaging the finished product.

The company then moved to the management of outsourced production. Companies provided design details and Li & Fung managed the manufacturing and delivery. For example, companies like The Limited would approach Li & Fung and discuss design plans for the upcoming season. Li & Fung would provide a sourcing plan and develop a regional sourcing capability that covered manufacturing in China, Taiwan, and Hong Kong.

The next step involved managing dispersed manufacturing. For example, an order placed for apparel manufacturing may involve sourcing fabric in Taiwan, cutting in Hong Kong, stitching in Thailand, and sourcing zippers and buttons from Japan and fabric shell from Germany. This garment might have to match with other garments sourced in other parts of the world and be delivered on time to a specified location. All of these shipments would have to fall within the specified import quotas into the United States or Europe.

Li & Fung takes no business risk but has access to over 1 million employees. The employees work for their independent owners but reserve about 30% of the capacity for access by Li & Fung. Li & Fung knows their capabilities and allocates work after demand unfolds. The ability to adjust capacity use to demand realizations permits faster turnaround of orders within the quotas. Also, since Li & Fung approaches the particular supplier with the expertise independent of location, they effectively manage dispersed production.

Victor Fung refers to the firm's capability as the "soft $3" of the supply chain. He explains that if a product that leaves a plant costing $1 ends up at retail for $4, the $3 represents the cost of inventory, forecast error, exchange rates, retail markup, and other factors. There is a much better chance at reducing the $3 than the $1. Li & Fung focuses on "creating a customized value chain for each order" ([82]). This represents a classic example of a pure supply chain company.

1.6.1 Li & Fung's Supply Chain Architecture

The Li & Fung supply chain consists of dispersed manufacturing capacity owned by independent apparel suppliers that provide flexible access to their capacity in return for lower selling costs. The customized supply chains created by Li & Fung for a manufacturer requires understanding the price vs. lead time trade-offs. Capacity is reserved by the supplier to accommodate demand as it unfolds. Trust between the supplier and Li & Fung and several years of continued growth enable this capacity to be reserved at no explicit cost. The ability to mediate between the information-technology-savvy Western retailers and the Eastern suppliers, operating at lower technology but at competitive price and quality levels, provides Li & Fung with its competitive advantage. Li & Fung enables supply chain efficiency, enabling improved forecasts, lower lead times, higher in-stock levels, and the ability to curtail orders for lower-demand volume products.

1.7 UNDERSTANDING SUPPLY CHAIN ARCHITECTURE AND ITS IMPACT—A CASE*

Industrial Chemicals faced a dilemma. The vice president of sales had a consultant's report that showed a significant sales opportunity as the North American Free Trade Agreement (NAFTA) became a reality. While the forecasts were known in the past to be a poor predictor of actual sales, sales had always managed to deliver long-term growth. Industrial needed to prepare for this expansion, and the lead time for plant and warehouse expansion was two years.

Industrial sold mainly through distributors, large and small. Orders from distributors generated a volatile demand at Industrial's warehouse (Figure 1.1). To optimize manufacturing, Industrial's plants produced in large lots periodically (Figure 1.2). To ensure a high in-stock availability, Industrial's warehouses carried a high level of inventory (Figure 1.3). All of this resulted in large levels of finished goods inventory at Industrial and thus demanded high levels of working capital. The demands for additional capacity would strain an already precarious business situation.

But before approving the expansion, Industrial's management wanted a supply chain audit of the entire system. This meant an analysis of all physical and informational flows throughout the system. Industrial wanted a complete analysis of every step in the supply chain, inside and outside the company, to identify performance improvement opportunities. This included new contracts, accounting allocations, and new responsibilities. Suggestions for improvement could cut across the supply chain and across functional areas.

A first step was to understand the link between orders received by Industrial and demand faced by Industrial's customers. Ten key distributors comprised over 80% of Industrial's sales. Separating the order streams indicated that these ten distributors generated the bulk of the order volatility faced by Industrial. The remaining 20% of the demand volume observed by Industrial was a quite steady (Figure 1.4).

FIGURE 1.1 Orders received by the warehouse before agreements

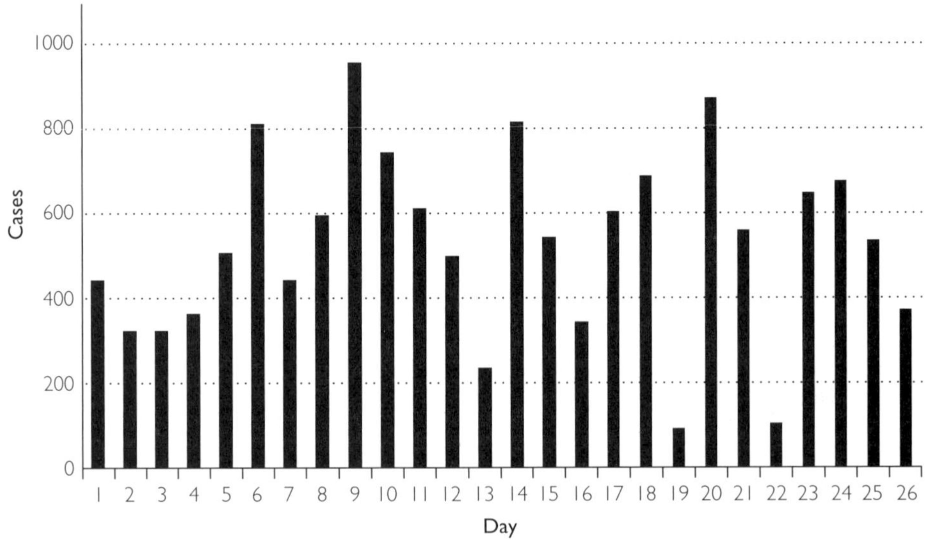

*This case is based on a description in Byrnes and Shapiro [13]. It is adapted here to fit the models and description of this text. Please refer to the article for a broader view to the organization.

FIGURE 1.2 Production at the manufacturing plant before agreements

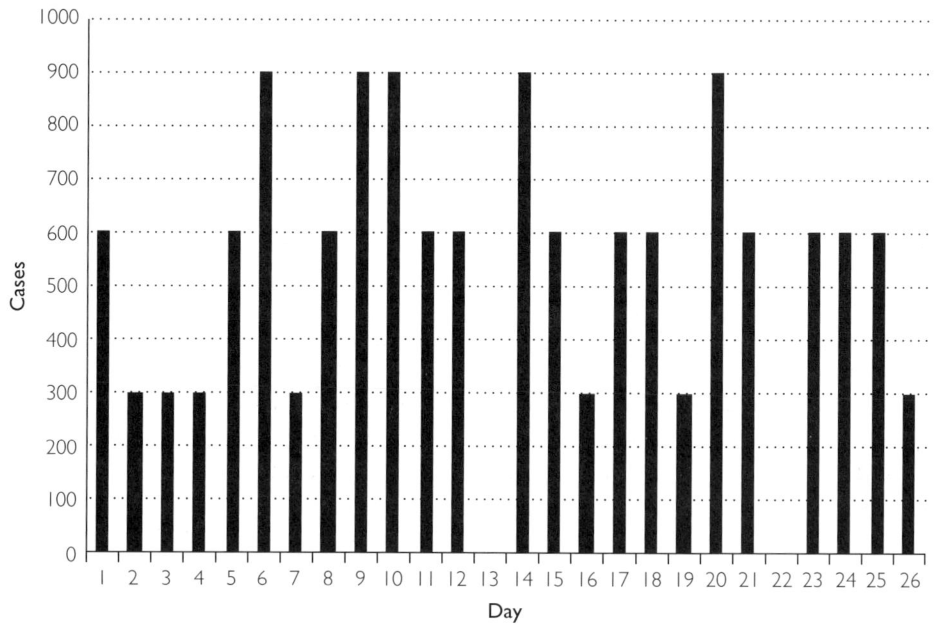

FIGURE 1.3 Warehouse inventory levels before agreements

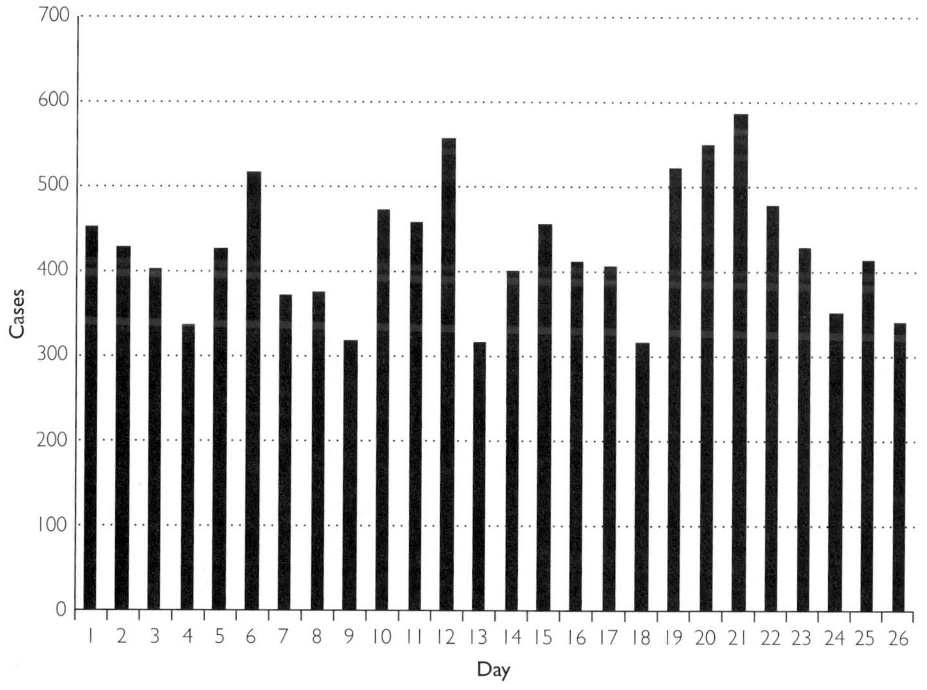

FIGURE 1.4 Orders split into large and small distributors before agreements

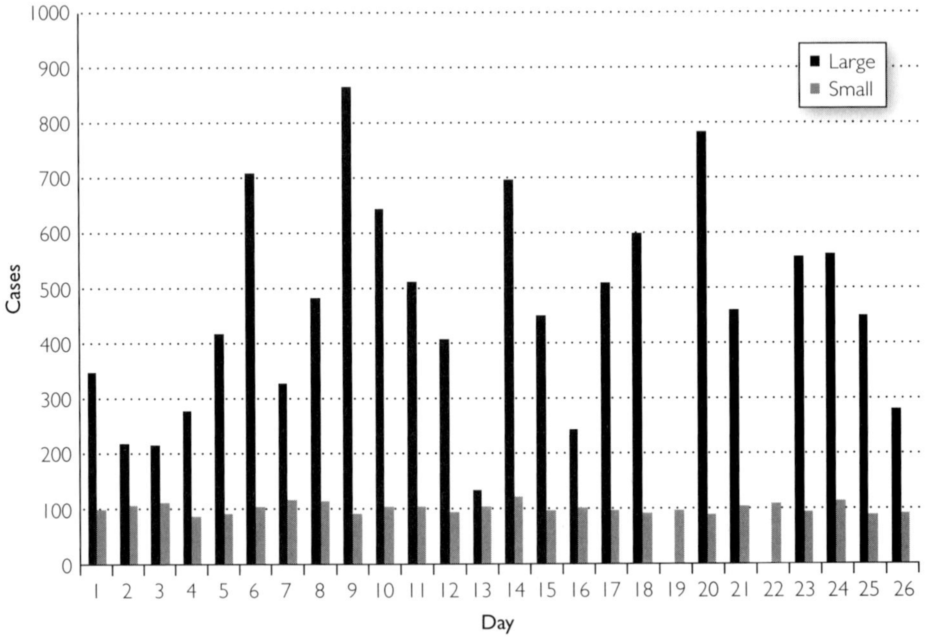

If orders to Industrial were volatile, could the demand faced by these distributors in turn be the cause of volatility? Meetings with these distributors indicated that their sales to small retail stores generated a reasonably steady demand to these large distributors. But Industrial had to identify why the distributors were ordering in such large quantities when their demand was steady. The secret turned out to be the transport cost that distributors were concerned with. Since Industrial offered large discounts for customer pickup, all distributors tried to create backhaul loads with their retail accounts and other product demands. In addition, sales offered discounts for large-volume purchases, which incented distributors to order large volumes to reduce their cost of goods sold and improve margins. Finally, Industrial offered generous return terms so that leftover product could be returned. This decreased distributors' need for careful planning. It was clear that choices made regarding the accounting and charging for customer services, sales incentives, and marketing programs all affected the demand volatility faced by Industrial.

How could Industrial get the same steady order that reflected the demand faced by distributors? Perhaps vendor-managed inventory (VMI) offered such a solution. The supply chain community had been reporting the benefits of such agreements for some time. Industrial decided to set up such agreements with the ten key accounts to stabilize demand through its supply chain. The process would essentially work by replenishing the volume that distributors shipped. But this also implied that there would be additional significant changes at Industrial's end to stabilize the supply chain. Long-term price agreements, taking over transport responsibility and establishing a coordinated transport system and eliminating specific programs for large buys were all part of this scheme. Industrial's management was committed to smoothing demand and implemented these programs. The results are shown in Figure 1.5 and Figure 1.6.

The result was a smooth order pattern Industrial that reflected the steady demand faced by the distributors (Figure 1.8). The stabilization of demand by the large distributors in turn meant that Industrial's total demand became smoother (Figure 1.5). As a result, the plant could reliably commit a portion of its capacity for steady production (Figure 1.6). As safety stock decreased, the warehouse inventory decreased by 70% (Figure 1.7). The result was that operating costs fell by 30%, and Industrial could reliably commit to supporting new sales zones with no need for new capital campaigns while maintaining its legendary service.

FIGURE 1.5 Warehouse orders after agreements

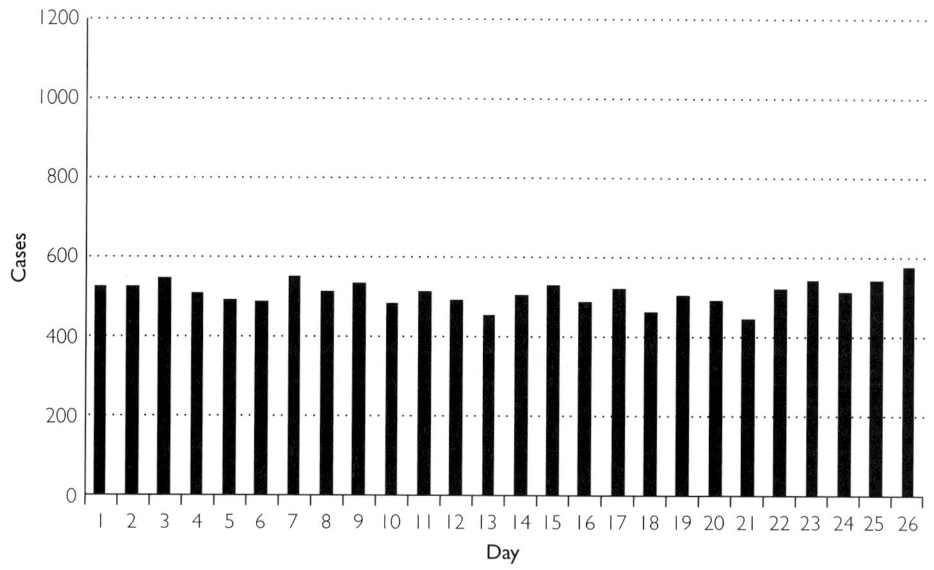

FIGURE 1.6 Production batches after agreements

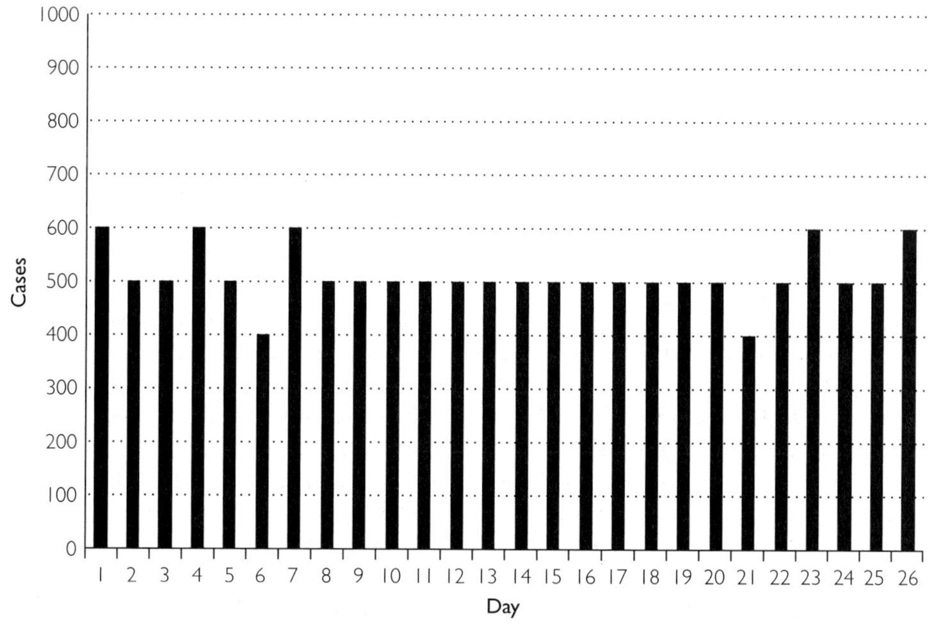

This example illustrates the benefit of thinking outside the box as defined by Industrial Chemicals and examining the root causes for order variation, i.e., the supply chain structure. But it also means moving to a bigger box, i.e., including more entities in the supply chain. The new perspective considers the link between demand variation and truck capacity driven by existing coordination agreements (backhaul discounts). The case shows the benefit of

FIGURE 1.7 Warehouse inventory after agreements

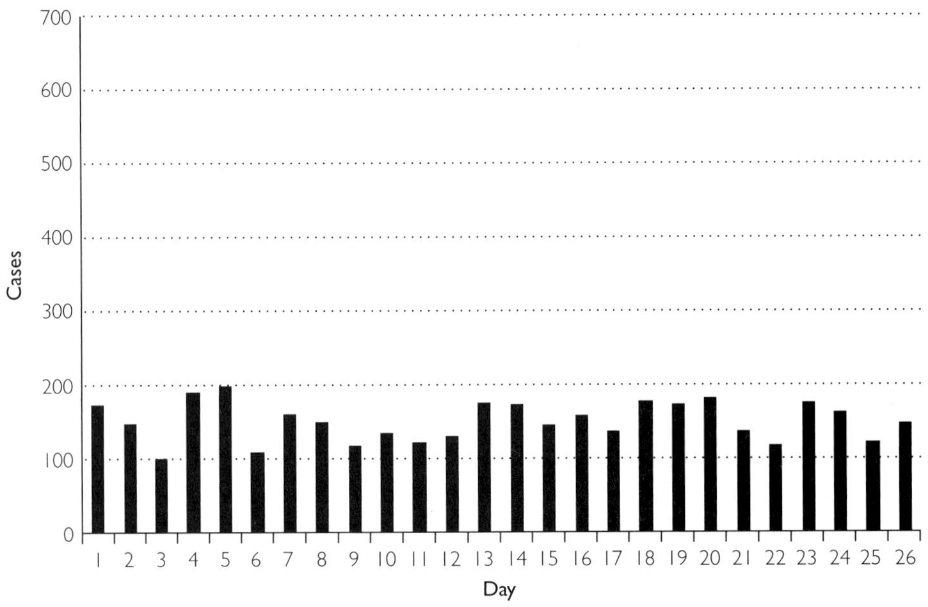

FIGURE 1.8 Split of orders after agreements

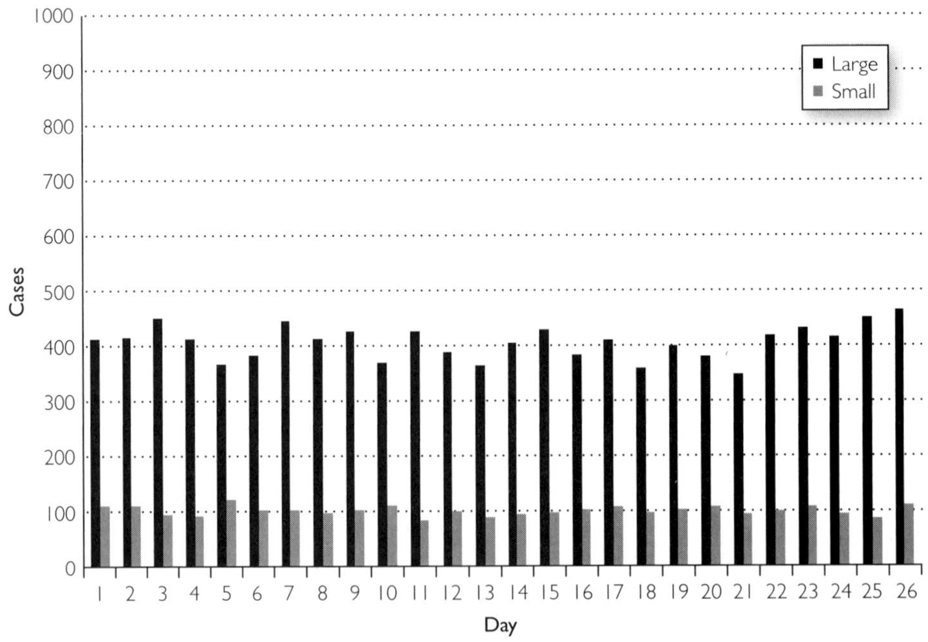

developing a coordination agreement between Industrial Chemicals and its customers, and the impact of the agreement on orders from distributors. Consequently, we see the ripple effect of such a change on the overall supply chain. This case provides a quick glimpse of the power of supply chain management to influence costs across functional areas of a company. The changes at Industrial impacted manufacturing, sales, logistics, and, by avoiding additional investments, the finance functions of the company. In short, integration across functional areas, both within and across company boundaries, provides supply chain opportunities. A 4C framework, which focuses on competitiveness, chain structure, capacity, and coordination choices across a supply chain, thus provides a succinct approach to understand the existing supply chain choices and to develop innovative alternatives.

1.7.1 Supply Chain Architecture at Industrial Chemicals

Industrial Chemicals has a supply chain that includes manufacturing plants, plant warehouse, distributor, and customers. Without changes in the existing supply chain architecture, expansion into a new market required new plants and warehouses. But a change in the supply chain architecture, through increased coordination with distributors, the introduction of vendor-managed inventory, and increased distributor demand information sharing, changed the product and information flows through the supply chain. Capacity was now freed up for expansion, and competitive costs were maintained. Solving the supply chain management problem for Industrial required dealing with coordination issues, adjusting capacity, and adjusting the competitive metrics of performance, thus influencing information and material flows throughout the supply chain. The changes in the supply chain architecture (i.e., the 4Cs) touched all functional areas of the company.

1.8 A SUPPLY CHAIN AUDIT

We will now focus on steps involved in completing an audit of a supply chain ([59]). The goals of this supply chain audit are to (1) understand the architecture of the current supply chain and (2) identify potential sources for improvement.

1.8.1 Mapping Chain Structure

The first step in a supply chain audit is to map chain structure and ownership as well as associated flows of physical products and information (orders) between members of the supply chain. The role of a supply chain map is to get a picture of the overall supply process and where the particular retail store fits. It reminds the manager that the current supply sources may need to evolve as the product characteristics change.

Key decisions at this stage involve the level of detail to include, e.g., a cross-product analysis rather than a focused analysis of an individual stock-keeping unit (SKU), the granularity of the data that will be considered (annual vs. monthly vs. daily flows), use of a finished goods inventory or work-in-process inventory, or whether the raw material and its sources will be included. These critical choices impact the 4C analysis.

As an example, imagine that you are inside a grocery store and want to understand the supply chain of finished goods upstream of this store. The supply chain map (Figure 1.9) starts at the store and works its way upstream. The store carries inventory, which is picked up and purchased by retail customers. The goal of the store is to make things convenient for customers by enabling them to get their demand satisfied immediately from store inventory (thus making their lead time zero). The store inventory ensures that customers do not have

FIGURE 1.9 Flows in a grocery supply chain

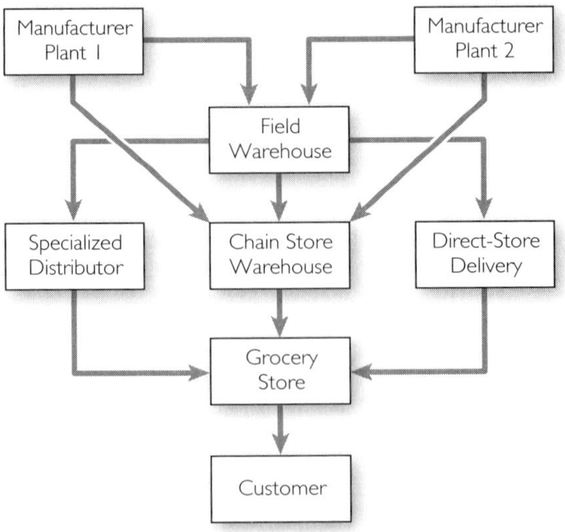

to worry about how the product got there, the associated 4Cs involved in making the product, moving it, and managing availability.

Upstream of the store, i.e., moving towards the manufacturer, there are numerous possible supply sources. The store can get its product from the chain store warehouse, which may have regular deliveries to the store. But the store can also get deliveries from wholesalers who support a particular manufacturer and deliver in bulk. The store can also receive deliveries from specialized distributors who may focus on a niche market, e.g., organics or special ethnic foods. Each of these sources in turn gets product from the plant warehouses or other sources. The plant in turn gets supplies from suppliers.

How does a store manager benefit by knowing where he fits into the grocery supply chain? Clearly it makes sense that for large-volume products, the store might try to get direct delivery from the plant warehouse. This reduces the lead time and handling and transport costs and generates a more efficient supply. But for small-volume products, with varying demand, it may be best to consider using specialized distributors who can deliver the required small volumes. Some manufacturers may be willing to manage the store shelves directly, as in the case of Coke, Pepsi, and Frito Lay. At the same time, some customers may be willing to take larger case sizes, thus reducing costs related to breaking bulk. Clearly, it might be to the store's advantage to match the product supply to its demand characteristics.

1.8.2 Capacity Audit

The next step in a supply chain audit is to examine how capacity is deployed by understanding its product-based allocation, which is related to design choices across locations and product types and across locations. Thus, we will first consider how products can be separated based on their demand volumes and consequent impact on capacity requirements. The next step will be to consider if product design specifications can be standardized to improve supply chain performance. Finally, the impact of a consolidation warehouse on required capacity will be considered.

Capacity and Product Characteristics

Next, focus on products handled by the supply chain and verify if the supply process matches product characteristics. If all SKUs are sorted in order of decreasing sales (i.e., from the highest to lowest sales levels) and the cumulative sales are plotted vs. the corresponding ranking of products, the data usually generates a Pareto distribution. Products can thus be divided into three categories: **A** products that represent 20% of the products but 80% of the sales volume, **B** products that represent 30% of the products and 15% of the sales volume, **C** products that represent 50% of the products and 5% of the sales volume.

How can the capacity associated with supply of products be adjusted to demand characteristics? Suppose the A products have high mean demand and low demand standard deviation (thus a low demand forecast error) while C products have low mean demand and high standard deviation of demand (thus a high demand forecast error). Suppose there is a choice between supplier 1, who operates with a high capacity utilization and thus has a four-week lead time but a price per unit of $10, and supplier 2, who has a high buffer capacity, low capacity utilization, and a one-week lead time but a price of $11 per unit. Given the low demand standard deviation, it might be optimal to avail of the efficiency of capacity utilization and its consequent lower costs by using supplier 1 for A products. Given the high forecast error for C products, it might correspondingly be optimal to use supplier 2 if the higher price and faster delivery is a better cost option to carrying safety stock.

This example suggests that supply chain costs can be decreased by adjusting the supply process to match product characteristics. Thus, in this step of a supply chain audit, the question is **Are the supply chain capacity and its deployment tailored to product characteristics? If not, how can supply chain costs be reduced by such adjustments?**

Capacity and the Role of Standardization

In many supply chains, products with similar form and function may end up having different specifications (e.g., consider the number of different power cords for cell phones). Such SKU proliferation can generate significant supply chain costs because each of these product variants has to be ordered, inventoried, accounted for, transported, and replenished. One reason for such proliferation across product selling segments may be the different design and procurement teams for each division that manages that segment. Standardization of components or product is an approach to manage capacity requirements to satisfy demand.

This is particularly true for a category of goods termed *maintenance, repair, and operating (MRO) supplies.* MRO refers to items that never end up in the product sold to the customer but that enable the manufacturing and distribution of the product. Examples include machine coolants, electrical fixtures, plumbing fixtures, paper, office supplies, supplies for environmental compliance of the plant and packaging material. In many cases, there is no engineering control of these product specifications, thus resulting in maverick buying or local decision making regarding specifications. The net result is a multitude of different specifications that can vary by location or even within a plant.

Standardization refers to identifying basic product specifications to gain the benefit of economies of scale as well as to increase supplier incentives for service. In many instances, standardizing parts permits vendors to reduce costs because it enables the vendor to use peddling routes (milk runs) to deliver products efficiently across locations. As a result, standardizing product specifications can reduce inventory by decreasing associated ordering costs, safety stocks associated with product forecast errors, as well as supplier lead time associated with eliminating supplier setups, which all lead to decreased supply chain costs. So the question is **Has the supply chain taken advantage of product design standardization to decrease costs?**

Capacity and the Role of Consolidation

Consolidation in a supply chain refers to the accumulation of product in a central location in order to take advantage of economies of scale in manufacturing, warehousing, and transportation. The basic economic reason for consolidation is to increase utilization of fixed capacity and thus gain the associated cost reduction. When many products share capacity, there is the opportunity to decrease delivery sizes across products, thus also decreasing inventory costs. Consolidation of orders also permits shipments to be potentially *cross-docked* (moved directly from inbound to outbound trucks) through careful coordination, also decreasing costs.

To evaluate if consolidation warehouses reduce overall supply chain costs, one has to balance the coordination costs associated with managing the timing of availability of products with the gains from sharing transport and providing deliveries to individual demand points that reflect their demand mix over time. So the question is **Has the supply chain taken advantage of product consolidation across locations to decrease supply chain costs?**

1.8.3 Coordination Audit

The next step is to consider a few standard opportunities to coordinate product flows and thus enable supply chain improvement. Assembly postponement is an approach to coordinate demand across products by creating a standardized design that is customized after demand for a specific product is realized. It permits better coordination of demand and supply by decreasing supply chain costs while enabling requisite variety. Geographic postponement is a similar strategy that stores product in a central location and moves it after demand is realized. Each of these strategies enables a closer link between demands realized and product creation or movement, thus leading to performance improvement.

Coordination Using Assembly Postponement

Assembly postponement refers to maintaining a product in a given state for as long as possible and customizing it after demand is realized. Thus, a set of products is replaced by a common platform product that is manufactured and customized only after demand is realized. Such an approach is also called *design for logistics*. This approach involves designing the product to reduce supply chain costs.

Consider the impact of redesign of the Hewlett-Packard (HP) Deskjet printer sold in Europe ([39],[79]). Before the project started, HP produced a separate model for each market in Europe and sent the manufactured product to its warehouse in Amsterdam for distribution to the retail segment. The warehouse satisfied retail demand from finished goods inventory. But given that product was shipped from the US plant to Europe by sea, the long lead time, coupled with demand variability, implied that high levels of safety stock had to be held in the Amsterdam warehouse.

HP's engineers developed a new printer design that permitted a generic printer to be made at the manufacturing plant. The generic printer was sent shrink wrapped in a pallet to the warehouse in Amsterdam where the customization and packaging would be done by loading the appropriate software and accessories. This design change resulted in lower transport costs, fresher and more recent packaging, lower inventories in Amsterdam, lower manufacturing costs at the plant, and higher in-stock levels. In addition, the lower inventory levels enabled faster introductions of new product and lower obsolescence costs. See Figure 1.10 for a representation of the concept.

But this change required that the designs maintain the product performance and reliability as well as result in reliable operation of the warehouse, whose new role included both light manufacturing as well as distribution.

There are many other examples of assembly postponement. The salad bar at a restaurant is a classic example of making the customer assemble their desired salad on demand.

FIGURE 1.10 Assembly postponement of Deskjet printers

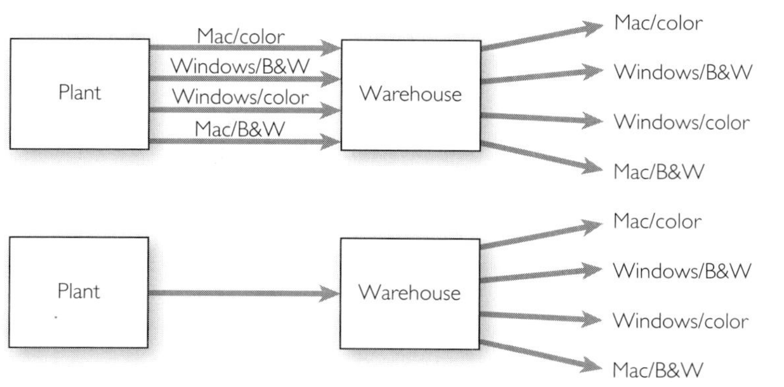

Hardware stores claim to carry over 30,000 colors of paint. But in most cases they carry only a small number of primary colors and additives and create the color on demand with the aid of software. Such assembly postponement permits lowering of supply chain costs while maintaining customer choice.

Thus, an important question for an existing supply chain is **Can assembly postponement, through product design changes, enable supply chain improvement?**

Coordination Using Geographic Postponement

Geographic postponement refers to delaying the movement of product to the demand location until after demand has occurred. If the customer lead time for delivery is short, this might require premium transportation. If not, the product may be moved to the customer demand point by normal transport modes.

A classic example is the supply chain for appliances sold by Sears in its retail stores ([116]). Customers went to a Sears retail store, selected an appliance, and then scheduled delivery using Sears delivery service. This meant that after purchase, lead time for delivery to the customer was about one week. Sears supply chain managers realized that retail stores did not need to carry as much store inventory, given the customer delivery lead time. Orders could be placed to a central location after retail orders for appliances were received. The products could, in some cases, be manufactured after demands were realized. Appliances would then be transported to the region and coordinated with retail deliveries. Retail customers received deliveries without ever knowing where the inventory was located. Geographic postponement thus enabled lower inventories, higher service level, and smoother new product introductions (and therefore easier handling of product recalls).

Such approaches to improving supply chain performance are common in the computer industry, where expensive parts required to fix computer systems are stored in a central location and shipped either overnight or on the next flight out to deal with mainframe failures for critical applications. For example, Federal Express (FedEx) has a division called Critical Parts Supply that permits manufacturers to warehouse product in Memphis with immediate automatic shipment by FedEx on customer demand.

The supply chain audit question is **Can geographic postponement be used in this supply chain to improve performance?**

Coordination using Speculative Capacity

Speculation refers to decisions (regarding inventory or capacity) made in advance of demand realization. Price variation may suggest use of speculation as a strategy, with purchases during low price points in anticipation of price increases. Long lead times for supply may suggest buffer safety stock and thus speculative inventory. Uncertain demands may require capacity buffers or speculative capacity. Product supply disruptions may imply stocks to be purchased whenever product is available. Seasonal demand or supply may demand that products are purchased and inventoried when "in season." Inventories may also have to be held to smooth production.

Consumer examples of speculative inventory include decisions to stock up on grocery products during a sale. Similarly, Chapter 9 on grocery supply chains highlights optimal retail warehouse purchases during trade promotions, with large increases in inventory and thus additional required warehouse capacity. Firms that build up inventory in anticipation of a strike or production disruptions during changeover use speculative capacity to buffer the impact.

Thus, the supply chain audit question is **Can speculative capacity or inventory be used to improve supply chain performance?**

1.8.4 Competitiveness Metric of the Supply Chain

What is the basis of competition for the supply chain? For purposes of illustration, we will use cost as a metric of performance, but many other possible choices (e.g., time, days of inventory) could also be the relevant metric. Consider the cost impact on the product as it moves through the supply chain. Examine how costs are added as each of the entities in the supply chain impact the product.

We provide an example for a medical supply manufacturer in Japan. This manufacturer first mapped the supply chain (Figure 1.11). The supply chain (on the left side of the figure) showed that the manufacturer produced the product and sold it to distributors. The distributors carried products made by this supplier as well as products made by many other suppliers. By providing one-stop shopping for all products, the distributors made procurement easy for the health care providers. The health care providers sold products to health care professionals, who in turn used them to treat patients.

The medical supply manufacturer asked a consulting firm to identify the total costs as the product moved through the supply chain. The right side of Figure 1.11 shows the costs added due to warehousing, transportation, inventory, and administration as the product moves through the supply chain. The data showed that about 45% of the costs were added after the product left the manufacturer.

FIGURE 1.11 Medical supply system before changes

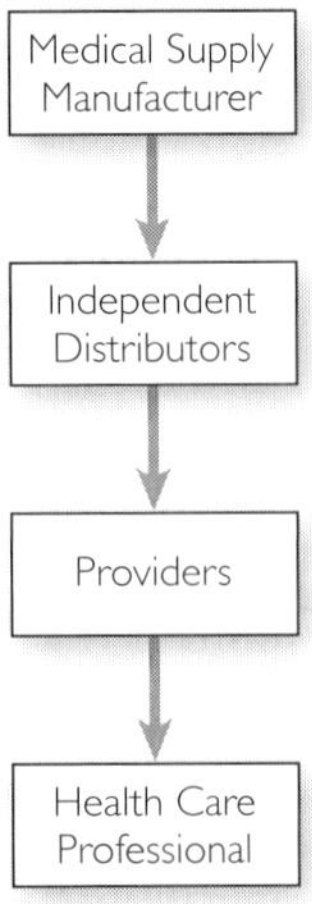

Channel Costs (Millions)

	Manufacturer	Distributors	Providers	Total
Warehousing	$10.3	$7.1	+	$17.4+
Transportation	21.2	8.3	–	29.5
Inventory	9.2	12.2	9.3	30.7
Administration	6.3	4.0	+	10.3
	$47.0	$31.6	$9.3+	$87.9+

The question now is **Which of the supply chain entities is affected by these added costs?** For the manufacturer, these added costs meant lower margins as well as greater potential for competitors to enter the market. The end customers (patients) cared because the supply chain inefficiencies meant higher costs.

But what could be done to improve the supply chain? The manufacturer studied the source of the costs and decided that the problem was the *one-size-fits-all* approach implied by the original supply chain. Because all products followed the same path in going from the manufacturer to the customer, the associated supply was not matched to demand patterns.

An alternative approach (Figure 1.12) was to permit multiple approaches to get the product to downstream customers, relative to the nature of the demands. Thus, a wholesaler who ships large volumes of product to a large health care provider could get product directly without going through a distributor. In some cases the product could be shipped directly to the health care professional, thus eliminating some steps in the process.

The net effect of the changes in the supply chain was to provide a more finely tuned link between supply and demand by product type. The impact on the supply chain was projected to be $14 million (out of $87.9 million spent). The impacts on individual steps in the supply chain are as shown in Figure 1.12. This example shows how supply chain structure and its adjustment can impact cost competitiveness.

1.8.5 Impact of Competitors on the Supply Chain

Consider how competitors impact a supply chain ([59]). Use the following questions to check performance relative to competitors.

1. How do our product attributes match customer requirements? How do our competitors' product attributes match customer requirements?

   The goal of this question is to understand whether there are differences in the extent to which our offerings and the offerings of the competition match the attributes demanded by our customers. The relevant attributes could include the extent of product customization to buyer requirements, the buyer-delivery flexibility vs. the delivery offered, and buyer preferences for the level of

FIGURE 1.12 Medical supply system after changes

Revised Structure

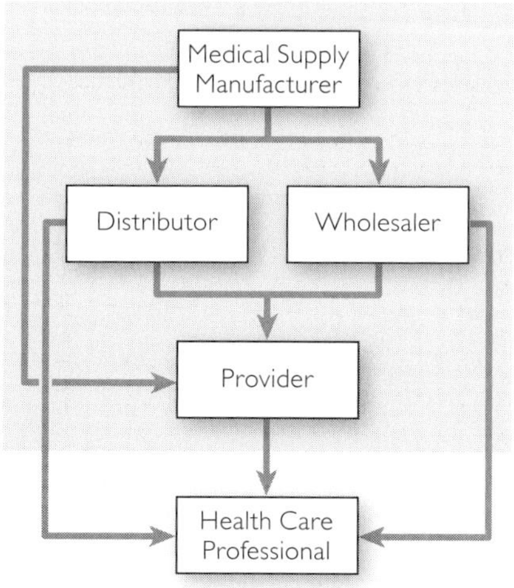

Channel Costs (Millions)

	Old System	Integration	Reduction
Warehousing	$17.4	$15.0	$2.4
Transportation	29.5	26.9	2.6
Inventory	30.7	22.6	8.1
Administration	10.3	9.2	1.1
	$87.9	$73.7	$14.2

involvement in the supply chain vs. the level currently offered across the industry.

2. How do our competitors offer the service they do or how do the customers perceive they offer it?

   The goal of this question is to compare customer perceptions of service offered by our competitors to the service we offer. Can differences in perceived service be traced to strategic choices in product attributes we make vs. those made by our competitors? As an example, if we offer customized products while our competitors offer off-the-shelf solutions, then we should expect customers to face higher lead times for our products vs. our competitors' products. After analyzing the response to this question, one should decide whether to maintain or adjust product characteristics to match the competition.

3. Where in the product life cycle do our products sit, and how have we adjusted our supply chain strategy to match? Where are the competitors' products located in their life cycle?

   It is clear that the operation of a supply chain during product introduction and ramp-up is quite different from the operation during product phase-out. As the product reaches the end of its life cycle, it may be appropriate to reduce inventories throughout the chain at the expense of slightly higher lead times (through, for example, geographic postponement). At the same time, pricing of new and old products may have to be managed to permit new product demand to grow without being cannibalized by old products. All of this requires a planned supply chain strategy for product phase-in and phase-out. This step checks if these strategies are in place in the supply chain. By considering the life cycle position of our products and comparing it to our competitors' products, we ensure that our supply chain is competitive through time.

4. How coordinated are the supply chain choices with the company strategy? How does this differ from our competitors? If our competitors have a coordinated supply chain and we do not, then the relative efficiency of competitors may require coordination of our supply chain. Note that the coordination of all competing supply chains does not guarantee improved profits, but only suggests a competitive necessity. The decision then is whether to continue to engage as needed or to change market focus.

1.9 CHAPTER SUMMARY

This chapter focused on examples of supply chains and their underlying supply chain architecture, using a 4C conceptual framework. The 4Cs refer to chain structure and ownership, capacity, coordination, and competitiveness. The supply chain audit permits an understanding of current choices and an approach to evaluate alternate choices for supply chain architecture. The goal of this chapter was to explain the 4C choices made in different successful supply chain contexts.

1.10 PROBLEMS

1. Precise is an automobile subassembly company located in Lafayette, IN. The company has requested a supply chain audit to enable it to identify ways to improve its performance, given the economic downturn. Data regarding the supply chain are provided below.

Precise imports ten components—five from suppliers in China and five from suppliers in Europe. An examination of these suppliers shows that all of them use a component supplied by a supplier located in Kokomo, IN. In turn, the supplier in Kokomo imports components from suppliers in India. The products made by Precise are shipped to automobile assembly plants located across the United States. Currently all products are made to assembly plant forecast, and Precise carries inventory to hedge against demand and delivery fluctuations. All deliveries are direct from supplier to Precise, i.e., point to point and full loads. Shipments are made using the cheapest mode of transport (i.e., by ship) and thus have a lead time of six weeks.

Precise competes to provide just-in-time (JIT) delivery to the assembly plant and is responsible to provide a 100% service level. Any delivery delays cause the assembly plant to shut down. To prevent this, Precise purchases delivery guarantee contracts from trucking companies that make deliveries within specific time windows.

Precise has been facing price and delivery competition from Prompt, a new vendor. Prompt delivers a less customized product to the assembly plant, a simpler design that can be supplied to a greater variety of assemblers. However, Prompt permits a smaller delivery time window and has located a warehouse near many of the assembly plants to provide faster turnaround at lower cost.

All deliveries to assembly plants are with wholesale price contracts. This has often resulted in Precise being forced to make decisions that are not optimal for the company in order to keep up with the competition.

Provide a supply chain audit of the system along with suggestions to improve performance.

2. Read the following and then answer the questions.

Under the just-in-time II (JIT II) system developed by Bose Corporation, the supplier provides an in-plant person who resides in Bose's facility. The in-plant representative coordinates the placement of orders from Bose with his company and does concurrent planning and adjusts order deliveries to serve Bose's demands. In turn, Bose provides an evergreen contract that lasts for a period of time (e.g., four years), requires some price reductions, and permits the in-plant personnel to participate in product design, material selection, and access to all Bose personnel and meetings.

Bose has used JIT II for a number of products. Note that under JIT, suppliers still get forecasts and have to use those forecasts to make decisions. However, forecasts are imprecise, often off by 10% to 15%, which requires suppliers to scramble. JIT II takes the next step from JIT by permitting in-plant personnel and hence suppliers to have an idea of demand trends before the orders are placed.

An in-plant from a supplier of plastic components suggests that under JIT II he be allowed to see demand data and have the flexibility to adjust shipment timings and quantity so that the supplier production runs are efficient. He can also build up inventory in anticipation of other orders to his manufacturing system. This concurrent planning is a major source of benefits for this supplier.

An in-plant from a transportation provider claims that her terminals at Bose permit information to replace Bose inventory. Knowing when the deliveries are expected allows Bose to reliably use in-transit inventory to satisfy production demand so that the company can operate with low physical inventories. Also the transport company can possibly gain work from Bose's suppliers and customers.

About 65% of Bose's customers are located outside the United States. An in-plant import and export specialist at Bose has data regarding order shipments and deliveries. Quick and timely access to information enables him to manage the international shipping operations and plan and react to contingencies.

An in-plant from a printing company works with orders from Bose's departments and coordinates the order placement, scheduling, and receipt between Bose departments to minimize overhead costs. Fixed prices reduce any need for Bose personnel.

Bose's senior management believes that JIT II enables Bose to have control without investing in vertically integrated assets.

2a. Provide a 4C Supply Chain Audit of this case.

2b. How does JIT II help the supplier? What tradeoffs does the supplier have to consider in choosing whether or not to be involved in JIT II with Bose?

2c. How does JIT II help Bose?

2d. Can the JIT II scheme be structured to benefit both Bose and the supplier? Explain.

2e. How is JIT II different from JIT?

2f. For what products would you expect JIT II to be suitable? For what products would it not be suitable? Explain.

Supply Chain Management Impact at Best Cookies

SCENARIO 1

Best Cookies is a manufacturer and distributor of cookies sold for fundraising purposes. Students go around to homes, selling these cookies. As these cookies are purchased, the students earn money from the sales for their organizations. Best Cookies gets orders from schools, churches, Little League clubs (similar to Girl Scout Cookies). These organizations are Best's customers. Best manufactures these cookies and creates a customized package with the name of the school or club and the specific fundraising activity. Orders are grouped together by customer, and Best ships one package containing the customer order, to each customer. These products are sold on consignment. Thus leftover product can be returned to Best Cookies.

In reality Best stores some "bright" packs at regional distribution centers (DCs). Large shipments go from Best's plants to the regional DCs and are shipped from there in small loads to individual customers. Last-minute orders are shipped from the DC, and small-volume labels are printed manually at the DC.

SCENARIO 2

Best has realized that demand for food purchased to support fundraising activity is declining. Best has thus created a new product, a catalog containing gift wrap, bows, and cookies that will be carried to homes by students. Individuals place their orders, which are transmitted to Best. Best orders the wrapping paper and bows from an Asian supplier who has an eight-month lead time. Packages are not customized for each school. However, Best now creates a pack of orders for each student who generates the orders. The student opens the box, chooses what was ordered by a particular home, delivers the product, and picks up the money. Goods are no longer sold on consignment by Best; all orders are received by Best and consist of firm individual orders. Picked orders are shipped to schools. The individuals placing orders now wait two weeks to receive their order.

CASE QUESTIONS

1. Provide an audit of the supply chain for scenario 1.
2. What should a supply chain manager "manage" in scenario 1 to generate a profitable system? What are the key bottlenecks in scenario 1?
3. Provide an audit of the supply chain for scenario 2.
4. What should a supply chain manager "manage" in scenario 2 to generate a profitable system? What are the key bottlenecks in scenario 2?
5. Should Best Cookies change the supply chain and move to the system in scenario 2? Explain your recommendation.

Winstar Gear—Uncovering Value in the Supply Chain

It was 7 a.m. on Monday, and Joe Morgan, CEO of Winstar Gear, entered the conference room agitated. He was a senior member of the local chamber of commerce and was scheduled to receive a businessman of the year award that weekend. What had upset him was a feature article in *Purchasing Index* magazine that focused on Winstar Gear with the headline "Custom Gear Manufacturer Fails Competitiveness Test." The same article was being reprinted in the local newspaper the day Joe was scheduled to receive his award. A copy of the article is attached below.

Custom Gear Manufacturer Fails Competitiveness Test

Winstar Gear, headquartered in Lafayette, Indiana, finished tenth out a possible ten in a study of gear manufacturers. The study was carried out by staff at *Purchasing Index* magazine, read by 50,000 purchasing professionals. The study analyzed ten gear manufacturers who produce 60% of the dollar sales in that category. Winstar scored a 4 out of a maximum of 10 in a supply chain capability index. The data for the analysis were collected from a survey of 5,000 purchasing professionals. A consultant, Hans Preckel, was quoted, "Obviously Winstar does not get it when it comes to supply chain management. Most modern CEOs recognize that developing an effective supply chain demands boardroom attention. I wonder if Joe Morgan knows the metrics of his supply chain or even if it is aligned with his customer's needs. He may be losing the market tomorrow and not even know it today."

"I have five reporters wanting to know if I have an effective supply chain strategy," thundered Joe. "And I want all of you to help me provide answers." Joe surveyed the room filled with his senior management team: Pat Methany, CFO; Jill Zwetz, VP Finance; Pedro Garcia, VP Marketing and Sales; and President Barney Sanders. Missing from the group was Jim Brush, VP Operations, who had resigned unexpectedly and gone off to explore the Andean mountains.

"I want you folks to generate some answers, and I want metrics, numbers, graphs, analysis—everything you can get done by the end of this week. We are going to hit the business hard with facts—and we WILL have a plan. What's more, I want us to sponsor a more detailed study that explains things to our stakeholders—and in plain English with no jargon. We will develop an SCM strategy that shows where we stand and how we will improve. That's it folks—you have work to do. With no Jim Brush to depend on, it's up to you all to shoulder this load. Barney will coordinate, but each of you has to pitch in and learn in a rush."

Barney took over. "What is supply chain management? I want each of you to write down what it means to you and to us as a company. Do a logistics audit and explain if we have one supply chain or many different ones. Do we have different products requiring different supply chains? Finally, recommend some things we can start planning right away. If required, we will create a new VP of supply chain management who can get things done for us."

Jill Zwetz spoke. "As far as I can tell, our customers gave us a great rating on value. We were top of the heap. But I do think we went too far with our attempts at keeping our distributors happy." Pat Methany concurred. "Being all things to all people is hurting our business. Do we need to provide superlative service even to our cost-conscious customers?" Pedro Garcia was the lone dissenter: "We are responding to what our competition is offering to our customers. Winstar does not sell products on an island. We are out there offering more to win orders. We'd better figure out how to do that and make money—not cut service and expect sales to remain where it is."

Winstar sold a mix of custom gears as well as off-the-shelf regular sizes—a commodity. Joe believed in being a full-service provider. "After all," he said, "every machine or product used a mix of custom and off-the-shelf gears and I want OEMs to come to us for all of their needs." Margins were 50% in the custom gear segment but orders required delivery of the entire kit of gears in the order. Commodity gear had 10% margins. In reality all custom gear consisted of four types, and Winstar satisfied customer orders from finished gear inventory at its warehouses.

Winstar was also a player in the machine tools aftermarket. Winstar sold through distributors who provided entire catalogs to their customers and inventoried regular sizes, but passed along orders for unique sizes. Winstar also had a fleet of salespeople who called on machine tool shops and delivered door to door if needed. There was also a hobby crowd of repairmen who ordered from the website.

Tables 1.1 to 1.6 provide more data regarding the supply chain.

Competition had been pushing Winstar Gear to offer four-day delivery to their larger distributors of all products. Smaller machine shop operators were also demanding faster turnarounds—the salespeople promised one week, but it often took longer. Distributors demanded priority processing, discounts, and full order delivery—no split shipments.

Understandably, production wanted long runs of product to reduce costs. Jim Brush had permitted plant managers to focus on one gear type each. Given there were four gear types, that meant that focused manufacturing at each plant as shown in Table 1.5. Each plant had a warehouse in its town, and that warehouse carried inventory of all of the four gear

TABLE 1.1 Annual product sales, in units

Gear Number	Annual Units Sold	
A	296,400	These four are custom gear numbers.
B	312,000	
C	468,000	
D	338,000	
141	185,714	These are commodity gear numbers.
151	185,714	
161	185,714	
171	185,714	
181	185,714	
191	185,714	
OTHERS—Commodity	185,714	

TABLE 1.2 Weekly demand information

GEAR/REGION	WEST		EAST		MIDWEST		SOUTH	
	Mean	Std Dev	Mean	Std Dev	Mean	Std Dev	Mean	Std Dev
A	2,000	1,000	700	400	1,000	500	2,000	100
B	3,000	1,000	1,000	250	1,000	500	1,000	250
C	1,000	300	4,000	1,000	2,000	500	2,000	1,000
D	500	200	3,000	200	2,000	500	1,000	100
Commodity	5,000	1,000	8,000	1,000	10,000	1,000	2,000	500

TABLE 1.3 Cost of components for custom gears

Component	$ Cost
Steel	20
Labor	20
Machine additives	3
Packaging	2

TABLE 1.4 Holding cost (includes storage and cost of capital) and transport cost

Holding cost	25% per year	
Transport cost	5	Dollars per unit from warehouse to customer
	2	Dollars per unit from plant to consolidation warehouse if full truckload
	5,000	Truck capacity

TABLE 1.5 Locations and lead times

Plants	Warehouse Locations	
West	Oakland	
East	Philadelphia	
MidWest	Chicago	
South	Atlanta	
Lead Time		
From Plant to Warehouse	5	days
From Supplier to Warehouse for commodity gear	4	days
Picking at Warehouse	1	day
Transport From Warehouse to Customer	2	days

TABLE 1.6 Inventory at regional warehouses

	West	East	MidWest	South
A	9,592	6,837	7,296	5,459
B	9,592	6,148	7,296	6,148
C	6,378	9,592	7,296	9,592
D	5,918	5,918	7,296	5,459

types. The warehouse manager placed orders in batches of 10,000 gears at the plant. The plant operated in a make-to-order manner and took five days from order placement to delivery at the warehouse. The average delivered cost of custom gears was $50 per unit. Winstar used a carrying cost of 50% of the value of inventory.

But Jim Brush had negotiated delivery terms for commodity gears: Winstar got delivery at the warehouse four days after order placement. The average delivered cost for commodity gears was $20 per unit. The supplier had offered a price of $10 per unit if orders were in batches of 10,000 units, but Jim Brush had brushed aside that option.

The warehouse took on average one day to pick and pack orders; because most orders were for a mix of commodity and custom gears, that meant that orders were shipped four days after receipt. Shipments to the customer were on a less-than-truckload basis, and the trucking company delivered the product to the customer within two days from pickup.

Customer (distributor) orders were all different: each distributor offered four different designs meant to appeal to different customer needs. While these differences were cosmetic, they resulted in significant set-up time differences. These different gears were thus made at each of the different plants.

New designs in the market had appeared recently, termed *vanilla gears* which could be made upfront and finetuned using inserts. Winstar had investigated these designs, and the available report claimed that with such a design change, each plant could produce all four gear types for its local region. The warehouse would then require an extra day of light manufacturing to assemble the required gear type.

Logistics had also studied combining all of the inventory into one location in Indianapolis, which had been gaining a reputation as a logistics center. The available report suggested closing all four warehouses and opening one warehouse in Indianapolis to serve the entire country. Such a scheme would lower inventory costs but increase transportation lead time to ship to the customer from two days to three days. Commodity gear suppliers were willing to ship to the Indianapolis warehouse (in fact they preferred it due to the potential larger orders) within four days. However, delivery to the customer would now take three days instead of two.

A transportation consultant had provided a report suggesting that Winstar shut its current warehouses and set up four new consolidation warehouses near customer locations. This would increase inventory a bit but lower transport costs because shipments to this warehouse would be in full truckloads. The lead time for delivery to the customer could be cut to one day, and the commodity suppliers would ship directly to these consolidation warehouses. However, lead time for delivery from the plants to these warehouses would be six days instead of the previous five days.

A design consultant had suggested getting distributors to standardize their designs. His new design included the features of all four gears currently sold. This "supergear" could be made at each plant and shipped to the customer along with the commodity gears. The production cost for these supergears would be 20% higher.

A procurement department study suggested carrying inventory of commodity gears and buying in full truckloads. This would lower the average price for Winstar to $10 instead of $20 per unit as well as permit a lowering of customer lead time.

One report had even studied the unthinkable—violating Joe Morgan's dictum that all gears in an order should be delivered to the customer as one package. Suppose the commodity suppliers could ship commodity gears direct to the customer and Winstar could ship the more detailed gears it manufactured. That would permit a four-day lead time for customer orders.

Barney had commissioned a study of Winstar's competitors, and a thorough report was presented to the group. The report provided data regarding products offered by competitors that overlapped Winstar's offerings. Atlas Gear, for example, focused only on the custom gear market and offered incredible delivery terms and flexibility but at a 20% higher price point. Atlas could turn orders around within 48 hours. Nexus Gear focused on commodity purchases and could beat Winstar's prices by 25% but offered two-week delivery. Wintel Gear offered kits of gears based on standard configurations. These kits offered quick delivery of standard sets of requirements that covered about 50% of the orders with multiple lines. Customers would now require about two days to assemble the required gear at their facility, but Wintel could deliver within five days.

Barney concluded the meeting by saying, "The bottom line—I want each of you to generate a one page executive summary that provides a logistics audit of our supply chain. We need ideas for improvement that can be implemented right away. We need analysis, numbers, anything we can generate by the end of this week. I have included a bunch of readings, data, etc., in the folder in front of you. See you Thursday afternoon at 3 p.m."

WINSTAR GEAR'S CURRENT STRATEGY

Breakdown of Inventory by Warehouse

CUSTOM GEAR INVENTORY	WAREHOUSES			
	Oakland	Philadelphia	Lafayette	Atlanta
"A" Gear	9,592	6,837	7,296	5,459
"B" Gear	9,592	6,148	7,296	6,148
"C" Gear	6,378	9,592	7,296	9,592
"D" Gear	5,918	5,918	7,296	5,459
Total Custom Gear Inventory: **115817**				

Breakdown of Costs per Gear Type in USD ($)

Gear Type	Plant (Manufacturing)	Transport to Warehouse	Warehouse (Inventory)	Transport to Customer	Total Cost
Custom Gear	45	5	2.05	5	57.05
Commodity Gear	20	0	0	5	25

FORECASTED OUTCOME OF ASSEMBLY POSTPONEMENT STRATEGY

Breakdown of Inventory by Warehouse

CUSTOM GEAR INVENTORY	WAREHOUSES			
	Oakland	Philadelphia	Lafayette	Atlanta
'Vanilla' Gears	11,704	10,160	9,592	9,778
Total Custom Gear Inventory: **40,602**				

Breakdown of Costs per Gear Type in USD ($)

Gear Type	Plant (Manufacturing)	Transport to Warehouse	Warehouse (Inventory)	Transport to Customer	Total Cost
Custom Gear	40	5	0.60	5	55.60*
Commodity Gear	20	0	0	5	25

*The $55.60 includes a $5 warehouse cost to covert vanilla gear to required final form.

FORECASTED OUTCOME OF GEOGRAPHIC POSTPONEMENT STRATEGY

Breakdown of Inventory by Warehouse

CUSTOM GEAR INVENTORY	WAREHOUSES
	Main Warehouse
"A" Gear	10,472
"B" Gear	10,385
"C" Gear	12,025
"D" Gear	7,678
Total Custom Gear Inventory: **40,560**	

Breakdown of Costs per Gear Type in USD ($)

Gear Type	Plant (Manufacturing)	Transport to Warehouse	Warehouse (Inventory)	Transport to Customer	Total Cost
Custom Gear	45	5	0.72	10	60.72
Commodity Gear	20	0	0	5	25

FORECASTED OUTCOME OF SPLIT SHIPMENTS STRATEGY

Breakdown of Inventory by Warehouse

CUSTOM GEAR INVENTORY	WAREHOUSES			
	Oakland	Philadelphia	Lafayette	Atlanta
"A" Gear	9,592	6,837	7,296	5,459
"B" Gear	9,592	6,148	7,296	6,148
"C" Gear	6,378	9,592	7,296	9,592
"D" Gear	5,918	5,918	7,296	5,459
Total Custom Gear Inventory: **115,817**				

Breakdown of Costs per Gear Type in USD ($)

Gear Type	Plant (Manufacturing)	Transport to Warehouse	Warehouse (Inventory)	Transport to Customer	Total Cost
Custom Gear	45	5	2.05	5	57.05
Commodity Gear	20	0	0	0	20

FORECASTED OUTCOME OF CONSOLIDATION STRATEGY

Breakdown of Inventory by Warehouse

CUSTOM GEAR INVENTORY	WAREHOUSES			
	Oakland	Philadelphia	Lafayette	Atlanta
"A" Gear	10,030	7,012	7,515	5,503
"B" Gear	10,030	6,528	7,515	6,285
"C" Gear	6,509	10,030	7,515	10,030
"D" Gear	6,006	6,006	7,515	5,503
Total Custom Gear Inventory: **115,817**				

Breakdown of Costs per Gear Type in USD ($)

Gear Type	Plant (Manufacturing)	Transport to Warehouse	Warehouse (Inventory)	Transport to Customer	Total Cost
Custom Gear	45	7	2.10	5	59.10
Commodity Gear	20	0	0	5	25

FORECASTED OUTCOME FOR STANDARDIZATION STRATEGY

Breakdown of Inventory by Warehouse

CUSTOM GEAR INVENTORY	WAREHOUSES			
	Oakland	**Philadelphia**	**Lafayette**	**Atlanta**
'Standard' Gears	12,342	10,653	10,031	10,234
Total Custom Gear Inventory: **43,260**				

Breakdown of Costs per Gear Type in USD ($)

Gear Type	Plant (Manufacturing)	Transport to Warehouse	Warehouse (Inventory)	Transport to Customer	Total Cost
Custom Gear	54	5	0.92	5	64.92
Commodity Gear	20	0	0	5	25

FORECASTED OUTCOME OF SPECULATION STRATEGY

Breakdown of Inventory by Warehouse

CUSTOM GEAR INVENTORY	WAREHOUSES			
	Oakland	**Philadelphia**	**Lafayette**	**Atlanta**
"A" Gear	9,592	6,837	7,296	5,459
"B" Gear	9,592	6,148	7,296	6,148
"C" Gear	6,378	9,592	7,296	9,592
"D" Gear	5,918	5,918	7,296	5,459
Commodity Gear	9,108	9,108	9,108	7,054
Total Custom Gear Inventory: **150,195**				

Breakdown of Costs per Gear Type in USD ($)

Gear Type	Plant (Manufacturing)	Transport to Warehouse	Warehouse (Inventory)	Transport to Customer	Total Cost
Custom Gear	45	5	2.05	5	57.05
Commodity Gear	10	0	0.26	5	15.26

CASE QUESTIONS

1. Map the current supply chain at Winstar Gear.
2. What "problem" does Winstar Gear face? How is the supply chain impacted by the current situation at Winstar?
3. Do a Pareto analysis by product to explore the relative impact of SKUs.
4. Summarize the cost and lead time associated with each of the possible strategies (i.e., postponement (assembly and geographic), split shipments, standardization, speculation, and consolidation).
5. How do competitor choices differ from Winstar's choice of Supply Chain Structure? What aspects of these choices influence Winstar's supply chain decisions?
6. What recommendation would you offer to Winstar?

Chapter 2

Chain Structure

This chapter focuses on supply chain structure and ownership, one of the Cs in the supply chain framework. The chain structure is the backbone or the pipeline through which information and material flow in the supply chain. It is the process map of a supply chain that typically crosses many independent company boundaries. Once a supply chain map is generated, the location of entities, as well as ownership, and the connections to the rest of the supply chain architecture influence the observed lead times, costs, incentives, and thus performance, of the supply chain.

Our goal in this chapter is to understand commonly observed supply chain structures and discuss their potential impact on performance. Key supply chain features include the number of links in the chain, the locations where capacity is shared, the level of flexibility of the entities and their impact, the impact of chain structure and capacity, the impact of uncertainty on performance of the network and finally, how country boundaries interact with flows across the chain.

2.1 CHAIN STRUCTURES

The following are commonly used supply chain structures.

2.1.1 Serial Supply Chain

A serial supply chain consists of a number of entities that work sequentially to deliver product. In a serial supply chain, any given node's supply is affected by the decisions of upstream entities, and that node's demand is generated by downstream entities. Serial supply chains provide a simple supply chain structure, but it often implies use of a one-size-fits-all strategy that can generate significant costs if products and customer segments can be differentiated. Thus, it is clear that managing a given node, even in a serial supply chain, is complex due to the need to anticipate how information and incentives are incorporated into actions by other participating entities.

The example provided earlier in the book (Figure 1.11) described the supply chain for a medical device manufacturer. In that example, products flow from the manufacturer to a distributor to a health care provider to a health care professional and finally to the patient. This is a serial supply chain: the product flows through a series of steps to reach the patient.

2.1.2 Assembly Structure

An assembly structure is one in which products from separate suppliers or plants are combined to form subassemblies, which in turn are combined to form the final assembly. Figure 2.1 shows a sample assembly supply chain. Automobile industry manufacturers, such

FIGURE 2.1 An assembly supply chain

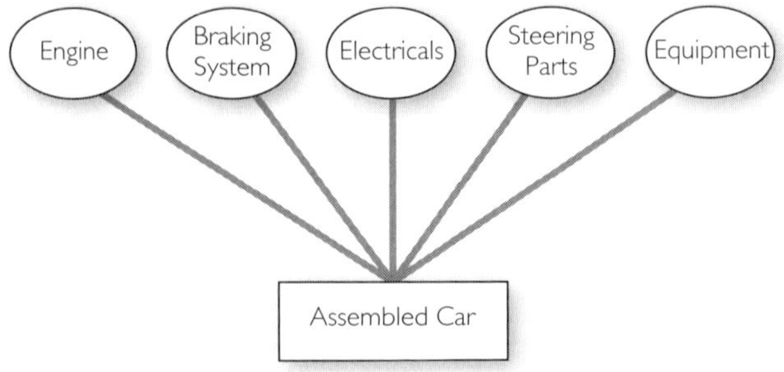

A Car Assembly Structure

as Toyota, Honda, and Ford, all use tiered purchasing arrangements, in which subassemblies from one set of suppliers are combined at the next level until the final car assembly, thus generating an assembly structure of suppliers. In such structures, the complete "kit" of parts from all suppliers is necessary to complete assembly. Thus, a key task for the operation of an assembly structure is coordinating the deliveries from all suppliers to produce a unit of a finished product.

2.1.3 Distribution Structure

In a distribution supply chain, products flow out in a fan-shaped structure to the retailers. Consider the example of a warehouse and retailers in Figure 2.2. Even if the retailers serve independent markets, the retail supplies are linked because the warehouse inventory policy affects the supply to otherwise independent retailers. But the presence of the warehouse may generate significant benefits to the supply chain by enabling bulk commitments by the wholesaler or plant, which can deliver to the warehouse, followed by a distribution to retailers as their demands unfold. The warehouse thus offers the benefits of "demand risk pooling" and enables geographic postponement of the deliveries to retailers. We will analyze the impact of such risk pooling in Section 2.3.

FIGURE 2.2 A distribution supply chain

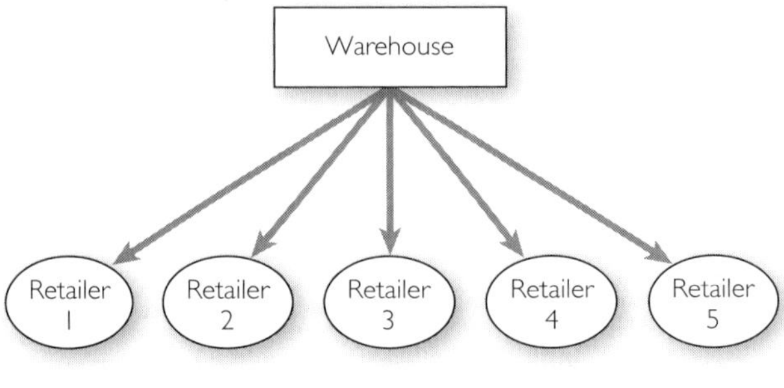

2.1.4 Assembly Followed by Distribution

Many supply chains have an assembly structure for product manufacturing followed by a distribution structure for product distribution. The assembly structures enable economies of scale in transportation and assembly, while the distribution structure enables efficiencies in matching finished goods inventories with product demand across retail locations.

2.1.5 Network Structure

In more general contexts, the components and products flow through a network. Figure 2.3 shows component suppliers (S), intermediate subassembly plants (I), assembly plants (A), distribution centers (W), and customer zones (C). The locations of these entities may be spread across the world. The main benefit from such a network structure is the flexibility to adjust flows to reflect demand, cost, and competitiveness. If the network flows cross country boundaries, then decisions made by each country location regarding exchange rates, duties, and tax structures impact the profitability implied by the supply chain.

FIGURE 2.3 A supply network

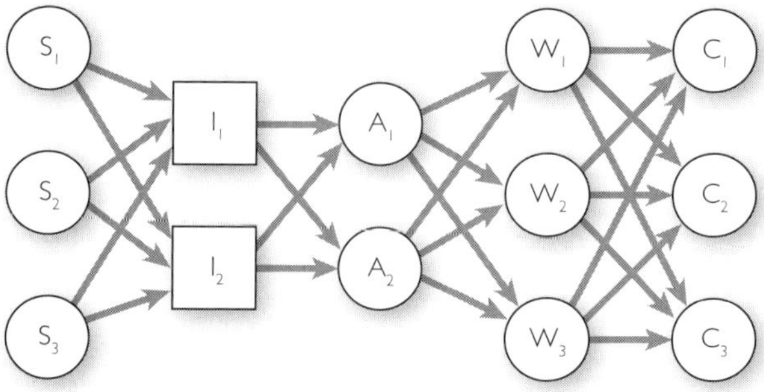

2.2 ORDER VARIABILITY IN A SERIAL SUPPLY CHAIN: THE BULLWHIP EFFECT

Consider a set of n independent entities (nodes) in a serial supply chain, shown in Figure 2.4. Node 1 is closest to the customer, and Node 1 is supplied by Node 2, Node 2 is supplied by Node 3, and so on. Now suppose that Node 1 faces a demand of μ every period. Suppose each node faces a lead time L to get product from its supplier immediately upstream. Finally, suppose that each node carries a pipeline inventory (sum of all physical

FIGURE 2.4 Chain for the bullwhip effect

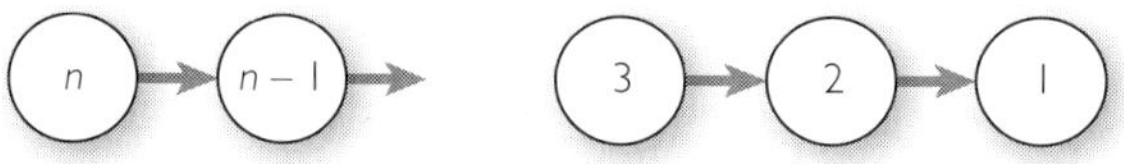

inventory, plus orders or material in transit) of $(L + S) \times$ DemandForecast, where S is the safety stock factor at that location. Thus, if every node passed along the demand forecast it faced, each node would have a pipeline inventory of $(L + S) \times$ DemandForecast.

But suppose customer demand were to increase suddenly by K units. For simplicity, suppose Node 1 changes its demand forecast to $\mu + K$. It would immediately order to satisfy the current demand and to fill the pipeline; thus the order placed to Node 2 would be $\mu + K + ((L + S)K)$, which can be written as $\mu + K(L + S + 1)$. In turn, the order placed by Node 2, following the same logic, would be $\mu + K(L + S + 1)^2$. The order placed by the nth node is, in turn, $\mu + K(L + S + 1)^n$. Notice the polynomial growth as we move upstream. This growth in orders is called the *bullwhip effect* and occurs because every node faces a demand that is partly in response to the current order and partly an attempt to fill up the pipeline.

What would happen if all nodes shared the downstream demand information? In such a case, every node would see the underlying demand. Thus, the order adjustment would cover the demand faced and would not be confused with the pipeline inventory increase. Thus, the order faced by node n would be $\mu + K((L + S)n + 1)$. The increase in order due to lack of demand information can thus be described as

$$\frac{(L+S+1)^n}{((L+S)n+1)}$$

This increase reflects the exponential growth in orders in response to lack of information in a fragmented supply chain. As mentioned in Chapter 1, this is called the bullwhip effect. Thus, even in a serial supply chain, lack of transparency can create undesirable volatility even when each entity behaves optimally, thus generating the bullwhip effect. The consequences of such volatility are increased capacity, inventory, delivery lead time, and costs.

2.3 DISTRIBUTION SUPPLY CHAINS: RISK POOLING AND INVENTORY IMPACT

Consider a distribution supply chain consisting of a set of n downstream retailers linked to a common source warehouse. There is a common inventory pool at the warehouse shared by all downstream locations. Suppose the supplier lead time is L. If every retailer faced a demand with a mean of μ and a variance of σ^2, then the common pool of inventory at the warehouse would be $(nL\mu) + (Z\sigma\sqrt{Ln})$, where the Z refers to the standard normal value whose cumulative probability is the service level offered to retailers, and L is the supply lead time (see the Tools section in Chapter 15 for details).

If each individual retailer carried its own inventory, it would maintain an inventory level of $L\mu + (Z\sigma\sqrt{L})$. Thus the total system inventory would be $n(L\mu + (Z\sigma\sqrt{L}))$. The pooled inventory includes a safety stock of $Z\sigma\sqrt{nL}$ while the individual locations would generate a safety stock of $Z\sigma n\sqrt{L}$. Thus, the role of the warehouse in a distribution supply chain is to decrease the buffer capacity by a factor of $\sqrt{n}$. This $\sqrt{n}$ effect is a rule of thumb to estimate the benefit of consolidating inventory in a supply chain.

2.4 OPTIMIZING THE SUPPLY CHAIN NETWORK

A typical supply chain network is shown in Figure 2.3. Designing a supply chain involves choosing facilities, capacity, and deployment to maximize competitiveness. Steps to optimize a supply chain are described below.

2.4.1 Collect Supply Chain Network Data

The first step is to collect the relevant data regarding costs and demands faced by the supply chain. For a typical supply network, such as the one shown in Figure 2.3, some of the data that will affect performance of the chain are:

1. Products and their production requirements
2. Cost to get raw material to each producing plant
3. Component production costs
4. Inter-plant transport costs
5. Assembly costs at each plant
6. Cost of transporting finished goods to warehouses
7. Warehousing costs at each distribution center
8. Customer zone demands by product

Note that there are important managerial accounting decisions that precede this data collection. These include decisions regarding appropriate average costs and flows. How should these average costs per unit be chosen, given data regarding the past history of transactions and associated costs? What values will convince current managers that these costs are truly those associated with their transactions? The typical validation check is to evaluate the costs generated by the model for the current history of flows and compare it with the current costs to see if it provides an acceptable representation.

2.5 PURPOSE OF THE MODEL

The role of the supply chain design model is to answer the following questions:

1. Where should intermediate and final products be produced?
2. What interplant shipments of intermediate products should occur?
3. How many distribution centers (DCs) should be included?
4. Where should these DCs be located, and what should be the planned capacity?
5. Which plants should supply each of the DCs?
6. Which DC should supply a specific customer zone?

Describing the chain structure, a network in this case, along with all the associated data that capture the performance impact of flows, enables an understanding of the impact of interactions between flows in the system and their effects on costs and capacity.

2.6 A NETWORK FLOW EXAMPLE

Consider the example network shown in Figure 2.5. This example is from a presentation by Jeffrey Karrenbauer from Insight Consulting, distributed in one of my classes. The supply chain consists of two plants, P1 and P2, that can each supply the demands at warehouses W1 and W2, which in turn can supply each of three customer zones, C1, C2, and C3. Demands at C1, C2, and C3 are 50,000, 100,000, and 50,000 units respectively.

FIGURE 2.5 A sample network with data

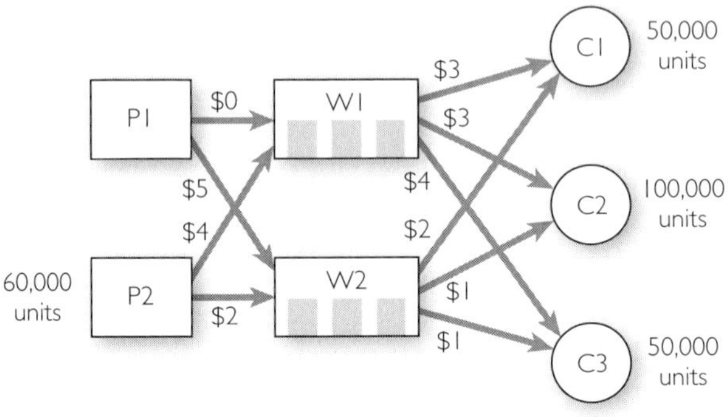

Warehouses W1 and W2 have no capacity constraint. The capacity at plant P2 is 60,000 units. The costs per unit are provided for each link between plants and warehouses and between warehouses and customer zones.

2.6.1 A Least-Cost-per-Lane Solution

A least-cost-per-lane solution ignores the network structure and chooses the minimum-cost warehouse to supply each customer zone, i.e., each customer zone gets delivery from the closest warehouse. In turn, the warehouses are supplied from the closest plant subject to capacity constraints. For the network shown in Figure 2.5, the corresponding decisions regarding how much each plant produces, the quantities shipped to each warehouse, and the quantities shipped by each warehouse to customer zones are shown in the Figure 2.6.

The cost associated with these decisions is obtained by multiplying the decisions with the corresponding costs on each lane to obtain a total cost of $1,070,000. But notice that when the first set of decisions was made by the customer zones, the zones did not consider which plants supply the warehouses. In addition, when the customer zones chose their closest warehouse, the deployment of the capacity of plant P2 is not accounted for. Thus, the resulting decision may not generate the lowest-cost decision for the supply chain. The key takeaway from this example is that myopic, single-stage optimal decisions may not generate the best result throughout the entire supply chain. But how much can the solution be improved?

FIGURE 2.6 Results using a least-cost-per-lane solution

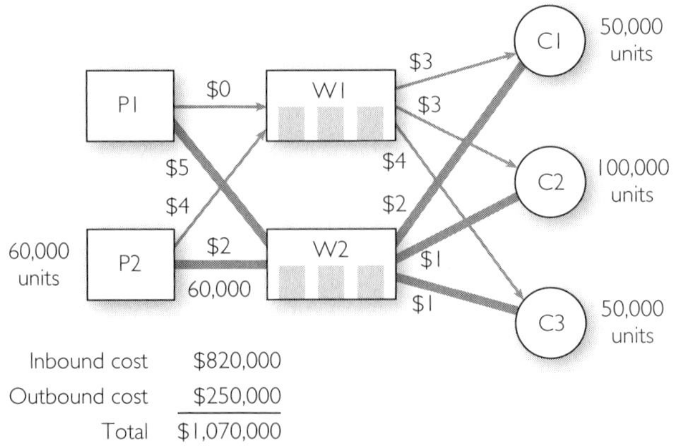

2.6.2 A Least-Cost-Path Solution

A first step to improving the solution is to consider the total cost per unit along the chain from the plant through the warehouse to the customer zone. There are twelve possible chains:

(P1, W1, C1), (P1, W1, C2), (P1, W1, C3), (P1, W2, C1),

(P1, W2, C2), (P1, W2, C3), (P2, W1, C1), (P2, W1, C2),

(P2, W1, C3), (P2, W2, C1), (P2, W2, C2), (P2, W2, C3).

The cost per unit associated with each of the paths is, in dollars, 3, 3, 4, 7, 6, 6, 7, 7, 8, 4, 3, and 3, respectively.

Given the costs of these paths, the optimal decision for each customer zone would be for C1 to pick W1, C2 to pick W2, and C3 to pick W2. In turn, warehouse W1 is supplied 50,000 units by plant P1, and warehouse W2 is supplied 60,000 units by P2 and 90,000 units by P1. Given these flows, the associated cost can be verified to be 870,000, which is lower than the earlier solution.

Note that unlike the solution in the earlier section, this approach takes account of the cost along the entire path from the plant to the warehouse to the customer zone. However, it still does not account for plant P2's capacity when making the customer zone sourcing decision. Thus, a possible reason for the absence of a lowest-cost solution for the supply chain is that we may not have allocated plant P2's capacity optimally across the warehouses.

2.7 SOLVING THE MODEL USING LINEAR PROGRAMMING

In this section, we describe the optimal solution to the problem using linear programming as a solution tool. Details of the solution are provided in Section 15.1, the Tools section. The linear programming model takes a "global" look at the problem and incorporates the path of flows, the capacity impact, and the benefit to taking multiple paths of flows to balance use of capacity and satisfying demand.

The results of using Microsoft Excel Solver (one of many possible analytical tools) on the optimal solution are shown in Figure 2.7. The results show that the optimal cost to satisfy demands can be decreased to $600,000. The key to achieving this solution is to choose which warehouse supplies customer zone C2 and thus how the plant capacity will be used.

FIGURE 2.7 Optimal solution for the network

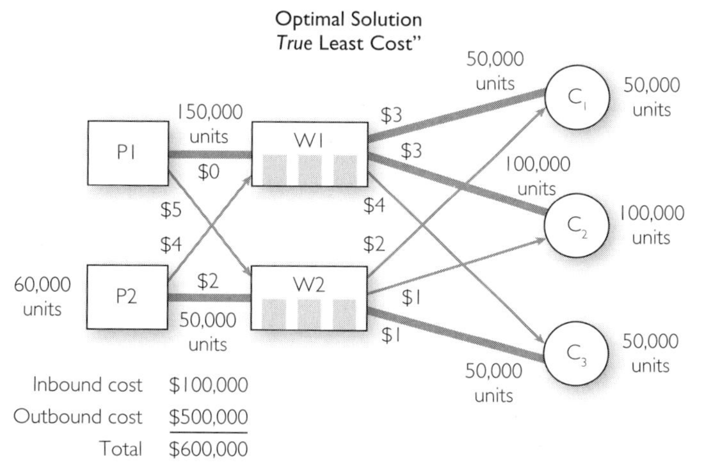

The linear programming tool is a first step in uncovering possible choices to operate a supply chain that may differ from the usual heuristics that do not account for the chain structure. Often the solution generated exposes opportunities that may not have been considered. At other times, the solution enables an understanding of the value of changes to a supply chain, such as addition of new supply sources or warehouses, that may further improve performance.

In addition, the optimization model also provides sensitivity analysis that can be used to understand the impact of capacity or demand changes.

2.8 EVALUATING THE EFFECT OF FIXED COSTS IN THE SUPPLY CHAIN EXAMPLE

Consider the earlier example, but include the possibility of closing plants and warehouses given fixed costs associated with each facility. During supply chain network design, such facility decisions will have to be made to optimize supply chain costs. Suppose the following capacities and fixed costs are associated with each of the plants and warehouses (Table 2.1).

There are three possible decisions regarding plant capacity: (1) keep both plants open, (2) keep plant 1 only open, or (3) keep plant 2 only open. Similarly we have three possibilities for the two warehouses: (1) keep both warehouses open, (2) keep warehouse 1 only open or (3) keep warehouse 2 only open. Closing plants or warehouses gives us fixed cost reductions but potentially decreases the flexibility to respond to changing cost or demand situations.

How would we evaluate the effect of potentially closing plants or warehouses and the impact on flexibility to respond to changing circumstances? The details of the implementation in Microsoft Solver are provided in Section 15.2. The results obtained are summarized in Table 2.2.

TABLE 2.1 Capacities and fixed costs for the example network

Facility	Capacity (Units)	Fixed Cost
P1	250,000	300,000
P2	220,000	280,000
W1	250,000	100,000
W2	200,000	90,000

TABLE 2.2 Results of plant and warehouse closings

Facilities Open	Cost ($)
(P1, P2, W1, W2)	1,370,000
(P1, W1, W2)	1,140,000
(P2, W1, W2)	1,120,000
(P1, P2, W1)	1,330,000
(P1, P2, W2)	1,320,000
(P1, W1)	1,050,000
(P1, W2)	1,640,000
(P2, W1)	1,830,000
(P2, W2)	1,020,000

Note that the optimal decision is to close plants P1 and W1, leaving plant P2 and warehouse W2 open. But this decision assumes that all costs, demands, and capacities are known. What if some of the parameters are not known with certainty?

2.9 THE IMPACT OF POSSIBLE COST SCENARIOS

When decisions are made regarding long-term capacity and network structure, it may be useful to consider possible future changes in the demand or cost scenarios when making choices. Assuming that once capacity is eliminated, it cannot be recovered easily (except after a long lead time), the reduced capacity levels may prevent access to the benefits that could accrue from having the flexibility to adapt product flows to match cost or demand levels at a future point in time.

To illustrate this idea, consider an alternative to the problem described earlier: a new transport company decreases costs from P2 to W1 to \$1/unit from W1 to C1, C2 and C3 decrease to \$1/unit, \$0.5/unit and \$0.5/unit respectively. Such a cost decrease may occur because of an arrangement with a trucking company that does extensive backhaul along these routes. Note that if we had closed P1 and W1 based on costs in the previous section, then we would operate only with P2 and W2, and our costs would have continued to be \$1,020,000.

However, if all plants and warehouse capacities remain, then the model can be optimized with the new cost parameters. The new optimal solution is to operate only P1 and W1 and thus have a cost of \$895,000. If there was an 80% chance of such a cost change, then the expected cost with all plants open would be $(0.2 \times 1{,}370{,}000) + (0.8 \times 895{,}000) = 990{,}000$. Thus, the slack capacity offers the flexibility to respond to such cost-reducing opportunities and decreases expected cost.

This example suggests that excess capacity in a network can provide the flexibility to react to changing cost or demand conditions. As we shall see later, when demands and costs are generated by scenarios and thus lack certainty, building in slack capacity throughout the network may preserve the flexibility to deal with parameter changes.

2.10 CHOOSING SUPPLY CHAIN STRUCTURE UNDER UNCERTAIN FUTURE SCENARIOS

Decisions regarding capacity and flexibility of plants in an automobile supply chain have to anticipate parameters several years out into the future. This is true for large assembly plants that take several years to construct and involve commitments to local governments to remain open for several years.

The article "A Scenario-Based Approach to Capacity Planning" ([36]) is motivated by capacity configuration decisions at General Motors (GM). The decisions involved choosing the appropriate type and level of production capacity at each of several locations, termed *capacity configuration*. But future demands for specific car types (large vs. small, fuel efficient vs. comfortable, etc.) are affected by several fundamental parameters such as oil prices, federally mandated miles per gallon laws, the state of the economy, and so on. Thus future demands can be described as being generated by demand scenarios unfolding over time.

Given an existing type and level of capacity at each plant, changing the configuration involves changeover costs. The resulting configuration can then produce a number of different product types, with associated fixed and variable costs, as the specific product demands unfold. Because the capacity decisions affect not just expected profits but also their variability, GM chose the decision that best maximized expected profit, subject to a limit on downside risk (which controlled the variability of profits). Downside risk is a prescribed target profit that has to be generated with large linear penalties for falling short of the target, but that gives no benefits to beating the target.

The paper [36] suggests that balancing expected profit with downside risk causes capacity choices to value the benefit of flexible resources in the supply network.

2.11 ESTIMATING SYNERGY ACROSS MERGED SUPPLY CHAINS

This section focuses on identifying synergies across merged supply chains. Our example involves a major US drug manufacturer and distributor that decided to form an alliance with a European counterpart. The alliance was expected to generate significant cost reductions and efficiency improvements as products were rationalized, production locations, and warehouses consolidated, and so on. But how much value could be realized by such actions, given the details of each company's supply chain?

The supply chain was complex and involved seven countries, two plants, twenty-one distribution centers, ten candidate distribution centers, 5,700 SKUs, and multiple channels of distribution. There was substantial overlap in plants and warehouse locations across both companies, with the US company having six plants and eight warehouses and the European company having four plants and seven warehouses.

The first step was to pull historical transaction data and recreate the costs associated with every possible flow through the merged supply chain. Validation of these data in the model was accomplished by comparing the costs generated by the model with the current flows and observed costs. The next step was to optimize the model and use it to recommend a configuration for the merged system. The resulting model was subject to several what-if analyses dealing with changes in freight costs, service-level requirements, warehousing costs, regulation outcomes for transport, changes in financing costs, and other factors.

The analysis described above is typically used to estimate the synergy-related savings associated with merging supply chains and is often a key justification for mergers.

2.12 RATIONALIZING SUPPLY CHAIN EVOLUTION

Often a company's supply chain is the result of a historical accumulation of assets or expansion in response to growth. In such contexts, revisiting the rationale for the existing network structure reveals opportunities to improve performance.

Consider an example provided by Dr. Jeffrey Karrenbauer in one of my classes. The company, XYZ, was founded in 1930, and started with one plant near New York City and one distribution center on the outskirts of Chicago. The market area covered the states bordering New York and the MidWestern states. In 1930, transportation to customers generated a significant portion of total logistics costs, compared to warehousing and inventory carrying costs. However, by 1980, the company had grown its market to include customers across the continental United States, thus evolving to five plants and seventeen distribution centers. Over 11,000 customers placed more than 100,000 orders per year. The company offered a 98% service level within seven days and had twelve major product categories with two separate production technologies. Supply chain costs as a percent of sales had grown from 5.8% in 1970 to 8% in 1980 and were growing faster than manufacturing costs. Similarly, inventory turns had declined from 7.5% in 1970 to 6% in 1980.

The company had tried many strategies. Edicts to decrease inventory had resulted in arbitrary inventory cuts, which had driven up manufacturing and transport costs while reducing inventory costs and reducing the level of customer service. Next, to solve the service problem while lowering transport costs, additional warehouses were introduced. This step decreased transport costs but increased warehousing and inventory costs. Adjustments of the rail and truck movements decreased transport costs while increasing warehousing costs and inventory costs. Then plant warehouse space was eliminated to add more equipment. This decreased manufacturing costs but increased transport costs due to the need to ship product out as it was manufactured, also increasing field warehousing costs and associated inventory costs.

Examination of the supply chain network focused on questions such as (1) How should inventory be stratified and positioned in the network?; (2) How many distribution centers should there be, and where should they be located?; (3) Should new plants be added, and if so where?; and (4) Which plants should make which products in order to have the greatest impact on the supply chain? In addition, the analysis was used to evaluate the impact of contingencies such as (1) the effect of trucking deregulation, which happened in the United States in the early 1980s, on full truckload and the consequent impact of less-than-truckload freight costs on XYZ; (2) the impact of increasing delivery lead times; (3) the impact of increases in the cost of financing inventory; and so on.

The main goal of the model was to understand the impact of capacity changes in the system on the supply chain. The model solution recommended changes in the network—a 20% reduction in the number of distribution centers, an 8% increase in the return on assets, and an improvement in the customer service offered, while decreasing inventory. An interesting component of the model was its ability to quantify the impact of managerial choices on the supply chain that were different from the optimal solution.

2.13 THE GLOBAL TAX IMPACT OF SUPPLY CHAINS

As global supply chains cross country boundaries, their structure impacts taxes and profitability. Consider the consequences of chain structure as illustrated by the Digital Equipment Corporation ([1]). In 1991, Digital Equipment Corporation served over 250,000 customers worldwide, with $14 billion in revenues coming from eighty-one countries outside the United States. The company had thirty-three plants in thirteen countries, along with thirty distribution and repair centers. The company produced a full range of minicomputers and mainframes but was also vertically integrated to produce chips, memory, disks, power supplies, cabinets, cables, keyboards, and other equipment. However, between 1988 and 1993, Digital had to make significant changes to its supply chain, in response to declining product volumes.

A study done over an eighteen-month period ([1]) recommended a decrease in the number of plants worldwide from thirty-three down to twelve. The recommendation included restructuring and adjusting plant production and associated equipment. The global supply chain model included tradeoffs between product transit time, associated costs, capacity, and, in addition, costs associated with crossing country boundaries, such as duties and taxes.

The study examined three types of duty drawbacks ([1]): (1) duty drawback for "re-export in the same condition," (2) duty drawback for "re-export in a different condition," and (3) duty drawback for "domestic goods returned in a different condition." As an example, see Figure 2.8 below. In the example, printers entering Europe from China had a 4.9% duty. When these printers were re-exported to Brazil, the printers were eligible for a duty drawback for "re-export in the same condition." This applied even if the printers exported were different, as long as they were fungible. Similarly, Europe imported liquid crystal displays (LCDs) from Taiwan but exported laptop computers. The shipments to Taiwan were eligible for duty drawback in Europe because of "re-export in a different condition." The

FIGURE 2.8 Supply chain flows in a global context

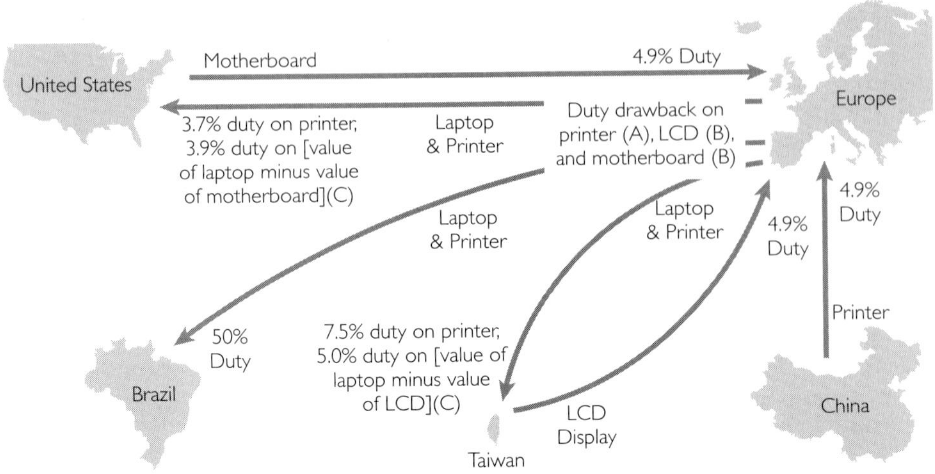

Duty drawback and duty avoidance are worth modeling. Shown are three ways to take advantage of import duty relief. When printers imported from China enter Europe, a duty of 4.9% is due. Europe also imports LCD displays from Taiwan and motherboards from the United States to manufacture laptop PCs which it exports to Taiwan and the United States. Laptop PCs with printers are exported from the United States to Brazil. Because the printers from China went through Europe and were ultimately shipped to Brazil, they are eligible for European duty drawback for re-export in the same condition. Usually the same printers imported into Europe from China need not be re-exported to Brazil; they need only be fungible, that is, equivalent. Europe imports LCDs from Taiwan, then re-exports them to Taiwan in laptop computers. It avoids the 4.9% LCD duty due in Europe because of re-export in a different condition. The LCDs reimported into Taiwan also create an opportunity for duty avoidance for domestic goods returned in different condition.

Source: Arntzen, B., Brown, G.G., Harrison, T.P., Trafton, L.L. Global Supply Chain Management at Digital Equipment Corporation. *Interfaces,* 25(1):69–93, January-February 1995.

LCDs, when reimported to Taiwan as laptops, were eligible for duty drawback in Taiwan for "domestic goods returned in a different condition." Duties ranged from 0%–200% for specific products, but the typical duty rates were in the range of 5%–10%.

The study ([1]) reported that implementation of the recommendations reduced the cost of raw materials and purchased components by $225 million and logistics costs by $150 million over eighteen months. By June 1995, annual logistics costs had decreased by $200 million and annual manufacturing costs had decreased by $167 million. This occurred even though the number of units shipped from the remaining locations increased dramatically. Managing the supply chain structure while accounting for tax consequences can thus generate significant financial benefits to a firm.

2.14 CHAPTER SUMMARY

This chapter focused on the impact of the chain structure on a supply chain's performance. The supply chain links supply locations, intermediaries, and final demand points and thus influences possible adjustments in information and material flow in response to costs or demand shifts. The impact of different supply chain structures were discussed. The bull-whip effect and the risk-pooling effect illustrate the impact of chain structure, visibility, and inventory pooling. The tools presented in this chapter show how supply chain optimization can enable cost reductions. The scenario-based planning approach permits the incorporation of risk in the choice of supply chain structure. Global operations require consideration of duties and duty drawbacks, which can affect the net costs of operation. Finally, mergers or alliances affect the cost structure of the new entity, and rationalization or synergy requires managing the combined supply chains. This chapter thus provides a detailed focus on one of the Cs—supply chain structure.

2.15 PROBLEMS

1. The Optima Corporation owns two plants, each with a capacity to produce 2,000 units of either product A or B. The net profit per unit to produce and ship each of these products from these plants is shown in Table 2.3. Demand for each of these products can take values of 1,000 or 3,000 with equal probability.

TABLE 2.3 Net profits

	PLANTS	
PRODUCTS	**1**	**2**
A	7	10
B	6	4

What is the expected profit associated with the current capacity configuration? Can you justify why the capacity at these plants is sometimes larger than the demand?

2. The INTL Corporation currently sells product in two countries: the United States and Germany. Annual demand for its product (a widget) in Germany is 100,000 units, and the annual demand in the United States is 100,000 units.

In 1990, the production costs and selling prices in each of the countries were as shown in Table 2.4.

TABLE 2.4 Production cost and selling price

	Production Cost	Selling Price
Germany	210 marks	275 marks
United States	$150	$170

The exchange rate in 1990 was 1.6 marks per US dollar. Transportation cost between the two countries per unit was $10. Duties for product shipped into either country was 10% of production cost. INTL has plants in each of the countries. Each plant has a productive capacity of 220,000 units.

2a. Assume that in 1990 each plant produced enough to satisfy local demand with no transfers between countries. What is INTL's profit (in dollars) associated with this strategy?

2b. Assume that INTL has to choose one plant to satisfy all of the demand in both countries in 1990. Which plant would you recommend? Provide the associated profit in dollars for the chosen strategy. Is this strategy better than a local production strategy?

2c. In 1997, the production costs in each of the countries (in 1997 currency) were as shown in Table 2.5.

TABLE 2.5 Production cost and selling price per unit in 1997

	Production Cost	Selling Price
Germany	300 marks	320 marks
United States	$180	$200

The exchange rate in 1997 was 1.4 marks per US dollar. Evaluate the profit impact of the local production strategy and the single plant strategy using costs in 1997. Assume that transport costs and duties remain at the same level as in 1990. Which strategy would you recommend for 1997?

2d. What capacity configuration would you recommend to INTL to maximize its profitability across 1990 and 1997; i.e., would you recommend that both plants be kept open or that one of the plants should be closed (if so, which one)? Explain your answer. (Assume that 1 1997 dollar = 85 cents in 1990 dollars.)

3. The Maxpro Company has plants in two cities: Lafayette, IN, and Osaka, Japan, and sells a specialty powdered chemical in 100-lb. bags. Since the chemicals produced at both plants are identical, either can be used to satisfy demand. Production cost per 100 lbs. in US dollars, is $25 in Lafayette and 3,960 yen in Osaka. Production capacity is 9,000,000 lbs. in Lafayette and 7,000,000 lbs. in Osaka. Maxpro ships to customers from its DCs in Osaka (for Asian demand), Frankfurt (for European demand), and Lafayette (for US demand). Demand in each of the zones is as shown in Table 2.6.

TABLE 2.6 Demand in Lafayette, Frankfurt, and Osaka

	Demand (in lbs.)
Lafayette	5,000,000
Frankfurt	4,000,000
Osaka	3,000,000

The retail price for a 100-lb. bag (expressed in local currency) is $100 in Lafayette, 150 euro in Frankfurt, and 17,000 yen in Osaka. If the chemical is shipped from Lafayette to Europe, it is sent via inland freight from Lafayette to the New York port, from New York (by ship) to Hamburg, and then moved by inland freight from Hamburg to Frankfurt. Similarly, if Lafayette ships to Osaka, the chemical is shipped from Lafayette to the New York port, from New York (by ship) to the Japan port, and from the Japan port via inland freight to the DC in Osaka. Similarly, goods from Osaka to Frankfurt would go via inland freight to the Japan port, from the port to Hamburg, and then via inland freight to Frankfurt. The cost of shipments by sea, in US dollars, is as shown in Table 2.7 (per 100-lb bag)

TABLE 2.7 Cost of shipping, in US dollars

	New York Port	Hamburg	Japan
New York port	0	30	40
Japan port	40	30	0

Inland shipments between the ports and the DC locations are as shown in Table 2.8.

TABLE 2.8 Cost of shipping, in US dollars

		Inland Freight
New York City	Lafayette	5
Hamburg	Frankfurt	10
Japan port	Osaka	5

Shipments between countries incur duties as a percent of value as shown in Table 2.9.

TABLE 2.9 Duties as a percent of value

	Lafayette	Frankfurt	Osaka
Lafayette	0	25	15
Osaka	10	20	0

Exchange rates are as follows (1 USD = 132 yen = 1.14 euros)

FROM	TO: USD	TO: yen	TO: euro
USD	1	132	1.14
yen	0.0075	1	0.0086
euro	0.87	115	1

3a. Provide a matrix of the profit in US dollars per 100 lbs. for production at each plant and sale at each of the DCs.

3b. What will be the optimal solution that maximizes profits for Maxpro? What is the associated profit in dollars for Maxpro?

3c. A consultant suggests that the exchange rates may change to those shown in Table 2.10.

TABLE 2.10 Exchange rates

	TO		
FROM	USD	yen	euro
USD	1	165	1.14
yen	0.006	1	0.0075
euro	0.87	132	1

What is the impact of these new exchange rates on the profits associated with the solution in 3b?

3d. Given the new exchange rates in 3c, what is the optimal solution?

3e. What is the benefit to having excess capacity (as against reducing the capacity in Osaka to 3,000,000 lbs.) in the system if exchange rates in the future were similar to those in 3a with a 50% probability or those in 3c with a 50% probability?

Chapter 3

Competition

The focus of a company is to be competitive in the marketplace and thus be profitable. A competitive supply chain has to provide customers with the expected or superior performance. But what does it mean to be competitive? The competitiveness of a supply chain refers to two aspects of the supply chain: (1) the link between a supply chain's choice of its competitive metric and the corresponding choice of its architecture and (2) the impact of competitors on a supply chain's performance. While successful firms in every industry often have unique capabilities, an important question for every firm is to adjust its supply chain architecture to remain competitive in the presence of a changing environment.

The examples in Chapter 1 describe the unique capabilities of Amazon.com, Li & Fung, Cemex, and Zara. In each of these cases, these firms chose specific supply chain architectures to impact their competitiveness. Fine [40] identifies industry clockspeed, i.e., the time between significant product or supply chain shifts, as affecting the choice of the competitive supply chain architecture. His description of the US bicycle industry shows several shifts between vertically integrated and fragmented supply chains between 1890 and 1990. Whenever a dominant player was vertically integrated, pressures to improve components forced disintegration, as assembly of components created competitiveness. At the peak of such fragmentation, a vertically integrated company with unique offerings became the dominant competitor. The lifecycle of a competitive supply chain architecture thus depends on the industry clockspeed.

One of the key messages in this chapter is that the choice of performance parameter and the level of competition will have a significant impact on supply chain performance. Similarly, the presence of competitors, whose strategies may be unknown, may cause a supply chain to be operated differently than in the absence of such competitors.

3.1 SUPPLY CHAIN COMPETITIVENESS

There are many possible proposed measures of supply chain performance. The Supply Chain Operations Reference (SCOR) [106] model is a consensus view across member companies of how to operate a supply chain. The model focuses on the series of activities in a supply chain, i.e., plan, source, make, deliver, return. The basic approach of the SCOR framework is to document current performance, benchmark comparable companies, and identify approaches to incorporate best-in-class approaches. The associated list of metrics is exhaustive and covers all the transactions in a supply chain. Given that the SCOR metrics are evolving over time, we will focus on generic metrics.

3.2 SUPPLY CHAIN METRICS OF COMPETITION

3.2.1 Time-Based Competition

One measure of competition is response time or speed of response. Blackburn [7] and Stalk [114] describe firms that compete on delivery speed. One example is Atlas Door, an industrial door company that coordinated its supply chain to offer custom door delivery (for reactors or furnaces) within two weeks, when the industry standard was over four months. Atlas performed at this level by coordinating order quotation and scheduling production, holding excess capacity and tools, synchronizing all components so that a complete kit was delivered to the construction site. Atlas's market share increased rapidly to 80% of the industry volume within five years, with a 15% price premium.

Similarly, quick-response programs in the apparel industry focused on decreasing apparel delivery lead time. The competitive benefit of lead-time reduction has been estimated to be equivalent to the profit associated with a 40% demand increase. In short, time can generate money for the supply chain.

3.2.2 Resilience

Resilience refers to the ability to restore performance rapidly following an adversity. Sheffi [112] describes how companies can create a resilient supply chain. Nokia's response to the fire in a Phillips semiconductor plant in Albuquerque, NM, a key component supplier, illustrates resilience. Unlike other cell phone manufacturers who also used the same plant, Nokia immediately recognized the criticality of the problem and coordinated with Phillips to allocate components and synchronize the recovery and ramp-up of production. Thus, Nokia's resilience enabled it to minimize the detrimental effects of the disruption. How should supply chains be structured to build in resilience to disruptions? Iyer and Zelikovsky [63] suggest building flexibility, agility, and real options into supply chain facilities as a way to develop resilience in a supply chain.

3.2.3 Triple A Supply Chains

Lee [78] describes three specific features of a supply chain: agility, adaptability, and alignment. Agility refers to the ability to adjust to unexpected changes in demand or supply. Adaptability refers to the ability to adjust supply chain structure to deal with shifts in products, technologies, and so on. Alignment deals with adjusting incentives or coordinating to improve supply chain performance. Seven-Eleven Japan is one company that manages its supply chain to develop all three capabilities. Its performance during the Kobe earthquake was testament to this capability. When the transportation infrastructure was destroyed, Seven-Eleven continued to deliver product, even on motorcycles, to keep shelves stocked for customers.

3.2.4 Environmentally Responsible Supply Chains

McDonough and Braungart [87] focus on the impact across the entire lifecycle of the product from manufacture to reuse. They provide several examples in which the choice of chemicals, technology, installation, and other factors affects the environmental impact of the supply chain. Their goal is to minimize the supply chain's detrimental impact on the environment. McDonough recommends that building supply chains that behave like biological systems, such that one entity's waste is another entity's input. Realizing such a goal will require closed-loop supply chains that recycle product across generations and thus reduce waste generated.

3.2.5 Balanced Variety

In a study of Toyota's supply chain management systems, Iyer, Seshadri, and Vasher [64] describe a v4L framework, which comprises velocity, variability, visibility, and variety along with leadership. They describe Toyota's supply chain choices as a balance of these four Vs, which requires involvement across the employee base as well as coordination across entities in their supply chain, from dealers to manufacturing to transportation to suppliers. As an example, Toyota's careful mix planning, which selects the variety of products that will be offered in each region, enables decreased variability and increased velocity while providing a high level of quality. This framework permits an understanding of supply chain differences across products offered (i.e., Scion, Lexus, and Toyota) and how they vary by geographic location (i.e., United States, Europe, and Japan).

3.3 THE IMPACT OF ALTERNATE PERFORMANCE METRICS

To understand how choosing different performance metrics will impact a supply chain, consider a supply chain with a single manufacturer that supplies a retailer. The manufacturer produces and sells the product at a per-unit price of c and a production lead time of L_m. It costs c_1^t to transport the product to the retailer with a lead time of L_m^t. The result is total lead time of $L_m + L_m^t$ (manufacturing time and transport time) and a cost of $c + c_m^t$ to a single retailer, who in turn adds a markup α. The retailer incurs a holding cost h per unit of product and per unit time. The customer incurs a cost of c_c^t and lead time L^c to get the product to his or her location.

3.3.1 Minimum Purchase Cost

If the manufacturer and retailer were to carry no inventory and all production and orders followed customer order placement, the product purchase price paid by the customer would be minimized. In the absence of any inventory in the system, the cost per unit product for the customer is $\alpha(c + c_m^t) + c_c^t$, and the lead time for delivery to the customer is $L_m + L_m^t$. The customer will then have to hold inventory at his or her location to cover demands over $L_m + L_m^t + L_c^t$ or wait for the product. Notice that this corresponds to a make-to-order system at the manufacturer and assumes that the lead time $L_m + L_m^t$ permits the manufacturer to produce and deliver to the retailer at minimum cost. Similarly, we assume that receiving and shipping to the customer enables the retailer to manage his or her operation at the lowest cost. Finally we assume that the markup charged by the retailer, α, is competitive.

If the goal of the supply chain is to minimize purchase cost, then this approach offers a supply chain structure that enables that performance metric to be minimized. But will the customer wait for delivery in such a system? If not, alternate configurations will be appropriate.

3.3.8 Global Supply Chains

In today's global operations environment, competitive suppliers are expected to follow manufacturers to different locations around the globe and provide product with consistent quality and delivery metrics. How should a supplier position a supply chain structure to succeed in such an environment? Should operations be established in all of the locations where the manufacturer plans to operate? Should alliances be established with local suppliers to supply this manufacturer? Or should logistics companies be used to supply locally but from central manufacturing locations? Each of these questions provides interesting alternatives to be competitive on the global access dimension. Given the need to coordinate supplies and manufacturing, such global supply chains may involve joint capital investments, risk sharing agreements, and so on.

In summary, an important decision for a supply chain is the metric of competition. We have identified several different metrics that have significant impacts on the supply chain structure. The key takeaway is that the metric of competition will affect the supply chain structure chosen. This suggests that prior to evaluating supply chain structures, it is important to understand the metric of competition.

3.4 IMPACT OF COMPETING SUPPLY CHAINS

Thus far, we have focused on alternate performance metrics and associated supply chain architecture. Now we will consider the impact of competitors who independently make decisions to maximize their performance. The presence of competitors may often benefit individual customers but may also decrease the profitability of supply chain entities. A key concept is that competing supply chains generate "equilibrium" results, in which each supply chain makes decisions independently, anticipating but not knowing decisions by competitors. There are several ways that supply chains affect the competing choices and performance of a given supply chain.

For example, the presence of competing retailers offers a customer the choice of visiting the competition if one retailer is out of stock. In anticipation of such "spillover" customers, as well as the increased options for their own customers, retailers can adjust their inventory. An individual retailer's supply chain choice is an equilibrium response to competing retailer's choices.

In other words, competing retailers offer the customer the option to take advantage of many possible pools of capacity, as we will discuss in Chapter 4 on capacity. We described competitive effects on service level in this section, but the same idea can be considered for any metric in the supply chain.

3.5 INVENTORY LEVELS IN THE PRESENCE OF COMPETITORS

To develop intuition regarding the optimal inventory levels carried by retailers in the presence of competitor, consider a retailer's inventory decision when faced with uncertain demand. Because the general model is complicated, we will develop our intuition using a numerical example. Consider a single retailer who faces a single period of uncertain demand, as illustrated in Table 3.1.

TABLE 3.1 Sample demand distributions

Demand	Probability	Cumulative Probability
10	0.20	0.20
20	0.20	0.40
30	0.20	0.60
40	0.10	0.70
50	0.15	0.85
60	0.15	1.00

Assume that Retailer 1 buys the product from a supplier for $1 per unit and has a retail price of $3.80 per unit. Assume that holding cost for leftover inventory is $0.2 per unit. If this were a profit-maximizing retailer, the marginal cost per unit short (C_s) is $2.80 and the marginal cost of excess inventory (C_e) is $1.2. Thus the critical fractile $\left(\frac{C_s}{C_s + C_e}\right)$ is 0.70, suggesting an optimal inventory level of 40 units. The associated expected profit is $64, with the following calculation:

$$(-1 \times 40) + (0.2 \times 3.8 \times 10) + (0.2 \times 3.8 \times 20) + (0.2 \times 3.8 \times 30)$$
$$+ (0.1 \times 3.8 \times 40) + (0.15 \times 3.8 \times 40) + (0.15 \times 3.8 \times 40)$$
$$+ (-0.2 \times 30 \times 0.2) + (-0.2 \times 20 \times 0.2) + (-0.2 \times 10 \times 0.2)$$

Retailer 2, in the same market region, has a similar demand distribution from a separate primary market. Assume that customers who face a stockout at Retailer 1 go to Retailer 2 and vice versa. Thus, the demand faced by Retailer 1 for a given inventory level held by Retailer 2 is obtained as the sum of Retailer I's primary demand plus spillover demand from Retailer 2. Given an inventory Q = 40 held by Retailer 2, the spillover demand received by Retailer 1 has the distribution shown in Table 3.2.

TABLE 3.2 Spillover demand distributions

Spillover Demand	Probability
0	Demand for retailer 2 is ≤ 40 i.e., 0.7
10	Demand for retailer 2 = 50 i.e., 0.15
20	Demand for retailer 2 = 60 i.e., 0.15

The total demand faced by Retailer 1 is the sum of primary demand and spillover demand from Retailer 2. If the rows represent the level of primary demand and the column the spillover demand, then the following matrices provide the different possible values of total demand and the associated probability of occurrence of each of these events (see Table 3.3).

TABLE 3.3 Primary and spillover demands

PRIMARY DEMAND		SPILLOVER DEMAND		
		0	10	20
	Probability	0.7	0.15	0.15
10	0.20	10	20	30
20	0.20	20	30	40
30	0.20	30	40	50
40	0.10	40	50	60
50	0.15	50	60	70
60	0.15	60	70	80

The corresponding probability of each total demand occurrence, given that Retailer 2 carries an inventory of 40 units, is shown in Table 3.4.

TABLE 3.4 Joint probability of demand outcomes

PRIMARY DEMAND		SPILLOVER DEMAND		
		0	10	20
	Probability	0.7	0.15	0.15
10	0.20	0.14	0.03	0.03
20	0.20	0.14	0.03	0.03
30	0.20	0.14	0.03	0.03
40	0.10	0.07	0.015	0.015
50	0.15	0.105	0.0225	0.0225
60	0.15	0.105	0.0225	0.0225

Given the two matrices above, the demand distribution faced by one of the retailers given the other retailer's inventory of 40 units can be summarized as shown in Table 3.5.

Since Retailer 1 will now choose an inventory level to optimize profits, i.e., one that attains the service level of 0.7, the optimal inventory choice is an inventory of 50 units. The associated expected profit for Retailer 1 is thus \$76 (repeat the same calculations as before but with the probability distribution from above and an inventory of 50 units). Using Retailer 1's inventory of 50 units, we can go back and calculate the profits for Retailer 2 as \$67.60, taking into account the spillovers from Retailer 1 to the Retailer 2.

We can now repeat this process for different levels of inventory chosen by Retailer 2 and the optimal decision by Retailer 1. Let Q_2 be the inventory chosen by Retailer 2 and Q_1^* be the optimal response of Retailer 1. Recall that we just calculated that when $Q_2 = 40$, we get $Q_1^* = 50$ and the profit for Retailer 1 as 76; correspondingly for Retailer 2, the profit was \$67.60. Table 3.6 shows the optimal response of Retailer 1 to every choice by Retailer 2 and the associated profits for each retailer.

TABLE 3.5 Total probability of demand outcomes

Total Demand	Probability	Cumulative Probability
10	0.14	0.14
20	0.17	0.31
30	0.20	0.51
40	0.13	0.64
50	0.15	0.79
60	0.14	0.9325
70	0.05	0.9775
80	0.02	1

TABLE 3.6 Expected responses and profits for retailers 1 and 2

Fix Q_2	Optimize Q_1^*	$EP(Q_1^*)$	$EP(Q_2)$
10	70	119.2	28
20	60	99.2	48
30	50	84.8	62.4
40	50	76	67.6
50	50	68.2	68.2
60	40	64	72.4

Given that both retailers would keep adjusting their inventories in response to each other, what is the equilibrium inventory? It is the point at which, given Retailer 1's decision, the decision made by Retailer 2, fed back to Retailer 1, generates the same decision. Such an equilibrium is called a *Nash Equilibrium*, in honor of economist John Nash.

Note that from the table above, this equilibrium level is 50 units. When Retailer 2 chooses an inventory of 50 units, so does Retailer 1, and thus the decision for Retailer 2 remains the same in response. We can identify an equilibrium level of inventory for both retailers to be 50 units. Note that this inventory level is higher than the level in the independent retailer system, but with a higher level of expected profit. Thus, for this example, competition to satisfy demand from one's own customer base and spillover demand from other retailers leads to higher profits and higher inventory levels for all retailers.

This suggests that a higher inventory level and the higher associated effective service level is the outcome in a competitive environment. This happens because of the opportunity to both sell leftover product to satisfy the spillover demand from the other retailer and gain the higher revenue from satisfying its primary demand. Thus, in this case, competition provides benefits to the customer in the form of improved service and manifests itself in the form of higher retailer profits.

This also means that in a competitive environment, efforts to implement schemes such as inventory pooling among retailers may have limited success.

3.6 COMPETITION ACROSS PRODUCT ATTRIBUTES

How do products with different attributes impact demand? Given customer responses to different attributes, how should a manufacturer position products in the attribute space? What is the impact of promised lead time on capacity required?

To examine this question, we provide an example context and then provide details of a model. The example is based on work done by Iyer and Sommer [62] for the Indiana Department of Transportation. The goal of the study was to understand the effect of improving transportation infrastructure in southern Indiana on competitiveness of the local industry. Southern Indiana's Dubois County is home to a thriving commercial furniture industry. In the furniture supply chain, product flows from forest owners who grow the trees to lumber distributors to veneer manufacturers to component suppliers to furniture manufacturers to retailers and to the final customers.

Each of these steps of the supply chain was governed by an independent association that focused on maximizing its performance. Data analysis showed that logistics costs (primarily transport costs) were between 5% and 20% of cost at each step of the supply chain. In addition, most companies had suppliers deliver inbound product; thus the cost of product included the inbound transport costs. This suggested that if there were five stages in the supply chain and a 10% reduction in logistics cost at a stage, the supply chain as a whole might save 5% of cost—a significant improvement in competitiveness.

A model developed by Boyaci and Ray [11] was used to develop insights for this project. The model describes a context where a retailer sells two different products to a market characterized by price and delivery lead time. Suppose that, for Customer Product 1, the retailer chooses a lead time L_1 and price p_1, while for Product 2 there is a fixed, long lead time L_2 but a choice of price p_2. Given these parameters, customers adjust their choices and thus generate demand rates for each of the two products, as follows:

$$\lambda_1 = a - \beta_p p_1 + \theta_p(p_2 - p_1) - \beta_L L_1 + \theta_L(L_2 - L_1)$$

$$\lambda_2 = a - \beta_p p_2 + \theta_p(p_1 - p_{2)} - \beta_L L_2 + \theta_L(L_1 - L_2)$$

These demand relations suggest that demand for one product is decreasing when product price increases and product lead time increases. But this same product attracts customers from the other product's demand if its price and lead time are lower. Now consider the cost associated with delivering this demand within the promised lead time. Given an exponential service time, the lead time distribution for retailer j is exponential, with a rate $\mu_j - \lambda_j$ (from standard single-server exponential interarrival and exponential service-time models), thus the service rate μ_j required to guarantee a lead time L_j can be expressed as $\lambda_j - \frac{ln(1-\alpha)}{L_j}$, where α is the desired service level within lead time L_j.

Finally we can express the expected profit for each retailer as $(p_1 - m)\lambda_1 + (p_2 - m)\lambda_2 - A_1\mu_1 - A_2\mu_2$. In this expression, A_1 and A_2 represent the per unit per unit of service costs for the service rates μ_1 and μ_2, respectively, and m represents the manufacturing (e.g., material) cost per unit of product. The retailer will have to choose optimal values of p_1, p_2, L_1, and L_2 so as to maximize profits across the two products.

We present the results using an example, to provide intuition regarding the interaction across products. Results of the model are shown in Figure 3.1. The x-axis shows the impact of changes in the cost associated with offering a lower lead time for custom products, and the y-axis shows the corresponding on optimal lead times, pricing, total demand, and profitability. Consider the impact of logistics improvements and manufacturing changes so that A_1, the cost per unit time to deliver custom products, decreases (i.e., moves to the left on the x-axis). The graphs suggest that if A_1 decreases, it is then optimal to lower prices for custom products (Figure 3.1a), lower lead times offered (Figure 3.1b), thus increase demand for such products (Figure 3.1c), and significantly improve profitability (Figure 3.1d).

FIGURE 3.1 Impact of reducing cost to lower lead time

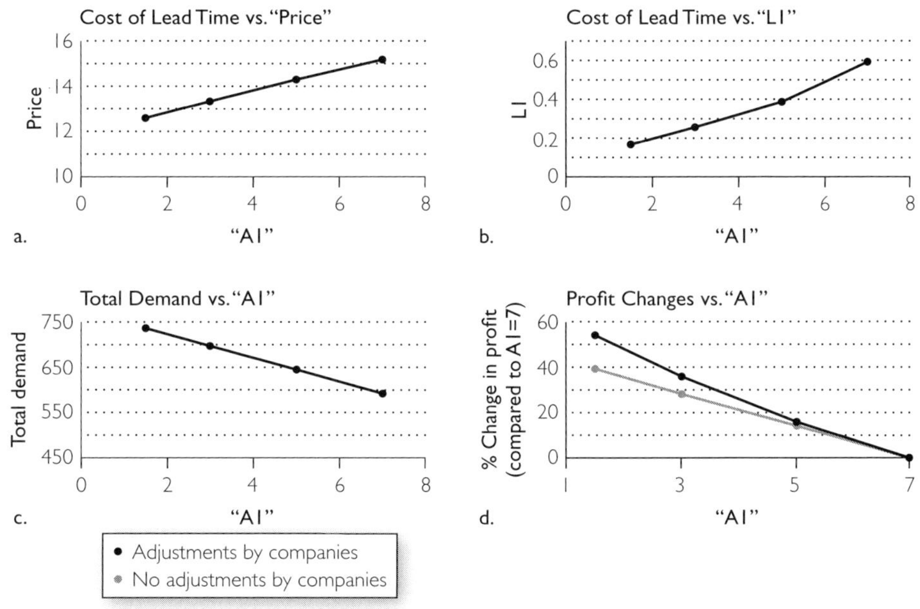

Figure 3.1d also shows that changing the product mix by adjusting lead times and pricing can be very beneficial: notice the upper versus the lower line. In other words, efforts to reduce delivery lead times can improve industry profitability by permitting a shift to faster-response, higher-margin products supplied competitively.

The model described earlier was used to link improvements in local logistics, interpreted as decreasing A_1, to their impact on competitiveness (improved profitability).

3.7 ADVANCE ORDER DISCOUNTS UNDER COMPETITION

Manufacturers often offer advance order discounts to attract retailers. Consider a supply chain where two retailers offer products to their separate customer bases. As is the practice in many industries, suppose one of these retailers offers a price discount for those who place orders in advance of the season. This discount may attract a portion of the demand from both retailers, depending on the relative size of the discounts offered by each retailer as well as the fraction of the customer base that will be sensitive to such early demand placement. Note that all deliveries take place during the season. This section provides a short summary of the model (details are in the paper [86]) and a numerical example.

As an example, consider Retailers 1 and 2, whose joint demand has the distribution in Table 3.7.

While their in-season demand levels are correlated, both retailers have to order inventory in advance in the start of the season and thus face their own independent single-period demand uncertainty models (newsvendor models). Let x_1 and x_2 refer to the discount factor for early orders, thus the retail prices are px_1 (for Retailer 1) and px_2 (for Retailer 2) for early orders.

TABLE 3.7 Joint probability of demand for Retailers 1 and 2

Demand 1	Demand 2	Probability
4	4	0.2
4	12	0.3
12	4	0.2
12	12	0.3

Note that in the absence of any advance orders, Retailer 1 faces a demand of 4 with probability 0.5 and 12 with probability 0.5. Similarly, Retailer 2 faces a demand of 4 with probability 0.4 and 12 with probability 0.6. If the retailer price during the season is \$1/unit, retailer cost is \$0.6/unit, salvage value of leftover inventory is \$0.4/unit, the optimal service level planned by each retailer is $\frac{p-c}{p-s} = 0.67$. Thus Retailer 1 and Retailer 2 would order 12 units and obtain expected profits of 2.4 and 2.88 respectively.

Suppose Retailer 1 offers an advance order discount of 30%, i.e., $x_1 = 0.7$. Also assume that $a = b = r_{1e} = r_{1s} = 0.4$. Note that when such a discount is offered, the fraction of demands that are observed are $R_{11} = 0.168$, $R_{12} = 0$, $R_{22} = 0$, $R_{21} = 0.168$. Thus we get the following set of values for the early demands: $D_{11} = R_{11}D_1 + R_{21}D_2$, where D_{11} is the advance order observed by Retailer 1 and D_{21} is the regular season demand. Similarly, D_{22} is the regular season demand observed by Retailer 2 (see Table 3.8).

TABLE 3.8 Expected profit for Retailer 1

D_1	D_2	Prob	D_{11}	D_{21}	D_{12}	D_{22}	Expected Profit Retailer 1
4	4	0.2	1.344	3.328	0	3.328	1.465
4	12	0.3	2.688	3.328	0	9.984	1.866
12	4	0.2	2.688	9.984	0	3.328	1.866
12	12	0.3	4.032	9.984	0	9.984	4.396

Thus the expected profit across all possible demand realizations is the product of the probabilities in the third column and the associated expected profit in the last column which is 2.545. The expected profit for Retailer 1 when $D_{11} = 1.344$ is $(px_1 - c)D_{11} + (p - c)D_{21} = (1 \times 0.7 - 0.6) \times 1.344 + (1 - 0.6) \times 3.328 = 1.4656$. Similar calculations apply when $D_{11} = 4.032$. However, when $D_{11} = 2.688$, the demand during the season can take values of 3.328 or 9.984 with respective probabilities of $\frac{0.3}{0.3+0.2} = 0.6$ and 0.4 respectively. To provide a service level of 0.67, Retailer 1 will thus order to cover D_{11} and order 9.984 units to cover the uncertain demand. A newsvendor expected calculation for the in-season demand generates an expected profit of 1.597. Thus the total retailer expected profit when $D_{11} = 2.688$ is obtained as $[(1 \times 0.7 - 0.6)2.688] + 1.597 = 1.866$.

However, since Retailer 2 does not offer an advance order, the observed demand would be 3.328 and 9.984 with probabilities of 0.4 and 0.6 respectively. Thus Retailer 2 would order 9.984 units and get an expected profit of 2.396. The results show that Retailer 1 benefits from offering the advance orders because its expected profit increases from 2.4 to 2.545. Retailer 2 observes a profit decrease from 2.88 to 2.396.

Similar analysis will show that if Retailer 2 were to offer an advance order at a discount of 30%, i.e., $x_2 = 0.7$, and Retailer 1 did not, then the expected profit for Retailer 2 would increase (from the original 2.88) to 2.94. Retailer 1, on the other hand, would observe its expected profit decrease to 1.996. The analysis shows that the retailer who offers an advance order sees a benefit, to the detriment of the other retailer.

But suppose Retailer 1 offers an advance order; is it in Retailer 2's incentive to also offer an advanced order? We can analyze this question by considering the case when both retailers offer an advance order discount of 30%, i.e., $x_1 = x_2 = 0.7$. Consider the same parameters as earlier, i.e., $a = b = r_{1e} = R_{11} = R_{22} = R_{21} = 0.4$. The table provided can be used to verify that we get the values in Table 3.9.

TABLE 3.9 Expected profits for Retailers 1 and 2

D_1	D_2	Prob	D_{11}	D_{21}	D_{12}	D_{22}	Exp Profit Retailer 1	Exp Profit Retailer 2
4	4	0.2	1.152	2.848	1.152	2.848	1.254	1.254
4	12	0.3	2.304	2.848	2.304	8.544	1.597	2.28
12	4	0.2	2.304	8.544	2.304	2.848	1.597	2.28
12	12	0.3	3.456	8.544	3.456	8.544	3.763	3.763

Thus the corresponding expected profit for Retailer 1 is 2.178 and the corresponding profit for Retailer 2 is 2.52. These values are obtained by taking the product of the probability and expected profit. Thus, when both retailers offer an advance order discount, they see their expected profits drop from the original values of 2.4 and 2.88 to the new values of 2.178 and 2.52. Thus, competition can improve individual supply chain performance, but when matched by competitors, can create a prisoner's dilemma outcome (bad for all) when both retailers engage in the same action.

This example illustrates the counterintuitive effects of competition: it can cause actions that can worsen overall performance even when it would have been beneficial in a monopolistic context. The bottom line for companies is that not all actions can generate the planned beneficial outcome in the presence of competition.

3.8 CHAPTER SUMMARY

This chapter showed how the choice of metric of competition and the existence of competitors affects the performance of a supply chain. The first part of the chapter examined the many alternate metrics that can determine performance, including costs, profitability, service, variety, and lead time. Each of these alternate metrics implies different choices for supply chain architecture as well as for the details of operation. In addition, in the presence of competitors, agreements that are good for the supply chain in a monopolistic setting may be bad for the supply chain in a competitive environment. Thus one may find an industry supply chain stuck in a bad equilibrium with frequent harmful promotions or advance order discounts, unable to pull itself out of this state due to competitive pressures. This chapter thus suggests that competitiveness can be a significant driver of supply chain performance.

Chapter 4

Capacity

Capacity refers to the designed maximum flow of work through a facility over a period of time. When used in the context of a warehouse, capacity refers to the amount that can be shipped in a given time period, every hour or day, for example. For truck transportation, capacity refers to the quantity that can be moved in a trip. For a retail store, capacity may refer to the maximum amount of inventory that can be held at the store or the maximum number of customers that can be served per hour to satisfy demand.

However, the available capacity in a period of time consists of a hardware decisions (those that deal with physical constraints) as well as software decisions (those that deal with scheduling or forecasting aspects of deployment). For example, at the business school I teach in, the physical space and classrooms in a new building were designed with a plan to accommodate a maximum of 250 students in any given year of our two-year MBA program. The associated room capacities then represent the hardware decision with respect to capacity. However, the actual deployment, i.e., classes offered, schedules, and enrollment of students, is adjusted as conditions evolve. These factors represent the software associated with the use of capacity. Often the hardware and software decisions are comingled during use and are thus difficult to disentangle.

A quick example regarding the hardware vs. software aspects of capacity occurred in a project dealing with deployment of Chicago's garbage trucks ([32]). The capacity of trucks (weight and volume) to pick up garbage was an input to the analysis. But we realized that if a garbage truck picked up garbage and, in the middle of the day, went to a dump site to drop it off and returned to continue garbage pick-up, it could pick up double its designed capacity during a single day. In other words, the deployment of the truck affected the daily garbage pick-up capacity. The same capacity increase is true if employees work overtime or if subcontracted capacity can be seamlessly added. Our first focus is on the hardware decision regarding capacity. This will be followed by a discussion of some of the software decisions to increase capacity.

Consider contexts when capacity decisions have to be made in advance of demand realization. In the apparel industry, capacity has to be chosen eight to twelve months ahead of demand. In the auto industry, plans for capacity configurations at plants are made several years in advance. For infrastructure decisions, such as highway construction, decisions may be made fifteen to twenty years in advance. In a just-in-time delivery context, decisions may be made four hours in advance ([64]). Clearly the main question is the extent of demand uncertainty when decisions are made and the consequences of having an inadequate level of capacity. In addition, if the capacity decision maker is different from the information provider, incentive effects have to be considered. Hence the need for coordination agreements (as discussed in Chapter 5). However, the availability of alternate sources of capacity, albeit at a higher cost, can relieve the pressure to commit to capacity in advance.

In other contexts, there may be a number of demands on capacity at the same time. In such cases, performance of the supply chain is affected by how this temporal supply-and-demand mismatch is resolved. Such contexts can best be viewed as queues, where requests for capacity await access to that capacity. Even in such cases, the configuration of access to capacity affects performance. In a queueing context, choice of priorities for different arrival streams can affect the realized performance; thus, matching priorities to the level of demand uncertainty may reduce overall inventories in a supply chain.

If the temporal demand levels can be forecast, then a dynamic adjustment of capacity to synchronize with demands may enable performance improvement without a significant increase in capacity levels. As an illustration, allocating employees to temporally staggered shifts can be a mechanism to manage the impact of demand variation.

This chapter will illustrate several capacity contexts and provide tools to effectively select and deploy capacity.

4.1 CAPACITY CHOICE IN THE PRESENCE OF DEMAND UNCERTAINTY

Consider a company that is planning capacity but is unsure of the potential demand for products. Suppose the cost per unit of capacity is \$25. Next, if demand is satisfied, the company gets revenue of \$100 per unit. Leftover capacity can be used to satisfy secondary demand but generates revenue of only \$10 per unit. There is sufficient capacity for this secondary demand. For purposes of clarity, assume that demand can take the values with associated probabilities as shown in Table 4.1.

TABLE 4.1 Demands and associated probabilities

Demand	Probability
100	0.6
300	0.3
500	0.1

Now suppose the company were to obtain a capacity of 300 units. The associated expected profit can be calculated as

$$(-25 \times 300) + (100 \times 100 \times 0.6) + (100 \times 300 \times 0.3) \\ + (100 \times 300 \times 0.1) + (10 \times 200 \times 0.6) = 11{,}700$$

Repeating this exercise for each of the possible choices of capacity, i.e., 100, 300, and 500, provides the results in Table 4.2.

TABLE 4.2 Capacity choices and associated expected profit

Capacity	Expected Profit
100	7,500
300	11,700
500	10,500

Table 4.2 suggests that an optimal capacity is 300 units. Thus the company will forgo some of the demand when the demand is 500 units. This decision maximizes the company's expected profit. It is also clear that if the company cares about unsatisfied demand and its effect on future customer arrivals, then there has to be a mechanism to account for the cost of this unsatisfied demand—perhaps by including a goodwill cost for unsatisfied demand. (This cost is the net present value of the margin associated with future lost sales caused by the unsatisfied demand this period.) If a goodwill cost is included, it may be optimal to increase capacity, depending on the level of this goodwill cost, to increase expected profits.

The decision described above is commonly termed the *newsvendor model*. The optimal capacity decision can be obtained by identifying two costs: the marginal cost of excess capacity, C_e and the marginal cost of capacity shortage, C_s. In the example above, the marginal cost of excess capacity is $C_e = 25 - 10 = 15$, while the marginal cost of capacity shortage is $C_s = 100 - 25 = 75$. Thus the ratio is $\frac{75}{75+15} = 0.83$. The optimal capacity decision is to identify the lowest capacity level that guarantees that the probability of satisfying the cumulative demand is at least 0.83. The corresponding decision is to choose a capacity of 300, which provides a probability of 90% probability of satisfying cumulative demand that is less than or equal to 300.

Now suppose it is possible for the company to obtain a perfect forecast of demand and then choose capacity. In such a case, it is optimal to choose a capacity level that matches demand. Such a context is called the perfect-information expected profit. The expected capacity would be

$$(100 \times 0.6) + (300 \times 0.3) + (500 \times 0.1) = 200$$

For this example, the expected profit under perfect information would be

$$((100 - 25) \times 100 \times 0.6) + ((100 - 25) \times 300 \times 0.3) + ((100 - 25) \times 500 \times 0.1) = 15{,}000$$

The profit impact of demand uncertainty is thus 15,000 – 11,700 = 3300, or 28.2% of expected profit. This example shows how demand uncertainty interacts with capacity to affect profit. It also shows the potential value of perfect information, obtained through sources such as market surveys, expert forecasts, and test markets.

This example also shows that one response to demand uncertainty is to add a capacity buffer, e.g., (300 – 200) = 100 units. The associated buffer is a hedge against demand uncertainty. Thus whenever capacity in a system is observed to be far greater than observed demand, it may in fact represent an optimal buffer size and an option to serve potential demand.

4.2 CAPACITY CHOICE GIVEN LEAD TIME

This section presents an example to illustrate the capacity impact of long lead times. Consider a manufacturer who faces demand for a fashion product that can take one of two levels, low and high. If the demand level is high, then the demand is expected to follow a uniform distribution between six and ten units. If the demand is low, then it is expected to be uniformly distributed between one and five units. Given the nature of manufacturing, capacity decisions have to be made many months in advance of demand. At the point in time that a capacity decision is made, suppose the manufacturer does not know if demand will be high or low, but the best estimate is that demand will be high or low with a 50% probability.

Suppose the cost of capacity for a certain manufacturer is \$100 per unit and has to be incurred in advance, independent of actual demand. Suppose the revenue associated with satisfying demand is \$200 per unit. The maximum quantity that can be produced is limited to the available capacity. Any unused capacity can be used to satisfy demand for low-margin products but yields a revenue of only \$20 per unit. Any unsatisfied demand is estimated to have a goodwill impact of \$200 per unit.

Given the lack of information regarding the demand level, the demand faced by the manufacturer is illustrated in Table 4.3.

TABLE 4.3 Demand faced by the manufacturer

Demand	Probability
1	0.1
2	0.1
3	0.1
4	0.1
5	0.1
6	0.1
7	0.1
8	0.1
9	0.1
10	0.1

Given that $r = 200$, $c = 100$, $s = 20$, and $g = 200$, the value of $C_s = r + g - c = 300$ and $C_e = c - s = 80$. Thus the optimal service level is $\frac{C_s}{C_s + C_e} = 78.9\%$. Given this service level, the optimal capacity choice for the manufacturer is to choose a capacity to manufacture eight units. Using the same approach as in earlier sections, the expected profit associated with this capacity choice can be calculated to be \$236.

Now suppose the manufacturer has access to data from related markets that enable a reliable estimate of whether the demand level is high or low. How does this affect the choice of capacity? Note that if the capacity decision has to be made when demand is low, it is optimal to have a capacity of four units to ensure a service level of 78.9%. Similarly when the demand is high, it is optimal to have a capacity of nine units to ensure a service level of 78.9%. Thus the expected capacity chosen is $(0.5 \times 4) + (0.5 \times 9) = 6.5$ units. In addition, because the capacity level is chosen to be synchronized with demand level, the expected profit when demand is low (with a capacity of four units) is \$144, and the expected profit when demand is high (with a capacity of nine units) is \$644. Thus the expected profit across demand levels is $(0.5 \times 144) + (0.5 \times 644) = \$394$.

This example shows the close interaction between information, lead time, and capacity choice in the presence of demand uncertainty. In the absence of information, capacity buffers are optimal. However, lower lead times may permit better demand information, thus leading to a better match between demand levels and capacity. This enables additional capacity to be planned when there is an upside potential associated with high demand and simultaneously lower capacity when demand levels are anticipated to be low. The net result is a higher profitability with lowered average capacity levels.

4.3 CAPACITY CHOICE TO MAINTAIN SERVICE LEAD TIME

Often, orders placed in a supply chain face lead times for delivery based on the presence of supply or capacity constraints. We provide a model to understand the source of such lead times—in this case, it is due to capacity (or supply) and demand mismatches.

Consider a single location of capacity, such as a warehouse or manufacturer. Orders arrive to this location, and the facility operates in a make-to-order manner. Service is provided in order of arrival. The time to produce or service a given order follows an exponential distribution with parameter μ. If the orders come from many independent sources, then they can be described statistically as a rate. From a technical perspective, the interarrival rate (time between successive arrivals) of orders to this location can be expressed as an exponential distribution with a rate parameter λ. Thus orders arrive at a rate of λ orders per time unit, and the location can produce μ orders per time unit.

It can be shown that the probability that the location is busy or producing an order is $\frac{\lambda}{\mu}$. The ratio $\frac{\lambda}{\mu}$ is also known as the system load, often denoted by $\rho = \frac{\lambda}{\mu}$. The expected time an order spends in the system is

$$L = \frac{1}{\mu - \lambda}$$

Therefore the expected time an order spends in the queue waiting for service is

$$L_q = \frac{1}{\mu - \lambda} - \frac{1}{\mu}$$

A quick glance at the expressions shows that for the system to be stable (i.e., have lead times that are finite), the arrival rate of orders must be less than the service rate of orders. The difference between these two rates is the "buffer capacity" that the system needs to carry to deal with temporal supply-and-demand mismatches. How big should this buffer capacity be? Intuition suggests that the faster the need to respond, the higher the buffer capacity. To understand this idea, note that if the lead time has to be guaranteed to be lower than a fixed value, on average, then the service rate has to be proportionally larger than the arrival rate, i.e., $\mu = \lambda + \frac{1}{L}$. Note also the inverse relationship between lead time and service rate required. This means that as the system is forced to commit to faster service, the service rate grows exponentially larger than the arrival rate.

Every time you drive by a fire station, you observe the capacity that is idle but ready to deploy; this is buffer capacity that can be deployed as soon as a fire alarm is heard. This buffer capacity is the price that has to be paid to ensure prompt response.

A well-known result called Little's law yields the expected number of orders in the system:

$$N = \lambda L = \frac{\lambda}{\mu - \lambda}$$

and the expected number of orders in a queue:

$$N_q = \lambda L_q = \frac{\lambda^2}{\mu(\mu - \lambda)}$$

To illustrate these ideas, consider a numerical example with four orders arriving per hour to a location that can serve these orders at a rate of six orders per hour. The queuing template spreadsheet (available in the course CD and website) computes that the average lead time is 0.5 hour, or 30 minutes, and that there are an average of 2 orders in the system. The lead time for an order consists of an average service time of 10 minutes (or $\frac{1}{6}$ hour) and an average time spent waiting in the queue of 20 minutes. The average time spent waiting in the queue is directly affected by the buffer capacity in the system, i.e., the inverse of difference between the service rate (the capacity) and the arrival rate. Thus, a higher buffer capacity decreases order lead time. However, a higher buffer capacity also implies a lower capacity utilization.

Table 4.4 summarizes the effect of increasing the arrival rate of students while maintaining the service rate of six orders per hour. For each pair of arrival and service rates, the

TABLE 4.4 Average WIP and lead time for different arrival rates

Arrival Rate	Average Work-In-Process	Average Lead Time
4	2 orders	0.5 hours
4.5	3 orders	0.667 hours
5	5 orders	1 hour
5.5	11 orders	2 hours
5.75	23 orders	4 hours
5.95	119 orders	20 hours

queueing template (provided in the book website) was used to obtain the average work-in-process inventory and the average lead time.

Observe that as the ratio of arrival rate to service rate increases, the capacity utilization at the location increases, but the corresponding lead time faced by a customer increases. As an example, when the arrival rate increases to 5.5 orders per hour, the expected lead time is now 2 hours, even though the service time (on average) is only 10 minutes. Thus, for high arrival rates (5.95 per hour), the waiting time in the system is 20 hours, while service time remains 10 minutes. This example shows that lead time consists of both service time and time spent waiting to access capacity. Intuitively, such congestion mimics the delays one faces during rush hour traffic, i.e., road flow capacity remains constant while demand for that capacity grows, thus creating congestion.

But what can be done to decrease such congestion effects? The following sections suggest possible remedies.

4.4 IMPACT OF MANY CAPACITY UNITS OPERATING IN PARALLEL

Consider a system consisting of *mc* independent capacity units operating in parallel, all capable of providing service to an arriving stream of orders, which are processed in order of arrival. Orders are allocated to the first available unit of capacity. Assume (as before) that the service time is exponentially distributed. The arrival of orders to the system has an interarrival time that is exponential with parameter λ. As stated earlier, from a theoretical perspective, this model of order arrivals approximates the combination of many independent order sources.

For such a system, there exist standard templates to analyze performance, such as the expected number of orders in the system, the expected lead time for an order, and so on. We will use such a template to apply the model to develop insights into the configuration of capacity.

4.4.1 Understanding the Benefits of Capacity Pooling

Consider a company with two independent locations, each of which serves orders for its own geographic territory. Each location receives, on average, about 4.375 orders per hour at each center, and each location has the capacity to process 5 orders per hour. There is some extra capacity to deal with demand and supply fluctuations, the same as described in the earlier section. The queuing template provides the expected lead time for an order and the expected number of orders waiting to be processed and verifies that the system will have an average work-in-process of 7 orders, and orders will face an average lead time of 1.6 hours. Across both locations there will be 14 orders in the system.

Now consider an option to combine the two locations and share their capacity. For now, assume that the location that delivers the product is irrelevant to satisfying the requirements of the order. Thus, the orders can take advantage of situations when queues exist at one location while the other location is free. Notice that under this pooled capacity system, the queueing template shows that the total pool of customers across both locations faces an arrival rate of 8.75 orders per hour. Suppose the service rate at each office, 5 orders per hour, remains the same. Using the queuing template with two locations, it can be seen that the resulting system will have 7.46 orders on average in work-in-process inventory and an average lead time of 0.853 hours.

Thus, as long as the pooled order stream can be served by any location, at the same rate, lead time is decreased by about 50% with the same capacity. This is the benefit of pooling capacity in a supply chain. But how did the same capacity, deployed differently, have such a significant impact on performance? Notice that in a pooled capacity system, any available unit of capacity can be used to satisfy a waiting order. This flexibility to use a larger pool of capacity at any time prevents queues, improving the performance of the supply chain.

4.5 IS SPLITTING CAPACITY APPROPRIATE? THE IMPACT OF ORDER-RELATED SERVICE CHARACTERISTICS

The earlier section showed that pooling capacity can benefit the supply chain. But there are cases where splitting capacity may improve the system. To illustrate this issue, consider a supply chain where orders have different service requirements. When such orders share a location, a set-up time or change-over time is introduced in order for the location to accommodate the requirements of disparate customers.

As an example, consider a supply chain with 16 machines that process orders placed by customers. Customer orders form a common queue and are allocated to the first available machine. The set-up time or change-over time for each customer order is 14.25 minutes. The service time after setups is 30 minutes. The total order arrival rate across all customers is 20 orders per hour. With a common queue, using the queueing template, we can see that the average lead time is 1.132 hours.

Consider an alternative in which customer orders are split into four similar groups (i.e., orders grouped together are similar to each other and thus incur lower change-over times), so that each group thus has an arrival rate of 5 orders per hour. Correspondingly, suppose the machines are divided into four sets of four machines, and each set only deals with a limited set of customer order requests. As a result, suppose the set-up time between orders in each group (because these orders are similar) decreases to 3 minutes per customer. Using the queueing template, the lead time for customers now drops to 0.773 hours.

Thus, even though the benefits of pooling capacity have been sacrificed, the supply chain benefits from the increased productivity of the specialized capacity. Therefore, even though capacity pooling increases potential access to capacity, the associated mix of tasks to be done at pooled locations may affect the supply of capacity available and thus worsen system performance. In other words, capacity configurations have to balance the benefits of pooling with the benefits of splitting capacity.

This idea of creating supply chains with unique characteristics constitutes one of the basic ideas behind the development of cellular manufacturing systems.

4.6 IMPACT OF A SERIES OF STAGES WITH CAPACITY: A SERIAL PRODUCTION LINE

The earlier sections considered a single stage of capacity. However, orders often have to be processed by many separate stages in order to be completed. Consider a supply chain where a given customer order has to go through a sequence of *MS* stages for the order to be served. The customer order starts at the first stage and moves from stage to stage (from stage 1 to stage *MS*) until all service is completed.

Suppose now that each stage (labeled $i = 1, 2, \ldots, MS$) has mc_i machines working in parallel. Suppose the time for a customer order to be served by a machine at stage i is exponentially distributed with parameter μ_i. Then, if orders enter the first stage with interarrival time that is exponential with parameter λ, it can be shown statistically that they enter all stages with the same rate, λ. Thus, each stage can be analyzed independently. The expected lead time for a customer is the sum of lead times in each stage,

$$\text{Total lead time} = \sum_{i=1}^{MS} L_i$$

where L_i is the lead time for stage i.

To understand this analysis, consider a manufacturing system that processes orders using a make-to-order approach. This means that order processing begins only when the order reaches a certain stage. Suppose each order has three tasks that have to be done in series. All orders go from stage 1 to stage 2 to stage 3. Suppose stage 1 has one machine that does task 1 at the rate of 5 orders per hour. Stage 2 is done by three machines working in parallel, each operating at the rate of 1.4 orders per hour. Stage three is done by two machines operating in parallel, each operating at a rate of 2.2 orders per hour. Suppose job orders arrive at a rate of 4 orders per hour. What is the total lead time for an order to be processed across all the stages and delivered to the customer?

The total lead time is computed by taking each stage, evaluating it separately with the same arrival rate of orders, and adding up the resulting values. For stage 1, with a service rate of 5 orders per hour, an arrival rate of 4 orders per hour, and one machine, the lead time (from the queueing template) is 1 hour. For stage 2, with a service rate of 1.4 orders per hour, three machines working in parallel, and the arrival rate of 4 orders per hour, the lead time (from the queueing template) is 5.27 hours. Similarly, for stage 3, with a service rate of 2.2 orders per hour and two machines working in parallel, the lead time is 2.61 hours. The total time for an order to pass through all three stages is the sum of these lead times: 1 + 5.27 + 2.61, or 8.8 hours. Notice that the number of stages and the capacity at each stage influence the overall lead time observed by the customer.

The purpose of this section is to highlight the link between plant capacity configuration and the consequent impact on customer order lead time. Once the linkage is understood, the next step is to find a way to restructure capacity to improve lead time performance.

4.7 LEAD TIME IN A MANUFACTURING SYSTEM WITH ORDER BATCHES

Consider demand that consists of orders, where each order is for a batch of Q units. These orders are generated by the customer, for example, a retailer, either to (1) replenish manufacturer finished goods inventory or (2) represent an accumulation of customer demands for the product when the manufacturer carries *no* finished goods inventory. The main reason that manufacturing and ordering are done in batches is to optimize the impact of set-up times on the machine.

Consider production in batches of size Q units, where it takes t_s time units to set up a batch for production and t_p time units to produce each unit in a batch. The production time for a batch of Q units is modeled as exponentially distributed with a mean production batch rate of $\mu = \dfrac{1}{t_s + (t_p Q)}$. If D is the demand rate faced by the retailer, W is the number of independent inventory sites whose orders are supplied by this machine, and Q is the order batch size, then the arrival rate of order batches is $\lambda = \dfrac{WD}{Q}$. Note that the manufacturing lead time is given by the lead time for the corresponding queueing system.

Consider an example of the Instock store that sells ten different types of products. Demand for each product each day follows a normal distribution with a mean of 50 units and a standard deviation of 25 units. All these products are produced by a manufacturer who carries no finished goods inventory, i.e., operates a make-to-order system.

The manufacturer has 3 machines working in parallel, and production of a product requires a set-up time of 30 minutes and a processing time of 2 minutes per unit. This implies a set-up cost of $50. The cost per unit of product charged by the manufacturer is $25/unit. Instock's holding and storage cost are estimated to be 10% of the cost per unit. Assume that production occurs 8 hours per day, 5 days per week, 50 weeks per year, and that Instock's service level is 95%.

Question 1: What should be Instock's order size be for each product?

Answer 1: The order size is obtained as the economic order quantity:

$$EOQ = \sqrt{\frac{2 \times 50 \times 50 \times 50 \times 5}{0.1 \times 25}} = 707.1 \approx 708 \text{ units}$$

Question 2: What is the order arrival rate faced by the manufacturer?

Answer 2:

$$\lambda = \frac{50 \times 10}{708} = 0.707 \text{ orders/day}$$

Question 3: What is the lead time to fill a product's order?

Answer 3: All products require processing on 1 machine. All 3 machines are capable of processing all products. Thus

$$mc = 3$$

$$\mu = \frac{1 \times 60 \times 8}{(30 + (2 \times 708))} = 0.3319 \text{ orders/day}$$

Read off the value from the queueing template for 3 machines working in parallel and the arrival rate and service rate as obtained earlier. Thus, the lead time is

$$L = 4.77 \text{ days}$$

Question 4: Provide an inventory policy for Instock. Provide the average inventory level and associated holding cost at Instock.

Answer 4: If Instock were to follow a quick-response (Q, r) policy, the reorder level r would be

$$r = (50 \times 4.77) + (Z_{0.95} \times 5 \times \sqrt{4.77}) = 256.4 \text{ units}$$

$$Q = 708 \text{ units as before.}$$

Also, the average inventory level at Instock is

$$Q + r - \mu L = \frac{708}{2} + 256.4 - (50 \times 4.77) = 372 \text{ units}$$

Thus, across the 10 products, the average inventory level is

$$372 \times 10 = 3{,}720 \text{ units}$$

The holding cost faced by Instock is

$$0.1 \times 25 \times 3{,}720 = \$9{,}300/\text{year}.$$

Question 5: The manufacturer is considering a reorganization of his machines. The new system will have 2 machines dedicated to producing 7 products and the remaining 1 machine dedicated to producing 3 products. Set-up time to change-over between products would now be 5 minutes. Consequently, the setup cost per order will be \$5.

Provide the impact on Instock's inventory level and the manufacturing lead time.

$$Q = \sqrt{\frac{2\times 5\times 50\times 50\times 5}{0.1\times 25}} = 223.1 \approx 224 \text{ units}$$

We first examine the effect on the 7 products that share 2 machines.

$$\lambda = \frac{50\times 7}{224} = 1.563 \text{ orders/day}$$

$$c = 2$$

$$\mu = \frac{1\times 60\times 8}{(5+(2\times 224))} = 1.059 \text{ orders/day}$$

Read off the values from the queueing template as

$$L = 2.07 \text{ days}$$

$$r = (50 \times 2.07) + (Z_{0.95} \times 5 \times \sqrt{2.07}) = 115.33$$

$$Q = 224 \text{ units as before.}$$

Also, the average inventory level at Instock is

$$Q + r - \mu L = \frac{224}{2} + 115.33 - (50\times 2.07) = 123.83 \text{ units}$$

For the 3 products that share a machine, we have

$$\lambda = \frac{50\times 3}{224} = 0.6696 \text{ orders/day}$$

From the queueing template, we get

$$L = 2.56 \text{ days}$$

$$r = (50 \times 2.56) + (1.65 \times 5 \times \sqrt{2.56}) = 141.2 \text{ units}$$

The average inventory level for each of these three products is

$$\frac{224}{2} + (141.2 - (50\times 2.56)) = 125.2 \text{ units}$$

$$\text{Overall inventory level} = (123.83 \times 7) + (125.2 \times 3) = 1{,}242.42 \text{ units.}$$

$$\text{Holding cost} = 0.1 \times 25 \times 1{,}242.42 = \$3{,}106.07$$

Reduction in holding costs as a result of this reorganization of machines is

$$\$9{,}300 - \$3{,}106.07 = \$6{,}193.93$$

Notice that in this example, adjustments in capacity impacted both the lead time at the manufacturer as well as the consequent buffer inventory at the retailer. In addition, changing the capacity configuration and lowering the set-up time also decreased the incentive to batch as well as the system inventory and lead time.

4.8 TAILORED LOGISTICS SYSTEMS

In section 4.5 we suggested that grouping similar tasks together may enable a supply chain to perform effectively. Fuller et al. ([43]) describes examples where tailoring the supply chain to product characteristics improved performance significantly. In an applied context, Eisenstein and Iyer ([33]) describe their intervention in the Chicago Public Schools logistics system. The main change they suggested was to split the system, which originally processed all orders with a common pool of capacity. The new system consisted of two separate tailored logistics systems and associated capacity, each of which provided service to its own set of orders.

How can tailored systems improve a supply chain? To provide some intuition, consider a manufacturer who receives orders for two products. Orders for product 1 arrive at the rate of λ_1 orders per day. Orders for product 2 arrive at the rate of λ_2 orders per day. The number of orders received each day $\lambda = \lambda_1 + \lambda_2$. Both products share a common production facility that produces products at the rate of μ per day. Assume that each order is for Q units of product and that $\mu = \frac{1}{A+(tQ)}$, where A is the setup time and t is the production time per unit.

If orders are processed in their order of arrival (first in, first out), the lead time for any product order is

$$L = \frac{1}{\mu - \lambda}$$

Suppose that demand per day for the first product follows a normal distribution with a mean of m, and a standard deviation of σ_1. Also the second product demand has a mean of m_2 and a standard deviation of σ_2. Assume that $\sigma_1 \geq \sigma_2$.

The average inventory level across the two products is $Q+\left(Z_{ser}\sigma_1\sqrt{L}\right)+\left(Z_{ser}\sigma_2\sqrt{L}\right)$.

What can the manufacturer do to decrease inventory levels for these products?

Suppose we manage the production facility so that we prioritize product 1 over product 2. Thus orders for product 1 are processed before we process orders for product 2.

The impact of providing higher priority for product 1 is to generate a lead time for product 1, L_1, as follows:

$$L_1 = \frac{1}{\mu} + \frac{\lambda}{\mu(\mu - \lambda_1)}$$

Also the lower priority for product 2 generates a lead time for product 2, L_2, as follows:

$$L_2 = \frac{1}{\mu} + \frac{\lambda}{(\mu - \lambda)\times(\mu - \lambda_1)}$$

The new average inventory levels across both products is

$$Q+\left(Z_{ser}\sigma_1\sqrt{L_1}\right)+\left(Z_{ser}\sigma_2\sqrt{L_2}\right)$$

Can prioritization of orders improve the system performance? Consider a numerical example with demand rates for each of the two products that are $m_1 = 140$ units per day and $m_2 = 60$ units per day, and variability of $\sigma_1 = 125$ units and $\sigma_2 = 25$ units. Next, assume that the batch size for both products is 100 units. Thus, the order batch rate from each product would be $\lambda_1 = 1.4$ orders per day and $\lambda_2 = 0.6$ orders per day respectively for a total arrival rate of 2 orders per day across both products. Given the batch size, suppose the set-up time for an order is 0.1 days and the processing time per unit is 0.003 days. The corresponding service rate for any order batch of 100 units is 2.5 orders per day, or $\frac{1}{0.1+(0.003\times 100)}$.

Notice that if both products were accessing capacity in order of arrival with no priority, they would both face the same lead time of 2 days. The corresponding impact on their safety stock would be 363.05 units for the first product and 72.61 units for the second product (obtained using the formula $Z\sigma\sqrt{L}$). Thus the total safety stock inventory across both products would be 435.66 units.

However, if we prioritize access to capacity for product 1 (which has a higher variability), then the new lead times, using the formulas provided earlier, would be $L_1 = 1.12$ and $L_2 = 4.03$ days. With these lead times, notice that the corresponding safety stock for the first product would be 272.55 units (which decreases from the earlier case), while the safety stock for the second product would be 103.15 units (which increases from the earlier case). Note that the total safety stock inventory across both products is now 375.72 units. This decrease in inventory reflects the benefit of tailoring access to the supply chain based on product demand characteristics. Notice that giving priority to the more variable product permits its lead time to decrease, thus decreasing the safety stock for that product. But clearly this comes at a cost to the less variable product, whose lead time increases but at a slower rate. Thus, we have traded off lead time customization for an aggregate decrease in the overall inventory.

In other words, it may be worth reconsidering how orders get access to capacity. Tailoring the access to capacity based on product characteristics can improve the overall supply chain performance.

4.9 THE MAKE–BUY DECISION AND CAPACITY

In the earlier sections, we considered how to improve performance by splitting capacity or tailoring access to capacity. We expand the notion of providing different paths for orders to a supply chain by examining the choice of the mix of orders a company may choose to make vs. the orders that they may subcontract in a supply chain.

A procurement manager has access to both capacity within the company as well as capacity at a subcontractor. All orders accepted have to be satisfied per company policy. Thus revenue is fixed, and maximizing profit implies minimizing cost. With each order the manager has to decide how much the company should make and how much it should buy, so as to minimize the costs to satisfy product demand. To illustrate this scenario, consider an example and an associated process to make the optimal decision ([100]).

Company Makebuy has just received an order for making three different kinds of products: A, B, and C. Each product must be processed on two machines: X and Y. Table 4.5 summarizes the requirements for the three models.

TABLE 4.5 Product volume and processing requirements on each machine

	Product A	Product B	Product C
Number ordered	2,000	1,000	500
Hours required on X per unit	2	3	1
Hours required on Y per unit	1	1	1

However, the company has only limited capacity on machines X and Y, given prior commitments. The available capacity during lead time for machine X is 6,000 hours, while the capacity for machine Y is 3,000 hours. The company has the option to buy the products from an outside contractor, who charges the following and can deliver within the lead time. Table 4.6 summarizes the costs for the company.

TABLE 4.6 Company costs for make vs. buy for each product

	Product A	Product B	Product C
Costs per unit to make	$40	$73	$100
Costs per unit to buy from outside	$55	$93	$125

How should the order be produced: what mix of make vs. buy should be used to minimize costs? This decision can be made by framing the problem as a linear program and using available solution packages, e.g., the Solver package in Excel. To frame the problem, we define a set of decisions X_{i1}, $i = 1, 2, 3$ as the amount of products 1, 2, and 3 that are made in house and X_{i2}, $i = 1, 2, 3$ as the amount of products 1, 2, and 3 that are subcontracted. Let c_{ij}, $i = 1, 2, 3$ and $j = 1, 2$ refer to the costs associated with each of the decisions (Table 4.6) and d_i refer to the quantity of product i demanded.

Then the goal is to minimize $\Sigma_{ij} c_{ij} X_{ij}$.

There are two constraint sets that have to be satisfied. We need to have enough product to satisfy the demand for each product, i.e.,

$$\Sigma_j X_{ij} = d_i$$

We also need to check that we do not exceed the available capacity on each of the machines X and Y, i.e.,

$$(2X_{11}) + (3X_{21}) + (1X_{31}) \leq 6000$$

$$(1X_{11}) + (1X_{21}) + (1X_{31}) \leq 3000$$

The model described above is a linear program and can be solved using the Solver model in Excel. The solution to this model is shown in Table 4.7.

TABLE 4.7 Optimal make vs. buy decisions for products

	Product A	Product B	Product C
Units to make	2,000	500	500
Units to subcontract	0	500	0

Note that in the solution, the cost per unit to subcontract product B is \$20 (i.e., 93 – 73), while the cost of outsourcing product A is \$15 per unit. Why is it optimal for the company to outsource product B instead of product A? It is clear that product B uses more bottleneck resources, i.e., the capacity of machine X, than product A. In other words, the make–buy decision now requires identifying the internal bottleneck resource and then finding the best way to minimize cost using the internal resource. The linear programming tool enables this bottleneck resource to be identified and generates the optimal make–buy decision.

This section thus suggests that careful choice of the products that use up internal capacity vs. those that can use externally available capacity should consider the marginal benefit per unit of the bottleneck internal capacity. Such an analysis gets complicated because the bottleneck resources are, in turn, defined by the mix of products that are made vs. outsourced. The use of tools such as linear programming enables this issue to be resolved by considering the entire problem simultaneously. Such tools enable the optimal choice of bottleneck resources that minimize supply chain costs.

4.10 CAPACITY AS AN OPERATIONAL HEDGE TO REGULATORY CHANGES

When capacity is chosen in a global supply chain, it may be necessary to anticipate possible opportunities that may arise as countries change their trade agreements, for example. Having locations that can make use of the operational flexibility can have benefits. But all this means paying a price in terms of current performance in order to position the supply chain to have a higher level of average performance. To illustrate such issues, we provide a numerical example.

Company ABC has two plants manufacturing product A. The first plant is located in Illinois, while the second plant is located in Germany. Both plants have a capacity of 500,000 units per year. These plants have been built primarily to serve two markets: the United States and Europe. The unit production cost at the Illinois plant is $1 per unit, while the unit production cost at the plant in Germany is $1.25 per unit. The product demand for the US market is 250,000 units per year, while the demand for the European market is 200,000 units per year. The cost of transporting between Europe and the United States is $0.10 per unit. Also, the average import duty for goods imported into Europe is 30%, while there is no import duty for goods imported to United States. Also, for the purpose of maintaining uniform quality, company ABC has decided that each demand region will be supplied by a single plant only.

Consider possible solutions to the production and sourcing decisions under the above cost structure.

Sourcing decision:

1. US market

   If supplied by the Illinois plant, unit cost is $1.

   If supplied by the German plant, unit cost is $1.25 + 0.1 = $1.35.

   The product is cheaper if supplied by the Illinois plant.

2. European market

   If supplied by the Illinois plant, unit cost is $1 + 0.1 + 0.3 = $1.4.

   If supplied by the German plant, unit cost is $1.25.

   The product is cheaper if supplied by the German plant.

3. Optimal production decision

   The Illinois plant produces 250,000 units per year.

   The German plant produces 200,000 units per year.

Now suppose that Europe were to adopt a free trade agreement and drop the import duty. How would the production and sourcing decisions change?

Sourcing decision (under Free Trade Agreement with Europe)

1. US market

   If supplied by the Illinois plant, unit cost is $1.

   If supplied by the German plant, unit cost is $1.25 + 0.1 = $1.35.

   It is thus optimal to be supplied by Illinois plant.

2. European market

   If supplied by the Illinois plant, unit cost is $1 + 0.1 = $1.1.

   If supplied by the German plant, unit cost is $1.25.

   It is again optimal to be supplied by the Illinois plant.

3. Optimal production decision

   The Illinois plant produces 450,000 units per year.

   The German plant has no production.

Next, suppose the German plant has improved its efficiency, and hence its production costs have dropped to $0.85 per unit. How would your production and sourcing decisions change? What is the value of excess capacity at the German plant under this scenario?

Sourcing decision

1. US market

   If supplied by the Illinois plant, unit cost is \$1.

   If supplied by the German plant, unit cost is \$0.85 + 0.1 = \$0.95.

   It is optimal to supply the US market from the German plant.

2. European market

   If supplied by the Illinois plant, unit cost is \$1 + 0.1 = \$1.1.

   If supplied by the German plant, unit cost is \$0.85.

   It is optimal to supply Europe from the German plant.

3. Optimal production decision

   The Illinois plant has no production.

   The German plant produces 450,000 units per year.

What do all these alternative capacity configurations suggest? All along, if we carry excess capacity, we can avail of these opportunities as they arise. The extra capacity does not have to remain idle; it needs to remain flexible so that it can be used when conditions are right. This example shows how excess capacity in a global supply chain provides a "real option" that can be exercised as business conditions unfold. Eliminating excess capacity will reduce the options available to operate a global supply chain.

4.11 TEMPORAL ADJUSTMENT OF CAPACITY THROUGH CHOICE OF EMPLOYEE SCHEDULES

Finally, consider how availability of capacity across time can be adjusted through choice of capacity in shifts, when employees represent the source of capacity. This view of capacity is temporal and thus adjustable. Such models come under the general topic of tactical scheduling. Scheduling models specifically focus on taking available shifts for personnel and attempt to have sufficient people in each time period (e.g., half-hour or one-hour intervals) to cover projected demand over time. For a comprehensive description of techniques for solving such systems, please see ([100]).

Many systems, e.g., nursing, the airline industry, and travel planning, involve daily demand that displays significant variation. However, for convenience, the staff may have to be scheduled around standard shifts. The main scheduling problem is to minimize costs while maximizing utilization of the staff across the hours of the shift.

Consider the following scheduling model: Let the day be divided into N time periods (say half-hour intervals). Let d_i be the demand (in number of staff) required in time period i (where $i = 1, 2, ..., N$. Let a_{ij} be equal to 1 if a person working on shift j is available in period i. Let c_j be the cost for a person to work in shift j. Let x_j be the number of people in shift j.

The problem we want to solve is the following:

$$\text{Minimize } \Sigma_j c_j x_j.$$

$$\Sigma_j a_{ij} x_j \geq d_i \text{ for all } i = 1, 2, ..., N$$

$$x_j \text{ are restricted to be integer values.}$$

The solution allocates people to shifts in a way that allows us to provide adequate staff during each time period of the day. We now provide an example to illustrate this model.

Consider a service system that has divided time during the day into 6 periods. Demand for service personnel each period is as follows: {5, 8, 15, 12, 8, 13}. Each person works three periods, and there are five possible shifts as follows:

Shift 1: Work periods 1, 2, 3 Cost = \$100/person
Shift 2: Work periods 2, 3, 4 Cost = \$90/person
Shift 3: Work periods 1, 3, 4 Cost = \$120/person
Shift 4: Work periods 4, 5, 6 Cost = \$105/person
Shift 5: Work periods 2, 5, 6 Cost = \$125/person

We thus formulate the model with

x_1 = number of people working shift 1
x_2 = number of people working shift 2
x_3 = number of people working shift 3
x_4 = number of people working shift 4
x_5 = number of people working shift 5

The equations are

$$\text{Minimize } ((100 \times x_1) + (90 \times x_2) + (120 \times x_3) + (105 \times x_4) + (125 \times x_5)$$

$$x_1 + x_3 \geq 5$$

$$x_1 + x_2 + x_5 \geq 8$$

$$x_1 + x_2 + x_3 \geq 15$$

$$x_2 + x_3 + x_4 \geq 12$$

$$x_4 + x_5 \geq 8$$

$$x_4 + x_5 \geq 13$$

$$\text{All } x_1, x_2, x_3, x_4, x_5 \geq 0$$

If we set this program up in Excel and solve it, we generate the solution

$$x_1 = 5, x_2 = 10, x_3 = 0, x_4 = 13$$

The corresponding cost is \$2,765.

Notice that under this scheme, we have the following number of people each period:

$$\{5, 15, 15, 23, 13, 13\}$$

Thus, in periods 2, 4, and 5, we have more staff than we need.

This model shows that it may make sense to have more capacity than required in some periods in order to save overall costs to cover demand across all periods. In other words, since the shifts are not flexible to the specific demand requirements over time, the extra slack capacity in some periods enables the supply demand mismatch to be solved cost effectively. It is thus worth considering the allocation of shifts to employees to optimize overall supply costs.

4.12 CHAPTER SUMMARY

In this chapter we focused on the drivers of capacity and the impact of capacity on supply chain performance. Capacity affects service levels offered and lead times experienced by customers. In the presence of long lead times to establish capacity, forecast error may lead to required buffer capacity for optimal performance of the supply chain. The capacity configuration that optimizes performance requires careful consideration of the impact of pooling on set-up and processing times. Excess capacity in a supply chain network may provide an option that can be exercised if parameters change. In the presence of capacity constraints, competition for capacity may result in local decisions generating nonoptimal outcomes. Finally, in the presence of varying demands, a carefully optimized temporal capacity plan may generate competitive outcomes.

4.13 PROBLEMS

1. Bank4 is a local bank with an automatic teller machine (ATM) on a college campus. It has a steady demand for cash, at the rate of $2,000 per day. It costs Bank4 $50 to have a private security company go to the ATM and stock it with cash. The cost of capital that Bank4 estimates for money is an annual rate of 15%.

1a. How much cash should be placed in the ATM during each trip to minimize Bank4's annual holding and cash-filling costs? How frequently should the ATM be replenished in a year? What will be the average amount of cash in the ATM?

1b. Currently the ATM can hold $50,000. Bank4 currently fills up this ATM during each trip. What is the percent increase in Bank4's annual holding and cash-filling costs (over the optimal) as a result of this policy?

1c. Bank4 operates two ATMs on campus. Each of these ATMs faces similar demands and costs. Bank4 could shut down the two ATMs and have one new location that is as easily accessible to all customers who use ATMs. This new ATM will also cost Bank4 $50 to fill up, demand at this new ATM will be the total demand across the two old ATM locations, and holding costs will remain the same rate of 15% annually.

How much cash should be placed in the ATM during each trip to minimize Bank4's annual holding and cash-filling costs? How frequently should the ATM be replenished in a year? What will be the average amount of cash in the ATM?

1d. Does the new single-location ATM decrease Bank4's costs over the old two-location ATM system? Explain.

2. The Parts Company has a single central warehouse that supplies parts to four regional warehouses. We will focus on the inventory policies for the TX54 spring, which is sold to customers from the five regional warehouses. Parts purchases the TX54 from a manufacturer for $50 and sells it at the regional warehouses for $75. Parts estimates an annual carrying cost equal to 25% of the value of product in inventory. Demand faced by the central warehouse each week has a mean of 400 units and a standard deviation of 150 units.

The central warehouse estimates that the cost to place an order with the supplier is $1,000. The central warehouse maintains a service level of 99%. Lead time to get delivery from the supplier is four weeks.

2a. Provide a (Q,r) policy at the central warehouse. Provide the associated average inventory level at the central warehouse.

2b. Given that orders to the central warehouse come from four regional warehouses, suppose the central warehouse were shut down and all orders were placed directly by each regional warehouse. Each regional warehouse faces a weekly demand of 100 units and a standard deviation of 75 units. The regional warehouses have to provide a service level of 99%.

Assume that ordering cost for each regional warehouse is $1,000 and delivery lead time is four weeks. Provide the associated (Q,r) policy for each regional warehouse and the associated total average inventory level across the four regional warehouses.

2c. Does eliminating the central warehouse decrease or increase average inventory levels for Parts? Explain.

3. The Optima Corporation strives to create products (widgets) that meet customer requirements. Currently Optima makes 60 different SKUs. Optima satisfies customer orders from finished goods inventory. Demand for each of the 60 products is at a rate of 16 widgets per day.

As finished goods inventory depletes, Optima places orders with its manufacturing plant. Orders are in batches of 80 widgets of the same type. Making the widget requires doing three tasks, and the entire order moves together through each task.

Task 1 can be done by any one of 3 machines. Orders line up and are processed in order of arrival and go to the first available machine. Set-up time is 30 minutes, and processing time is 1 minute per widget.

After task 1 is completed, orders line up to be processed for task 2. Task 2 can be done by any one of 6 machines operating in parallel. Set-up time is 2 hours and processing time is 1 minute per widget.

After task 2 is completed, orders go to task 3. Here there are 3 machines operating in parallel, and orders go to the first available machine. Set-up time for task 3 is 1 hour, and processing time is 30 seconds (i.e., 0.5 minutes) per widget.

3a. What is the lead time to complete all three tasks for an order of widgets placed by the finished goods inventory manager?

3b. Closer analysis of the products shows that 40 of the SKUs are similar and the remaining 20 are similar. A consultant suggests splitting the capacity and creating two cells. However, as before, each widget order will be for 80 units of a given type. Demand for an SKU would still be 16 units per day.

Thus cell 1 would process orders for the first 40 SKUs. Task 1 would have 2 machines operating in parallel, task 2 would have 4 machines operating in parallel and task 3 would have 2 machines operating in parallel. Set-up times drop to 50% of their earlier levels. Thus set-up time for the first task is now 15 minutes; for the second, 1 hour; and for the third, 30 minutes. Processing time per unit remains the same.

Cell 2 would process orders for the remaining 20 SKUs. Task 1 would have 1 machine, task 2 would have 2 machines operating in parallel and task 3 would have 1 machine. Set-up times drop to 50% of their earlier levels. Thus set-up time for the first task is now 15 minutes; for the second, 1 hour; and for the third, 30 minutes. Processing time per unit remains the same for all tasks as in 3a.

Provide the values of lead times for cells 1 and 2 in this new configuration. Do lead times decrease or increase? Explain.

4. The Fit Corporation makes two types of widgets that are sold at a retail store. Demand for the widgets (each week) is as shown below:

Demand (units)	Widget 1	Widget 2
100	0.2	0.2
200	0.2	0.3
300	0.5	0.3
400	0.1	0.2

Thus Fit faces an average demand of 250 widgets per week for each of the two widgets. The widgets cost \$40 per unit to produce. The retail price is \$70 per unit. All orders are placed by the retail store at the start of the week and are delivered immediately to the store. If the retail store runs out of stock, Fit purchases a widget from a competitor at a cost of \$100 per widget and supplies it to the customer. The customer pays (as before) a price of \$70 per widget. Weekly holding cost is 10% of the cost of the widget. Yearly demand for widgets is 13,000 widgets.

4a. Assume that Fit's retail store places orders once a week. Provide an inventory for each product and associated average inventory level at the store.

4b. An engineer at Fit has figured out a way to produce a generic widget that can perform the functions of the earlier two widgets. Thus Fit's retail store would have to store only one SKU of this new widget and yet satisfy all of the demand for the two widgets. Assume that the demand distributions remain the same as in 4a and that customers are willing to use the new widget instead of the old widgets. Production cost of this new widget is still \$40. The other costs are as before.

Assume that Fit's retail store follows a weekly ordering policy, and provide an inventory policy for the new widget and the associated average inventory level at the store.

4c. Does the total average retail inventory level (across all widgets) decrease if Fit adopts the new widget to satisfy demand? Explain.

5. The Holix Corporation has two separate processing centers for credit applications. Each credit application passes through three steps: step 1—background credit check, step 2—credit risk profile analysis, and step 3—credit level approval and communication to client. The processing time for each of the stages is 20 minutes for credit check, 50 minutes for credit risk profile analysis, and 14 minutes for credit approval and communication. The set-up time between successive applications for each step is 10 minutes. While both processing center take similar steps, they each deal with different types of applications: processing center 1 evaluates residential customers and processing center 2 evaluates commercial customers.

5a. Each of the two processing centers is organized in exactly the same manner and receives the same average number of applications per day. For example, processing center 1 gets about 30 applications per 8-hour day. The first step in center 1 has 2 employees working in parallel. The second step has 4 employees working in parallel, and the third step has 2 employees working in parallel. What is the average lead time to process an application through all three steps in each processing center?

5b. Holix is considering merging these two operations into one system. The new system faces a total arrival rate of 60 applications per 8-hour day. The first step would now have 4 employees operating in parallel, the second would have 8, and the third would have 4. Processing time per step per employee would remain the same. However, the set-up time is anticipated to increase to 11.5 minutes. What is the average lead time to process an application through all three steps in this merged processing center? Why does this merger of processing centers generate the lead time observed?

5c. A consultant suggests that the new center should be split into four separate teams, each team consisting of four employees. The teams would work on one application at a time and complete all steps. Each team would thus operate as a single-server queue with a processing time of 25% of the total processing time for all three steps, i.e., each of the four team members would do 25% of the processing. Since the team does all steps for an application, set-up time is expected to decrease to 5 minutes.

Because some applications are very similar, they can be split into four types. Each of the four teams would expect to get 15 applications per 8-hour day.

What is the impact of this method of organization on lead time? Explain the result.

5d. Summarize conditions under which each of the three modes of operation would be the appropriate choice.

6. The First Bank of Lafayette has a common office for mortgage and commercial credit processing. The process involves several departments: data collection, data verification, loan pricing, loan closing, and loan maintenance. For each of the departments, there are a number of clerks working in parallel. All requests pass through each of the 5 stages.

Stage	Number of Clerks	Set-up Time	Processing Time
Data collection	6	20 minutes	10 minutes
Data verification	4	25 minutes	3 minutes
Loan pricing	4	15 minutes	10 minutes
Loan closing	4	4 minutes	20 minutes
Loan maintenance	6	10 minutes	20 minutes

6a. Data regarding orders received shows 40 orders per day for mortgage processing and 20 orders per day for commercial credit. Given that all orders are processed in order of arrival and that every order has to go through all 5 stages, provide the average lead time for First Bank to complete the process. Assume 8 hours of work per day, 5 days per week, and 50 weeks per year.

6b. A re-engineering study indicates that the first three steps differ considerably for mortgage processing and commercial credit. The study suggests splitting the processing into two separate departments with their own separate capacity. While processing will still go through 5 stages, the number of clerks allocated to mortgage processing for each of the stages will be 4, 3, 3, 3, 4, respectively, and the number of those allocated to commercial loans will be 2, 1, 1, 1, 2, respectively. Set-up times will drop by 80% as a result. What will be the implied lead times for each of the two departments?

7. The Quick company sells 6 types of widgets. Weekly demand for each widget type is normally distributed with a mean of 50 units and a standard deviation of 25 units. Quick currently purchases widgets 1, 2, and 3 from supplier A and widgets 4, 5, and 6 from supplier B. The fixed ordering cost to order a widget is $50. Holding cost for a widget is assessed at an annual rate of 25%. Each widget costs a wholesale price of $5. Quick would like to see happy customers, so Quick plans to be in stock 95% of the time for every widget type. Supplier A has a single machine that produces widgets 1, 2, and 3. The set-up time for an order of widgets (of a given type) is a mean of 200 minutes. The machine then takes a mean of 12 minutes to produce 1 widget. The same parameters hold for supplier B and widgets 4, 5, and 6.

7a. Provide a (Q,r) inventory policy for the widgets. Also provide the overall average inventory holding cost at Quick across the 6 widgets.

7b. A buy-out specialist Fast is planning to buy suppliers A and B and merge their capacity. The new plant will have both machines. The widget orders will be assigned to the first available machine. Because of increase in product variety the set-up time is now 300 minutes (instead of 200 minutes from 7a). The variable production time remains 12 minutes. How does this capacity configuration affect the inventory policy at Quick? What will be the impact on the overall average inventory holding cost at Quick across the 6 widgets?

7c. Fast has proposed modifying the designs for widgets. A new widget A will replace widgets 1, 2, and 3. A new widget B will replace widgets 4, 5, and 6. These new widgets will satisfy all of the demand for the original 6 widgets. Set-up time drops to 200 minutes, and the two-widget (A and B) orders go to the first available machine. Provide the impact on inventory policy at Quick and average inventory holding costs.

Chapter 5

Coordination

The Oxford Dictionary ([96]) defines the verb *to coordinate* as to "bring together the different elements (of a complex activity or organization) into a harmonious or efficient relationship." To coordinate, a supply chain manager may have "to negotiate with others in order to work effectively" or "to match or harmonize" ([96]) the needs of multiple constituents. For supply chains, coordination of flows of physical goods, information, and money is challenging because modern supply chains frequently have several independent owners with individual goals. Thus, coordination of disparate entities is a key feature of a supply chain's architecture and has an impact on observed performance and therefore on competitiveness. The performance of a supply chain is often difficult without coordinating agreements. An appropriate coordination mechanism, along with associated sharing rules, can often result in improved performance across all supply chain entities.

The first step in developing coordination agreements is to identify the goals of individual decision makers in the supply chain and the associated observed performance in the absence of any agreements. Then, consider the best possible performance of the supply chain, as if all ownership were with one entity. The difference between these two measures of performance indicates the maximum value that can be released by the use of coordination agreements. A supply chain coordinating agreement is an agreement that adjusts performance of each of the independent decision makers such that the total supply chain performance matches that generated by a single owner of the system. The key difference between a coordinated supply chain and a vertically integrated supply chain is that independent ownership of the entities in the supply chain is maintained, but coordination agreements enable an overall performance that matches that of a system with a single owner.

One possible goal for coordination agreements is to generate Pareto-improving performance, i.e., no party to the agreement is worse off and at least one is strictly better off. The example in Chapter 6 focuses on such an agreement.

While this chapter assumes coordination to be a good thing to do, there are contexts in which no coordination is assumed to be best. Some of these examples appear in the context of humanitarian logistics and arise primarily due to different mandates across participating entities (some of these issues will be highlighted in Chapter 13 on humanitarian supply chains).

This chapter will provide tools and associated concepts to develop coordination agreements. First, some specific examples to illustrate the use of coordination agreements.

5.1 THE COAST GUARD AND THE VALUE OF COORDINATION

The following project is described in detail in Deshpande, Iyer, and Cho ([27]). The United States Coast Guard (USCG) protects the US coastline, using ships and airplanes. The Coast Guard operates twenty-six air stations, which are spread across the coast. Each air station operates a subset of ten different aircraft types. There are over 200 aircrafts across these twenty-six air stations, consisting of fixed-wing and rotary-wing aircrafts. The focus of the study was the Aircraft Repair and Supply Center (ARSC) located in Elizabeth City, North Carolina.

The process of operation of the supply chain is as follows. When aircraft parts fail, they generate demand for replacements, also called service parts, which are supplied from the local inventory at air stations. This inventory is replenished by the central warehouse facility at Elizabeth City. In 2001, the total number of individual parts managed at the central facility exceeded 60,000, and the total value of the inventory exceeded $700 million. When working parts are shipped from the warehouse to the air station to satisfy aircraft demand, the salvageable broken components from all air stations, are shipped back to the warehouse for repair and reuse. The aircraft from all air stations also come for periodic overhaul (depot maintenance) to the Elizabeth City facility, and thus generate demand for parts. Of the total parts in the system, about 6,000 are repaired both internally and by outside commercial vendors. The total annual budget for parts purchases, parts repair, and depot-level maintenance exceeds $140 million.

All repair and supply activities were subject to detailed tracking in two separate databases: Aviation Computerized Maintenance System (ACMS) and Aviation Maintenance Management System (AMMIS). The ACMS database tracks all individual parts installed on individual aircraft, flags the required maintenance, and records the history of repairs using each part's unique serial number. The AMMIS database in contrast tracks every step of the process once the part comes off the aircraft. It tracks demand requisitions (orders) placed to the warehouse, and the shipment of good parts to the air stations and maintenance facility, as well as the receipt of failed parts (carcasses), their shipment to vendors or in-house for repair, and their induction back into the system. Historically, there was no connection between the AMMIS and ACMS systems, and there was no advance information regarding impending demands or repair lead times.

The project by Deshpande, Iyer, and Cho ([27]) describes an effort to coordinate these two sets of information. The models developed connected the two databases. The consequent data were used, along with part age signals, to adjust inventory levels and thus reduce supply chain costs. But how does this scheme work? An indicator level was set for each part so that whenever the part reached a threshold age, a part age signal was sent to the ARSC facility. Given these part age signals, the inventory levels of repaired components could be adjusted to repair both in anticipation of demand and following the rest of demand. This required a correlation between the signal and the demand over the repair lead time. Figure 5.1 shows the empirical data regarding the correlation between demand and signal for different thresholds for the main gearbox. Intuitively, the optimal threshold is the one that maximizes the correlation because it provides the best signal regarding impending demand.

The resulting system, customized for each one of forty-one prototype products, permitted coordination between part maintenance data and inventory data. In this context, coordination used part age signals to adjust the inventory level and thus improve overall system performance. Savings due to moving to a signal-driven inventory system were estimated to be 18%–22% of inventory costs. In short, data sharing between maintenance and inventory systems and consequent coordination of the repair inventory permitted higher service levels with lower inventory.

FIGURE 5.1 Correlation between signal and demand for different thresholds

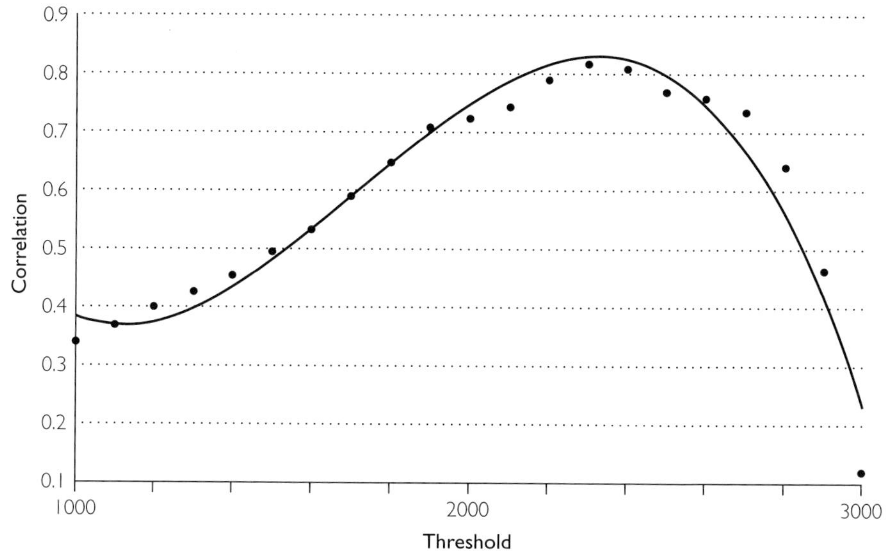

5.2 INDUSTRIAL REVENUE SHARING AGREEMENTS

Revenue-sharing agreements are an approach to supply chain coordination. For example, Lorain County in Ohio and a wind turbine installer established a revenue-sharing agreement that states that the county will receive 20% of the revenues from energy generated in return for land leases ([122]). GoodmanSparks in the United Kingdom supplies, installs, and maintains coin-operated laundry equipment in return for a share of the revenues generated when students use the facilities ([46]). In the aviation industry, Lucas Aerospace entered into contracts with Rolls Royce to supply engine and fuel control systems for the new generation of Trent engines. Under the terms of the deal, Lucas would invest $122 million and receive 3%–5% of the total revenues from the engines ([89]).

To provide an example that is closer to the customer, consider the problem faced in past years by Blockbuster Video, a renter of videotapes ([47]). Movie studios had charged video rental companies $65 to $100 per tape. Blockbuster and other rental companies had an exclusive time window before the tapes were sold to other channels (such as cable and video-on-demand). Blockbuster had to choose the number of copies of a given movie to stock to maintain profitability. Most retail data showed that stockouts were about 30% in the industry with poor availability.

Then a revenue-sharing solution came on the market, pioneered by Rentrak, an information services company. Rentrak negotiated with movie studios to introduce a pay-per-transaction revenue sharing program. Under the program, studios were paid close to $8 per tape initially and close to 40% of the $3 rental fee per transaction. The impact on the industry was substantial. Retail tape inventory increased, stockouts were cut in half, and retailer revenues soared. Film studios, too, now obtained a large fraction of their revenues from retail sales. In all, revenue sharing represented a win–win proposition. Large stores such as Blockbuster Video avoided Rentrak and struck deals directly with movie studios.

Smaller stores could go to Rentrak, which aggregated their demands and thus provided scale economies.

But disagreements among supply chain partners caused Disney to sue Blockbuster, alleging accounting irregularities that failed to account for hundreds of thousands of tapes under a 1997 revenue-sharing agreement and suggesting that Disney was cheated out of $120 million. Blockbuster denied the allegations. Independent video retailers sued Blockbuster and the studios, claiming that the studios were discriminating against the independents in violation of the Robinson–Patman Act. The case was dismissed in US district court.

Soon Blockbuster announced that it would not be renewing the revenue-sharing deals in the industry. The key reason was that DVDs entered the market and were sold at $15 per unit. Blockbuster did not sign any revenue-sharing contracts for DVDs. In addition, because the DVDs did not incur as many costs (such as rewinding), DVD rentals were $1.20 vs. $1.80 for a video. In fact, both Blockbuster and the studios competed to sell DVDs to the public. It was projected that the net result of the cancellation of revenue-sharing contracts would be to increase DVD prices, thus helping both Blockbuster and the studios. But customers could buy DVDs from mass merchants rather than renting or buying from Blockbuster, creating a whole new set of supply chain challenges.

The main message is that revenue-sharing agreements need an effective information system to guarantee compliance. But, as we shall see later in this chapter, they enable supply chain coordination and can thus generate Pareto-improving outcomes for participating companies.

5.3 HUMANITARIAN LOGISTICS AND COORDINATION

Historically, the United Nations Joint Logistics Committee (UNJLC) was a coordination body within the United Nations (UN) system whose goal was to coordinate logistics across independent agencies both the UN and governmental and nongovernmental organizations (such as the Red Cross). Over the years the UNJLC has played a key role in deconflicting and debottlenecking in several contexts, as the following examples illustrate.

As described in a case written by Levins, Samii, and Van Wassenhove ([81]), when relief organizations were rushing in to provide aid in Afghanistan, a landlocked country, many organizations attempted to enter the country through Uzbekistan and send supplies on barges down the river. Hundreds of relief organizations tried to enter Afghanistan, each operating independently, which created such chaos that the Uzbek government shut down access to Afghanistan. The UNJLC played the role of "traffic cop," improving the situation by establishing a regular barge schedule and smoothing the flow of aid through the Uzbek entry point. Coordinating the independent relief organizations increased capacity and decreased lead time for everyone. Such a role can be considered as *coordination by command,* i.e., a centralized external scheduler who delivers value to all parties by coordinating the system and improving overall performance.

Another case written by Samii and Van Wassenhove ([103]) describes a situation when the World Food Program (WFP) was shipping in food for hungry Rwandans, while the United Nations High Commissioner of Refugees (UNHCR) was shipping out Rwandan refugees from the war-stricken areas. Given the floods, the main mode of transport was by air. WFP was flying in food and flying out empty, while the UNHCR was flying in empty and flying out full. The UNJLC coordinated the schedules across the two agencies so that the WFP aircraft flew back with refugees, while the UNHCR aircraft flew in food supplies. The adjustments in flight schedules had to take into account loading issues and food and refugee arrival at each end, as well as safety and security. But coordination enabled improved utilization and higher capacity at about the same cost. This is called *coordination by consensus* across the relief organizations.

In yet another case by Samii and Van Wassenhove ([102]), in Afghanistan, they describe a UNJLC website that provided security and weather updates, requests for logistics shipments (similar to a ride board in most campuses), road conditions, and more. The remaining coordination was left to individual agencies who used this information to seek out interested parties to share resources. This minimal coordination is termed *coordination by default*.

The previous examples illustrate three forms of coordination: (1) coordination by command, a centralized approach; (2) coordination by consensus, cooperative Pareto-improving solutions; and (3) coordination by default, or no coordination except perhaps information sharing. In Chapter 13 we will discuss possible reasons for each form of coordination.

5.4 A MODEL OF COORDINATION

Consider a supply chain consisting of a single manufacturer who produces a product and sells it to a retailer, who, in turn, sells the product to the final customer. Suppose that in order to produce the product, the manufacturer has to choose to reserve a capacity level K at a cost per unit of c_k. Retail price per unit is r, the wholesale price is set at w, and the cost per unit to manufacture is set at c. This notation and description we follow is from Ozer and Wei ([97]).

Three important characteristics are (1) the timing of data received by manufacturer and retailer, (2) the extent of information shared, and (3) the timing of decisions. The capacity decision is made by the manufacturer and the orders are placed by the retailer.

5.5 MANUFACTURER CHOOSES CAPACITY

This section includes scenarios in which the retailer waits for demands to be known before ordering. The manufacturer orders at time 0, before the demands occur. Assume that retail demand follows a distribution with mean μ and standard deviation σ. The retailer orders at L, after observing demand. Decisions have to be timed so that capacity is reserved by the manufacturer in advance of retailer order. However, the manufacturer selection of capacity will then restrict the retail demand that can be satisfied. This suggests the need to coordinate decisions made by the manufacturer with those that are ideal for the retailer.

5.6 SUPPLY CHAIN PROFIT

Once the manufacturer and retailer decisions are made, the combined profit across the two firms is termed the *supply chain profit*. Notice that when the profits of the manufacturer and retailer are added together, the wholesale price level does not affect this total as it is merely a transfer payment from the retailer to the manufacturer. The supply chain as a whole thus attempts to choose a capacity level K that will maximize supply chain profit.

Intuitively, the supply chain manager chooses a capacity level that sets the expected revenue associated with increasing capacity equal to the expected cost associated with increasing capacity. Thus, following the newsvendor model, the optimal capacity has to satisfy

$$\text{Probability}(\text{Demand} \leq K_C) = \frac{r - c - c_k}{r - c}$$

This capacity level K_C and the associated supply chain profit maximize the profits of the supply chain.

Consider an example with a retailer whose demand follows a uniform distribution with values between 8 and 22 (see Table 5.1). The probability of demand taking each value between 8 and 22 is equal to $\frac{1}{15}$. Suppose $r = 4$, $w = 2$, $c = 0.6$, $c_k = 0.5$. Following the steps defined earlier, the optimal service level for the supply chain is $\frac{r - c - c_k}{r - c} = 0.852$. Thus the optimal capacity level is obtained as $K = 20$, using the values in Table 5.1.

The corresponding supply chain profit can be calculated as 40.32. Table 5.2 shows the steps in this calculation for the supply chain profit. The first column shows the demand; the second the probability associated with each demand level (equal to $\frac{1}{15}$); and the third column, the cumulative probability. The fourth column shows the revenue for each demand realization, i.e., the minimum of the demand and the capacity ($K = 20$) times the revenue of $4 per unit of demand satisfied. The fifth column provides the cost to reserve capacity, i.e., $c_k K$. The sixth column shows the cost to execute the capacity cMin(Demand, K). The seventh column shows the product of the net profit for each demand realization times the probability. The sum of the entries in the last column provides the expected profit = 40.32.

Notice that the manufacturer and retailer are separate companies so they need some mechanism to attain this maximum profit. The next few sec-

TABLE 5.1 Demands and associated probabilities

Demand	Probability	Cumulative
8	0.067	0.067
9	0.067	0.133
10	0.067	0.2
11	0.067	0.267
12	0.067	0.333
13	0.067	0.4
14	0.067	0.467
15	0.067	0.533
16	0.067	0.6
17	0.067	0.667
18	0.067	0.733
19	0.067	0.8
20	0.067	0.867
21	0.067	0.933
22	0.067	1

TABLE 5.2 Calculation of supply chain profit; $r = 4, w = 2, c_k = 0.5, c = 0.6, K = 20$

Demand	Prob	CumProb	Revenue	CapCommit	Execution	Profit×Probability
8	0.067	0.0667	32	10	4.8	1.147
9	0.067	0.1333	36	10	5.4	1.373
10	0.067	0.2	40	10	6	1.6
11	0.067	0.267	44	10	6.6	1.8267
12	0.067	0.333	48	10	7.2	2.053
13	0.067	0.4	52	10	7.8	2.28
14	0.067	0.467	56	10	8.4	2.507
15	0.067	0.533	60	10	9	2.733
16	0.067	0.6	64	10	9.6	2.96
17	0.067	0.667	68	10	10.2	3.186
18	0.067	0.733	72	10	10.8	3.413
19	0.067	0.8	76	10	11.4	3.64
20	0.067	0.867	80	10	12	3.867
21	0.067	0.933	80	10	12	3.867
22	0.067	1	80	10	12	3.867

tions will explore several agreements and determine if they attain the maximum supply chain profit. If they do so, such agreements are said to be coordinating agreements. If they do not, they are considered to be agreements that generate an uncoordinated supply chain.

5.7 WHOLESALE PRICE AGREEMENTS

Consider the case when the manufacturer and retailer are separate companies, each optimizing their profits. Because the manufacturer has to choose capacity to optimize his profits, he will consider the wholesale margin $w - c - c_k$ associated with a sale as against the loss associated with wasted capacity of c_k. The manufacturer will thus choose capacity to offer a service level of Probability(Demand $\leq K_w$) = $\frac{w-c-c_k}{w-c}$. Given this manufacturer choice of capacity, the retailer's profits are affected because his supply is constrained by the manufacturer's choice of capacity.

Consider the supply chain example discussed earlier, but for this decentralized supply chain decision-making environment. Using the numerical example from the earlier section, the manufacturer's optimal service level is $\frac{2-0.6-0.5}{2-0.6} = 0.643$. Using the probabilities in Table 5.1, this service level implies a capacity decision by the manufacturer of $Kw = 17$. Notice that $K_w \leq K_C$, i.e., the manufacturer invests in less capacity than is desired by the entire supply chain. The impact of this underinvestment in capacity is that the retailer's expected profit is now 28, the manufacturer's expected profit is 11.1, and the supply chain profit, which is the sum of manufacturer and retailer expected profits, is 39.1. The details of this calculation are shown in Table 5.3.

TABLE 5.3 Wholesale price agreement calculations for the manufacturer; $r = 4$, $w = 2$, $c_k = 0.5$, $c = 0.6$, $K = 17$

Demand	Prob	CumProb	Revenue	CapCommit	Execution	Profit×Probability
8	0.067	0.067	16	8.5	4.8	0.18
9	0.067	0.133	18	8.5	5.4	0.273
10	0.067	0.2	20	8.5	6	0.367
11	0.067	0.267	22	8.5	6.6	0.46
12	0.067	0.333	24	8.5	7.2	0.553
13	0.067	0.4	26	8.5	7.8	0.6467
14	0.067	0.467	28	8.5	8.4	0.74
15	0.067	0.533	30	8.5	9	0.833
16	0.067	0.6	32	8.5	9.6	0.9267
17	0.067	0.667	34	8.5	10.2	1.02
18	0.067	0.733	34	8.5	10.2	1.02
19	0.067	0.8	34	8.5	10.2	1.02
20	0.067	0.867	34	8.5	10.2	1.02
21	0.067	0.933	34	8.5	10.2	1.02
22	0.067	1	34	8.5	10.2	1.02

TABLE 5.5 Manufacturer expected profit calculations a take-or-pay contract; $r = 4, w = 1.95, c_k = 0.5, c = 0.6, K = 20$, payback credit = 0.35

Demand	Prob	Cumulative	Revenue	Cap Commit	Exec Cost	Credit	Profit×Prob
8	0.067	0.067	15.6	10	4.8	4.241	0.3360
9	0.067	0.133	17.55	10	5.4	3.887	0.4025
10	0.067	0.2	19.5	10	6	3.534	0.468
11	0.067	0.267	21.45	10	6.6	3.181	0.535
12	0.067	0.333	23.4	10	7.2	2.827	0.601
13	0.067	0.4	25.35	10	7.8	2.4741	0.668
14	0.067	0.467	27.3	10	8.4	2.120	0.734
15	0.067	0.533	29.25	10	9	1.767	0.801
16	0.067	0.6	31.2	10	9.6	1.4133	0.867
17	0.067	0.667	33.15	10	10.2	1.060	0.934
18	0.067	0.733	35.1	10	10.8	0.706	1.0004
19	0.067	0.8	37.05	10	11.4	0.353	1.066
20	0.067	0.867	39	10	12	0	1.133
21	0.067	0.933	39	10	12	0	1.133
22	0.067	1	39	10	12	0	1.133

TABLE 5.6 Retailer expected profit calculations a take-or-pay contract; $r = 4, w = 1.95, c_k = 0.5, c = 0.6, K = 20$, payback credit = 0.35

Revenue	Cost	Capacity Credit	Profit×Prob
32	15.6	4.241	0.810
36	17.55	3.887	0.970
40	19.5	3.534	1.131
44	21.45	3.181	1.291
48	23.4	2.827	1.451
52	25.35	2.474	1.611
56	27.3	2.120	1.771
60	29.25	1.767	1.932
64	31.2	1.413	2.092
68	33.15	1.060	2.252
72	35.1	0.706	2.412
76	37.05	0.353	2.573
80	39	0	2.733
80	39	0	2.733
80	39	0	2.7333

FIGURE 5.3 Manufacturer, retailer, and supply chain profits with payback for different K values

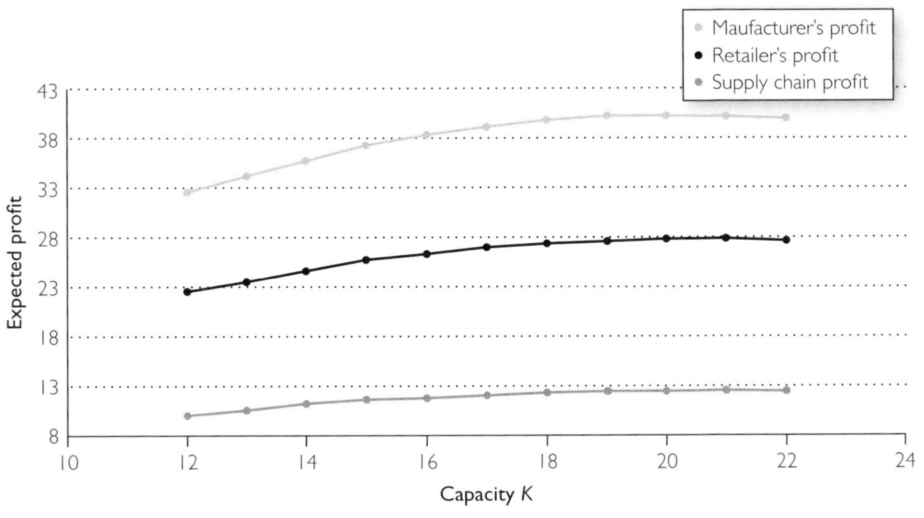

the sum of the manufacturer's and retailer's profits now match the single supply chain profit, thus generating a coordinated supply chain. In summary, not only is the supply chain coordinated, but the manufacturer's profits increase from 11.1 under the wholesale price agreement to 11.82. In addition, the retailer profit increased from 28 to 28.5. Since both manufacturer and retailer see their profits increase under this agreement, such agreements are called **Pareto-improving agreements**. In addition, the supply chain profit attains the maximum possible for the supply chain, thus the payback agreement coordinates the supply chain. Figure 5.3 shows the effect of different K values on the manufacturer's and retailer's profits, as well as the supply chain profit. Notice that the manufacturer's optimal K (when equal to 20) now coincides with the optimal K_C for the supply chain as in the earlier section.

Why does the payback contract coordinate the supply chain? Notice that the effect of the payback agreement is to adjust the wholesale price and the payback rate to get the manufacturer to choose a capacity that is optimal for the supply chain. In effect, the retailer creates an incentive for the manufacturer for carrying excess capacity by covering part of the downside risk, thus controlling the supply chain. Hence the agreement generates supply chain coordination. Note also that for each setting of w, there is a setting of τ that coordinates the supply chain. The main difference between alternate pairs of w and τ is that they correspond to the different possible splits of the total supply chain pie of profits. Also, for a given wholesale price level as in the previous section, there often exists a w and τ combination that can increase profits for both manufacturer and retailer.

5.9 CAPACITY RESERVATION CONTRACTS

Another possible contract is one in which the retailer is charged p per unit to reserve capacity and then w to use this reserved capacity. The manufacturer builds this reserved capacity and the retailer then uses capacity based on the observed demand. Intuitively this agreement spreads the risk between retailer and manufacturer. Since the retailer absorbs some of the manufacturer's risk, this contract has the potential to coordinate the supply chain.

5.11 RETAILER ABSORBS RISK

In all the examples discussed until this point, the manufacturer chose capacity and thus absorbed supply chain risk. Consider the case where the retailer has to order ahead of observing demand (i.e., at time L before the start of the season), while the manufacturer produces this certain order. The retailer thus absorbs all demand risk through its choice of inventory. Given that demand is variable, this demand risk manifests itself at the end of the season through either excess inventory that has to be salvaged or shortages that generate opportunity costs.

5.12 SUPPLY CHAIN PROFIT

The main difference between this case and the case when the retailer orders after observing demand is that the supply chain, too, has to make decisions before observing demand. Thus, all orders have to be placed and produced at L units of time before the start of the season. The effect is that the retailer places orders for K units of inventory, the manufacturer produces the entire order and incurs $c + c_k$ per unit, and the supply chain has inventory ready before the season demand unfolds. The supply chain expected profit is $rMin(Demand, K) - (c + c_k)K$. This profit is maximized by a choice of K that offers a service level of $\frac{r - c - c_k}{r}$.

Consider the same example as before, with the manufacturer costs of $c + c_k = 1.1$, $w = 2$, and $r = 4$ and the demand uniformly distributed between 8 and 22. The optimal supply chain service level is $\frac{4 - 0.5 - 0.6}{4} = 0.725$. The corresponding optimal inventory is thus $K_c = 18$. Table 5.9 shows the corresponding calculations for the maximum supply chain profit, which is equal to \$37.53.

TABLE 5.9 Supply chain expected profit calculations when the retailer absorbs risk; $r = 4, w = 2, c_k = 0.5, c = 0.6, K_c = 18$, optimal service level = 0.725

Demand	Prob	CumProb	Revenue	CapCost	Cost
8	0.067	0.067	32	19.8	0.8133
9	0.067	0.133	36	19.8	1.08
10	0.067	0.2	40	19.8	1.3467
11	0.067	0.267	44	19.8	1.613
12	0.067	0.333	48	19.8	1.88
13	0.067	0.4	52	19.8	2.147
14	0.067	0.467	56	19.8	2.413
15	0.067	0.533	60	19.8	2.68
16	0.067	0.6	64	19.8	2.946
17	0.067	0.667	68	19.8	3.213
18	0.067	0.733	72	19.8	3.48
19	0.067	0.8	72	19.8	3.48
20	0.067	0.867	72	19.8	3.48
21	0.067	0.933	72	19.8	3.48
22	0.067	1	72	19.8	3.48

Note that since the supply chain is forced to make decisions before demand realization, the expected profit in this case is lower than the case discussed earlier, when decisions regarding execution of capacity were made after demand realization.

5.13 WHOLESALE PRICE AGREEMENT

Suppose the manufacturer and retailer were separate entities, linked only by the fact that the retailer has to pay the manufacturer a wholesale price of w per unit for the product and place the entire order in advance of demand realization. The manufacturer, in turn, produces the entire order in advance and incurs a cost of $c + c_k$ to produce each unit.

The retailer's expected profit would thus be equal to $rMin(Demand, K) - wK$ while the manufacturer's expected profit would be equal to $(w - c - c_k)K$. The optimal service level desired by the retailer to maximize its profit is thus equal to $\frac{r-w}{r}$. This order size by the retailer is produced and delivered by the manufacturer.

Consider the example described in the previous section with the same demand and cost parameters. The retailer optimal service level would thus be $\frac{4-2}{2} = 0.5$. The corresponding retailer order would be $K = 15$ units. Table 5.10 shows the retailer's expected profits for the order of 15 units. The retailer's profit is obtained as \$22.53. The manufacturer expected profit will be $(2 - 0.5 - 0.6) \times 15 = 13.5$.

The retailer's and manufacturer's profits and supply chain profits for different K values are shown in Figure 5.4. In Figure 5.4, notice that the retailer's expected profits are maximized at $K = 15$, as we calculated earlier. However, at that inventory level, the supply chain profit, which is the sum of manufacturer's and retailer's profits is \$36.03, which is lower than the maximum supply chain profit obtained earlier. This is observed in Figure 5.4, which shows that the maximum supply chain profit is attained at $K = 18$, rather than at the inventory decision of $K = 15$ obtained in this case.

TABLE 5.10 Retailer expected profit calculations for wholesale price agreement when the retailer absorbs risk; $r = 4, w = 2, c_k = 0.5, c = 0.6, K = 15$, optimal service level = 0.5

Demand	Prob	CumProb	Revenue	CapCost	Profit×Prob
8	0.067	0.067	32	30	0.133
9	0.067	0.133	36	30	0.4
10	0.067	0.2	40	30	0.667
11	0.067	0.267	44	30	0.9333
12	0.067	0.333	48	30	1.2
13	0.067	0.4	52	30	1.467
14	0.067	0.467	56	30	1.733
15	0.067	0.533	60	30	2
16	0.067	0.6	60	30	2
17	0.067	0.667	60	30	2
18	0.067	0.733	60	30	2
19	0.067	0.8	60	30	2
20	0.067	0.867	60	30	2
21	0.067	0.933	60	30	2
22	0.067	1	60	30	2

FIGURE 5.4 Manufacturer, retailer and supply chain profits for different *K* values when retailer bears the risk

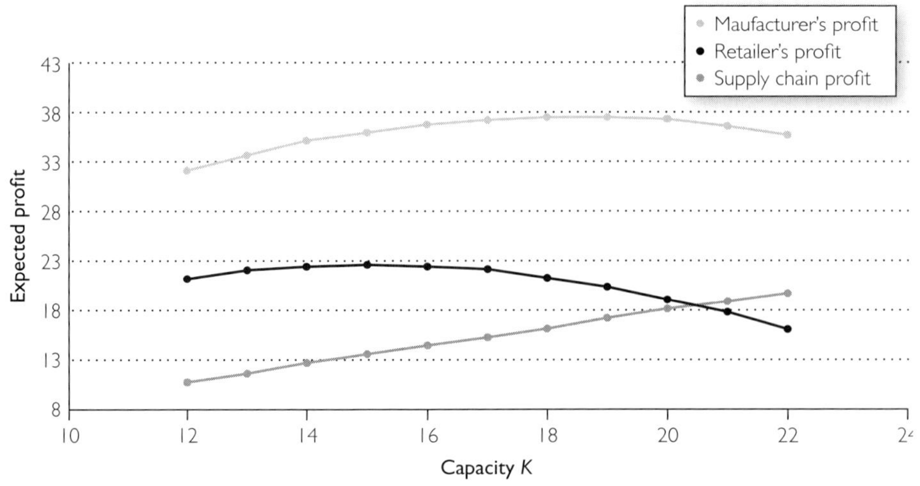

This difference in supply chain profit arises because of double marginalization, i.e., the retailer does not see the supply chain margin associated with each sale realized or lost and thus makes inventory decisions that are lower than the supply chain optimal decisions (for service levels > 0.5).

How does the problem change from the discussions in earlier sections where the manufacturer absorbs all risk? Notice that all of the contracts we discussed earlier can now be considered for this case. As before, double marginalization will prevent the supply chain from being coordinated with a wholesale price only contract. A payback contract now becomes a returns contract, where the manufacturer takes back leftover product from the retailer with an associated payment for returns. The payback contract can coordinate the supply chain in this case. The capacity reservation contract also coordinates the supply chain, in this case due to its equivalence to the returns contract, as discussed earlier.

5.14 RETAILER INFORMATION IMPROVEMENT

Consider the case where the retailer realizes that if he or she could wait to place an order at L_1 ($< L$) closer to the start of the season, better information would be available. Assume that the demand levels are low, medium, or high. Suppose a low demand level implies that the realized demand takes values (uniformly) between 8 and 12; a medium demand level has values between 13 and 17; and a high demand level has values between 18 and 22. In addition, suppose the demand level is low, medium, or high with probability $\frac{1}{3}$. Suppose the demand level is known to the retailer L_1 units of time before the start of the season. The manufacturer produces the order placed by the retailer.

How would permitting the retailer to order at L_1 affect manufacturer and retailer profits compared to the values under the wholesale price agreement in the earlier section? If all costs remain the same as in the previous sections, the retailer would continue to choose an order, given the demand level, that generates a service level of 0.5. Thus, if the demand level is low, the retailer orders 10 units; if medium, the retailer orders 15 units; and if high, the retailer orders 20 units.

If we calculate the expected order received by the manufacturer, it is $(\frac{1}{3}\times 10) + (\frac{1}{3}\times 15) + (\frac{1}{3}\times 30) = 15$ units. Thus the manufacturer's expected profit remains $(2 - 0.5 - 0.6)15 = 13.5$. Note that while the manufacturer's expected profit remains the same, the manufacturer does absorb more risk than before, because his order could be lower or higher than 15 with a probability of $\frac{2}{3}$.

The retailer adjusts his or her order with the known demand level. Calculating the expected profits for each demand level as shown in Table 5.11, we get the retailer profit under a low demand level of \$17.60, under a medium demand level of \$27.60, and under a high demand level of \$37.60.

The retailer's expected profit across all the possible demand realizations is thus $\frac{17.6+27.6+37.6}{3} = 27.6$. Notice that this increases the retailer's expected profit above the value generated when orders had to be placed at time L, while the manufacturer's expected profit remains the same as before. How did the retailer's expected profits increase? Better information when retailer orders are placed permits the supply to be more responsive to demand. This improved matching of supply to demand increases retailer profits.

TABLE 5.11 Retailer expected profit calculations under information improvement

Low Demand Level; $r = 4, w = 2, c_k = 0.5, c = 0.6, K = 10$, retailer optimal service level = 0.5

Demand	Prob	CumProb	Revenue	Inventory	Profit×Prob
8	0.2	0.2	32	20	2.4
9	0.2	0.4	36	20	3.2
10	0.2	0.6	40	20	4
11	0.2	0.8	40	20	4
12	0.2	1	40	20	4

Retailer profit under low demand is \$17.60.

Medium Demand Level; $r = 4, w = 2, c_k = 0.5, c = 0.6, K = 15$, retailer optimal service level = 0.5

Demand	Prob	CumProb	Revenue	Inventory	Profit×Prob
13	0.2	0.2	52	30	4.4
14	0.2	0.4	56	30	5.2
15	0.2	0.6	60	30	6
16	0.2	0.8	60	30	6
17	0.2	1	60	30	6

Retailer profit under medium demand is \$27.60.

High Demand Level; $r = 4, w = 2, c_k = 0.5, c = 0.6, K = 20$, retailer optimal service level = 0.5

Demand	Prob	CumProb	Revenue	Inventory	Profit×Prob
18	0.2	0.2	72	40	6.4
19	0.2	0.4	76	40	7.2
20	0.2	0.6	80	40	8
21	0.2	0.8	80	40	8
22	0.2	1	80	40	8

Retailer expected profit under a high demand is \$37.60.

We will discuss such contexts in Chapter 10, which is focused on the apparel industry. In the apparel industry, quick response is a movement that tries to get orders placed closer to the start of the season. In Chapter 10 we will discuss a number of coordinating agreements to generate Pareto-improving agreements under quick response.

5.15 CHAPTER SUMMARY

This chapter focused on coordination as an important component of supply chain management. We presented three cases focused on coordination decisions to develop a problem context. We then discussed several supply chains that were uncoordinated but could be coordinated using Pareto-improving agreements. We also showed that the availability of better information can decrease demand risk, better match demand and supply, and thus improve supply chain profits.

In later chapters, we will highlight the coordination mechanisms used in the contexts of specific industries. For example, in Chapter 6 on transportation, we discuss the Reynolds Metals case and the associated truck volume commitment contract. In Chapter 8 on purchasing, we discuss cases where design specifications are coordinated with supplier capability. In the grocery context (Chapter 9), we discuss coordinating promotions and associated inventory decisions. In the apparel industry context (Chapter 10), we discuss service level agreements to implement quick response. The key message is that in many supply chain contexts coordinating agreements can deliver significant improvements that all involve expanding the supply chain profit pie, thus enabling Pareto-improving profit situations.

5.16 PROBLEMS

1. Brian Williams is a supply chain manager at Bricks, a hardware retailer. In an effort to streamline his supply chain, he decided to focus on one hot-selling SKU for the upcoming season, the tedwig. Demand for the tedwig for the upcoming season is shown in Table 5.12.

TABLE 5.12 Tedwig demand

Demand (units)	Probability
100	0.2
150	0.3
200	0.2
250	0.2
300	0.1

Tedwigs are currently purchased from a supplier, Mortar, for $5 per unit and are sold for $12 per unit. Any leftover tedwigs are discarded by Bricks. It costs Mortar $2 per unit to manufacture one tedwig.

1a. Find the optimal service level that Bricks should offer, the associated inventory of tedwigs, and the optimal expected profit for Bricks. Find the associated expected profit for Mortar. What is the total expected profit for the supply chain in this system?

1b. Brian is considering the following recommendation provided by Buck Rogers, an MBA intern at Bricks. Buck suggests that there may be a coordination agreement that can improve profits for Bricks and Mortar. He recommends that Bricks offer the following agreement to Mortar.

"Mortar will get to increase the wholesale price to $6 per unit but will guarantee to take all leftover product from Bricks with a payment of $4.80 per unit. In return, Bricks will choose its optimal inventory level, and Mortar will thus get the associated expected profit."

Find the optimal service level that Bricks should offer, as well as the associated expected profit for Bricks. Find the associated expected profit for Mortar. Identify the expected supply chain profit given this agreement.

1c. Can we devise any other agreement that can increase the supply chain profit above the value in 1b? Explain why or why not.

2. A manufacturer Best has to commit to reserving capacity at a per-unit capacity cost of $1.50 per unit. The retailer, Smart, places orders after demand unfolds. Production by Best then costs $2 per unit produced, and the number of units produced cannot exceed the reserved capacity. The wholesale price charged by Best to Smart is $7 per unit. Smart sells the product at retail at $12 per unit.

The demand faced by Smart is described in Table 5.13.

TABLE 5.13 Demand for Smart

Demand	Probability
10	0.2
11	0.2
12	0.2
13	0.15
14	0.05
15	0.1
16	0.1

2a. Given this cost structure, (i) what is the optimal service level and capacity that Best would reserve to maximize its expected profit? (ii) Given Table 5.14 below, identify the associated expected profits for Best and Smart. (iii) Provide the associated supply chain expected profit. Is this supply chain expected profit maximized? If not, explain why.

TABLE 5.14 Best and Smart expected profit for different capacity choices

Capacity	10	11	12	13	14	15	16
Best exp profit	35	37.5	39	39.5	39.25	38.75	37.75
Sart exp profit	50	54	57	59	60.25	61.25	61.75

2b. Suppose Smart and Best are part of the supply chain. If a supply chain manager were to choose the optimal supply chain service level for Best, what would be that service level? What are the associated capacity choice for Best and associated expected profits for Best, Smart, and the supply chain?

Is this supply chain profit different from that in 2a? Explain why or why not.

2c. A supply chain consultant suggests that Best should lower the wholesale price to $6.90 and charge Smart a payback for leftover capacity to coordinate the supply chain. All other costs and prices remain the same as 2a, Best has to commit to reserving capacity at a per-unit capacity cost of $1.50 per unit. The retailer, Smart, places orders after demand unfolds. Production by Best then costs $2 per unit produced, and the number of units produced cannot exceed the reserved capacity. The wholesale price charged by Best to Smart is $6.90 per unit. Smart sells the product at retail at $12 per unit.

Possible values of the payback charge are $0.70 per unit, $0.80 per unit, or $0.90 per unit. What payback charge per unit should Smart offer Best so that Best chooses the supply chain with optimal capacity? Table 5.15 provides Best's expected profit for different payback charges. Thus, for example, the first row shows a payback charge of $0.70 per unit and the value under the capacity choice of 10 shows that Best's expected profit would be 34.

TABLE 5.15 Best's expected profit for different capacity choices

Payback charge	10	11	12	13	14	15	16
0.7	34	36.56	38.28	39.16	39.41	39.45	39.07
0.8	34	36.58	38.34	39.28	39.605	39.725	39.435
0.9	34	36.6	38.4	39.4	39.8	40	39.8

What payback charge will both coordinate the supply chain and generate expected profits that are greater than the results in 1a for both Best and Smart? What are the corresponding expected profit values? How did we manage to generate such Pareto-improving profits for both firms?

2d. Another consultant suggests that Best should provide an early order discount to incent Smart to reserve capacity in advance of demand. Will such a scheme coordinate the supply chain? Explain why or why not.

3. The Zebra company is a retailer of zany merchandise. The supplier of this merchandise, Props, receives orders from Zebra that are highly variable in their timing, reflecting Zebra's demand. To stimulate sales, Zebra uses retail price promotions that create demand variance but has an expected revenue associated with such pricing patterns of $20,000 per day.

The retail mean demand is 2,000 units per day and associated standard deviation is 750 units per day. Orders to Props face a lead time with a mean of 10 days and a standard deviation of 5 days. Zebra would like to offer a 98% service level to retail customers. Also, Props requires Zebra to order in truckload quantities. The truck capacity is 6,000 units. Holding cost is $0.50 per unit per day.

3a. Given these parameters, what should be the inventory policy at Zebra? What is the associated expected profit for Zebra?

3b. A consultant suggests that Zebra reduce price variation and thus eliminate retail demand variance. The associated impact is that expected revenue drops to $18,000 per day. However, the impact is that mean demand is 1,500 units per day and demand standard deviation is 50 units per day.

The supplier, Props, can now deliver all orders with certainty in exactly 10 days. Orders remain in full truckload quantities. What will be the impact on Zebra's reorder level? What is the associated inventory holding cost at Zebra?

What is the effect of this new scheme on Zebra's expected profits over the original system in 3a? Should Zebra switch to this system to maximize profits?

4. The Green company is a retailer of gourmet bottled pickles that purchases its products from Whole, a gourmet food manufacturer. Green buys units (from Whole) at a price of $15 per unit and sells them to customers at $45 per unit. Currently Whole produces to Green's order and delivers all requirements at the start of the period. Leftover inventory at the end of the season incurs a holding cost of $5 per unit and can be salvaged for $5 per unit. If Green does not have inventory, then demand is lost. Whole's production cost is $10 per unit.

TABLE 5.16 Demand distribution

Demand (units)	Probability
100	0.2
200	0.3
300	0.2
400	0.3

4a. Given this agreement, how many units should Green stock to satisfy demand? What is the associated profit for Whole and Green and for the supply chain?

4b. If Whole and Green were one integrated company, how many units would be stocked? What is the associated profit for the supply chain?

4c. Why is there a discrepancy between 4a and 4b? What steps would you recommend to improve profits for Whole and Green?

5. Fit is a retailer of women's apparel. In an attempt to keep with current trends, Fit coordinates with a manufacturer, Trim. In advance of the season, Fit communicates the custom fabric that will be used that season, and Trim purchases the fabric in advance. The cost of the fabric is $10 per unit of finished apparel. Since apparel cannot be stitched without the fabric, Fit is constrained by the inventory purchased by Trim. When the season begins and demand is realized, Fit orders from Trim. It costs an additional $25 per unit for the fabric to be converted to the final retail product. Trim gets paid $50 per unit. Fit then sells the product at retail for $100 per unit. The retail demand faced by Fit is shown below in Table 5.17.

TABLE 5.17 Fit's retail demand

Demand	Probability
100	0.2
150	0.2
200	0.25
250	0.2
300	0.15

5a. What is the optimal service level that the manufacturer, Trim, would choose? Given that choice, provide Trim's expected profit. Then provide the corresponding expected profit for Fit. Also provide the associated total supply chain profit for these decisions.

5b. Suppose Fit and Trim were to choose a service level and an initial inventory of cloth that would maximize supply chain profit. What would be the optimal supply chain service level and associated inventory and supply chain profit? Is this supply chain profit higher or lower than the supply chain profit in 5a? Explain.

5c. Fit asks Trim to increase purchase of fabric to the level in 5b. Will such a level of inventory increase Trim's profit over the level in 5a? Explain.

5d. Fit suggests a take or pay contract. Under this scheme, Fit will pay Trim the amount of $8 per unit for all leftover cloth. In addition, Fit will pay Trim $48 per unit for every unit purchased from Trim. In return, Fit asks Trim to guarantee a 100% service level. If Trim were to accept this contract, what would be Trim's expected profit? What would be Fit's expected profit? What would be the supply chain expected profit? Did these profits increase compared to 5a? Explain.

6. A manufacturer produces widgets at a cost of $3 per widget. These widgets are sold to a retailer at a wholesale price of $5 per widget. The retailer in turn sells these widgets to customers at a retail price of $12 per widget. Widgets left over at the end of the period are salvaged at a price of $2 per widget. Demand each period follows a normal distribution with a mean of 100 units and a standard deviation of 50 units. You may use Table 5.18 to get the *Z* value for a given service level.

TABLE 5.18 Service level and *Z* values

Service Level	*Z* value
0.6	0.25335
0.65	0.38532
0.7	0.5244
0.75	0.67449
0.8	0.84162
0.85	1.03643
0.9	1.28155
0.95	1.64485

6a. If the manufacturer owns the channel, i.e., both the manufacturing capacity as well as the retailer, provide the optimal level of inventory that will be carried and the associated service level offered to customers.

6b. If the manufacturer and retailer are separate companies, provide the optimal service level offered to customers and associated optimal retail inventory.

6c. Why are the two service levels different?

6d. Can the manufacturer structure an agreement so that the retail service level is the same as in 6a? Explain.

7. The Slick manufacturing company plans capacity and produces to orders placed by a retailer Fresh. Fresh collects orders for widgets during the season and places orders with Slick for manufacturing and delivery during the planned customer lead time. Slick has to plan capacity in advance. Reserving capacity costs Slick $1.50 to reserve capacity to produce 1 unit of product. In addition, after reserving the capacity, if demand is received, then production costs to create the product using the reserved capacity costs an additional $2 per unit.

Fresh pays Slick a wholesale price of $5 per unit. Fresh in turn sells the product to customers at a retail price of $10 per unit. Any capacity not used is wasted. Demand faced by Fresh has the following distribution, as shown in Table 5.19.

TABLE 5.19 Fresh's retail demand

Demand	Probability
10	0.1
11	0.2
12	0.3
13	0.2
14	0.1
15	0.1

7a. Suppose Slick were to choose its optimal capacity. What capacity choice will maximize Slick's profits, and what is the associated service level? What is the associated expected profit for Slick at that capacity? What is the corresponding expected profit for Fresh? What is the total supply chain profit? You may use Table 5.20 below to obtain the expected profits for each company.

TABLE 5.20 Expected profits at different capacity choices

Capacity Chosen	10	11	12	13	14	15
Manufacturer expected profit	15	16.2	16.8	16.5	15.6	14.4
Retailer expected profit	50	54.5	58	60	61	61.5

7b. Consider a choice of capacity that will maximize overall supply chain profits. What is the associated optimal capacity choice and service level? What is the corresponding supply chain profit? Is this profit different from the profit in 7a? If it is different, then explain why. (You may use the tables in 7a.)

7c. A Supply chain researcher suggests the following contract. Fresh will pay Slick $4.95 per unit as the wholesale price, but Fresh will pay Slick $1.165 per unit of left-over capacity.

Given this payment, what capacity should Slick choose as its profit-maximizing choice, and what is the associated service level? What is the associated expected profit for Slick? What is the expected profit for Fresh associated with this capacity choice by Slick? Are these expected profits larger than the profits in 7a? If so explain why. What is the total supply chain profit? How does it compare with the results in 7b?

You may use Table 5.21 to get the expected profits for each company.

TABLE 5.21 Expected profit at different capacity choices

Capacity Chosen	10	11	12	13	14	15
Expected profit manufacturer	14.5	15.77154	16.68615	17.06538	17.1	16.93154
Expected profit retailer	50.5	54.92846	58.11385	59.43462	59.5	58.96846

Chapter 6

Transportation

The role of transportation in a supply chain is to change the physical location of products and get supplies to the demand location. Transportation in the United States in 2012 was a $760 billion industry, with truck transportation accounting for 78% of domestic movement ([12]). A large portion of this market, around 70%–80%, is accounted for by contract trucking, where a trucking company operates as a dedicated carrier for the user during trips. The location of suppliers, intermediate processing plants, final assembly plants, finished-goods warehouses, customers, and so on, and their respective decision making regarding the transportation carriers used, determine the chain structure that has to be supported by transportation flows. The choice of transport mode (truck, rail, or air), and the associated capacity, e.g., container size, wagon load, or truckload, determine the size of shipments and thus the frequency of deliveries required to satisfy demand. The nature of the coordinating contract, e.g., spot capacity, core carrier programs, volume commitments, and so on, determine the impact of coordination agreements on transportation flows. Finally, the performance of a transport mode is determined by the metrics of its competitiveness, i.e., minimum cost, on-time delivery guarantees, dynamic routing, downstream services, as well as the availability of credible alternative carrier choices and their capacity.

Of the $1.2 trillion spent in 2010 in the United States on logistics costs, with $2.06 trillion of inventory, transport accounted for over 63% of the total expense ([12]). The industry is competitive, with over 10,000 trucking companies declaring bankruptcy over a two-year period. Indeed, it is probably appropriate to visualize a mode management terminal as similar to the National Aeronautics and Space Administration's (NASA's) flight control center, with streams of data flowing into a central hub, and dispatch decisions being fed back to truck drivers, with everything being monitored by a global positioning system (GPS) for location and speed.

A similar transport picture exists in Europe, where trucks account for about 75% of surface freight, while trains provide less than 20% of the capacity. The river primarily plays the role of feeder traffic for merchant shipping—but has the potential to play a much bigger role in the future. Auto companies such as Nissan and Honda use inland barges, an effective approach to transport about 30%–40% of their automobiles. Reports suggest that Nissan achieved this efficiency by using barges to transport vehicles from Amsterdam, the Netherlands, to Warth, Germany, and then delivering them by truck to their final destination ([94]).

Intuitively, it is clear that each mode choice has its unique cost structures, shipment volumes, and delivery lead times. Large-volume shipments at low transport costs per unit with long lead times favor rail. Smaller-volume shipments with higher costs per unit and faster delivery favor truck. An even more rapid delivery requirement with significantly higher costs per unit favors air. Barge shipments by river and shipments by sea further differentiate transportation cost choices. The appropriate question then is how to integrate transportation into a supply chain's architecture.

6.1 TRANSPORTATION TRANSACTIONS AND SUPPLY CHAIN ARCHITECTURE INTERACTIONS

6.1.1 Chain Structure

Because the role of transportation is to move product between supply chain locations, the locations of entities in the supply chain and the magnitude and frequency of material flows have a significant impact on this function. The nature of material flows also impacts the choice of transportation mode and thus the shipment size that proves most economic. In addition, the location of suppliers and customers affects the feasibility of backhaul (or continuous) moves, that is, shipments on trucks during their return to the source, as a means to reduce overall costs. In a global supply chain, the wide dispersion of locations means that different transport modes and their associated lead times will impact overall supply chain cost. There may also be cost differentials in different directions. In 2006, the cost to move a 20-foot container from the United States to China was $200, while the cost to ship a container from China to the United States was $1400, about seven times higher [44]. Such distortions have significant impacts on optimal supply chain flows.

6.1.2 Capacity

Transport capacity varies by choice of transportation mode. Shipments by sea are measured by container size, shipments by rail use wagon capacity, shipments by truck involve full truckload, and shipments by air may vary depending on the trade-off between weight and volume. In addition, while air shipments may provide the lowest lead time for transit, costs are such that these shipments usually involve light, smaller-volume quantities. The truck capacity decisions associated with transportation may involve planning the number and location of trucks, location and capacity of crossdocks, and capacity of terminals, roads, and tracks. Finally, routing choices for transportation can impact the timing and capacity available in a supply chain.

6.1.3 Coordination

A shipper and a shipping company can coordinate based on advance information regarding planned shipments, the creation of preferred carriers who manage the bulk of the loads, delivery window guarantees, and so on. Crossdocking is a process that involves linking truckload arrivals from different suppliers to truckload deliveries to retailers in order to convert static inventory into rolling stock, thus decreasing overall inventory levels and delivery lead times. Implementing crossdocking requires coordination of deliveries within specified time windows, linking containers from truck to rail, and allowing volume and schedule commitments to enable continuous routes. For rail shipments, coordination issues include planning routes, tracking containers along routes, managing blocking and bracing, coordinating local pickup or delivery at both ends, and shipment preparation. Shipments by barge involve coordinating material handling at the barge terminal and managing hand-offs to trucks at terminals. Finally, many shipping companies guarantee delivery within specified time windows, which generates contractual or pricing agreements to guarantee their feasible execution.

6.1.4 Competitiveness Measures

For shippers and transportation providers, an important metric is the total supply chain cost of transportation transactions. This total supply chain cost includes the effect on both transport costs and associated inventory costs. In addition, measures of performance include delivery lead time, percent on-time delivery or delivery within time windows, and schedule flexibility to accommodate shipment reschedules. Given the large volume of shipments that occur on dedicated contract trucking, there is scope for use of information, coordination agreements, and associated capacity commitments to improve performance across a supply chain. Competing carriers sell bundled routes to minimize shipper costs.

6.2 A SHIPPING COMPANY CONTEXT

ABC Rail faced the following problem: How should the company convince shippers of the benefit of its services relative to other modes of transport? How could the company adjust its schedules to be competitive in the marketplace? Reducing costs for rail shipments involves maximizing the number of wagons hitched to the engine, because once a trip is chosen and all labor, fuel, and track access charges are evaluated, the goal is to minimize costs. Each successive wagon thus increased the cost to ABC Rail by a small margin, hence the benefit of long trains.

While rail offered low transport costs, it also involved larger delivery sizes and longer transit times and thus higher inventories across the supply chain. In addition, waiting to ship loads meant that shippers faced a longer and potentially more variable lead time. This impact on lead times increased costs for the shipper. How should ABC Rail generate competitive schedules that could win business while still being profitable?

Perhaps it would help to view the decision from the perspective of the shipper. The shipper had to contend with the transport costs, inventory costs, other incidental costs as a total supply chain cost effect. Would it help if ABC enabled customers to evaluate the total supply chain cost of alternatives? If salespeople for ABC Rail could get an idea of competitive total supply chain cost by customer route, then ABC could identify how to adjust schedules and decide the number of wagons to wait for in order to beat the competition. Such an approach, repeated over and over across customers, would generate a customer-responsive train freight schedule. ABC had heard of an initiative by Burlington Northern called ShipSmart, which offered a similar service to shippers. Should ABC Rail use such an approach?

6.3 TOTAL SUPPLY CHAIN COSTS AND THE IMPACT OF TRANSPORTATION MODE

Consider a retailer in location B who purchases product from a supplier in location A. Customer demand at location B is satisfied from stock at a warehouse at B. The retailer takes possession of goods at A and arranges transport, manages inventories and order placement, and so on. The retailer can choose any mode of transport to get product from A to B. How should the retailer take account of total supply chain costs in making this decision?

There are three separate categories of costs that are considered:

1. **Transport Costs:** These costs are a function of transportation mode used. Assume that full truck- or full carload shipments are used and that transport capacity is not shared with any other products. This minimizes transport cost per unit on the route and therefore is the natural choice for transportation managers who seek to minimize transport costs alone.

   Given its larger capacity, rail transportation will be lower per unit shipped than truck, thus a goal to minimize transport costs will result in choice of large loads moved infrequently. If the transport capacity is C and the demand rate is D, the transport cost per unit for full load shipments is $\frac{KD}{C}$.

2. **Inventory Costs:** This cost category examines the effect of transit times (both mean, variance, and shipment size) on inventory. Under this category, we consider three sets of inventory levels.

   a. **In-transit Inventory:** This refers to goods that are on the trucks or railcars in the process of being moved from the source to destination. The average value of in-transit inventory is just the demand rate times the transit lead time: $D \times L$. This inventory level increases as the average transit time increases. Note that in-transit inventory is independent of the shipment size. This is because the inventory policy is assumed to follow a replenishment system whereby the order releases track demands. Thus doubling the shipment size merely halves the shipment frequency, leaving the in-transit inventory unchanged. The cost of this in-transit inventory is thus $h \times D \times L$ where h is the holding cost per unit of inventory.

   b. **Cycle Stock:** This refers to inventory levels required to satisfy expected demand. Thus, if we assume there is a constant and an average demand each period, the average inventory level is half the order size per cycle. If there are Q units in each delivery, the cycle stock will be $\frac{Q}{2}$ (see the section on economic order quantity [EOQ] in Chapter 15 for details). The cost associated with the cycle stock will be $h\frac{Q}{2}$.

   c. **Safety Stock:** This refers to inventory required to meet variable demand or effects of transit time variance. Typically the safety stock level is chosen to guarantee a certain probability of having no stockout. Assuming a normal distribution of demand over the delivery lead time, a standard deviation of demand over lead time of σ_{DL}, and an in-stock probability of *ser* (the service level), the safety stock is $Z_{ser}\sigma_{DL}$. The associated holding cost is $hZ_{ser}\sigma_{DL}$.

3. **Blocking and Bracing Costs:** These are costs applicable for rail car shipment where the product in the car must be "carefully packaged to prevent damage" for protection. This is usually a per-shipment charge.

6.4 AN EXAMPLE PROBLEM

Fixit is a hardware chain focused on do-it-yourself customers. Fixit operates in the Pittsburgh area and has a distribution center that receives shipments from its supplier, Acme, located in Seattle, Washington. Demand at Fixit each month is 30,000 packs of bulky widgets. Currently shipments from Acme to Fixit are sent by truck. The capacity of a truck is 5,000 packs. Transit time for the truck from Seattle to Pittsburgh is 5 days. In addition, analysis of the data shows that the lead time has a standard deviation of 2 days.

Fixit's accounting group has estimated that the annual holding cost is 20% of the cost of the product. Acme supplies a case of widgets for a price of $15 per pack. Assume a desired service level of 95% and a current safety stock of 1 day of inventory at Pittsburgh to counter delivery lead time variation. The cost for a truckload shipment from Seattle to Pittsburgh, by third-party carrier, is $3,000.

6.4.1 Truck Shipments

1. **Transport Cost per Month:** Given Fixit's demand of 30,000 packs per month and the truck capacity of 5,000 packs, the system needs $\frac{30{,}000}{5{,}000} = 6$ shipments/month. The monthly cost of these truck shipments is 6 × $3,000 per truckload = $18,000 per month.

2. **Inventory Related Costs:**

   a. **Cost of In-Transit Stock:** The monthly demand of 30,000 packs, with each pack spending an average of 5 days in transit, implies that we have $\frac{30,000 \times 5}{30} = 5,000$ packs of in-transit inventory. Using a holding cost of 0.20 × \$15 per pack per year or $\frac{\$0.20 \times 15}{12}$ per pack per month = \$0.25 per pack per month, we get a holding cost of \$1,250.

   b. **Cycle Stock Cost:** Since order size is one truckload, cycle stock is $\frac{5,000}{2}$ or 2,500 packs. Thus the monthly holding cost of cycle stock is \$0.25 × 2,500 = \$625.

   c. **Safety Stock Cost:** The safety stock covers the demand during the variability of lead time and is expressed as $Z_{service}\sigma D$, where σ is the standard deviation of lead time (in days) and D is the daily demand. Thus the safety stock carried at Pittsburgh to deal with transit time variability is 1.65 × 2 × 1,000 = 3,300 packs. The holding cost of this safety stock is 0.25 × 3,300 = \$825.

   Thus total supply chain inventory cost is \$1,250 + \$625 + \$825 = \$2,700.

Thus total supply chain cost is \$18,000 + \$2,700 = \$20,700.

6.4.2 Total Supply Chain Costs Using the Existing Rail Option

Railcar, a rail brokerage that works closely with railroads to schedule shipments, has made Fixit an offer to move product. Railcar also coordinate schedules with the railroads to improve supply chain costs for shippers. The current offer by Railcar is a shipment price of \$6,000 for one wagonload of widgets from Seattle to Pittsburgh. The capacity of a wagon is 15,000 packs. Transit time is expected to be 15 days with a standard deviation, based on current performance, of 10 days.

If Fixit were to use rail to ship product from Seattle to Pittsburgh, what would be the impact on total supply chain costs?

1. **Transport Costs per Month:** As before, we take the average of the rail shipments each month and multiply it by the cost per rail shipment to get $\frac{30,000}{15,000} \times 6,000 =$ \$12,000 per month.

2. **Inventory Costs:**

   a. **Holding Cost of In-transit Inventory:** The in-transit inventory is obtained as $\frac{30,000 \times 15}{30}$ = 15,000 packs. The corresponding holding cost is 0.25 × 15,000, which is \$3,750.

   b. **Holding Cost of Cycle Stock:** The cycle stock level is $\frac{15,000}{2}$ = 7,500 packs. Thus, the holding cost of this cycle stock is 0.25 × 7,500 = \$1,875.

   c. **Safety Stock Holding Cost:** The safety stock held to compensate for transit time variability is 1.65 × 10 × 1,000 = 16,500 packs. Thus the holding cost of this safety stock is 0.25 × 16,500 = \$4,125.

   The total of supply chain inventory costs is \$3,750 + \$1,875 + \$4,125 = \$9,750.

The total of supply chain costs for shipping by rail is \$12,000 + \$9,750 = \$21,750.

Notice that the total of supply chain costs for the the rail proposal is more than truck. However, the observed train average lead time and associated lead time variance is based on the current mode of minimizing costs to ship by rail. This suggests that using rail mode creates a lead time due to the need to maximize the number of wagons and to route the wagons to minimize costs. This is similar to trying to minimize costs for a set of trips made by airplane—often the cheapest route involves going through airline hubs. However, as in the airline case, it may be possible to reduce lead time, increasing the transportation cost, and yet make it profitable for the shipper. The shipper can choose alternate modes of transportation, resulting in market pressure, which requires the train schedules to be competitive and profit maximizing rather than cost minimizing and thus potentially not generating revenues. We explore such an adjustment in Section 6.4.3.

In particular, consider an alternate proposal for the rail option, whereby the trains travel at a lower average lead time that is less variable. Since transport cost per unit of train shipments is low, these lower average lead time and less variability could reduce both the in-transit inventory holding costs to ship by rail and the associated safety stock. We examine next the impact of these changes on the total supply chain cost experienced by the shipper.

6.4.3 A Revised Rail Option

Railcar has developed another shipping proposal by coordinating with the railroads so that the cost to ship remains the same but delivery performance is improved. Railcar's proposed schedule drops the transit time to 10 days and the variation in transit time to 3 days. This may increase actual rail operating costs but may also increase revenues if it generates supply chain costs that are more competitive than truck shipments. What is the impact of this schedule on total supply chain costs at Fixit?

1. **Transport Costs:** The transport costs per month remain the same as in the previous scenario: $\frac{30,000}{15,000} \times 6,000 = \$12,000$ per month.
2. **Inventory Costs:**
   a. **In-Transit Inventory Costs:** The in-transit stock is $\frac{30,000 \times 10}{30} = 1,000$ cases with a holding cost of $\$0.25 \times 1,000 = \$2,500$.
   b. **Cycle Stock Costs:** The level of cycle stock is determined by the shipment size and is $\frac{15,000}{2} = 7,500$ packs. The associated holding cost is $\$0.25 \times 7,500 = \$1,875$.
   c. **Safety Stock Costs:** The safety stock held to compensate for transit time variability is $1.65 \times 3 \times 1,000 = 4,950$ packs. Thus the holding cost of this safety stock is $0.25 \times 4,950 = \$1,237.50$.

   The total of supply chain inventory costs is $\$2,500 + \$1,875 + \$1,237.50 = \$5,612.50$.

The total supply chain cost is $\$12,000 + \$5,612.50 = \$17,612.50$.

6.4.4 Mode Choice and Its Impact on the Supply Chain

The example above shows the impact of competing modes of transport, creating schedule changes that increase the competitiveness of rail. In this case the chain structure involved four companies: Acme, the transport company (and possibly a transport broker like Railcar), Fixit, and Fixit's customers. Railcar had to identify its competitiveness by examining the impact on total supply chain costs. Railcar then had to coordinate with railroads to adjust their schedules so that transit times could be improved and variation decreased. The larger capacity for rail shipments provided a lower cost per unit but correspondingly increased Fixit's cycle stock inventory in Pittsburgh. Railcar was able to improve the supply chain architecture because it understood the impact of the current supply chain architecture on Fixit's mode choice decision and adjusted the architecture to become competitive relative to other mode choices.

6.5 USING COORDINATION AGREEMENTS TO IMPROVE TRANSPORTATION SYSTEMS

Coordinating agreements can be implemented between a shipper and a transport provider to improve performance. Consider a supply chain consisting of suppliers, manufacturing plants, and customer locations. In the original system, suppose each plant runs as an independent profit center, choosing its own transportation. To create scale economies as well as increase the fraction of line and backhaul routes, an alternate system can be implemented to coordinate across locations and with a transport company. Consider the potential impact on the system as it transitions from independent transport choices to a corporate load control center that enables performance improvement.

There are several companies that face such a transition, especially during establishment of a core carrier program. There is an important difference between centralization of transportation and coordination of transportation. Under a centralized system, a central entity decides how to handle all loads. Under a coordinated system, the load control center offers possible delivery times and defines associated costs, but the individual locations make the final decision. Thus in a coordinated system, individual profit centers decide on the tradeoff between customer service and related costs and revenue benefits.

6.6 REYNOLDS METALS AND CORE CARRIER PROGRAMS

This section summarizes the article in [88]. In 1988, Reynolds Metals Corporation was a $6.2 billion company that carried a variety of aluminum-intensive products—from aluminum foil to airplane parts. Reynolds had 120 shipping locations and 5,000 shipping destinations and used 200 van and flatbed carriers. Reynolds prided itself on being a decentralized corporation where the local plant manager chose the transport with an emphasis on quick delivery to meet customer schedules. Reynolds spent $80 million in transport costs. Transport was handled by over 200 trucking companies, each working with a particular location or shipping lane. The net results were low use of continuous loads, low volume discounts due to the small volume with each trucking company, and poor on-time delivery performance. Reynolds management wanted to realize the benefits of coordination between loads without eliminating the flexibility afforded to each location.

Reynolds needed to create a corporate logistics entity to provide reduced costs and improved service. The company created a load control center (LCC) to coordinate loads across locations and offer larger volumes to trucking companies without centralizing decision making. When a location was planning to ship a load, the LCC would choose a trucking company, quote a price, and provide an estimated delivery time to the shipping location. LCC would then select from a small subset of trucking companies that would get an annual volume commitment in return for lower prices and a higher service level. Next Reynolds needed to identify a way to share demand risk (for trucks) with the trucking company so as to improve performance for both shipper and shipping company.

The LCC needed to identify loads in opposite directions that could be combined to create continuous moves. This would enable reduction of deadhead moves (return trips without a load) by the trucking company and thus reduce costs for Reynolds and the trucker. Such moves require flexibility regarding ship times and delivery times, a decision that only the local manager can make. Suppose the LCC could offer the opportunity to reduce shipping costs by coordinating loads. Assuming local plants are profit centers, the choice for a location is based on the benefit of lower shipping costs vs. the flexibility to deliver the loads. In addition, if the LCC could guarantee delivery reliability and tracking of deliveries by pooling all transactions, that increases the benefits for individual locations.

Reynolds achieved a $7 million annual reduction in transport costs, which consisted of a 70% reduction due to volume buying, and a 30% due to a 600% increase in continuous moves while increasing on-time delivery from 80% to 95%. This was achieved along with reducing the number of transport companies from 200 to 5 van carriers and 8 flatbed carriers. How are such dramatic improvements achieved within a corporation?

6.7 COORDINATING FREIGHT OPERATIONS—CORE CARRIERS AND PARETO IMPROVEMENT

To understand the benefit of a coordination approach to improve performance, consider a change from an arm's-length relationship to one that is based on a risk-sharing agreement in the transportation context. We show that risk-sharing coordinating agreements can improve the performance of both the shipper and the carrier, thus generating Pareto-improving performance. Pareto-improving performance requires that no participants to the agreement are worse off, and at least one of them is better off, than before.

Recall the Reynolds Metals case discussed in Section 6.6. This example shows how a volume commitment can be used to get a cost reduction and improved service while generating Pareto-improving benefits for the carrier.

6.7.1 The Impact of Truck Volume Commitment—An Example

Consider a supply chain consisting of a manufacturer (Smart) who requires trucks to pick up material from one location every day to be delivered to a customer. The number of trucks required by Smart varies daily. A histogram of the history of daily truck usage indicates the following probability distribution (Table 6.1):

TABLE 6.1 Daily truck usage

Trucks Required	Probability
0	0.2
1	0.2
2	0.2
3	0.2
4	0.1
5	0.1

The data above suggest that a trucking company providing trucks faces demand risk because on 20% of the days Smart will require no trucks, while on 10% of the days Smart will require 5 trucks. The next step is to understand how a carrier has to plan capacity to make trucks available to Smart. Smart has contacted a trucking company (Quick) that will supply these trucks. Smart notifies Quick of the trucks it will need on a given day, and Quick sets them aside the day before they are needed. It costs Quick $100 to make a truck available. The current agreement between Smart and Quick is as follows: If Smart uses a truck on any day, Smart pays Quick $200 per truck. However, if a truck requested by Smart is not available at Quick, Quick pays Smart a penalty of $200 per truck. In that case, Smart has to pay a spot rate (market rate without a contract) for transportation of $900 per truck to have shipments handled by another trucking company.

6.7.2 Profits at Quick and Costs to Smart with No Coordination

Question 1: How many trucks will Quick commit to maximize its expected profit each day?

Note that Quick and Smart are separate companies, each seeking to optimize their performance. Thus, Quick will choose a planned capacity to maximize its profits. Suppose Quick commits T trucks. The corresponding expected profit for Quick is as follows:

$$-100T + \sum_{i=0}^{T} 200 \times i \times p_i + \sum_{i=T+1}^{5} 200 \times T \times p_i - \sum_{i=T+1}^{5} 200 \times (i - T) \times p_i$$

Suppose $T = 3$, the expected profit for Quick, is as follows:

$$-100 \times 3 + \{(200 \times 0 \times 0.2) + (200 \times 1 \times 0.2) + (200 \times 2 \times 0.2) + (200 \times 3 \times 0.2)\}$$
$$+ \{(200 \times 3 \times 0.1) + (200 \times 3 \times 0.1)\} - \{(200 \times 1 \times 0.1) + (200 \times 2 \times 0.1)\} = 0$$

A summary of Quick's expected profit under different numbers of committed trucks is as follows (Table 6.2):

TABLE 6.2 Expected profit with no coordination

Trucks Committed	Quick's Expected Profit
0	−420
1	−200
2	−60
3	0
4	−20
5	−80

Thus committing 3 trucks maximizes Quick's expected profits.

Note, of course, that the problem faced by Quick is a classic newsvendor problem. The optimal solution to the newsvendor model is to first determine the cost per unit short, C_s, and the cost per unit of excess inventory, C_e. In this case, C_s is equal to the sum of lost profits plus the penalty = (200 – 100) + 200 = 300. Also, C_e is equal to the cost of the truck (assuming that it has to be held on standby the whole day and thus cannot be deployed for other purposes) = 100. Thus the optimal critical fractile $\frac{C_s}{C_s + C_e} = \frac{300}{300 + 100} = 0.75$. The lowest capacity that provides this desired service level is three trucks (observe that at three trucks, the cumulative probability is 0.8). The optimal capacity thus coincides with the results observed from Table 6.2.

Question 2: What is the impact of Quick's decisions on Smart's costs?

Given Quick's decision to reserve 3 trucks, Smart's expected cost is as follows:

$$(0.2 \times 1 \times 200) + (0.2 \times 2 \times 200) + (0.2 \times 3 \times 200) + (0.1 \times \{(3 \times 200)$$
$$+ (1 \times 900) - (1 \times 200)\}) + (0.1 \times \{(3 \times 200) + (2 \times 900) - (2 \times 200)\}) = \$570$$

Note that if demand by Smart is for three or fewer trucks, the entire demand is satisfied by Quick. If demand is for four or five trucks, then Quick satisfies the demand for three trucks, and the unfulfilled demand is satisfied by Smart from the spot market with associated penalty payments by Quick. While this maintains service level for Smart's customers, it does require Smart to scramble to satisfy demand.

6.7.3 Impact of a Volume Commitment by Smart

Can an agreement between Smart and Quick improve their respective performance measures, i.e., increase expected profits for Quick and decrease expected costs for Smart? In order to devise such an agreement, consider the fact that Quick has to balance the potential revenues from high truck demand with the potential costs associated with unused trucks if demand is low. One approach is for Smart to decrease demand risk for Quick by offering a take-or-pay contract in return for a higher service level commitment.

Consider the following contract: "Smart guarantees use of at least two trucks every day, i.e., Smart will pay Quick at least $400 every day, even if Smart does not need two trucks. In return, Smart demands a 100% service level from Quick."

How will this affect Quick's expected profits and Smart's costs? Note that under this scheme, Quick has to commit at least two trucks.

Quick's expected profit is as follows:

$$= (-100 \times T) + \Sigma_{i=0}^{2} 400 \times p_i + \Sigma_{i=3}^{T} 200\, ip_i + \Sigma_{i=T+1}^{5} 200 \times T \times p_i - \Sigma_{i=T+1}^{5} 200 \times (i - T) \times p_i$$

TABLE 6.3 Expected profit with volume commitment

Trucks Committed	Quick's expected profit
2	60
3	120
4	100
5	40

The table shows that to offer a 100% service level, Quick has to reserve five trucks and that Quick can commit up to five trucks and still improve its expected profit.

The impact of Quick's commitment of five trucks on Smart's expected costs is as follows:

$$(400 \times 0.2) + (400 \times 0.2) + (400 \times 0.2)$$
$$+ (0.2 \times 3 \times 200) + (0.1 \times 4 \times 200) + (0.1 \times 5 \times 200) = \$540$$

The results show that the agreement between Quick and Smart results in an increase in expected profit for Quick from $0 to $40 and a decrease in expected costs for Smart from $570 to $540. Thus, in this example, both Quick and Smart improve their performance and Smart's service level from Quick increases from 80% to 100%. Such an agreement can be considered to be Pareto improving.

Note that similar calculations show that if Quick commits three trucks, Smart's costs are $690; if Quick commits four trucks, Smart's costs are $590. Thus only a 100% service level commitment by Quick creates a Pareto-improving system.

The example discussed shows that take-or-pay commitments can potentially permit both cost reductions and service-level improvements. The Reynolds case suggests that the company saw significant performance improvement as a result of a combination of both volume commitments as well as coordinated volume buying due to the aggregation of moves throughout the system. The example suggests that adjusting the supply chain architecture (changing the coordination agreement and thus adjusting the capacity) can improve the competitiveness of the supply chain as a whole.

6.8 E-COMMERCE AND TRANSPORTATION

The transportation industry was impacted by the rise of the dot com companies and consequent use of competition across carriers as a mechanism to improve transport costs for a shipper. In these markets, transport services face an important spatial dimension that affects costs ([111]): (1) where a truck ends its journey affects how valuable it is to handle follow-on loads and (2) the ability to develop balanced networks allows carriers to maintain equipment regularly at fixed locations and get their drivers home frequently and predictably. Thus the bids offered by a carrier to a shipper depend on how the loads carried for one shipper will interact with loads carried for other shippers in order to permit effective utilization of the carrier's assets over time. E-commerce hubs for transportation use auctions as a mechanism to increase the range of participants, thus potentially lowering costs.

6.9 TRANSPORTATION AUCTIONS

Transport costs depend on the location of the pickup and delivery points and thus rely on the spatial link to other routes served by the trucks. In addition, the cost to a trucking company to service a shipping lane from Chicago to Los Angeles (LA) depends on what is committed in the Los Angeles–to–Chicago direction. Thus, if another lane, say St. Louis to Chicago, is part of the return trip, then the transport company may be able to offer a better deal for the combined Los Angeles–to–Chicago and St. Louis–to–Chicago routes than for the sum of the individual routes bid separately ([77]).

Ledyard et al. ([77]) provide the following example that clearly illustrates the impact of spatial demand on costs. A retail company requires five truckloads from Los Angeles to Chicago, seven truckloads from Chicago to New Orleans, and ten truckloads from New Orleans to Los Angeles. One solution is to lease ten trucks and use them to complete the moves. But what if there are three trucking firms with the same costs but different customer bases? Firm 1 has five loads from Chicago to Los Angeles and a current return trip that generates a revenue of X. Firm 2 has ten loads from New Orleans to Chicago and a current return trip that generates a revenue of Y. Firm 3 has ten loads from New Orleans to Los Angeles and a current return trip with a return revenue of Z. If the cost to ship from Los Angeles to Chicago is $> X$, then any price that is such that $X <$ *price* $<$ *cost(LA to Chicago)* generates benefits to both Firm 1 and the retail company. Similarly Firms 2 and 3 would be willing to carry the loads for prices that exceed Y and Z respectively. However, notice that Firm 3 would be willing to transport loads from LA to Chicago and from Chicago to New Orleans for any price greater than Z + *cost(LA to Chicago to New Orleans)* – *cost(LA to New Orleans)*. Notice that the price for a lane is a function of the revenue currently generated for the return legs for travel by the three firms, which in turn is affected by the revenues generated in the outgoing legs of travel. This spatial link between loads shipped currently and the impact of the economics of return moves makes the transport industry pricing decisions complex.

In practice, the shipper would seldom know about the revenues earned during the return trips for transport firms. Auctions allow transport companies to reveal as much of this information as possible out of a desire to win the bid. The following examples provide such initiatives at two companies.

6.9.1 Sears Logistics Service

Sears Logistics Services (SLS) is a wholly owned subsidiary of Sears, Roebuck and Co., and is one of the world's largest procurers of trucking services. SLS controls the movement of products from vendor to distribution center to stores. Ledyard et al. ([77]) describe an application of combined value auctions for transport services at SLS. This approach was used to purchase 1,390 lanes of transport services for \$597 million. Over a three-year period, SLS saved more than \$84.75 million by running six such auctions.

An outline of the approach used is as follows: A subset of fourteen national and regional carriers was identified and given exclusive rights to provide a sealed bid during the auction. At the end of the round, the auctioneer announced provisional winners and revealed all the winning bids. The next round was open only to the winning set of carriers, who would bid against the current provisional winners. If total acquisition cost did not decline by a fixed percent over the previous round, the just-completed round would be declared the final round.

The bids submitted by carriers were input into a computer simulation that modeled a shipping lane scenario. The winning bids adequately provide transportation while preventing the total number of trucks from exceeding carrier specified capacity. The goal was to maximize the surplus for the shipper, defined as the amount below the shipper's reservation price. The details of the model used to select the winning bids and allocation will be provided in section 6.9.3.

The key decisions that supported this transportation auction include the description of the ending round, the training of suppliers as they put together bids, and the process of selection of winning carriers between rounds.

6.9.2 The Home Depot

The Home Depot also uses transportation auctions ([34]). The Home Depot was founded in 1978 in Atlanta, GA. Home Depot is the world's largest home improvement retailer. The 1,000 stores are supplied by thirty-seven distribution centers in forty-five states. The supply chain includes over 7,000 suppliers who provide over 40,000 SKUs to stores and DCs across locations. Over 90% of the products move on trucks. In 1999, the company made 7.1 million less-than-truckload shipments and 219,000 full truckload shipments. These were expected to change to 4.7 million less-than-truckload and 877,000 full truckload shipments in 2003.

Until 1996, the Home Depot asked carriers to submit bids on a standard Excel spreadsheet. Procurement still continued by lane separately, and thus carriers were unable to make informed bidding decisions that reflected synergies across lanes. Carriers also did not have adequate visibility of demand across Home Depot's network.

A new bidding process was announced in January 2000. Before the bidding process started, carriers were provided data regarding origin and destination locations, lane details, and demand forecasts. Carriers were permitted to bid on individual lanes or on groups of lanes. Lane groups represented geographic areas or groups of facilities or were customized by the carrier to fit into an existing schedule. There were also no constraints on the number of bids for a lane and the combinations of bids that could be offered. Carriers were also allowed to specify constraints across bids so that the resources required were available. The penalty for not having the resources to service a winning bid was that the carrier lost all of the lanes that had been awarded.

The bids were accepted at sealed-bid, single-round auction. Once bids were submitted, Home Depot solved an integer program whose goal was to (1) provide service on all lanes; (2) allocate a lane to one single carrier; (3) select allocations that satisfied shipper and carrier constraints; and (4) meet nonprice goals such as carrier reliability, load balancing among carriers, preferences to incumbents, hub locations of carriers, safety ratings, and so on. In other contexts [111], the shipper may adjust shipper bids based on its on-time delivery performance and its importance to the recipient.

The model used by the Home Depot to choose successful carriers is described in Section 6.9.3. In October 2000, the bidding was carried out with 111 carriers. The bidding process was expected to involve one round only, but decisions were made for 80% of the lanes in round one. For the remaining 20% of the lanes, Home Depot held a second round of bidding and invited sixty-two bidders, of which thirty-six submitted bids. Even after this round, some lanes were not covered because Home Depot felt that carriers available for some lanes were not acceptable. The average number of carriers bidding on each lane was 14, with a minimum of two and a maximum of 33 across lanes. Home Depot claimed that it received lower rates, while carriers expressed satisfaction from the part of the business they were awarded.

6.9.3 Selecting Carriers

Given bids from many independent carriers that specify the rate by lane or by groups of lanes, the minimum expected number of trucks by lane segment, the demands for trucks by lane, as well as the maximum rate the shipper would be willing to pay per lane, the goal of the model is to help the shipper select a prescribed number of different carriers that will satisfy carrier demand at minimum cost.

Suppose R_l refers to the reservation rate for lane l (the reservation rate for a package k, R_k would be the sum of the reservation rates for the lanes in the package); b_{jk} refers to the minimum dollar amount needed by firm j to supply package k; u_{jk} refers to the capacity estimated by firm j for package k; $U(j)$ is firm j's total capacity; x_{jkl} is 1 if firm j's package k contains lane l as part of the package and 0 otherwise; $d(j,k)$ is 1 if firm j's package k is selected, 0 otherwise.

The model will seek to maximize $\Sigma_{j,k}(R_k - b_{jk})d(j,k)$
subject to

$$\Sigma_{j,k}x_{jkl}d(j,k) \leq 1 \text{ for all lanes } l$$

$$\Sigma_k u_{jk}d(j,k) \leq U(j)$$

$$d(j,k) = 0 \text{ or } 1$$

The model described above permits the shipper to incorporate carrier cost structure into the choice of carriers that will minimize costs. There have been several experimental investigations of such bidding schemes that will provide outcomes that maximize carrier surplus. The approaches used by Sears and the Home Depot represent two such schemes.

6.10 CHAPTER SUMMARY

For supply chains, transportation flows enable products or components to change location, thus enabling them to be used at their demand points. The timing of these transportation flows in turn interacts with transport capacity and chain structure to impact supply chain performance. Given this interaction, the total supply chain impact of a choice of transportation flows has to include transport costs, cycle stock costs, safety-stock costs, and in-transit inventory costs. For each possible transport mode, there are different impacts on associated capacity and transit time. Thus, optimal transport mode requires consideration of the impact of different components of the supply chain costs and thus may impact associated capacity. The core carrier program discussion shows how a coordination of transportation using a Pareto-improving contract with carriers can decrease supply chain costs and increase on-time delivery. Given that the carrier industry is competitive, a company can use auctions as a mechanism to permit transport bundles to be bid on by carriers, thus decreasing overall costs. This chapter focuses on transportation decision impact of capacity, coordination with carriers, chain structure, and competitive benefits—all the four Cs associated with effective supply chain management.

6.11 PROBLEMS

1. The Giant Corporation has a plant in Nashville, TN. The plant ships product to its customer in the suburbs of Indianapolis, IN. The trucking company Deal charges Giant $400 per truckload shipped from Nashville to Indianapolis. Deal has agreed to pay Giant a penalty of $500 if Giant calls for a truck and Deal does not have it. Deal has to plan for trucks a day in advance, and it costs $250 per truck for Deal to have a truck available.

Demand for trucks in Nashville has the following distribution (Table 6.4):

TABLE 6.4 Demand for trucks in Nashville

Trucks Required	Probability
0	0.2
1	0.1
2	0.3
3	0.2
4	0.2

1a. How many trucks will Deal plan to have in inventory to maximize its profits? What are the associated expected profits for Deal?

1b. Given Deal's truck commitment, what is the expected cost for Giant?

1c. An executive at Giant has found a company (Tiny) in a related industry who ships regularly from Indianapolis to Nashville. The company has costs and demand for trucks the same as Giant and gets the same service and costs from its trucking company.

The Giant executive suggests the following scheme. Both companies, Giant and Tiny, will contract with Deal. Every day Tiny will call Deal with its truck requirements from Indianapolis to Nashville, and Giant will report them to Deal. Assume that the trip from Indianapolis to Nashville and back can be done in a day. Depending on the trucks required, Deal will try to run a continuous route. Each continuous route will be charged $600 for the roundtrip. All single routes will be charged $400. (Thus for example if Giant needs two trucks (Nashville to Indianapolis) and Tiny needs one truck (Indianapolis to Nashville), the total charge will be $600 (for one continuous route) and $400 (one single route) = $1,000 for the total moves.)

The total charge will be shared between Giant and Tiny. In return, Deal will offer a 100% service guarantee.

Should Deal accept this scheme? Is this scheme good for Giant? Is this Pareto improving?

2. The Rapid trucking company works with Steel, a shipper. The trucking contract requires Rapid to provide or decline trucks requested by Steel with a payment per shipment of $120 per truck provided. To provide trucks to Steel, Rapid has to plan in advance and reserve trucks the previous day at a cost per truck of $60.

If Steel cannot get demand satisfied by Rapid, it will cost $200 to get the shipment completed by a spot carrier.

The demand for trucks at Steel each day can be described by the following distribution (Table 6.5):

TABLE 6.5 Demand for trucks at Steel

Trucks Required	Probability
1	0.2
2	0.3
3	0.3
4	0.1
5	0.1

2a. Given this contract, what is the profit-maximizing number of trucks Rapid should reserve, and what is the associated expected profit for Rapid?

2b. Given Rapid's decision in 2a, what is Steel's expected cost?

2c. A consultant offers the following contract: Rapid would reserve five trucks each day. For all trucks that Steel uses, Steel would pay Rapid at the rate of $120 per truck. It would cost Rapid $60 per truck to reserve trucks the previous day. If trucks are not used by Steel, Steel would guarantee to pay for up to two trucks that are not used at the rate of $60 per day. (Thus, for example if Steel only uses two trucks, Steel would pay Rapid $120 per truck for two trucks. In addition, since Rapid would have three trucks unused, Steel would pay for two of those three trucks at the rate of $60 per truck. On the other hand, if Steel used four trucks, Steel would pay Rapid $120 per truck for four trucks. In addition, since Rapid would have one truck unused, Steel would pay for one truck at the rate of $60 per truck.)

What is the impact of this contract on Rapid's expected profit?

What is the impact of this contract on Steel's expected costs?

Is this contract Pareto improving over the original system? Explain why or why not.

3. The Trip Company has two plants located in the north and south of Indianapolis, IN. Each plant currently contracts separately with its own carriers. These carriers are paid $500 per shipment picked up. If a carrier receives a call and cannot provide a truck, it pays Trip $300. Trip then uses spot market operators to move the product at a cost of $1,000. Demand, which is independent and identically distributed, is distributed as follows (Table 6.6):

TABLE 6.6 Demand at Trip plants

Demand Trucks	Probability
5	0.4
10	0.5
30	0.1

Trucks to be provided have to be reserved the previous day and cost $200 per truck.

3a. What will be the optimal service level target by each carrier. What will be the associated expected profit for each carrier?

6c. Trip has identified another division of its holding company that ships from its plant near Norfolk to a location near Atlanta. The truck demand distribution for that location (near Norfolk) is the same distribution as the demands generated by Trip's plant in Atlanta. Currently, these two locations (i.e., Atlanta and Norfolk) have different trucking companies with the same contract structure.

Quick proposes that if Quick got the contract from both locations, then the cost per truck for completing the route, charged to Trip's holding company, would be $400. However, if the trucks did a continuous move, Trip's holding company would get a discount of $50. Thus, doing one move from Atlanta to Norfolk and one move back would cost Trip's holding company 2 × 400 – 50 = $750. The cost to reserve a truck still remains $200 per truck for Quick. Quick also commits to provide a 100% service level. The probability of different demands from the locations are as in Table 6.10:

TABLE 6.10 Probability of different demands

Atlanta to Norfolk	Norfolk to Atlanta			
	0	1	2	3
0	0.01	0.04	0.02	0.03
1	0.04	0.16	**0.08**	0.12
2	0.02	0.08	0.04	0.06
3	0.03	0.12	0.06	0.09

The table provides the probability of a number of trucks in each direction. For example, the entry in **bold (0.08)** represents the probability that Trip needs 1 truck from Atlanta to Norfolk and 2 trucks from Norfolk to Atlanta. The cost will thus be 400 + 750 = $1,150 ($400 for the one-way trip and $750 for the continuous move).

What is the impact of this contract on Quick's expected profit? What is the impact on Trip's expected cost across the two shipment routes, Atlanta to Norfolk and Norfolk to Atlanta?

Is this a Pareto-improving contract over Trip's expected cost across the two separate shipment routes, i.e., twice the value in 6b? Explain.

7. Reliant is a manufacturing company with a plant in Indianapolis that ships to its customers using a trucking company, Fast. It costs Fast $250 per truck to reserve capacity the previous day in anticipation of Reliant's demand. If Reliant needs a truck that Fast has, Reliant pays Fast $400 per truck to ship product. If Fast does not have the truck, Fast pays a penalty of $300 to Reliant. It costs Reliant $900 to get a single truck from the spot market (of which $300 is subsidized by Fast so the net cost to Reliant is $600 per truck obtained in the spot market).

The demand for trucks required by Reliant is as follows (Table 6.11):

TABLE 6.11 Demand for trucks by Reliant

Truck Demand	Probability
0	0.3
1	0.3
2	0.2
3	0.2

7a. Given the pricing structure, how many trucks should Fast reserve? What is Fast's associated expected profit?

7b. Given Fast's reserved capacity, what is Reliant's expected cost?

7c. Reliant is part of a holding company, Big, that has another plant, Alliant, in the same region that has similar truck-demand and cost structures with its transport company (not Fast). Big's managers want to consolidate the demand from both plants, Reliant and Alliant, and contract with only Fast to provide service under the same terms. Since both Reliant and Alliant are in the same city, a common pool of trucks can satisfy the demand from both locations.

Given such an offer, how many trucks should Fast reserve? What is Fast's associated expected profit in this new system?

7d. Given the trucks reserved by Fast, what is the total expected cost to the holding company.

8. Bill Parcell was a supply chain manager at XYZ Corp. His decision today would determine XYZ's transportation procedure for moving finished goods from its eastern plants to its western DCs. Bill had three bids on his desk. Apart from the glossy covers and colorful binders, each bid represented a different transport mode to move goods from plants to distribution centers. The trucking company emphasized speed of delivery and competitive pricing. The rail company emphasized low transport costs and larger deliveries but had offered to sell him a delivery guarantee as part of his contract—he had to choose if he wanted to pay the additional fee. There was a new company that had suggested a combination of barge deliveries and truck deliveries. Bill had until the end of the day to put together a presentation for his executive committee and recommend a solution. But he knew that transport was just part of a supply chain process, and thus it had to be evaluated in that context.

XYZ's European operation had just made a bold move to pick a combination of transport by sea, barge, and rail to get goods from XYZ's east Asian plants to the Amsterdam DC. Management was thrilled by the cover-page focus on this decision by *European Shipper* magazine. Bill recalled an internal presentation that had laid out the logic for this choice and suggested the need to examine inventory and transport costs as a total cost view of the mode choice decision. He pulled the PowerPoint presentation from his desk and read through the contents. The major ideas were summarized in four figures, which showed (1) a map of flows; (2) cost per unit, shipment sizes, and lead times; (3) inventories at each location; and (4) demands at each location.

Bill wanted to create a similar summary of the impact of the offered bids on his total costs. This would enable him to justify his recommendation. It might also allow him to generate some improvements in each bid that would be feasible in the current economic environment. He knew that the rail company was hungry for more business. He also knew that truck competition was brutal, and truckers were willing to go to great lengths to win bids. Bill could also tap into other companies in the conglomerate that XYZ was part of, e.g., BAC Corp., to see if some joint efficiencies could be attained. He was aware of the description of Reynolds Metals and their success in creating a corporation-wide CLC center to drive efficiencies. They had reportedly managed to decrease costs and improve service to an incredible level.

Without any more data, describe the architecture of the supply chain faced by Bill Parcell, i.e., tell how each of the four Cs will be impacted by each of the three bids. How can potential changes in the architecture improve performance?

GoodFood Products: The Trucking Outsourcing Decision

Professor Inar Araspa sipped his cappuccino as glanced at the piles of reports on his desk. He had just returned late the previous night from a trip to the corporate offices of GoodFood Products with several reports and summaries of discussions with senior managers at GoodFood. He had promised a quick turnaround of his report to Bill Haskell, VP of Supply Chain Management at GoodFood, and had allocated the afternoon to do it. The goal this afternoon was to provide an analysis for GoodFood management to assist in their decision whether to outsource transportation to Pendelton or Ridgeway or to keep transport in house, as was the current strategy.

THE PROBLEM CALL

It had all started with a phone call from Bill Haskell the previous week. With soaring input costs and significant competitive pressures, GoodFood faced a tough financial year. Bill was charged with trying to free up cash by taking a close look at the $18.4 million spent on transportation to ship 700 million pounds of product over 13 million miles each year. Bill had been a student in an executive program taught by Dr. Araspa and had recalled a discussion on transportation outsourcing in one of the lectures. GoodFood was in the process of making a crucial outsourcing decision, and Bill had persuaded Inar to accept a short consulting assignment consisting of data exchange, a one-day trip to GoodFood's corporate office, and a short summary report.

GoodFood had two plants, one each in Auburn, AL, and Rome, GA, producing products that required refrigeration during transit and storage. Finished products were shipped to retail chain warehouses in a 500-mile radius from the Auburn plant. About 50% of the trucks required for transportation were provided by outside carriers hired on a spot basis. The remaining 50% of the requirements was met by a private fleet of trucks owned by GoodFood. The total miles driven each year across all the trucks was estimated as 13 million miles. A summary of GoodFood's costs for transportation is provided in Exhibit 1 on page 130.

Bill Haskell had read about significant cost reductions through transport outsourcing—with estimates from 15%–25% claimed by third-party logistics companies. Given the financial pressures at GoodFood, CEO Mark Freund had approved Bill's proposal to seek outside quotes for third-party logistics for the remaining GoodFood-owned trucks.

LEARNING FROM FRESHFOODS

Another division of the conglomerate that owned GoodFood, called FreshFoods, had faced a similar decision the past year. FreshFoods had one plant that shipped finished products to warehouses throughout the country and had (until last year) a private fleet of trucks to do the deliveries. The route structure at FreshFoods afforded significant opportunities for backhaul loads, but FreshFoods had not been successful with its backhaul operations. FreshFoods had decided to outsource its dedicated fleet to be managed by Pendelton Transportation, with great success. A copy of the report provided by FreshFoods was on Bill's desk, and Bill in turn had sent it along to Inar (see Exhibit on page 133).

In that location, Pendelton had started with FreshFoods' cost of $1.28 per mile but had managed, through careful choice of backhaul opportunities, to reduce costs to $0.81 per mile. The supply chain executive at FreshFoods claimed that Pendelton's management of the dedicated transport routes had invigorated the division, retained the bulk of the original FreshFoods drivers and trucks, provided superior customer service, and decreased costs. Pendelton had been provided an incentive to keep 7% of backhaul revenues—this had been sufficient to get a significant backhaul plan incorporated into the routing system.

DATA AND BIDS

With Mark Freund's approval, Bill had created a bid package for potential transport companies to provide bids to manage transportation for GoodFood. The package contained data on the volumes of loads shipped each of the last 30 weeks in Exhibit 3a on page 134. A large number of the loads involved consolidation of shipments from Rome at Auburn before transport. Of shipments out of Rome, about 75% of the volume was to Auburn. A summary of miles driven and total number of stops were included in the bid package. A copy of the current union agreement signed by GoodFood was provided in Exhibit 3b on page 134.

GoodFood encouraged each transportation company to provide the most competitive price while maintaining superior customer service and safety levels. Each of the bidding companies was given two weeks to send in bids to Bill Haskell, who would be the single point of contact at GoodFood for all bidders and would provide identical information to everyone. A restricted access website was set up for bidding companies to access relevant information.

Two companies sent in final bids by the prescribed due date—Pendelton Transport and Ridgeway Transport. One of the issues that had to be resolved were the payments to drivers who had to idle at the delivery location before deliveries were accepted by warehouses. Both bidders had been adamant that they could not be held responsible for these waiting delays and handling costs—GoodFood had agreed to accept those costs as a pass-through and maintain the same payments as currently agreed to in the union agreement. The trucks also used refrigeration fuel (termed *reefer fuel*), and transport companies could choose to include it in their bid or have GoodFood provide or pay for it at cost.

PENDELTON'S BID

Pendelton's bid details are provided in Exhibit 4 on page 136. The company provided two separate bids, one for trucks out of Rome and the other for trucks out of Auburn. Pendelton had also provided a bid assuming a minimum fleet miles guarantee of 5 million annual miles. Any shortfalls would incur a penalty, while excess miles would be charged at a reduced rate (see bid for details). Pendelton would pass along all the delay costs to GoodFood and also use reefer fuel provided by GoodFood. Tolls would be passed along at cost.

Pendelton had claimed great success at FreshFoods and promised a significant push to see that GoodFood received excellent service.

RIDGEWAY'S BID

Ridgeway chose to provide one bid across both locations (Exhibit 5 on page 136). This bid provided one per-mile rate across both locations. The assumed minimum annual miles was set as 7.1 million, with penalties for shortfall and reduced rates for exceeding the minimums. Ridgeway would cover all fuel costs with the exception of reefer fuel.

Comments by Ridgeway suggest that they expected the number of trucks required to be decreased by about 16.5% due to better route planning.

THE CONSULTANT'S REPORT

Professor Inar Araspa had all of this data readily available as electronic files on his laptop. He realized that all of the bids had to be converted to a common format so as to compare "apples to apples." Given the time available, he could not estimate how effective current routes were and the possible impact of optimization software to improve routing. He also knew that Bill Haskell had to decide to either accept one of the bids, force the bidders to face more competitive pressure in an attempt to improve their bids, or use the data to find ways to improve existing operations of the private fleet.

All of this had to be succinctly summarized and provided as a PowerPoint presentation that Bill Haskell could use for his meeting with Mark Freund next week. Inar was pensive as he opened up his documents and set to work. The cappuccino cup was empty and would be refilled soon.

EXHIBIT 1 GoodFood's Transportation Costs

SALARY & WAGES	(Used W-2 income for drivers and base rates for others)						
	Headcount	% of Total Cost	Expenses ($)	Cost/mile			
Tractor Drivers	56		2243155.83	0.17	Annual Miles	12983248	miles
Bob Drivers	22		635582.42	0.05	Annual Weight	653590674	lbs.
Wash & Grease	14		261002.25				
Dispatch Opns	7		211654.98				
Mechanics-A	8		193519.87				
Fleet Mgmt & Safety	4		138152.79				
Body Work	4		95992.00				
Garage Mgmt	2		74369.80				
Traffic Clerical	4		66503.07				
Mechanic Helper	3		56213.47				
Mechanic-C	2		38472.49				
Garage Clerical	2		37321.51				
Fueler	1		17996.65				
	129		4069937.12	0.31			
BENEFITS (34% rate)			1383778.62	0.11			
Total Labor Expense		29.75%	**5453715.74**	0.42			
TRANSPORTATION EQUIPMENT							
Lease & Rental Units :							
Trailer-Refrigerated			852000.00				
Tractors & Bob Trucks			1146747.00				
Thermokings			253.00				
Owned Units :							
Trailer-Refrigerated			10041.37				
Tractors & Bob Trucks			10533.46				
Other			4034.63				
		11.04%	**2023609.46**	0.16			
OTHER OPERATING EXPENSES							
Repair/Maint-Trucks			675000.00				
Repair/Maint-Trailers			59000.00				
Garage Operating Supplies			136000.00				
Tires & Tubes			193000.00				
Gas Oil/ Propane			99000.00				

Diesel Fuel-Taxable			727000.00				
Diesel Fuel-NonTaxable			294000.00				
Gas & Oil-Away			470000.00				
Driver's Travel Expenses			449000.00				
Insurance			274550.00				
License/Taxes/Permits			416700.00				
Utilities			27500.00				
Travel			1000.00				
Handtools			4000.00				
Office Supplies			18000.00				
Depreciation			24371.82				
	Total Other Operating Expenses	14.76%	**2706121.82**	0.21			
INTEREST EXPENSE							
Parts Inventory	($300,000 base)		19383.00				
Supplies Inventory	($50,000 base)		3230.50				
Fixed Assets	($42,000 base)		2719.18				
Fuel Inventory	($15,000 base)		969.15				
	Total Interest Expense	0.14%	**26301.83**	0.00			
OUTSIDE CARRIER EXPENSE							
Outside Carrier Freight	5,559,851 estimated miles		8895762.00	1.60			
Dedicated Carrier-SSK	1,010,264 actual miles		909237.60	0.90			
	Total O/S Carrier Expense	53.49%	**9804999.60**	0.76			
LESS BACKHAUL CREDIT		–9.19%	**–1685040.00**	–0.13			

PROFORMA EXPENSE SUMMARY for FLEET OPERATIONS (excludes O/S Carriers)				
[Used FY95 cost data for 48 weeks and projected balance.]				
			Total	
		Annual	GoodFoods	Cost
		Miles	Cost	Per Mile
		6,413,132		
		% of Total		
SALARY & WAGES	(Used W-2 income for drivers and base rates for others)			
	Headcount			
Tractor Drivers	56		$2,243,156	$0.350
Bob Drivers	22		635,582	$0.099
Wash & Grease	14		261,002	
Dispatch Opns	7		211,655	
Mechanics-A	8		193,520	
Fleet Mgmt & Safety	4		138,153	
Body Work	4		95,992	
Garage Mgmt	2		74,370	
Traffic Clerical	4		66,503	
Mechanic Helper	3		56,213	
Mechanic-C	2		38,472	
Garage Clerical	2		37,322	
Fueler	1		17,997	
	129		$4,069,937	$0.635
BENEFITS (34% rate)			1,383,779	$0.216
Total Labor Expense		61.85%	$5,453,716	$0.850
TRANSPORTATION EQUIPMENT				
Lease & Rental Units :				
Trailer-Refrigerated			852,000	
Tractors & Bob Trucks			1,146,747	
Thermokings			253	
Owned Units :				
Trailer-Refrigerated			10,041	
Tractors & Bob Trucks			10,533	
Other			4,035	
		22.95%	$2,023,609	$0.316
OTHER OPERATING EXPENSES				
Repair/Maint-Trucks			675,000	
Repair/Maint-Trailers			59,000	

Garage Operating Supplies			136,000	
Tires & Tubes			193,000	
Gas Oil/Propane			99,000	
Diesel Fuel-Taxable			727,000	
Diesel Fuel-NonTaxable			294,000	
Gas & Oil-Away			470,000	
Driver's Travel Expenses			449,000	
Insurance			274,550	
License/Taxes/Permits			416,700	
Utilities			27,500	
Travel			1,000	
Handtools			4,000	
Office Supplies			18,000	
Depreciation			24,372	
	Total Other Operating Expense	30.69%	$2,706,122	$0.422
INTEREST EXPENSE				
Parts Inventory	($300,000 base)		19,383	
Supplies Inventory	($50,000 base)		3,231	
Fixed Assets	($42,000 base)		2,719	
Fuel Inventory	($15,000 base)		969	
	Total Interest Expense	0.30%	$26,302	$0.004
LESS BACKHAUL CREDIT	excludes O/S TRK backhauls	−15.79%	(1,392,630)	(0.217)
TOTAL GOODFOOD FLEET EXPENSE		100.00%	$8,817,119	$1.375

EXHIBIT 2 Current Operations at FreshFoods by Pendelton Transport Based on Last Year

Tractor Single miles charge of $1.282 per mile	1,108,119 miles driven
Stops charged at $15.870 per stop	125 stops
Layovers charged at $40 per layover	328 layovers
Delay hours charged at $11.35 per hour	70 hours
Reefer hours $0.71 per hour	859 hours
Reefer standby of 0.22 per hour	677 hours

Mileage guarantee of 208,000 miles
Excess miles at $0.678 per mile
Deficit miles at 0.604 per mile
Total charges for previous year = $1,445,442.18

Actual cost per mile from October (previous year) to May (this year) was $0.89 per mile after backhaul adjustments. The backhaul revenue per week increased from $2,860 in November to $8,280 the following October with an average of $5,378 per week for the year. The annual backhaul revenue for the previous year was $295,782 and backhaul mileage credit was 84,733. Given 1,043,259 miles driven, the cost per mile (average) was $0.89.

EXHIBIT 3A Table of Current lbs Shipped and Stops per Month for Private Fleet

Week #	# Stops	Weight	Volume
1	596	3764622.04	118487.19
2	694	5109213.19	160378.94
3	703	4875061.83	150086.53
4	678	4817121.06	149109.08
5	661	5298256.25	165322.13
6	708	5327277.18	167391.37
7	741	5894998.83	181966.31
8	705	5513352.75	167979.00
9	661	5080183.16	160427.85
10	551	3749944.8	118951.78
11	702	5180895.25	164031.61
12	691	5915244.1	184058.26
13	687	5893458.07	179388.45
14	685	5519211.87	166782.22
15	694	5489595.02	168796.79
16	678	5516549.84	170337.60
17	685	5861412.98	180088.55
18	673	5849812.54	180953.52
19	668	5350821.7	168615.26
20	753	6366144.58	200499.75
21	509	4714898.71	166752.56
22	670	5581086.35	168790.18
23	659	5981954.58	186559.28
24	760	6102253.52	185720.55
25	728	6391333.24	188964.12
26	566	4280327.76	127401.61
27	600	4061949.82	123400.61
28	719	5084763.04	152901.57
29	622	4670751.32	138812.39
30	690	5799834.75	176483.49
	671.23333	Average	163981.285
	56.940134	Stdev	20848.08398

EXHIBIT 3B Current Agreement between GoodFood and Its Union Membership

Payments per mile (excluding benefits): $0.272
Stop off to load or unload: $16.50 per stop
Trip pay: $10.00 per trip dispatched
Allowance for loading or unloading

Average weight per stop	Rate per thousand lbs
< 600	2.45
601 to 900	2.35
901 to 1,500	2.15
1,501 to 3,000	1.95
3,001 to 4,500	1.75
4,501 to 6,000	1.55
> 6,000	1.40

Motel payments of $20.00 on required layover with motels designated by the company. Meal allowances of $6.00 for breakfast, $6.00 for lunch and $6.00 for dinner.

Delay time paid at the rate of $14.50 per hour if driver is not dispatched within 12 hours of the time the driver checks in. The driver will be paid for a maximum of 8 hours every 24-hour waiting period.

EXHIBIT 4A Pendelton's Bid for Rome, GA

Components	Charge	Annual Units	Annual $
Single Miles	1.12/mile	1,474,044	1,655,550
Stops	14.23/stop	3,068	43,670
Layovers	28.05/layover	2,392	67,089
Delay Hours	14.23/hour	0	0
Reefer Hours	0.70/hour	0	0
Mileage Guarantee			
Excess Miles	0.607/mile	0	0
Deficit Miles	0.515/mile	0	0
Total			$1,766,310

EXHIBIT 4B Pendelton's Bid for Auburn, AL

Components	Charge	Annual Units	Annual $
Single Miles	1.389/mile	6,300,000	8,754,977
Stops	22.3/stop	35,576	793,359
Layovers	27.03/ layover	10,345	279,659
Delay Hours	19.57/hour	0	0
Reefer Hours	0.70/hour	0	0
Unload Charge	1.89/ thousand lbs	211,028	399,306
Mileage Guarantee			
Excess Miles	0.607/mile	0	0
Deficit Miles	0.515/mile	0	0
Total			$10,227,304

Thus the estimated cost per mile is $1.62.

Assumptions:
Fuel cost assumed to be $1.00 per gallon, reefer fuel provided by GoodFood. Tolls passed through at cost. All delays, etc., billed as per current union agreements directly to GoodFood. Pendelton will aim to retain most of the current drivers. The existing freight management system will try to generate backhauls.

EXHIBIT 5 Ridgeway Transport bid

Transport cost per mile = $1.595
All miles over 7,120,000 per year at $0.96. This is a reduced price per mile.
All miles under 7,120,000 per year at $0.63. This is a penalty for miles not driven.

CURRENT VS. PROPOSED ASSETS BY RIDGEWAY		
Truck Types	**Existing**	**Proposed**
Power Tractors	76	65
Power Trucks	33	21
Reefer Trailers	151	131
TOTAL	260	217

Suggested savings of $0.05 per mile due to better controls over routes, etc. Reefer fuel provided by GoodFood. Tolls passed through at cost. Expected savings of 10%–15% due to route optimization and backhauls. Additional savings will come from joint optimization of moves by GoodFood and Ridgeway.

CASE QUESTIONS

1. Analyze the current operation at GoodFood. What is the total cost per mile and the component costs for the private fleet and the outsourced providers?
2. From Pendelton's bid, generate numbers that can be compared to the current system at GoodFood. What aspects of this bid would you negotiate further with Pendelton?
3. Summarize Ridgeway's bid and identify what aspects of the bid you would negotiate.
4. Suggest a decision for GoodFood and defend your recommendation.

Chapter 7

Warehousing

The use of just-in-time inventory at manufacturing plants and dispersed production of components have increased the need for inventory management and therefore warehousing operations in the supply chain. The *competitiveness* metrics of performance for a warehousing function include inventory turns, productivity (lines per hour), inventory availability, or cost performance. The location of warehouses within the *chain* structure assigns its role as a buffer against supply disruptions if it is located upstream or as a catalyst for efficient plant production scheduling while providing promised delivery performance if it located downstream. The *capacity* of the warehouse is determined both by its physical size and flow management capability, as well as the nature of the resources used for warehouse management: automatic, manual, or hybrid material handling systems. In addition, the number and locations of the warehouse doors determine the feasibility of handling crossdocking operations. Finally, *coordination* agreements (such as vendor-managed inventory) developed with suppliers impact the performance of the warehouse.

7.1 DELCO ELECTRONICS CASE

A study ([9]) described General Motors (GM) as carrying over $7.4 billion in inventory and incurring $4.1 billion in freight costs in 1984. The questions the study explores are the following: How could this total supply chain cost be decreased? Could the approach be used by decision makers throughout the GM system to impact supply chain costs and thus improve performance?

In 1984, Delco Electronics, which was a division of GM, faced a problem. Three component plants, in Matamoros, Mexico, Milwaukee, WI, and Kokomo, IN, supplied radios, heater controls, electronic modules respectively to thirty GM assembly plants located throughout the country. Figure 7.1 shows the location of the supplier component and assembly plants. The original supply chain configuration used full truckload shipments from component plants to a consolidation warehouse in Kokomo. From this consolidation warehouse, full truckload shipments containing a mix of radios, heater controls, and electronic controls were shipped to each assembly plant. Delco wanted to identify alternate ways that product could be moved from component plants to assembly plants to decrease the $11.2 million in inventory costs.

Figure 7.2 shows seven possible solutions for the problem. The routes examined included direct shipments from component plants to assembly plants, shipments through the warehouse, peddling (whereby trucks, originating from component plants, would make deliveries across various assembly plants), and combinations of such strategies. For each route, the shipment size could be full truckloads or the optimal shipment size. Figure 7.2 also shows the composition of transport and inventory costs in each of the seven possible logistics systems.

The alternatives described in Figure 7.2 indicate the many different ways to manage the network of warehouses and associated transportation. Each of these flows is impacted

FIGURE 7.1 The Delco Electronics supply chain subset

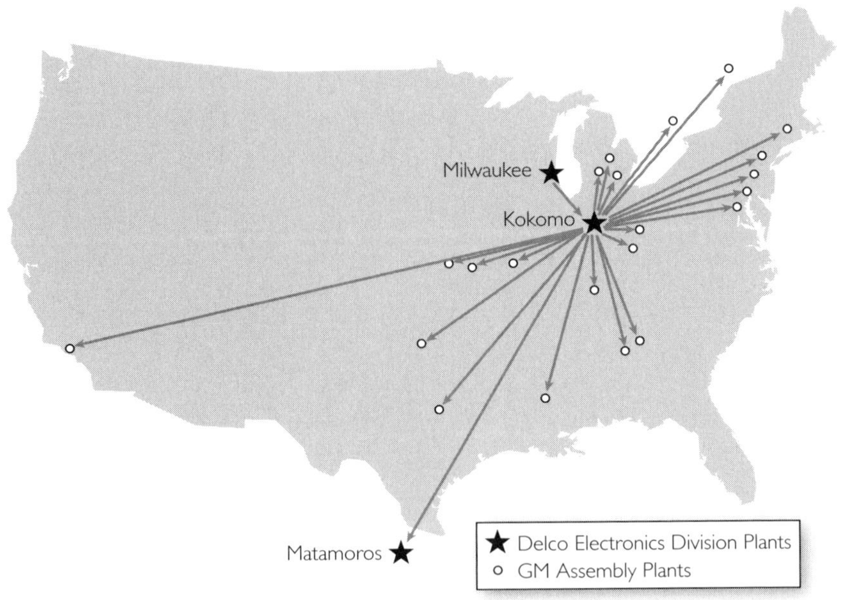

FIGURE 7.2 Seven possible solutions for the Delco Electronics supply chain

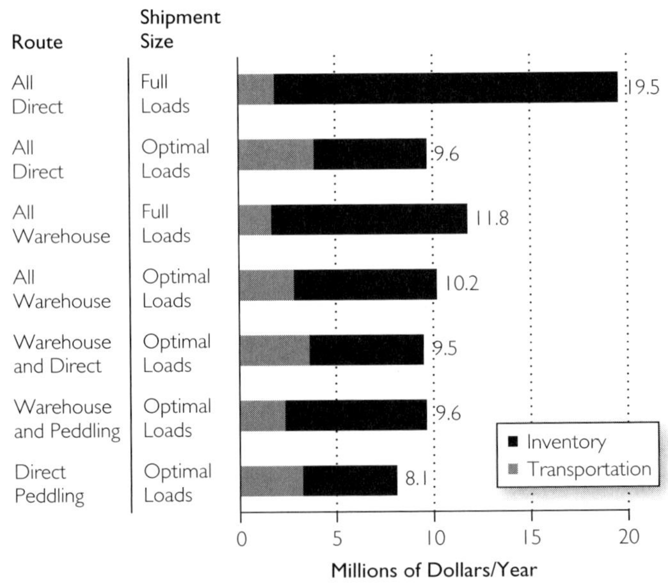

differently by business conditions, thus changing the ideal choice over time. The role of the analysis was to both identify and quantify the impact of each of these choices.

GM devised an easy to use software to calculate the costs for each of these alternatives. The resulting approach, Transpart II, has been used at over forty locations producing annual savings ranging from $35,000 to $500,000. When used at Delco, Transpart II saved over 26% of logistics costs for an annual savings of over $2.6 million. The implemented solution at Delco involved speeding up the material handling at the Kokomo warehouse from two days down to half a day and peddling out of the Milwaukee warehouse. Projected savings were expected to increase as holding costs increased.

7.2 MERLONI ELETTRODOMESTICII CASE

Merloni Elettrodomesticii is an Italian appliance manufacturer that sells white goods: washers, dryers, dishwashers, refrigerators, and so on ([56]). Merloni had promised all retailers delivery of orders within twenty-four hours. This arrangement was part of the guaranteed service that enabled Merloni to have a dedicated set of retailers who sold its product to the Italian consumer.

Merloni had five plants spread throughout Italy. Each plant had a focused product line with focused plants enabled substantial scale economics as well as a consistent approach to choice of technologies and equipment. The products from each plant were shipped to a central warehouse in Fabriano. From Fabriano, products were shipped to a network of seventeen regional warehouses, using long-haul trucks. Each regional warehouse then shipped orders to retailers within twenty-four hours of receipt of the order. Merloni carried a total of 14,330 units in finished goods inventory at the warehouses.

A bold experiment, the Transit point experiment, focused on the Milan warehouse, which was cleared of all inventory. Orders would be placed every day by the manager at Milan and transmitted to Fabriano. Trucks would be loaded and arrive in the morning at the Milan warehouse. Goods would be crossdocked into smaller trucks and delivered to retailers. With this new system, retailers continued to receive orders within twenty-four hours and were unaware of the change in regional warehouse inventory. This approach, if expanded through the Merloni network, had the potential to reduce operating costs by up to 80%. The new network required close coordination between regional warehouse, central warehouse, and plants to ensure product availability, minimal disruptions, and reduced costs.

7.3 LETIN ELECTRONICS CASE

Bill Rogers faced a problem. As warehouse manager for Letin Electronics, he knew that his presence in the logistics network facilitated system-wide cost reductions. Letin's five focused plants shipped to Bill's consolidation warehouse. Bill then shipped to twenty-five distribution centers that supplied large distributors of Letin's products. But the current corporate staff at Letin was hard pressed to generate a return on investment (ROI) for Bill's operation. Costs incurred by the warehouse and his component of costs as a percentage of sales were easy to calculate. But the system-wide return that he generated was more complicated. How could Bill justify that his costs actually saved money overall for Letin Electronics?

Bill suggested the following thought experiment: Suppose Bill's warehouse were shut down. How would Letin operate and supply its distribution centers? A quick calculation provided the total supply chain costs that would be incurred under this alternate system. Inventories would increase at distributors as Letin would try to manage transport costs by shipping full truckloads. Distribution centers would have to expand and carry more inventory of full truckload shipments from plants. Could the difference between the costs in that configuration and the current costs provide an estimate of the benefits of Bill's warehouse? If that difference were significant compared to Bill's costs of operation, would that generate an ROI that corporate could use to decide the fate of the warehouse? How robust would that decision be to changes in transport costs and holding costs?

7.4 PROBLEM ABSTRACTION AND ANALYSIS

Each of the three problem contexts described earlier has the following basic structure: A set of sources of supply has to be linked by a supply system to a set of demand locations. Figure 7.3 shows the supply and demand nodes for Delco (three supply nodes and thirty demand nodes). Merloni had five supply nodes and seventeen demand nodes. Letin had five supply nodes and twenty-five demand nodes. Notice that in the Delco case, the flows from supply to demand nodes consist of components used to assemble cars. In the Merloni and Letin cases, the flows consist of finished goods from assembly plants to locations closer to customers. But the abstraction of these problems has the same structure. What are possible ways to create a supply chain from these supply locations to the demand locations?

One approach is to focus on minimizing the transport cost per unit. Under such an objective, it is best to ship directly from supply to demand points. Figure 7.3 shows the direct shipping for the Delco supply chain, which would result in ninety shipping lanes. Figure 7.4 shows a direct shipping approach for the Merloni case that would result in 105 shipping lanes. Finally, Figure 7.5 shows the direct shipping lanes for Letin, which would result in 100 shipping lanes.

A second approach is to ship from all supply points to a single consolidation warehouse. Then mixed shipments would go from this warehouse to the demand locations. Figures 7.6 through 7.8 show the supply chain flows through a consolidation warehouse. Under such

FIGURE 7.3 Direct shipping for the Delco supply chain

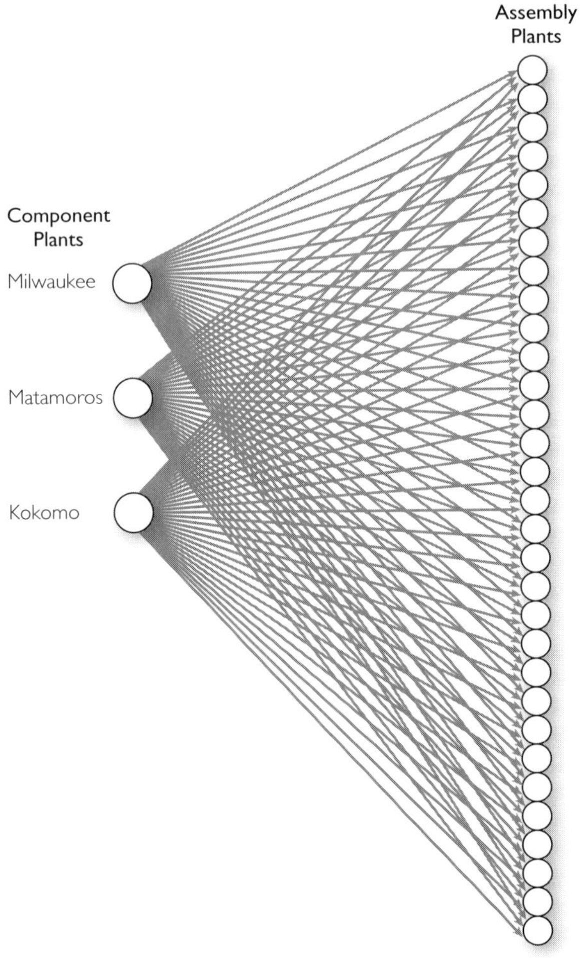

FIGURE 7.4 Direct shipping for the Merloni case

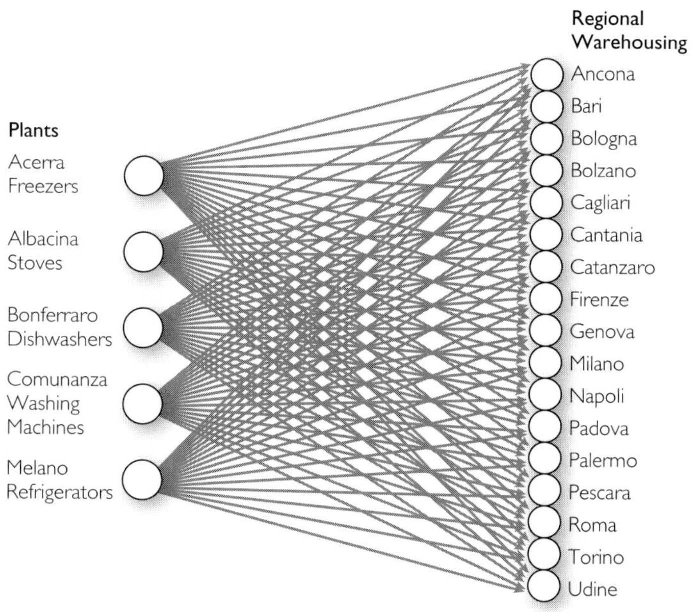

FIGURE 7.5 Direct shipping for the Letin case

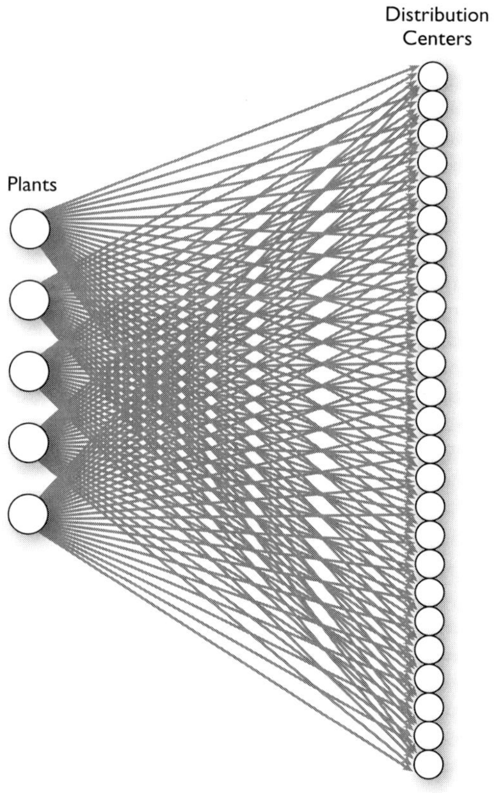

FIGURE 7.6 Consolidation warehouse for the Delco supply chain case

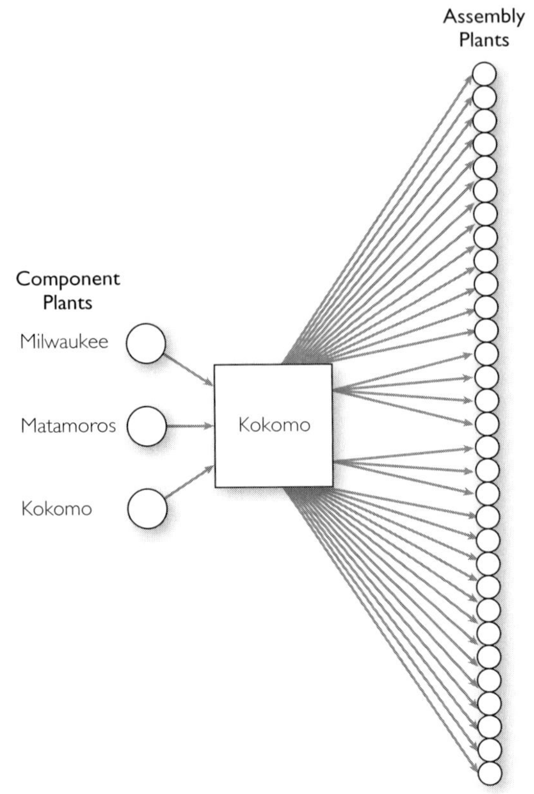

FIGURE 7.7 Consolidation warehouse for the Merloni case

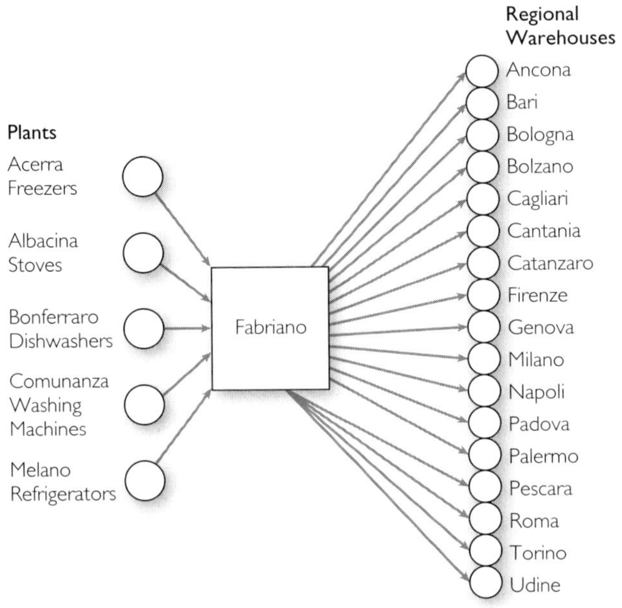

FIGURE 7.8 Consolidation warehouse for the Letin case

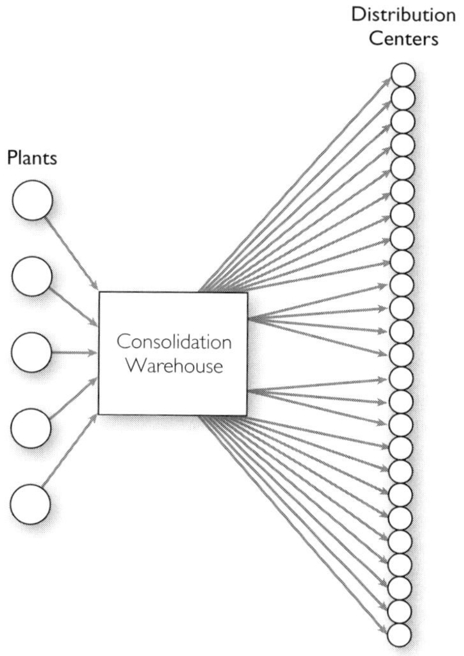

FIGURE 7.9 Delco supply chain with direct peddling routes

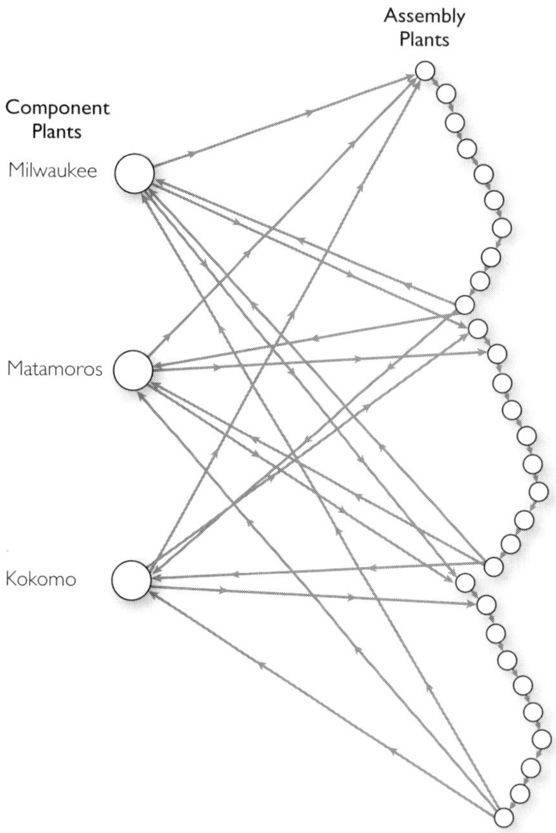

a supply chain, Delco would have thirty-three shipping lanes. The Merloni system would have twenty-two shipping lanes, and Letin would have twenty-nine shipping lanes.

A third approach would be to create routes that start from each supply location and visit a set of demand locations that would share the truck capacity (i.e., peddling routes). Figure 7.9 shows such a system for the Delco Electronic case. Under such a supply chain, the number of shipping routes would depend on the number of demand points sharing trucks from a common supply point.

In addition to the choices above, there can be a number of hybrid versions of the supply chain architecture. The appropriate choice clearly affects the performance of the supply chain architecture.

7.5 TOTAL SUPPLY CHAIN COSTS

Total supply chain cost is the sum of inventory, transport, warehousing, and routing costs. This cost is affected by the structure of the chain, capacity of transportation, required coordination between locations for managing consistent operation, and competitiveness of the mode used, which will affect costs and the competitiveness of the business environment, thereby affecting the desired service required.

The components of the total supply chain cost are

1. **Transport cost per unit time:** Across each shipping lane, suppose the capacity of transport is C. Let the amount shipped during each delivery be Q. To be feasible, we need to ensure that $Q \leq C$. Assume the demand that generates flows on this lane is D per unit time. Then to satisfy the demand rate, deliveries must be received every $\frac{Q}{D}$ periods. If the transport cost per delivery on this lane is K, then the transport cost per unit time is $K\frac{D}{Q}$.

   Notice that in the absence of any other costs, it is optimal to ship at full mode capacity.

2. **Cycle stock at demand points:** When demand points receive delivery, the quantity delivered is Q, described earlier. This delivered quantity may be greater than the demand each period. If so, the demand location carries cycle stock, which is the average inventory across successive deliveries.

   If profile of inventory is observed between successive deliveries, then note that the inventory starts at a level of Q and drops to zero just before the next delivery is received. (Note that in the presence of any uncertainty, safety stock would have to be carried over and above the cycle stock.) Given a demand rate of D, the time for the delivery to run out would be $\frac{Q}{D}$ periods. The average inventory level is thus the ratio of the area implied by the inventory, which is $\frac{Q^2}{2D}$ divided by the length of the cycle, which is $\frac{Q}{D}$ periods. This ratio is thus equal to $\frac{Q}{2}$.

   The holding cost per unit of product per unit time reflects the costs associated with carrying inventory. This marginal cost can include (1) the cost to finance this inventory or the opportunity cost associated with it, (2) the insurance costs against shrinkage or damage, (3) the obsolescence-related costs if the inventory has to be salvaged, (4) storage costs. These costs reflect the system-wide impact if inventory is carried in a supply chain.

3. **Intransit inventory costs:** When inventory is shipped from the supply point, we assume that title for the goods passes to the buyer, who then arranges all transport. Thus the buyer is responsible for the inventory of goods in transit between supply and demand points. What is the level of inventory in transit from the supply to demand points?

   Note that supply chains are replenishment systems, thus the average amount shipped should match the average demand. If the transport lead time were L, the average in transit inventory is LD. Notice that this is just Little's law from queueing theory, which says that the average work in process inventory is equal to the demand rate times the average lead time through the system.

   Given a holding cost per unit per unit time, the associated in transit inventory cost is hLD. Note that the average in transit inventory is independent of the shipment size Q but only depends on the transport lead time and the demand rate.

4. **Safety stock costs:** If the demand time, the transit time, or both are uncertain, it may be necessary to carry inventory as a buffer against demand uncertainty. As discussed earlier, the extent of this inventory buffer depends on the magnitude of the demand uncertainty during the supply lead time and the planned in-stock service level. If the planned in-stock probability is expressed as *service* and the demand over lead time has a standard deviation of σ_{DL}, then the safety stock level is expressed as $Z_{service} \times \sigma_{DL}$. (Note that we assume that demand follows a normal distribution as an approximation: there are more detailed models available.) The associated holding cost is $hZ_{service}\sigma_{DL}$.[1]

[1]If demand is normally distributed with mean μ_D and standard deviation σ_D and the lead time is normally distributed with mean μ_L and standard deviation σ_L, then the demand during the supply lead time is distributed with a mean $\mu_{DL} = \mu_D \times \mu_L$ and the standard deviation of demand during lead time is $\sqrt{\mu_L\sigma_D^2 + \mu_D^2\sigma_L^2}$.

7.6 COMPUTING TOTAL SUPPLY CHAIN COSTS—AN EXAMPLE

The Optima Corporation produces two different types of widgets, A and B. Each widget type uses two components, 1 and 2. Widget A requires two units of component 1 and one unit of component 2 per unit of widget A. Widget B requires two units of component 2 and one unit of component 1 per unit of widget B.

Widget A is manufactured at a plant in Boston, MA. The plant produces 100 units of widget A each day. Widget B is manufactured at a plant in Jersey City, NJ. The plant produces 100 units of widget B each day.

Component 1 is manufactured at a plant in Santa Fe, NM, and component 2 is manufactured at a plant in Portland, OR.

Products are shipped in full truckloads directly between plants: Full truckloads of component 1 are shipped from Santa Fe to the Boston plant and from Portland to the Jersey City plant. Similarly, full truckloads are shipped from the Portland plant to the Boston plant and from the Portland plant to the Jersey City plant (Figure 7.10).

Holding cost is estimated to be \$0.40 per component per day for both components. Both components have similar physical volume. Each truck can hold 3,000 components (of either component 1 or 2). Each truckload shipment costs \$4,000 between either pair of locations, i.e., Portland to Boston, Portland to Jersey City, Santa Fe to Boston, or Santa Fe to Jersey City. Travel time between any of the location pairs is estimated to be six days.

7.6.1 A Minimum Transport Cost Supply Chain

Notice that minimizing transport costs is equivalent to using a full truckload direct shipment system. The next steps will provide details of the total supply chain costs for this mode of operation.

Cycle Stock Costs: Given the full truckload shipments, the size of the deliveries of each component received by each assembly plant is 3,000 units. In the absence of demand uncertainty at each plant, the next truck delivery would be scheduled when the components in this delivery are consumed. This means that the inventory level cycles between 3,000 and 0 units. The average inventory is thus the average height of a right triangle whose height is 3,000 units and whose base is $\frac{3,000}{D}$ where D is the demand rate. Thus the average height of this triangle is $\frac{3,000}{2}$. This average inventory multiplied by a holding cost per unit per unit time provides the cost associated with cycle stock carried at the assembly plants.

FIGURE 7.10 The Optima direct shipping supply chain

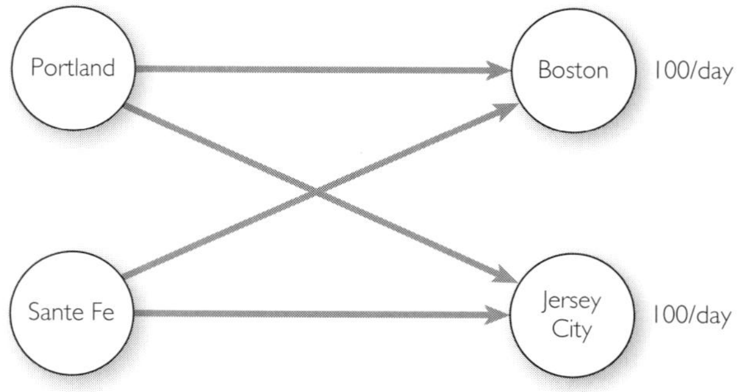

Thus, the holding cost of the cycle stock of component 1 at Boston is

$$0.4 \times 3{,}000/2 = \$600/\text{day}$$

(In the above calculation, 3,000 is the truck capacity, 3,000/2 is the average inventory level at Boston and 0.4 is the holding cost per day provided in the problem.)

Similarly, the holding cost of the cycle stock of component 2 at Boston is:

$$0.4 \times 3{,}000/2 = \$600/\text{day}$$

The holding cost of the cycle stock of component 1 at Jersey City is:

$$0.4 \times 3{,}000/2 = \$600/\text{day}$$

The holding cost of the cycle stock of component 2 at Jersey City is:

$$0.4 \times 3{,}000/2 = \$600/\text{day}$$

Thus total cycle stock holding cost across the two components and at the two assembly plants is \$2,400/day.

In-Transit Inventory Costs

The average in-transit inventory between any two locations is equal to

$$\text{Transit time} \times \text{Demand rate}$$

Notice that the equation above is Little's law, which states that the average number of units in a queue is the demand rate times the average lead time. Little's law links lead time to work in process inventory. In our case, the inventory in transit is work-in-process inventory between the component plant and the assembly plant where it is required. Once we get the average in-transit inventory, we merely have to multiply it with the holding cost per unit per unit time to get the holding cost associated with the in-transit inventory.

Using this relation, we get

In-transit inventory holding cost between Santa Fe and Boston (component 1):

$$0.4 \times 6 \times 200 = \$480/\text{day}$$

In-transit inventory holding cost between Portland and Boston (component 2):

$$0.4 \times 6 \times 100 = \$240/\text{day}$$

In-transit inventory holding cost between Santa Fe and Jersey City (component 1):

$$0.4 \times 6 \times 100 = \$240/\text{day}$$

In-transit inventory holding cost between Portland and Jersey City (component 2):

$$0.4 \times 6 \times 200 = \$480/\text{day}$$

Thus, total in-transit inventory holding cost between all component plants and assembly plants = \$1,440/day.

Transport Cost

We now focus on the average transport cost between every pair of locations in the supply chain. Shipment sizes refer to full truckloads and routes are direct from component plant to assembly plant. Thus the corresponding transport cost obtained is the minimum possible value.

Average transport cost per day from Santa Fe to Boston:

$$\$4{,}000 \times 200/3{,}000 = \$266.67/\text{day}$$

(In this calculation, \$4,000 refers to the cost for one truckload, 3,000 is the truck capacity, and 200 is the demand rate for component 1 at Boston.)

Average transport cost per day from Santa Fe to Jersey City:

$$\$4{,}000 \times 100/3{,}000 = \$133.33/\text{day}$$

Average transport cost per day from Portland to Boston:

$$\$4{,}000 \times 100/3{,}000 = \$133.33/\text{day}$$

Average transport cost per day from Portland to Jersey City:

$$\$4{,}000 \times 200/3{,}000 = \$266.67/\text{day}$$

Total transport costs = \$800.00/day

Thus the total supply chain cost across all locations = \$2,400 + 1,440 + 800 = \$4,640/day.

7.6.2 Optimal Shipment Sizes and Their Impact on Supply Chain Cost

Suppose Optima were to replace full truckloads by optimal shipment sizes. How would the optimal shipment sizes be determined? Given the symbolic description earlier, consider the expression for the total logistics cost for a component from its component plant to the assembly plant. This total logistics cost is expressed as

$$\frac{KD}{Q} + \frac{hQ}{2} + (hDL)$$

Figure 7.11 shows the three components of the total logistics cost. Given the shape of these costs, the optimal shipment size calculated above, if feasible, is the one at which the average transport cost equals the average holding cost. The corresponding shipment quantity is obtained as

$$Q^* = \sqrt{\frac{2KD}{h}}$$

FIGURE 7.11 Cost components and optimal shipping quantity

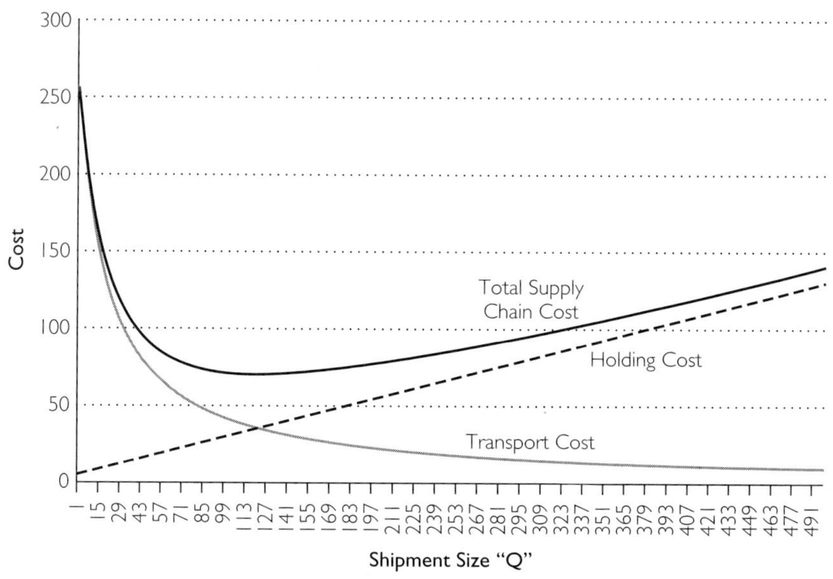

Note, however, that once this quantity is obtained, feasibility of implementation requires that this quantity not exceed truck capacity. If it does exceed capacity, then it is optimal to ship at full capacity. Thus the optimal shipment quantity would be set as minimum $\{Q^*, C\}$ where C refers to the truck capacity.

Thus the shipment sizes and the associated total supply chain costs for Optima can be computed as follows:

Optimal shipment size from Santa Fe to Boston (EOQ):

$$\sqrt{\frac{2 \times 4,000 \times 200}{0.4}} = 2,000$$

(In the above expression, \$4,000 is the fixed ordering cost for one truckload, 200 is the demand for component 1 at Boston each day, and 0.4 is the holding cost per unit per day.)

Note that the above computation suggests that it is optimal to ship at less-than-full truckload, thereby reducing truck capacity utilization.

Similarly, the optimal shipment size from Santa Fe to Jersey City (EOQ):

$$\sqrt{\frac{2 \times 4,000 \times 100}{0.4}} = 1,414$$

The optimal shipment size from Portland to Boston (EOQ):

$$\sqrt{\frac{2 \times 4,000 \times 100}{0.4}} = 1,414$$

The optimal shipment size from Portland to Jersey City (EOQ):

$$\sqrt{\frac{2 \times 4,000 \times 200}{0.4}} = 2,000$$

Note that since all of the optimal shipment sizes are below the truck capacity, it is optimal to ship these quantities. Recall, however, that trucking costs will still be assessed at full truckload levels.

Given these optimal shipment sizes, the associated costs are calculated as follows:

Cycle stock costs:

Boston (component 1) holding cost:

0.4 × 2,000/2 = \$400.00/day

Boston (component 2) holding cost:

0.4 × 1,414/2 = \$282.80/day

Jersey City (component 1) holding cost:

0.4 × 1,414/2 = \$282.80/day

Jersey City (component 2) holding cost:

0.4 × 2,000/2 = \$400.00/day

Total cycle stock holding cost = \$1,365.60/day

In-transit costs:

Verify that these costs remain the same, and the total in-transit cost = \$1,440.00/day

Transport costs:

Santa Fe to Boston (component 1):

\$4,000 × 200/2,000 = \$400.00/day

Santa Fe to Jersey City (component 1):

\$4,000 × 100/1,414 = \$282.80/day

Portland to Boston (component 2):

$$\$4{,}000 \times 100/1{,}414 = \$282.80/\text{day}$$

Portland to Jersey City (component 2):

$$\$4{,}000 \times 200/2{,}000 = \$400.00/\text{day}$$

Total transport cost = \$1,365.60/day

Total supply chain cost = \$1,365.60 + 1,440 + 1,365.60 = \$4,171.20/day

How did the total supply chain cost decrease even though the transport cost increased from the earlier value of \$800 to the new value of \$1,365.60? Notice that given the holding cost, optimizing the transport cost forced high levels of inventories at the assembly plants. Shipping less-than-truckloads increases the transport costs but decreases the corresponding inventory costs. The net result is that the total supply chain cost is decreased by changing the composition of the total cost. This trading off of local costs to decrease global costs is a basic idea in many supply chain management contexts.

The managerial implication is that to realize these savings, it is important to create accountability for these total supply chain costs whereby the supply chain manager has responsibility for the total cost. In the absence of such managerial responsibility, it is difficult to realize such adjustments and thus such savings. This is one of the reasons why supply chain management requires a senior management position that can affect such changes and thus realize supply chain savings.

7.6.3 Impact of Adding a Warehouse

Optima is considering the option of establishing a consolidation warehouse at Chicago. In the new system, full truckloads of components 1 and 2 would be shipped to Chicago from Portland and Santa Fe. These trucks would have a capacity of 3,000 units and would deliver to Chicago once every ten days.

The transport cost of a truckload is \$2,500. Travel time between locations is estimated to be three days.

Once every five days, a truck would leave Chicago with 1,500 units of component 1 and 1,500 units of component 2. This truck would travel three days. The Boston plant would receive 1,000 units of component 1 and 500 units of component 2, and the Jersey City plant would receive 1,000 units of component 2 and 500 units of component 1.

Holding cost at Chicago is also \$0.40 per component per day.

Provide the total logistics costs for this logistics system.

Figure 7.12 provides a map of the corresponding supply chain.

FIGURE 7.12 The Optima supply chain with the Chicago warehouse

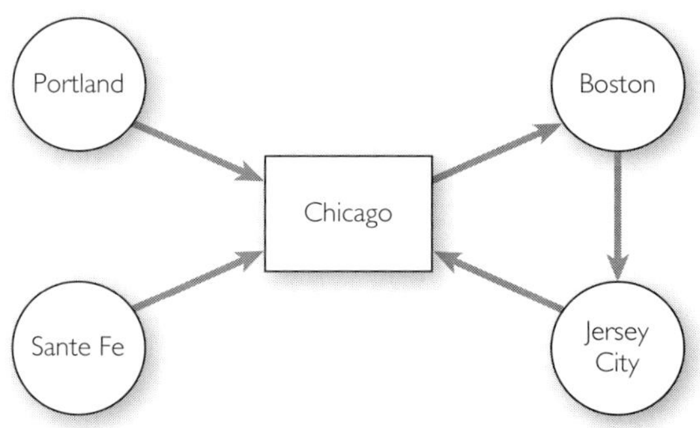

Given the role of the warehouse in Chicago and the shipment schedule, here are the calculations:

Cycle stock costs:

Boston (component 1):

$$0.4 \times 1{,}000/2 = \$200/\text{day}$$

Boston (component 2):

$$0.4 \times 500/2 = \$100/\text{day}$$

Jersey City (component 1):

$$0.4 \times 500/2 = \$100/\text{day}$$

Jersey City (component 2):

$$0.4 \times 1{,}000/2 = \$200/\text{day}$$

Chicago (component 1):

Note that Chicago receives a shipment of 3,000 units from Santa Fe every ten days and ships out 1,500 units every five days to the east coast. Thus the cycle stock at Chicago during every ten-day cycle is 1,500 units for the first five days of the cycle and zero units for the remaining five days. Thus the average cycle stock of component 1 at Boston is

$$((5 \times 1{,}500) + (5 \times 0))/10 = 750$$

The associated cycle stock cost = $750 \times 0.4 = \$300/\text{day}$

Chicago (component 2):

$$0.4 \times ((5 \times 1{,}500) + (5 \times 0))/10 = \$300/\text{day}$$

Thus, total cycle stock cost = \$1,200/day

Transport cost:

Santa Fe to Chicago:

$$\$2{,}500 \times 300/3{,}000 = \$250/\text{day}$$

Portland to Chicago:

$$\$2{,}500 \times 300/3{,}000 = \$250/\text{day}$$

Chicago to Boston and Jersey City:

$$\$2{,}500/5 = \$500/\text{day}$$

Thus, total transport cost = \$1,000/day

In-transit inventory costs:

Santa Fe to Chicago:

$$0.4 \times 3 \times 300 = \$360/\text{day}$$

Portland to Chicago:

$$0.4 \times 3 \times 300 = \$360/\text{day}$$

Chicago to Boston and Jersey City:

$$0.4 \times 3 \times 600 = \$720/\text{day}$$

Total in-transit inventory costs = \$1,440/day

Thus total logistics costs = $\$1{,}200 + 1{,}000 + 1{,}440 = \$3{,}640/\text{day}$

Note that this results in a \$1,000/day savings over the scenario in Section 7.6.1. These savings can be used to pay for the managerial expertise required to manage the warehouse and schedule routes at Chicago as well as to pay for any fixed costs to acquire the warehouse at Chicago.

How were these savings realized? They required sharing of the outbound trucks across components and across the assembly plants, using the consolidation warehouse to continue to have full truckload shipments, managing the warehouse to realize crossdocking savings, and so on. In short, the reduction in costs per day is the direct result of supply chain management actions in the modified system. Note that this estimate of savings per day can be treated as the return on investment in the costs related to supply chain management.

7.7 SUPPLY CHAIN ISSUES TO CONSIDER IN EUROPE

Europe is densely populated, with over 85% of the population of 335 million living within a 500-mile radius. But the presence of many independent countries in Europe and the consequent regulation and political boundaries create unique supply chain challenges. Reference [94] provides a summary of many issues that have to be considered in managing supply chains in Europe. Some of the major characteristics of European logistics are

- Many companies make extensive use of local warehouses, often with one warehouse in each country of operation.
- The supply chain keeps small amounts of widely dispersed inventory, which prevents pooling benefits.
- At the start of European integration, in 2002, a large fraction of the shipping (around 60% of trucking) was by private fleets, but third-party logistics (3PL) options were emerging. Pan-European carriers were also emerging as possible solutions.
- Most movement of product involves circuitous routing, with associated unreliable service, resulting in very expensive transportation. One estimate suggests that over 40% of the ton miles are driven empty. Before European integration efforts, about 35%–45% of the time was spent waiting at borders.
- When the European common market was initiated, the projected European Union single-market benefits were that rationalization of production and distribution would potentially generate around 45% of the supply chain efficiencies. These efficiencies would occur through improved utilization of resources and higher reliability levels.

What does all this mean for a supply chain manager in Europe? It means that spatial distance may not be an appropriate way to look at the supply chain because country boundaries may have an impact. It means that individual country specific rules regarding truck sizes and movement would need to be considered while planning the supply chain network. Coordination agreements to decide how orders are initiated and delivered could have a significant impact on costs. In short, the supply chain architecture in Europe would have to respond to the specific European logistics context.

7.8 MANAGING WAREHOUSE OPERATIONS

The next few sections focus on warehouse management examples and their impacts, including layout choices and their effects on crossdocking. Recall that crossdocking refers to using a warehouse (or transit location) as a coordination point to accept inbound shipments from suppliers and create outbound shipments to customers or stores or assembly plants with a mix of components. Successful crossdocking in a supply chain permits inventory to be converted to rolling stock, thus decreasing static inventories and permitting the inventory in transit to be used as de facto inventory with guaranteed availability at a specific location and point in time. Then the focus shifts to coordination of task allocation between workers in a warehouse. Section 7.12 examines a novel scheme in the literature called "bucket brigades" and its application to several applied contexts.

7.9 DESCRIPTION OF THE SEARS SHOE DISTRIBUTION CENTER

As described in [83], the Sears Shoe Distribution Center in Edison, NJ, a 408,000 square foot central distribution facility for footwear, opened in March 1996. The warehouse was planned to support 750 Sears stores nationwide. The warehouse received inbound shipments from over 100 suppliers. The estimated monthly shipment volume was 2.5 million pairs of shoes a month to seven regional DCs. Stores were permitted the flexibility to order inventory one pair at a time. Taking into account seasonal variations, the facility was planned to carry an inventory level of 9,000 active SKUs, but it was flexible enough to accommodate an additional 7,000 SKUs.

Orders from stores were sent electronically to the distribution center. A majority of the orders were from stores; however, the central buyers for Sears retailers also placed orders for shipments to stores, and there were orders for promotion items. Orders that were received were processed based on footwear type, given their different characteristics. The pick system had 14 pods with four carousels each and 180 locations in each carousel, thus generating a total of 10,800 locations that could handle the active SKUs in the system at any given time. The warehouse used a pick-to-light system, in which the next item to be selected is indicated by a spotlight as soon as the previous item in the list is picked. The warehouse order picker thus followed the lights to identify items in an order. As soon as workers filled a carton, it traveled to a conveyor for final sorting, was weighed as a final item verification check, and sealed, and a shipping label was attached. When the cartons were shipped, advanced shipping notices were sent to stores to provide notice regarding impending deliveries. There are several examples of such warehouse operational details in the articles provided in *Manufacturing and Material Handling* magazine.

7.10 THE WALMART DISTRIBUTION CENTER

In the United States, Walmart distributes products to its 3,000 stores from 158 distribution centers (DCs) ([129]). Individual DC locations may have over 12 miles of conveyor belts that facilitate the movement of goods: Inbound shipments from suppliers become outbound shipments to stores. Each DC supports around 100 stores within a 200-mile radius. A private fleet of trucks and 7,000 drivers convey goods from suppliers to stores, logging more than 700 million miles each year. Trucks using auxiliary power units enable savings in emissions and costs. This reduces the environmental footprint and lowers costs.

Walmart also focuses on reducing its environmental footprint within the warehouse. Changes to packaging, such as placing milk in caseless plastic containers ([130]) have eliminated crates or racks, resulting in a savings of $0.20 per gallon. Use of light-emitting diodes (LEDs) in refrigerated crates instead of fluorescent lights results in more efficient energy use. Products delivered to the stores are either in boxes or shrinkwrapped with recycled content, which is transported back to the DC by trucks.

In the DC, product is managed differently depending on whether it is a staple or a seasonal item. Staple items, such as toilet paper and toothpaste, are managed by supplier-provided managers who ensure that stores maintain high in-stock levels. Category managers look across products offered in a category to ensure effective forecasts and orders. Seasonal items are managed centrally by the buyer, who ships products to stores to balance observed demand and purchase efficiencies. Disaster response warehouses are maintained fully stocked to reduce response time for disasters. For detailed descriptions of both Walmart and several other warehouses, see [53].

The ideal location for product within the Walmart supply chain is the store, where goods can be purchased by customers, rather than in a warehouse. Over 100,000 suppliers, many of whom deliver daily, coordinate with DCs to keep product moving all the way to the store. Product brought into the Walmart DC is usually crossdocked and shipped out within 48 hours. Therefore the supply chain facilities are viewed as conduits for product flow rather than as storage units. By providing central buyers with the flexibility to adjust orders, crossdocking at Walmart can operate efficiently. Loads to stores can be optimized and balanced with store inventories. Goods arrive at store delivery docks during pre-planned nighttime periods.

Walmart's next supply chain goal is to integrate e-commerce and store inventory. Customers can place orders on the company website and pick items up at stores. However, in some areas, they can also order at the store and get same-day delivery for a fixed delivery charge. All of these alternate flows of product make the DC and store inventory a seamless supply chain for the customer.

7.11 CROSSDOCKING LAYOUTS

Crossdocking is an approach that seeks to consolidate inbound shipments from many sources to generate outbound transportation while eliminating the consolidation warehouse inventory. The goal of crossdocking is to have rolling stock that is transferred from incoming shipments directly to outgoing trailers without storing them in between. Shipments typically spend less than twenty-four hours waiting at intermediate facilities.

In a traditional consolidation warehouse, goods are received from vendors and stored. Some time later, when orders are received, goods are picked from inventory and sent to the destination. In a crossdock, goods arriving from the vendor have a customer assigned so that workers need only move the shipment from the inbound trailer to an outbound trailer bound for the appropriate destination.

One way to classify crossdocking operations is according to when the customer is assigned to an individual pallet or product ([51]).

> "In pre-distribution crossdocking, the customer is assigned before the shipment leaves the vendor, so it arrives to the crossdock bagged and tagged for transfer. In post-distribution crossdocking, the crossdock itself allocates material to its stores. For example, a crossdock at a Walmart might receive 20 pallets of Tide detergent without labels for individual stores. Workers at the crossdock allocate 3 pallets to Store 23, 5 pallets to Store 14, and so on." ([51], p. 1)

Crossdocks come in different shapes, with associated implications for performance. The Gue article provides a summary of crossdocking types and examples of successful crossdock facilities. Further research by Gue ([52]) suggests that aisle shapes can affect picking efficiency significantly by changing travel time to pick orders. They recommend consideration of V-, fishbone-, and chevron-shaped aisle configurations, which have the potential to reduce travel time by up to 20%. Clearly reduced pick travel times imply faster order turnaround and thus higher productivity of the warehouse.

7.12 ALLOCATING TASKS BETWEEN WORKERS IN A WAREHOUSE

Once a warehouse is configured and the crossdocking decisions made, productivity can be increased by changing how tasks are allocated to workers in the system. Bucket brigades are defined as "a way to organize workers on a flow line so that the line balances itself" ([6], p. 1). The order picking operation in a warehouse is a flow line. Items in the order are collected in a tote until the order is complete. The finished order is then packaged, labeled, and shipped, using the appropriate shipment mode.

Maximizing warehouse productivity requires balancing task allocation across workers. In many contexts, warehouse management systems are used to identify task content across orders and thus manage the system. Assembly lines are balanced using detailed algorithms. However, the bucket brigades proposed in [6] are self-organizing and thus have little need for centralized planning. The operational role of the supervisor is thus significantly reduced.

In a bucket brigade, the product is moved forward from start to finish by a collection of workers working in sequence. As the last worker finishes a product, he walks back and takes over the partially finished product from his predecessor, who walks back and takes over from his predecessor, and so on. The workers continue to move product forward.

If, in addition, workers are sequenced from slowest to fastest, they will probably gravitate to the optimal division of work so that throughput is maximized [6].

Some of the benefits to a bucket brigade system are the following:

1. The role of the supervisor is decreased substantially because bucket brigades make the line self-balancing.
2. The ability of bucket brigades to adjust themselves, without the need for supervisory or software intervention and associated delays, enables the lines to become agile and flexible.
3. Because the lines run optimally, throughput is increased with minimal work-in-process inventory.

Details of a game to illustrate the impact of bucket brigades are provided in [6].

7.13 BUCKET BRIGADES AT REVCO DRUG STORES, INC. (NOW CVS)

One implementation of bucket brigades reported in [6] was at the national distribution center of Revco in Knoxville, TN. Prior to bucket brigades, Revco faced productivity issues because of its reliance on temporary labor and on overtime during peak periods. Revco used a zone-picking system in which the pick line was partitioned into areas based on the assumption of identical workers; but, given their employee experience mix, the actual pick rates of its workers could vary by a factor of three. The result was that the allocations of work were always unequal and the pick lanes were imbalanced: the slowest pickers were frustrated at falling behind and the fastest pickers were underutilized.

The report described in [6] claims that the idea of bucket brigades was explained to the workers in about fifteen minutes one morning. When implemented at Revco's warehouse, bucket brigades reduced work-in-process inventory, which relieved congestion on the conveyor. The reduced congestion and more effective task allocation increased pick rates and accuracy.

Under the new system, supervisors could monitor the relative progress of different lanes and adjust allocation of workers to keep the lanes coordinated (to reduce sorting downstream). Bucket brigades simplified the shifting of workers from a fast lane to a slow one because there is no need to redefine zones. The research measured a 34% increase in pick rates at Revco when they shifted to a bucket-brigade-based task allocation.

The report in [6] states that

> "Weekly average pick rates were measured by Revco over most of a year (normalized to Revco's work standard 1.0). Prior to the introduction of bucket brigades, Revco was picking at about 95% of their own work standard. After bucket brigades, this rose to 134% of their work standard." (p. 3)

The application of bucket brigades at Revco suggests that even after the warehouse location and layout are defined, there continue to be opportunities to improve performance by adjusting task allocation across workers to become more flexible and demand driven.

7.14 CHAPTER SUMMARY

This chapter focused on managing the warehouse and associated flows in a supply chain as well as on the number of different ways flows from suppliers to users can be organized. It established that effective use of the warehouse to decrease supply chain costs often requires careful design and use of crossdocking as an operational tool. Finally, managing order picking can have a big impact on warehouse turn-around time. This chapter thus discussed how the chain structure, the capacity of transportation, and the coordination of material movement and inventory as well as workers in a warehouse improve the competitiveness of the supply chain.

7.15 PROBLEMS

1. The Bright Corporation assembles widgets at its two assembly plants located in Indianapolis, IN, and Huntsville, AL. Each assembly plant produces 25,000 assembled widgets per year. Each widget requires one unit each of three different components. Component 1 is produced in a plant in Salt Lake City, UT; component 2 is produced in a plant in Jacksonville, FL; and Component 3 is produced in a plant in Seattle, WA. Currently all components are shipped full truckload to a warehouse in Denver, CO. From that warehouse, full truckloads are shipped to the assembly plants. The inbound shipments to Denver thus carry components for all assembly plants. The outbound shipments out of Denver carry all components for an assembly plant.

Travel times between component plants and the warehouse and between the warehouse and assembly plants, as well as the distance in miles, are given below.

Route	Distance (miles)	Travel Time (days)
Salt Lake City–Denver	250	1
Jacksonville–Denver	1,750	3
Seattle–Denver	1,750	3
Denver–Indianapolis	1,083.33	3
Denver–Huntsville	1,083.33	3

The truck capacity is 8,000 units. The cost for a truck to operate on any route is calculated as 1,000 + (4 × distance in miles). Thus, for example, the cost for a truck to ship from Salt Lake City to Denver is 1,000 + (4 × 250) = $2,000. The holding cost per unit per year at assembly plants is $50/unit/year. The holding cost per unit per year at Denver is $12.50/unit/year. All in-transit inventory are charged a holding cost of $12.50/unit/year. Assume 300 days of operation in a year.

1a. Provide the transport costs, in-transit inventory holding costs, and cycle stock holding costs as well as the total supply chain cost for the current mode of operation.

1b. Bright wants to replace all shipments with optimal shipments while maintaining the routes. Provide the optimal shipment on each route as well as the associated transport costs, in-transit inventory holding costs, and cycle stock holding costs as well as the total supply chain cost for the optimal shipments approach to managing the operation.

1c. Bright is considering eliminating the warehouse in Denver and shipping full truckloads directly from component plants to the assembly plants. The associated travel time and lead time is provided below:

Route	Distance (miles)	Lead Time (days)
Salt Lake City–Indianapolis	1,000	4
Salt Lake City–Huntsville	1,000	4
Jacksonville–Indianapolis	2,000	6
Jacksonville–Huntsville	2,000	6
Seattle–Indianapolis	2,000	6
Seattle–Huntsville	2,000	6

The truck capacity remains 8,000 units, and the truck cost is calculated as before as 1,000 + (4 × Distance). In-transit inventory holding cost is \$12.50/unit/year, and the assembly plant holding cost is \$50/unit/year. Assume 300 days of operation in a year. Provide the transport costs, in-transit inventory holding costs and cycle stock holding costs as well as the total supply chain cost for this mode of operation.

1d. Bright is considering replacing all the shipments with optimal shipments. Under this approach, Bright would like to find the optimal shipments on each route as well as the associated transport costs, in-transit inventory holding costs, and cycle stock holding costs as well as the total supply chain cost for the optimal-shipments approach to managing the operation.

1e. Why are there differences across the four approaches to operating the supply chain? Which one would you recommend and why?

2. The Fleet Corporation has two assembly plants located in Los Angeles and San Jose, CA. These assembly plants produce widgets at the rate of 100 per day. Each widget requires two components, component 1 and component 2. Component 1 is produced at a plant in Atlanta, GA, and component 2 is produced at a plant in Chicago, IL. Currently components are shipped full truckload from the component plants to a warehouse in Kansas City. The travel time for trucks is 5 days, and truck capacity is 4,000 units. Each truckload costs \$2,000 in transport costs.

From the warehouse in Kansas City once every 10 days, a separate truck goes to each of the assembly plants carrying 1,000 units of component 1 and 1,000 units of component 2. The travel time for this leg is 5 days, truck capacity is 2,000 units, and transport cost is \$2,000. Holding costs charged per day for transit inventory and cycle stock at the assembly plants and at the warehouse are \$0.80/unit/day.

2a. Provide the costs associated with cycle stock, transport costs, and in-transit inventory as well as the total supply chain costs for the current model of operation.

2b. Suppose the shipments from the component plant to Kansas City were replaced by optimal shipments. Provide the impact on the costs associated with cycle stock, transport costs, and in-transit inventory as well as the total supply chain costs.

2c. A consultant suggests that Fleet should eliminate the warehouse and ship optimal loads direct from the component plants to the assembly plants. Truckload capacity is 4,000 units, but transport cost from each component plant to the assembly plant is \$3,500 with a transit time of 8 days. Provide the impact on the costs associated with cycle stock, transport costs, and in-transit inventory as well as the total supply chain costs.

2d. Another consultant suggests that Fleet should eliminate the warehouse and have a peddling route that would work as follows. Full truckloads would set out from each component plants every 10 days. For example, a truck carrying component 1 would start from Atlanta, travel to Los Angeles and drop off 1,000 units, and then travel to San Jose and drop off the remaining 1,000 units. A separate truck carrying component 2 would start in Chicago, travel to Los Angeles and drop off 1,000 units, and then travel to San Jose and drop off the remaining 1,000 units. Truck capacity would remain 2,000 units, transport costs are $4,000, and transit time is 9 days. Provide the impact on the costs associated with cycle stock, transport costs, and in-transit inventory as well as the total supply chain costs.

2e. Which of the 4 different options considered in questions 2a to 2d minimizes overall transportation costs? Which of the options considered in questions 2a to 2d minimizes overall inventory costs? Which of the options considered in questions 2a to 2d minimizes total supply costs? Explain.

3. The Prompt Corporation purchases product from two suppliers, A and B. Supplier A is located in Austin, TX, and supplier B in Carthage, TN. Supplicr A supplies component a and supplier B supplies component b. These components are used to make gizmos of two types, I and II. Gizmo I is made in Helena, MT, and Gizmo II is made in Duluth, MN. Each manufacturing plant makes 50 gizmos a day. Each gizmo requires 1 unit each of components a and b.

Currently loads are shipped full truckload from suppliers directly to plants. Trucks used have a capacity of 500 units and cost $2,500 per truckload shipped. Holding cost per component per day is $0.50. Transit time per route is 4 days.

3a. Provide the total supply chain costs for this system.

3b. Prompt has realized that it can obtain larger trucks with a capacity of 1,000 units for a cost of $3,500 per route and the same transit time of 4 days per route. If Prompt has these trucks, should all shipments be full truckload or less-than-full truckload? What will be the associated total supply chain costs to use these trucks with the appropriate level of loads on these trucks?

Are the costs lower than (3a)? Explain why or why not.

3c. Prompt has the option to use a warehouse in Kansas City to store product. Under this scheme (using the trucks with a 1,000 unit capacity), trucks would go from Austin to Kansas City and drop off full truckloads. Similarly trucks would go from Carthage to Kansas City and drop off full truckloads. Assume transit time drops to 2 days. Every 5 days, a truck would go from Kansas and drop off equal-size loads in Helena and Duluth. Assume transit time of 2 days to do this route. Assume that costs per route is $2,000 for each of the three routes, i.e., Austin to Kansas City, Carthage to Kansas City, and Kansas City to Helena and Duluth. Assume the same holding cost of $0.50 per unit per day at Kansas City.

What is the total supply chain cost for this system?

3d. Can Kansas City be converted into a crossdocking facility? If so, how would you adjust shipments? What are the corresponding total logistics costs?

4. The Right Corporation has three suppliers supplying components to its assembly plant in Atlanta, GA. Supplier 1 is located in Chicago, IL, Supplier 2 in Indianapolis, IN, and Supplier 3 in Nashville, TN. Each supplier supplies a different component. Demand for each component at Atlanta is 1,000 units per day.

Currently Right ships full truckload orders directly from the supplier plant to its assembly plant. The component suppliers produce in the quantities shipped and Right takes possession of goods at the supplier loading dock as it loads on Right's chosen trucking shipment time. Each truck can carry a maximum load of 3,000 units (across all three components—each component takes the same space and weight as the others). The cost for a truck route from the supplier to Atlanta is provided below.

From	To	Cost/Truckload	Transit Time
Chicago	Atlanta	$1,600	4 days
Indianapolis	Atlanta	$900	3 days
Nashville	Atlanta	$400	2 days

Holding cost at Atlanta is charged at a rate of $0.20/unit/day. The transit time provided for each route is the time from pickup at the supplier to delivery at Atlanta.

4a. Provide the cycle stock costs, the in-transit inventory costs, the transport costs, and the total supply chain costs per day for all direct full truckload shipments in this system.

4b. A logistics manager at Right suggests that the system can optimize total logistics costs by shipping optimal loads. What are the optimal shipment sizes for each route? What is the associated total supply chain cost?

4c. A consultant suggests that Right can have a peddling route that has a truck start at Chicago with 1,000 units of component 1, travel to Indianapolis and pick up 1,000 units of component 2, travel to Nashville and pick up 1,000 units of component 3, and then drop off all the 3,000 units at the assembly plant in Atlanta. Transit time for this peddling route would be 4 days. Atlanta would thus receive daily deliveries of 3,000 units, 1,000 of each component.

The cost for this peddling route would $2,500 per truckload. What would be the total supply chain cost for this system?

4d. Another consultant suggests that Right lease space at a warehouse near Memphis. Due to low demand, the warehousing costs at Memphis are $0.10/unit/day. All shipments would be full truckloads from the supplier plants to Memphis. The cost per truckload from each supplier plant to Memphis is as follows:

From	To	Cost/Truckload	Transit Time
Chicago	Memphis	$1,000	3 days
Indianapolis	Memphis	$600	2 days
Nashville	Memphis	$300	1 day
Memphis	Atlanta	$800	1 day

Every day, a shipment of 1,000 units of each component would go from Memphis to Atlanta. Transit times are provided. What is the associated total supply chain cost for this system?

4e. For each of the four options discussed earlier, provide the costs that are NOT included in the calculations. How might that affect your recommendation for Right corporation?

5. The Prompt Corporation owns two assembly plants, A and B. Plant A is located in Jacksonville, FL, and Plant B is located in Savannah, GA. Plant A produces a gadget, Gizmo 1, at the rate of 200 units per day. Plant B produces a gadget, Gizmo 2, at the rate of 50 units per day. Each gizmo requires one unit each of components 1 and 2 supplied by suppliers 1 and 2. Component supplier 1 is based in San Jose, CA, and component supplier 2 is based in Portland, OR.

Prompt buys components from suppliers and manages all logistics from then on. Currently, each supplier ships full truckload shipments directly to each plant. Truck capacity is 2,500 units. Transport cost per shipment per route is $1,000, and travel time is 6 days for each route between supplier and plant pairs. Holding costs are charged at the rate of $0.40/unit/day.

5a. Provide the total supply chain cost for the current operation.

5b. Suppose Prompt wanted to optimize shipments on each route. Provide the optimal shipment sizes on each route as well as the associated total supply chain cost for the system.

5c. A consultant suggests that Prompt open a warehouse in St. Louis, MO. Shipments would be full truckloads from each supplier to St. Louis. Every 10 days, a truck would go from St. Louis to Savannah and carry 1,000 units consisting of 500 units of component 1 and 500 units of component 2. Every 5 days a truck would go from St. Louis to Jacksonville, with 2,000 units for delivery consisting of 1,000 units of component 1 and 1,000 units of component 2. The St. Louis warehouse would crossdock when possible and carry inventory between inbound and outbound shipments.

Truck capacity remains 2,500 units. The shipments from each supplier to St. Louis cost $600 per shipment and take 3 days for delivery. The shipments from St. Louis to each plant cost $600 per shipment and also take 3 days for delivery. All holding costs are charged at $0.40/component/day.

Provide the total supply chain costs for this system.

5d. Another consultant suggests a complete peddling route that would operate as follows. A truck would start at Portland and pick up 1,250 units of component 2. This truck would travel to San Jose and pick up 1,250 units of component 1. The truck would go first to Savannah and drop off 250 units of component 1 and 250 units of component 2. The truck would then travel to Jacksonville and drop off 1,000 units of component 1 and 1,000 units of component 2.

Assume truck capacity remains 2,500 units. Cost per shipment across the entire route is $1,400. Travel time for the route Portland–San Jose–Savannah–Jacksonville is 6 days. For your analysis, ignore the travel time from Portland to San Jose and from Savannah to Jacksonville.

Provide the total supply chain cost for this system.

5e. For each of the three systems 5b through 5d provide the source of efficiency relative to the original system in 5a.

6. The Quad Corporation assembles tedwigs in an assembly plant in Louisville, KY. Tedwigs are complex products requiring a motor, a gearbox, and a panel, each made at supplier plants in Madison, WI, Columbus, OH, and Harrisburg, PA, respectively. Currently, all component suppliers ship full truckloads to a warehouse in Gary, IN. From Gary, IN, deliveries of all three components are made to the assembly plant in Louisville. Each truckload consists of a third motors, a third gears, and a third panels.

Truck capacity is 3,000 units of any component. Production at the assembly plant is 500 tedwigs per day. Travel distances (in miles) for the routes are provided below.

Route	Distance (miles)	Travel time
Madison to Gary	400	2 days
Columbus to Gary	600	2 days
Harrisburg to Gary	800	2 days
Gary to Louisville	400	2 days

The trucking company charges a fixed fee of $1,000 and a price per mile of 0.7 to transport loads. Thus the trip from Madison to Gary costs 1,000 + (0.7 × 400) = $1,280 per truckload. The holding cost at the Gary warehouse is $0.50/unit/day, and the holding cost at the Louisville plant is $1/unit/day. In-transit inventory is charged holding cost at the rate of the Louisville plant's holding cost.

6a. Provide the transport costs/day, the cycle stock holding cost/day, and the in-transit inventory holding cost/day as well as the total supply chain cost/day for the current mode of operation.

6b. A consultant has suggested eliminating the Gary warehouse and shipping direct in full truckloads. Truck capacity would remain 3,000 units. The trucking company's charges would also remain the same. However the distances would change to the following:

Route	Distance (miles)	Travel time
Madison to Louisville	700	3 days
Columbus to Louisville	800	3 days
Harrisburg to Louisville	1,000	3 days

Provide the transport costs/day, the cycle stock holding cost/day, and the in-transit inventory holding cost/day as well as the total supply chain cost/day for this mode of operation.

6c. If the shipment quantities were replaced by optimal loads, provide the impact on transport costs/day, the cycle stock holding cost/day, and the in-transit inventory holding cost/day as well as the total supply chain cost/day for this mode of operation.

6d. The transport company suggests that they could provide a long peddling route that will pick up components from all supplier locations and deliver them to the Louisville plant. The travel distance to cover all plants and deliver to Louisville would be 1,500 miles. The truck would pick up 1,000 units each of the three components and deliver to Louisville. Travel time would be 4 days. Provide the impact on transport costs/day, the cycle stock holding cost/day, and the in-transit inventory holding cost/day as well as the total supply chain cost/day for this mode of operation. (You may charge the in-transit holding cost based on the entire demand across all components and the Louisville plant's holding cost rate.)

6e. How should Quad decide among the four choices evaluated in 6a through 6d, i.e., what managerial considerations should affect its choice? Explain.

7. The Global Company has assembly plants that produce widgets located in Norfolk, VA, and in Boston, MA. Each widget requires one unit each of two components. Component 1 is produced at a plant in Shanghai, China, and component 2 is produced at a plant in Ningbo, China. Since both component plants are close to ports, each assembly plant (separately) receives full container-load shipments from each component plant. Container capacity is 4,000 units (of either component). Deliveries are to the Boston and Norfolk ports, which are close to the assembly plant locations. Thus there the transport costs from the component plants to the port in China and from the delivered port in the United States to the assembly plant are negligible.

The cost for a container to be shipped from Shanghai or Ningbo to Boston or Norfolk is $2,000 per container. Transit time is 30 days. Assume 5 days of operation each week and a production rate at each plant of 200 widgets per day. Also assume a holding cost of $0.20/unit/day across the system. Global takes possession of goods at the component supplier and thus incurs all costs in-transit.

7a. Global operates with all direct loads being shipped and full container shipments. Calculate the transport costs per day, the in-transit inventory costs per day, and the cycle stock costs at the assembly plants as well as the total supply chain costs for the system.

7b. Given these costs, do you expect there to be a benefit from optimizing loads? Explain. Provide the optimum shipment size for each link and the associated total supply chain costs. Why is it optimal not to ship full containers?

7c. A consultant to Global suggests that the company consolidate shipments in China at Ningbo and ship a full container once every two weeks from Ningbo. Thus, the component suppliers from Shanghai and Ningbo would deliver a full container once every two weeks to a warehouse near the port in Ningbo. Assume that the Ningbo supplier's transport cost is negligible, but the Shanghai supplier ships full truckloads. The truck capacity is 4,000 units, and the truckload cost is $200 per truck; transit time is negligible. The warehouse in Ningbo would carry inventory of one week's demand (across both plants) and crossdock one week's worth of demand to a container shipped from Ningbo to Elizabeth City, NJ. Transit time remains 30 days, and the cost of a container remains $2,000 with a capacity of 4,000 units. The warehouse in Ningbo incurs a holding cost of $0.10/unit/day; all other holding costs are as before, i.e., $0.20/unit/day.

When the container reaches Elizabeth, NJ, it is crossdocked on to trucks with a capacity of 200 units. One truck carries equal quantities of both components and goes to Boston; the other goes to Norfolk. Cost of transport by truck in the United States is $400/truckload, and transit time is one day.

Provide the total supply chain costs for this system.

7d. Which of the three possible systems would you recommend? What specific details have to be managed to realize the projected gains?

8. The Supply Company currently has two plants making two different components, 1 and 2. These plants, in Los Angeles (LA), CA, which makes component 1 and in Seattle, WA, which makes component 2, ship product to a warehouse in Kansas City (KC), MO. From Kansas City the trucks ship both components to plants in Boston, MA, and in Atlanta, GA.

It costs $2,000 per truckload shipped on any of the two possible routes (LA–KC, Seattle–KC). The truck capacity is 4,000 units, and its cost is $2,000 given the size of the business in the opposite direction of these routes.

To ship from the other two routes, i.e., KC–Boston or KC–Atlanta, it costs $2,500, and the truck capacity is 2,000 units. Travel time on each route is 5 days. Demand for each component at each plant is 200 per day. Holding cost at Boston, Atlanta, and KC is $0.25/component/day.

The trucks are currently shipped full from KC to each plant. Each truckload from KC to Boston carries 1,000 units of component 1 and 1,000 of component 2. Similarly each truckload from KC to Atlanta carries 1,000 units of component 1 and 1,000 of component 2.

8a. Supply currently ships all loads full truckload. What is the total logistics cost associated with this mode of operation?

8b. Supply would like to know if KC should be operated as a crossdocking facility that carries no inventory. What would be the total logistics cost associated with this mode of operation? Is it cheaper to carry inventory at KC? Provide an analysis to justify your conclusion.

8c. Management at Supply is considering eliminating the KC warehouse and shipping direct from LA–Boston, LA–Atlanta, Seattle–Boston and Seattle–Atlanta. Truck capacity would be 4,000 units, and trucking cost would be $5,000.

Holding costs and demands would be the same as before.

Supply is planning to ship optimal truckloads on each route. Provide the total logistics costs associated with this decision. Should Supply ship less than the maximum truck capacity? Provide an analysis to justify your conclusions.

9. The Zip Company purchases components from two suppliers: Supplier 1, with a plant in Seattle, WA, supplies component 1. Supplier 2, with a plant in Phoenix, AZ, supplies component 2. Both suppliers ship full truckload to a warehouse in Kansas City. From Kansas, full truckload shipments filled with 2,000 units of component 1 and 2,000 units of component 2 are shipped to Zip's plant in Cleveland, OH. A similar shipment is sent from Kansas to Zip's plant in Atlanta, GA.

Production rate for final products at Cleveland and Atlanta is 250 units per day. Each unit of final product requires one unit of each component. Truck capacity for all routes is 4,000 units. The inbound loads from component plants are crossdocked in Kansas so that Kansas carries no inventory. Transport cost per route per truckload is $1,000. Transport lead time for all routes is 2 days. In-transit holding cost per unit per day is $0.60. The holding cost at the Kansas warehouse is $0.60 per unit per day. The holding cost at the assembly plants in Cleveland and Atlanta is $1 per unit per day.

9a. Provide the total transport cost, in-transit inventory holding cost, and cycle stock holding cost as well as the total supply chain cost per day for the current system.

9b. Suppose Zip were to optimize the outbound loads from Kansas to each assembly plant. Provide the optimal shipment size out of Kansas. Provide the total transport cost, in-transit inventory holding cost, and cycle stock holding cost as well as the total supply chain cost per day for this system.

9c. Zip is considering eliminating the Kansas warehouse and shipping directly from component plants to each assembly plant using optimal shipment sizes. The cost per route per truckload is $1,750. Transit lead time per route is then 3 days. Provide the total transport cost, in-transit inventory holding cost, and cycle stock holding cost as well as the total supply chain cost per day for this system.

9d. Suppose you were advising Zip on the choice of a logistics system. Suggest a decision (across 9a, 9b, and 9c) and any additional analysis you would do before making a recommendation.

10. The Prompt Corporation has two assembly plants in Gary and Lafayette, IN. Components are supplied by suppliers. Component 1 is made by a supplier plant in Chicago, IL. Component 2 is made by a plant in St. Louis, MO. The assembly plants need 1 unit of each component 1 and 2 units of component 2 per unit of widget they manufacture. Each component is purchased from the component suppliers at a cost of $250 per unit.

The production rate at Gary is 100 widgets/day, and the production rate at Lafayette is 100 widgets per day. Annual holding cost at the assembly plants is 20% of component cost. Assume 50 weeks per year and 5 days per week of operation to calculate holding costs.

Currently the supply chain operates with all direct shipments being full loads. From the St. Louis component plant, one truck goes to Gary and another truck goes to Lafayette. The truck from St. Louis has a capacity of 3,000 units. The transit time for the truck from St. Louis to either assembly plant is 2 days, and the cost per truckload is $2,000. Similarly, from the Chicago plant, one truck goes to Gary and another truck goes to Lafayette. The truck from Chicago has a capacity of 750 units. The transit time for the truck from Chicago to either assembly plant is 2 days, and the cost per truckload to either plant is $1,000.

10a. Provide the cycle stock costs, holding costs, and transport costs per day per location. Provide the total supply chain costs. What cost does this shipping route and shipment size minimize?

10b. Prompt wants to identify the supply chain costs if it maintained the all-direct shipping but shipped optimal loads. Identify the optimal loads to be shipped on each route. Then identify the associated transport costs, in-transit inventory costs, and the holding costs at all locations and the total supply chain costs. Did the costs decrease under this system? Explain.

10c. Prompt has identified a transport company that is willing to pick up loads from both component plants and deliver to the assembly plants. Thus, one truck, with a capacity of 3,000 units, will pickup 2,000 units of component 2 from St Louis, travel to Chicago, pick up 1,000 units of component 1 from Chicago and deliver to the plant in Gary. Similarly, another truck, with a capacity of 3,000 units, will pick up 1,000 units of component 1 from Chicago, travel to St. Louis, pick up 2,000 units of component 2 from St. Louis and deliver the load to the plant in Lafayette.

The cost per truckload for each of these routes is $2,500. Assume that the holding costs are charged based on assembly plant holding costs and that transit times remain 2 days for each route.

Provide the cycle stock costs, holding costs and in-transit inventory costs under this system. Provide the total supply chain costs. Does this approach decrease costs or increase costs? Explain.

Winstar Gear and Supply Chain Configurations

WINSTAR CORPORATION: MANAGING THE SUPPLY CHAIN

Bill Donovan bounded up the stairs to his office on the fifth floor of Winstar Corporation's headquarters at One Corporate Drive in uptown Lafayette. His corner office with its all-glass side walls afforded a great view of the Wabash River with the courthouse cupola and the university buildings completing the view. It was Bill's prize for being named VP of supply chain management at Winstar.

Winstar Corporation was on a roll as far as Wall Street was concerned. From its humble beginnings as a manufacturer of gears, Winstar had transformed itself into a global conglomerate dealing with gears, machine tools, steel pipes, textiles, and software testing and packaging. Growth had been driven by acquisitions the last five years as Joe Morgan, CEO of Winstar, dazzled Wall Street with his financial wizardry. Joe knew that synergy and profitability would now come from improving Winstar's supply chain management. He had hired Bill Donovan to accomplish that.

As Bill settled down in his chair and looked at his email, he saw an urgent flashing message from his secretary. Joe Morgan had called a meeting of the senior management committee in one hour to discuss Winstar's operations in Eastern Europe. Bill pulled the folder with information about Winstar's recent acquisition, Lana Steel Pipe and Processing. Lana had operations primarily in the MidWestern United States, Southern Europe, and Eastern Europe. This was Winstar's only exposure to the Eastern European market, and Joe had great hopes for growth. Recent projections for growth in Eastern Europe were promising. If Hungary and the Czech Republic were admitted to the European Union, then growth would be far more dramatic. The steel pipe market in the United States was stable, but the future was far more volatile. Winstar's marketing managers had identified some great new customers in Hungary for Lana, and they were pushing for expansion in Budapest. All this was happening quickly, and Bill was expected to help frame things for the committee.

The meeting in Winstar's executive room on the 10th floor was animated. Joe Morgan laid out his expectations for Lana in Eastern Europe. Jim Weston, VP Marketing and Sales, provided his perspective on the growing market and the deals he was ready to bring in. Jean Lambert, VP Finance, wanted the group to be certain that the new assets that were expected to be funded would make sense, given Winstar's current asset utilization. Pat Merton, VP Operations, had proposals for three new plants and four warehouses that he expected to build all over Eastern Europe. Joe appointed Bill chair of the committee to recommend a plan for Winstar. He scheduled a meeting in exactly one week, and the meeting disbanded with everyone rushing out to catch flights that would take them to different parts of the world.

Bill took the stairs back to his office, loosened his tie and took a deep breath. He had one week to develop a plan, and he intended his report to be a classic primer on supply chain management at Winstar. This meant that he needed a plan, and he started writing down a process for him and his staff to follow. He called in his team of gung-ho managers: Sunil Pande, a new MBA hire; Brad Fife, his veteran manager; Jenny Cray, another new MBA hire; and Jill Stetson, new to Winstar but a veteran of the industry. He laid out the following plan:

1. First focus on how Lana is currently organized.
2. Do a what-if analysis following current organization for supply chains at Winstar's various divisions.
3. Examine Lana's demands from customers.
4. Put yourself in the shoes of the customers and see what Winstar can do to help customers.
5. See if there emerges some supply chain alternatives and determine the corresponding effect on the supply chain.

Bill allocated tasks to his managers and asked them to report back in two days.

The first report outlined current operations at Lana. Lana's pipe consisted of two parts: a steel pipe with a polymer core. The polymer had a patented honeycomb structure that permitted slow release of chemicals into the liquids flowing through the pipe. Precise control of these releases required careful manufacture of the polymer and precise fit of the polymer and the steel pipe. Lana's plant in Santa Fe, NM, specialized in the manufacture of steel pipe with an extra-smooth internal finish. Lana's plant in Portland, OR, focused on producing the polymer cores. These products were shipped to assembly plants in Cleveland, OH, and Philadelphia, PA. Each plant had assembly lines that combined the steel pipe and the polymer cores to create a special steel pipe used extensively in the chemical industry. The industry standard for pipe was 25 feet long and 12 inches in diameter. All of Lana's customers ordered in these standard units. Each assembled unit was estimated to have an average cost per unit of $500. However the plant in Cleveland created a pipe with two steel pipes sandwiching a polymer core. Thus each unit of finished product required two units of steel pipe and one unit of polymer pipe at Cleveland. The plant in Philadelphia produced a product with two polymer pipes sandwiching a steel pipe. Thus one unit of product in Philadelphia required two units of polymer pipe and one unit of steel pipe.

The transport lead time between any component plant and assembly plant was 6 days. Annual holding cost was charged at 25% of cost. But Brad also investigated the cycle stock at the assembly plants as well as the in-transit inventories on the trucks between the locations. He generated a chart with the supply chain cost for Lana's operations broken out into transport costs, in-transit inventory cost, safety stock cost, and cycle stock cost.

Bill was also aware that the group had focused on the mean demand. He recalled a conversation with a mid-level manager who had told Bill "Top management deals with the mean; middle management is left to deal with the variance." He resolved to also examine the variance and its impact. Also, should he go ahead and try to improve Winstar's internal operations, or should he also focus on customer demand, and what can be done to better understand it?

One number that bothered him was the report on safety stocks at Cleveland and Philadelphia. He first resolved to understand the logic for these finished goods inventories, starting with the Cleveland plant. Since the demand at this plant came from orders from the warehouse, he set the desired 98% in-stock probability as well as the plant lead time to identify the inventory levels he would expect in the warehouse. Table 1 shows the total demand faced by each of the assembly plant warehouses. Given that product was made in batches of 100 units of pipe and that production took 5 days, each plant satisfied demand from finished goods inventory. The warehouse carrying finished goods inventory carried product to hedge against lead time and to buffer against demand fluctuations. Bill realized that the inventory costs of the finished goods inventory were significant compared to the internal supply chain costs. But unless something could be done with orders, there was little hope for decreasing these costs. Bill derived the plant production based on the batch size and an optimal reorder point for the manufacturing plant. That allowed him to generate the warehouse inventory level. This meant that unless something changed in the orders or in the production system there was little hope for improving finished goods inventory at the assembly plants.

Bill decided that a supply chain focus had to be different than behaving like a distribution operation, which takes demands as orders that had to be filled without questioning the logic of the orders. As he recalled the description of logistics, he heard from a keynote speaker at one of the many logistics conventions he had attended in the past: "Logistics involves consideration of both information flows and material flows." So that meant that the team needed to understand orders for steel pipe a lot better than they currently knew at this point.

The next mission his team focused on was getting a handle on demand and understanding how the plants produced to satisfy this demand. He quickly discovered that warehouse demand varied dramatically from week to week. This made the average demand they had considered significantly different from the challenges faced on a daily basis; the *variance* to be handled by middle management. In response, the factory produced to optimize its production costs. Since steel pipe involved significant setups, this demand was satisfied primarily from stock. Production produced in a intermittent manner to satisfy this demand and to optimize its setup costs. His analysis generated factory production and warehouse inventory in response to demands faced by Cleveland.

These tables were the basis for the plant manager to demand more plant construction if new business in Eastern Europe were to come on board. New business meant more demand uncertainty and thus more fluctuating production plans. Unless Winstar was ready to compromise on customer lead times, which Joe Morgan absolutely would not tolerate, Winstar needed capacity and that meant plant construction. The warehousing manager correspondingly demanded more warehouse capacity to let the plants operate at an efficient level and deal with customer demands rapidly. These tables showed Bill that there was no other way to deal with Winstar's planned expansion unless . . .

Bill recalled that he had been exposed to logistics audits in an earlier assignment. He decided that Winstar needed to use a Pareto analysis to understand customer orders. Table 1 provides a breakdown of orders from a list of Winstar's customers for a 25-day period. Table 2 provides their annual orders. Bill wanted to find three large customers who generated about 80% of the orders at Cleveland.

Jenny suggested that Winstar could also talk to each of the three customers to examine how the customers' demands were related to the orders they placed with Winstar. Table 3 provides the customers' demands during the same 25-day period as Table 1. She would process the data, talk to the customer, and explain to the group the links between customer demands and their orders to Winstar.

Brad talked to the team about an article he read in *Purchasing Index* in which they described standing order agreements. He provided copies of the article to members of the group and suggested that Winstar consider such agreements with their large customers. Bill wanted a quick analysis of the feasibility of such agreements, and Brad offered to provide such an analysis.

Sunil suggested a thought experiment for the group: Suppose they could smooth orders from customers. How would the factory and the warehouse get affected? He agreed to provide an analysis of the effect.

Jill suggested that if they could free up factory capacity and warehouse capacity, Winstar might be able to supply its new markets and customers without any addition to its assets. Bill beamed with pride. He jumped up and exclaimed, "That's it! We need to show top management that supply chain management can deliver value to all VPs. And we need such a proposal by Monday!"

TABLE 1 Table of customer orders by day received by the Cleveland Warehouse

	CUSTOMER #												
Day	**1**	**2**	**3**	**4**	**5**	**6**	**7**	**8**	**9**	**10**	**11**	**12**	**TOTAL DEMAND**
1	54	0	44	5	0	0	5	0	0	5	0	0	113
2	38	0	0	0	5	0	0	5	0	0	5	0	53
3	55	0	0	0	0	5	0	0	5	0	0	5	70
4	117	0	0	5	0	0	5	0	0	5	0	0	132
5	0	53	0	0	5	0	0	5	0	0	5	0	68
6	0	58	6	0	0	5	0	0	5	0	0	5	79
7	33	0	7	5	0	0	5	0	0	5	0	0	55
8	0	16	50	0	5	0	0	5	0	0	5	0	81
9	0	0	26	0	0	5	0	0	5	0	0	5	41
10	83	0	6	5	0	0	5	0	0	5	0	0	104
11	60	0	47	0	5	0	0	5	0	0	5	0	122
12	0	0	81	0	0	5	0	0	5	0	0	6	97
13	0	0	11	5	0	0	5	0	0	5	0	0	26
14	213	0	45	0	5	0	0	5	0	0	5	0	273
15	51	0	53	0	0	5	0	0	5	0	0	6	120
16	86	0	49	5	0	0	5	0	0	5	0	0	150
17	128	9	0	0	5	0	0	5	0	0	5	0	152
18	0	7	15	0	0	5	0	0	5	0	0	5	37
19	0	25	60	5	0	0	5	0	0	5	0	0	100
20	0	10	0	0	5	0	0	5	0	0	5	0	25
21	121	0	4	0	0	5	0	0	5	0	0	6	141
22	0	3	7	5	0	0	5	0	0	5	0	0	25
23	42	148	86	0	5	0	0	5	0	0	5	0	291
24	0	12	61	0	0	5	0	0	5	0	0	6	89
25	0	11	30	5	0	0	5	0	0	5	0	0	56
Mean	43.2	14.0	27.5	1.8	1.6	1.6	1.8	1.6	1.6	1.8	1.6	1.76	100
Standard Deviation	55.5	31.9	27.6	2.44	2.38	2.38	2.44	2.38	2.38	2.44	2.38	2.63	67.26

TABLE 2 Annual orders from customers

Customer #	**1**	**2**	**3**	**4**	**5**	**6**	**7**	**8**	**9**	**10**	**11**	**12**	**TOTAL**
Demand	15739.36	5125.12	10017.28	655.2	582.4	582.4	655.2	582.4	582.4	655.2	582.4	640.64	36400
% of total Demand	43	57	84	86	88	89	91	93	94	96	98	100	
Pareto Chart													

TABLE 3 This table gives the DOWNSTREAM demands faced by the customers

	CUSTOMER #			
Day	1	2	3	Total demand faced by the rest of customers (4 through 10)
1	47	14	27	15
2	44	15	29	15
3	41	14	27	15
4	42	12	28	15
5	44	14	28	15
6	46	15	28	15
7	44	16	27	15
8	44	13	28	15
9	41	17	28	15
10	41	12	28	15
11	45	15	27	15
12	44	16	27	16
13	44	16	26	15
14	43	12	28	15
15	49	11	28	16
16	41	11	27	15
17	41	13	28	15
18	44	15	26	15
19	44	14	28	15
20	46	15	28	15
21	43	18	27	16
22	43	17	29	15
23	45	18	28	15
24	43	19	28	16
25	43	15	30	15
Mean	43.68	14.68	27.72	15.16
Standard Deviation	1.99	2.17	0.89	0.37

CASE QUESTIONS

1. Map the current supply chain at Winstar Corporation.
2. Generate tables describing the orders placed with the factory and the warehouse inventory levels over the 25-day period. Explain the logic for the observed variability.
3. Evaluate the impact of signing agreements with the major customers so that their demands would be passed through as orders for the new system on inventory levels and costs. Generate the impact on warehouse orders, factory production, and warehouse inventory.
4. What aspects of the new logistics system have to be *managed* for the new system to be successful? What are conditions under which the approach suggested in the case will not work?

Chapter 8

Purchasing

The purchasing function in supply chains focuses on the selection, contracting, design, and delivery of products from suppliers. Coordination with suppliers can generate significant benefits by leveraging supplier capability to adjust product specifications and required service. Purchasing managers can also leverage competition across suppliers to extract favorable contracts. If supplier capacity has to be reserved to guarantee supply, then competition across supplier types can be leveraged to optimize supply chain performance. This chapter will focus on coordination, competition, and capacity decisions within the purchasing function. The examples will illustrate the link between chain structure and the ability to effectively leverage the purchasing function.

The specific purchasing decisions include the make–buy decision for components and products, global location of sources for manufacturing and distribution facilities, and coordination with suppliers to maximize mutual benefit.

8.1 THE IMPACT OF SUPPLIER COORDINATION

As companies rely more on their suppliers to decrease overhead and asset levels, managing suppliers is now an important capability. To get a sense of the magnitude of the supplier's role, consider that, in the automobile industry, estimates suggest that Chrysler outsources over 80% of the parts it assembles into cars; Ford, over 65%; and GM, over 55%. In the electronics industry, Cisco System partners provide final assembly for almost half of its switches and routers ([68]). Table 8.1 (from [68]) shows that suppliers and buyers have closely intertwined relationships with one another across a range of industries, from automobiles to banking and electronics to pharmaceuticals.

It is clear that supplier networks can have a significant impact, particularly when the suppliers are the ones investing in technology and who have the design and testing capability required for the development of innovative products. A study by John Henke ([58], page 3) from Planning Perspectives calculates a Working Relations Index (WRI) that examines seventeen criteria under five broad categories related to the buyer–supplier relationship, OEM communication, OEM help, OEM hindrance, and supplier profit opportunity. The 2011 WRI considered 1,984 data transactions, and automakers could be awarded a total of 500 points. The WRI was 327 for Toyota, 309 for Honda, 271 for Ford, 247 for Nissan, 236 for General Motors, and 221 for Chrysler.

In a related context, an Original Equipment Suppliers Association (OESA)/McKinsey study suggested that interface costs between a supplier and OEM can be estimated to be 5.2% of total cost. The study also estimated that 80% of the waste in the auto industry was due to poor supplier management and was linked to product specifications, part complexity, and ineffective coordination of capacity and demand. The supply chain cost due to this

TABLE 8.1 Possible applications of our model

Industry/Activity	Buyer Resource Commitment	Supplier Resource Allocation
Auto Parts	Concept (Ford)	Design, manufacture (Johnson Controls)
Pharmaceuticals Manufacturing	Drug development (Merck, Pfizer)	Scale up and manufacturing (Catalytica)
Pharmaceuticals Contract Research	Basic research (Merck, Pfizer)	Research, testing (Covance, Quintiles)
IT Hardware	Concept (Cisco)	Subassembly, final assembly (Solectron)
Food and Beverage	Brand management (Coca-Cola, Redox)	Bottling, distribution (Bottlers, Korex)
Financial Services	Product, service design (PNC, First Union)	Transactions (MBNA)
dot.com Business	Business plan	Transactions processing and Customer Relationship Management (CRM)

waste was estimated to be $10 billion. Given these estimates, it is clear then that supplier management represents an important supply chain capability. The next few sections will focus on specific example to manage these costs.

8.2 SUPPLIER MANAGEMENT AT TOYOTA

The book *Toyota Supply Chain Management* ([64]) describes the auto manufacturer's supplier management practices. One important practice is to spend sufficient time during supplier selection to ensure that the vendor will mesh with Toyota's network. Suppliers join a *keiretsu,* a connected network, and can expect to work with other members to ensure competitiveness of the supply base. One such role is membership in a *jishuken* of suppliers, a gathering of executives who, through mutual criticism and applications, leverage the Toyota production system across their companies. But Toyota, in turn, provides a combination of group and individual assistance to the *jishuken* members, thus enabling them to have a higher output, lower inventory, and better quality than other suppliers in the automobile industry. An example cited in [64] is Toyota's CCC21 program that managed to cut costs by 30% and $10 billion over a five-year period.

One key component of Toyota's supplier selection is frequent interaction with suppliers. Over 85% of the suppliers in Japan are located within fifty miles of the assembly plant. In the United States, over 80% of the suppliers are within a three- to five-day lead time, with sequence suppliers (those that adjust their components to match specific requirements in a car such as seats, dashboards, etc.) located close to the assembly plant. This frequent interaction not only coordinates supplier production with Toyota's requirement, but also permits visibility and quality control.

Toyota both hosts supplier managers at their facility and sends their own managers to supplier facilities to iron out potential issues. Thus, [64] claims that the company manages the downstream supply chain to stabilize order volumes and thus decreases variability faced by its suppliers through careful choice of variety offered, visibility of its data across the supply chain, and a velocity that matches supply rate to demand rate.

8.3 COORDINATING BUYER–SUPPLIER CONTRACTS

Core buyers and their management of the buyer–supplier relationships for product specification and production at Ford Motor Company are described in [68]. Ford has over 350 core buyers responsible for overseeing the relationship with approximately 1,150 suppliers. These suppliers provide component parts or systems (e.g., brake pedals, seats, car audio systems), which are, in turn, assembled into Ford's cars. The core buyers evaluate supplier capability; negotiate component specifications, prices, and quantities; and decide if suppliers should be offered engineering assistance. While no costs are charged to suppliers, the procurement manager chooses how to deploy these scarce resources to deliver benefits to Ford.

An example in [68] describes the possible coordination between the OEM and supplier to reduce costs for a radio. As a starting point, product designers at Ford provide initial specifications regarding the radio; an estimate of variables such as the heat generated around it, the expected vibration, and so on; and details regarding the audio specifications. But these specifications are then translated into final specifications and manufacturing capability through interactions between Ford's engineers and the supplier's personnel, with the joint goal of producing a competitive radio.

Consider a single resource termed *engineering-hours.* These engineering-hours could be deployed in different ways. A quote from [68] summarizes these choices:

> Ford's engineering-hours might be employed to improve the initial design by using existing standards (e.g., the GAP standard dashboard cutout for head units), by eliminating/minimizing conflicts in the initial specifications (e.g., size and features), by applying design-for-manufacturing techniques, or by improving the communication of a given initial design (e.g., oral description versus written description versus digital files). Or, Ford's engineering-hours might be employed to cooperate with the supplier by testing prototypes in increasingly-sophisticated ways (e.g., CAD simulation) and providing the corresponding results to the buyer. Finally, Ford might employ its engineering hours independently, in parallel with the supplier's engineering-hours, on one or more of the steps in the transformation process.

The optimal level of supplier assistance will be described later in Section 8.12.

8.4 COORDINATING WITH SUPPLIERS AT BOSE CORPORATION: THE JIT II SYSTEM

The JIT II System ([28]) at Bose Corporation was championed by Lance Dixon while he was vice president of purchasing at the company. The Bose JIT II approach was different from the normal just-in-time approach (JIT) because it went further than a focus on inventory levels. Bose invited a supplier's employee to work as an in-plant representative, thus eliminating the need for a supplier to forecast buyer demands. The supplier was offered an "evergreen" contract that lasted over several years, an opportunity to access all of Bose's personnel and meetings and to influence designs during inception and an ability to do concurrent planning and concurrent design. In return, the supplier was expected to commit to price reductions and service improvements over the life of the contract.

Thus, under JIT II, Bose got a supplier employee, a reduction in purchasing overhead, a commitment to decreased prices, ideas focused on decreasing total costs rather than just component costs, better service and quality than market offerings, lower prices, and so on. As an example, a transport in-plant provided Bose an on-time delivery of 98%–99%, higher than the industry standard of 95%. Since over 60% of Bose's output was exported, an export–import in-plant specialist provided Bose with the ability to adjust shipments to meet shipping schedule changes and transit delays by identifying these changes early in the day and reacting appropriately. A metal-parts supplier who started direct meetings with Bose engineers provided suggestions for component redesigns and thus saved money for the supplier by using his existing tooling and decreased assembly costs to Bose. In effect, JIT II provided Bose virtual control over the supply chain without significant investments in assets. However, Bose only offers such an opportunity to suppliers who are already very competent and have delivered at a high level of reliability over time. No such agreements are made for acoustics and electronics, which remain in house.

Since supplier employees play a coordinating role, the corresponding buyer purchasing agent can be eliminated. Thus, Bose replaced a "market" read of supplier performance, through repeated supplier competition, with a nonmarket longer-term relationship. Consequently, it is important to project the potential cost reduction and service improvement over the life of the agreement and expect that in the contract. Choice of this commitment enables sharing of the cost reductions that are possible at the supplier end and sets expectations regarding how the supplier should leverage the increased access to the buyer real-time environment to reduce costs for the supply chain.

8.5 JAPANESE OEM SUPPLIER MANAGEMENT

Empirical studies suggest that Japanese original equipment manufacturers (OEMs) differ from US OEMs in their supplier-management practices. Japanese OEMs, in many instances, offer more flexibility to the supplier for part designs, but closely monitor manufacturing. The reverse seems to be true for US OEMs. Clark ([16]) states that black-box parts, "whose functional specification is done by the assemblers (buyers), while detailed engineering is done by parts suppliers," account for 62% of Japanese automakers' total procurement costs, but only 16% and 32% for US and European automakers, respectively. However, "detail-controlled" parts, which are developed entirely by the assemblers (buyers), from functional specifications to detailed engineering drawings," account for only 30% of Japanese purchases, compared to 81% and 54% for US and European automakers.

Empirical studies (see [68] for citations) describe three levels of involvement between the buyer and supplier. These are described as the drawing-supplied (DS) system, the drawing-entrusted (DE) system, and the drawing-approved (DA) system. Under the DS system, the OEM provides detailed drawings and the supplier manufactures parts to those specifications. Under the DE system, the supplier creates the drawings, but the OEM claims property rights to those drawings. Under DA, the supplier creates and owns the drawings and supplies the part to the OEM.

At Toyota between 1970 and 1990 the steering wheel remained a DA part, while interior parts were contracted as DS parts. For other components the level of supplier involvement changed, with weather strips evolving from being a DS part to becoming a DE part, while vibration-proof rubber evolved from being a DS part to being a DA part. It is thus clear that the level of supplier involvement evolves to adjust to the impact of the component's cost and quality on the final OEM product.

8.6 THE ALPS STRUCTURE FOR PROCUREMENT

Nishiguchi ([92]) describes the structure of purchasing used by Japanese OEMs as an Alps structure (that looks like the Swiss Alps). The auto assemblers are the peaks of the Alps structure. The first-tier suppliers, who have expertise in specific areas of component manufacture and systems development, form the first layer. Products they may handle include wire harnesses, instrument clusters, transmissions, radiators, and brakes. The second-tier subcontractors are smaller, with a lower systems capability level. They specialize in a smaller range of subassemblies: metal body parts, electrical relays, and seat frames. The third-tier subcontractors specialize in simpler parts such as small stampings for cores of motors and small plastic parts. The fourth-tier suppliers do simpler tasks such as preforming and sorting. The base of the Alps thus contains 30,000 to 50,000 small firms.

As described earlier, there is extensive delegation between the OEMs and the first-tier supply base for product designs. In addition, the same supplier may occupy different positions across tiers: for example a first-tier subcontractor to Honda may be a second-tier subcontractor for Nissan. Similarly a second-tier subcontractor to Nissan may be a first-tier supplier to Hitachi for computer components. This suggests that the tiered supply base is linked across many OEMs and products, thus generating an Alps structure.

The ability of suppliers to have a portfolio of customers enables flexibility of the supply base to absorb downturns in individual OEM volumes, thus providing the capacity adjustment flexibility for the OEMs. In addition, the ability for the base of smaller companies to easily adjust their production capacity by working longer hours and so on provides the ability to rapidly adjust upwards to demand increases.

8.7 EARLY SUPPLIER INVOLVEMENT (ESI)

Proactive purchasing groups typically consider the role of early supplier involvement (ESI) as a tool to improve the cost and quality performance of products. A paper by Zsidisin and Smith ([125]) summarizes the literature and a case study involving Rolls Royce (RR), which produces critical components for civilian and military aircraft. RR data suggests that 80% of product costs is locked during the design phase, thus demanding the need for suppliers to be involved during the design phase, given that the new-product development process lasts 10 to 20 years in this industry.

The key reason for RR to use ESI was the need to produce products at competitive prices, which required suppliers to use target costing approaches to produce competitive designs. The result was a set of suppliers and a collaborative approach to provide continued cost reductions during design and redesign. Legal liability and associated risks required sharing of expertise to reduce the risk of product failure and development of agreements to share gains, thus decreasing the risk of intellectual property rights concerns. Detailed tracking of supply base execution by tracking current suppliers enables choice of appropriate suppliers to be involved in ESI.

An important consideration is the supplier capacity availability to support production needs. Discussions with suppliers about their planning process, planned investments, and so on enables RR to be comfortable about supplier capacity availability. A key consideration for RR was whether the culture and philosophy of the supplier organization matched RR's culture and philosophy. A better match between RR and its suppliers' philosophy reduces the risk in new product development. Studies suggest that outcome-based management works best when risk is minimal for the product. However, behavior-based management focuses on approaches to decrease risk that then minimize the probability of problems arising. ESI plays the role of enabling the latter approach to managing suppliers.

8.8 CUSTOMER AND SUPPLIER COORDINATION AT RANE BRAKE LININGS

This section describes processes for customer and supplier coordination at Rane Brake Linings (RBL), Deming Award–winning brake lining supplier in India ([61]). One of RBL's customers introduced a new two-wheeler disc pad in the Indian market. While RBL produced the product to specifications, the pads were found to stick during use by the end customer. The customer reported the problem to RBL on 14 April, 2004. The two-wheeler

groups, and other institutional groups. However, as the Indian market opened up to global OEMs, market share started dwindling, and the company decided to focus on selling to the urban consumer. Since it did not have a product targeted to this customer, the company decided to produce a utility vehicle with a carlike feel.

The company's management decided that they did not want to be part of a global OEM's subsidiary but rather wanted to control the vehicle design and distribution. It decided to

> "develop a brand-new vehicle with nearly 100 percent supplier involvement from concept to reality for $120 million, including improvements to the plant. The new Mahindra Scorpio SUV had all of its major systems designed directly by suppliers with the only input from Mahindra being performance specifications and program cost." (Weilgat [123, p. 1])

One of the reasons that global supplier capacity was available in India was the slow growth of the passenger car market and thus the level of unused capacity with top-tier suppliers in India. This slack capacity could be leveraged by the suppliers to provide a competitive product in a short time frame.

> "To keep costs down, many Scorpio suppliers used existing components or components already in development. While much of what drivers see is new, some of the subcomponents are carryover products from something that was already engineered and tooled." (Weilgat [123, p. 3]).

Costs were also kept low because Mahindra (M&M) stuck to its original parameters for the project and didn't change specifications or content. In traditional purchasing arrangements competitors come in with different products, and automaker OEMs thus want to add features. M&M allowed suppliers to use their expertise, even if it meant using unproven processes. Suppliers also say the program cost them less in investment because they didn't have to constantly change the program. While the project was underway, M&M gave many of the suppliers existing M&M business so they would not have to wait until the new Scorpio entered production to become profitable.

The result was a product that was completely configured to M&M provided specifications, developed for $120 million (which was 20% of the costs faced by a global OEM), sold at retail at a price point between $12.5 thousand and $17 thousand.

> "M&M tied up with the best in the world in their respective areas of the global auto industry. Fukui, Japan, for the press shop; Fuji, Japan, for the dies; Korean company Wooshin for body shop; Fori Automation, USA, for the tester line for final assembly; Durr, Germany, for the paint shop; Lear, USA, for seats and interiors; Visteon, USA, for exteriors; Samlip, Korea, for suspension; and BEHR, Germany, for air conditioning and Renault for gasoline engines. M&M facilitated the development of the supply chain and assembly operations. The vendors set up facilities in and around the factory. The end result was a fully indigenous product with international quality at affordable price." [70, p. 2]

The next few sections will focus on a few abstractions of the procurement problem in an attempt to clarify the buyer's and supplier's roles in the relationship.

8.12 COORDINATING SUPPLIER UNDER AGENCY EFFECTS

Iyer, Schwarz, and Zenios [68] consider the agency effect and provide an example where supplier and buyer coordination affect set-up cost at the supplier. The buyer requires a product from the supplier at a fixed rate D per unit time. Demand is met from finished-goods inventory maintained by the supplier. Shortages are not allowed. Production is assumed to be instantaneous, but there is a production set-up cost and an inventory-holding cost, both incurred by the supplier.

In this context, the buyer is the principal who pays for the work and decides how much to help the supplier. The supplier is an agent who knows specifics regarding production and his capability (which is unknown to the buyer). The set-up cost depends on the buyer's specifications, which in turn, depend on the buyer's resource commitment, x_1, and on the supplier's set-up capability, ϕ. Thus the unknown supplier's capability creates an agency problem. The agent chooses the production lot size and thus influences buyer costs. The set-up cost will be denoted by $K(x_1,\phi)$. The supplier's decision is the production lot size, x_2. The holding cost is h per item per unit time. The supplier's cost function is $\frac{K(x_1,\phi)}{x_2}+\frac{h}{2}x_2$.

The supplier will choose the optimal lot size x_2 that minimizes his costs. Thus the corresponding supplier cost would be $\sqrt{2DhK(x_1,\phi)}$. Suppose that the setup consists of a number of steps, $N(x_1,\phi)$, that depend on agreed-upon product specifications and supplier capability. In addition, suppose that the cost of each step depends on supplier capability, $s(\phi)$, i.e., $K(x_1,\phi) = N(x_1,\phi) \times s(\phi)$.

The impact of buyer involvement on supplier costs depends on whether the cost relationship between buyer effort and supplier impact is one of substitutes or complements. Figure 8.1 shows an example of complements. In this case, if the buyer agrees to specification adjustments that reduce the number of set-up steps, and when the supplier's capability only influences the cost of each step but not the number of steps, the supplier cost decreases faster for a more capable supplier than for a less capable supplier for a given amount of buyer assistance. Such a context is described as a complementary buyer–supplier relationship. In this case, an increase in buyer involvement, an increase in x, makes the impact of capability on supplier cost steeper, which increases the cost of information for the buyer.

However, if the supplier's capability influences both the cost of each step and the number of steps, it is possible to generate a substitutes relationship, which allows the supplier cost to improve more for a less capable supplier than for a more capable supplier. Figure 8.2 shows that as the buyer involvement increases, the supplier capability impact on costs becomes less steep. In other words, supplier assistance helps the buyer decrease information-related costs.

Given the description above, buyers would tend to provide more assistance in a substitutes relationship than in a complements relationship. This is the result described in [68]. The example above suggests that buyers should consider the trade-off between

FIGURE 8.1 Supplier capability vs. production cost for complements

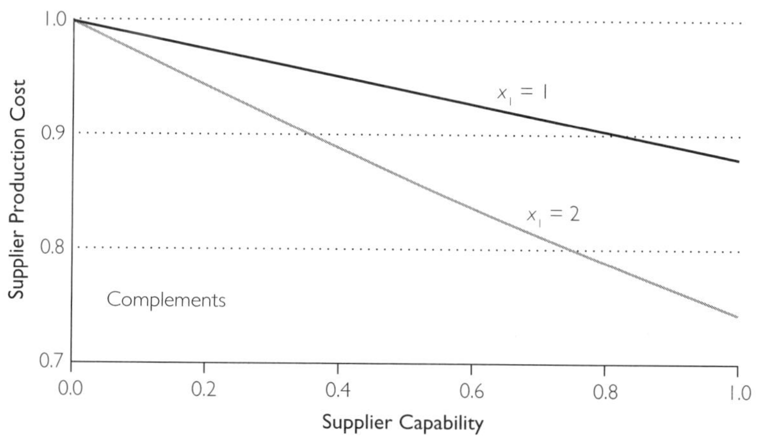

FIGURE 8.2 Supplier capability vs. production cost for substitutes

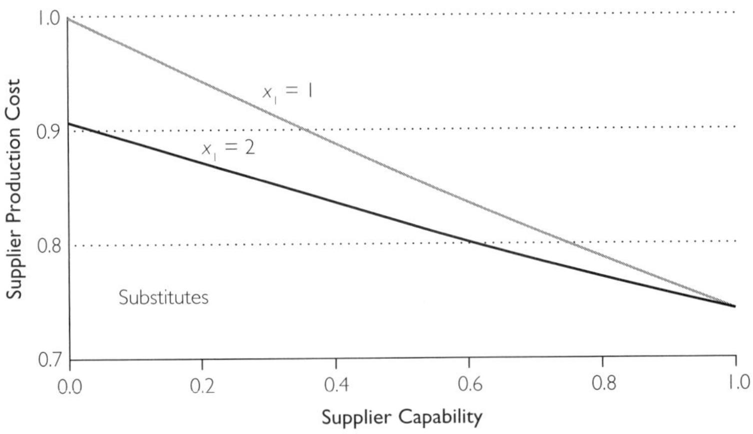

involvement with the supplier and its impact on the information rent, i.e., the difference in cost performance across suppliers with different capabilities. If buyer involvement flattens the cost curve across suppliers, that is, decreases cost differences across supplier capabilities, the relationship is one of substitutes, and it may be optimal for the buyer to expend effort to decrease supplier costs and benefit from the reduced information asymmetry related to contracting costs. On the other hand, if buyer assistance were to increase the cost differences across suppliers, then it may be optimal for the buyer to withhold assistance because it only serves to increase the cost impact of information asymmetry.

8.13 COMPETITION AND PURCHASING IMPACT

Earlier sections in this chapter highlighted the benefit of developing a relationship with a supplier, but such choices are made in a competitive environment. The mere existence of competition may enable better performance to be elicited from suppliers. How does competition across multiple suppliers benefit a purchasing manager? The next few sections focus on this question: Sections 8.14, 8.15, and 8.16 are a summary of material provided in [126].

8.14 THE SUPPLY CHAIN IMPACT OF DECENTRALIZED PURCHASING

Consider a supply chain consisting of a supplier who produces product at a cost per unit of s and then chooses a wholesale price w to sell the product to a buyer. The buyer, in turn, faces a retail demand curve, with the retail price p linked to retail demand q as $p = a - bq$. For the wholesale price to permit retailer incentive, assume $s < a$.

Suppose the supplier and buyer were making decisions independently to maximize their respective profits. The supplier quotes a wholesale price w, and the buyer chooses a retail price p and buys the required quantity q. The supplier's profit is described as $(w - s)q$ while the buyer's profits are $(p - w)q$. Given a wholesale price w, the buyer will choose a retail price $p = \frac{a+w}{2}$ as his profit maximizing retail price, and the associated purchased quantity purchased will be $q = \frac{a-p}{b} = \frac{a-w}{2b}$. Given this purchased quantity as a function of wholesale price, the supplier will choose an optimal wholesale price $w = \frac{a+s}{2}$. Notice that the prices chosen by each member of the supply chain result in a retail price level of $\frac{3a+s}{4}$ and a retail quantity of $q = \frac{a-s}{4b}$.

However, consider a centralized supply chain, with the buyer and supplier maximizing their joint profit. For such a supply chain, the associated retail price will be $\frac{a+s}{2}$ and a retail quantity of $\frac{a-s}{2b}$—decisions made by a monopolist. Note that the retail quantity is higher and the retail price lower than in the decentralized supply chain.

8.15 THE IMPACT OF SUPPLIER COMPETITION—THE WHOLESALE PRICE AUCTION

But what if there were two suppliers, each competing to win the contract? Suppose the two suppliers have production costs of s_1 and s_2, with $a > s_2 > s_1$. Consider a system in which the suppliers first compete on wholesale price, and the buyer chooses the appropriate retail price and quantity. If the two suppliers participated in an auction, then the wholesale price charged to the buyer would be s_2. This wholesale price is always smaller than the best that can be achieved in a decentralized supply chain, i.e., $\frac{a+s}{2}$ because $a > s_2 > s_1$.

Thus, supplier competition to obtain the order results in lower buyer prices than in a monopolistic supplier supply chain. The lower wholesale price increases buyer profits and decreases supplier profits.

8.16 WHOLESALE PRICE AND CATALOG AUCTIONS UNDER INFORMATION ASYMMETRY

Consider the situation where the buyer does not know the supplier production costs, but only knows that the costs are uniformly distributed between $\underline{s}$ and $\bar{s}$. Each of the two suppliers knows their own production cost but only the range of the true cost for the other supplier. All that the buyer knows is that the supplier's cost follows a uniform distribution between $\underline{s}$, *overlines*.

We first consider a *wholesale price* auction. In a wholesale price auction, the buyer announces his purchase quantity, choosing his retail price **before** he knows supplier bids. The buyer has to use his expectation of supplier costs while making the quantity decision. Each supplier has to post wholesale prices in response, and the buyer merely picks his best option. Though suppliers do not know each other's bids because an auction is used, the resulting wholesale price is $\max(s_1, s_2)$. For the suppliers to be competitive, their cost s has to be lower than the wholesale prices that each of them would offer the buyer if they were by themselves, i.e., each supplier's s_j is $< \frac{a+s_i}{2}$ (where $i = 1, 2$) in addition to having $s_i < a$. Assume that $s_1 < s_2$.

After some algebra (see [126]), it turns out that

$$q = \frac{a-2}{2b}$$
$$= \frac{2\overline{s} + \underline{s}}{6}$$
$$p = a - bq$$
$$w = \max(s_1, s_2)$$

However, under a *catalog* auction, the retailer gets to adjust the purchase quantity in response to the wholesale prices obtained. Thus, the suppliers first compete on wholesale price, and the winning price is s_2. The corresponding retail price is set as $p = \frac{a+s_2}{2}$ with the associated retail quantity determined as $q = \frac{a-p}{b}$. Notice that the associated buyer expected profit is greater than the expected profit obtained under the wholesale price auction. This is because the retailer fine-tunes the purchase quantity to the wholesale price and thus improves overall profitability. Corresponding the supplier's expected profit is lower.

The results discussed in this section suggest the need to adjust the type of auction to extract the benefit of supplier competition as well as compensate for the decentralized supply chain.

8.17 RESERVING SUPPLIER CAPACITY UNDER COMPETITION

Procurement managers may have to reserve capacity at suppliers before knowing their demand. Suppliers, in turn, face costs to reserve capacity and a cost to execute the order. The costs to reserve capacity are the fixed costs or commitments required to be incurred in advance of the demand realization due to operational lead times.

Given that suppliers have their individual cost structures, suppose these suppliers provide bids to the procurement manager. Each supplier bid consists of a price to reserve capacity (per unit) before demand realization and a price to execute (per unit) or produce and deliver after demand is realized, subject to the capacity limit that has been reserved. Given a set of supplier bids, how much should the procurement manager reserve with each of the suppliers, and how should the reserved capacity be used when demand is realized? In addition, given the procurement manager decisions, how should suppliers decide on their bids? This specific problem was analyzed by Martinez-de-Albéniz and Simchi-Levi ([85]). The remaining part of this section will provide an example to illustrate this auction.

Suppose there are suppliers 1–7 and a dummy supplier 8, whose costs are provided in Table 8.2. These costs are unknown to the procurement manager. Supplier 8 provides any leftover demand and charges the retail product price.

Consider an example set of bids from the seven suppliers, as shown in Table 8.3.

The first step is to use a scatter plot to plot the points with the execution price on the x-axis and the reservation price on the y-axis. Once this step is carried out, the lower envelope of these points is obtained by moving up as far up as possible such that all points are on or to the right of this envelope. This envelope is called the *convex hull* of these points. In other words, imagine a wind blowing a line made up of a light straw, or a straw line, from the upper right to the origin. The straw line will be pushed until it runs up against a set of points that restrict its movement further. The corresponding structure created by the straw line is the convex hull.

For the example provided earlier, plot the points using a scatter plot (see Figure 8.3) and identify that bids from suppliers 2, 4, 5, 7, and 8 are on the convex hull: they will be termed *active suppliers*. This means that it is optimal for the buyer to reserve capacity only

TABLE 8.2 The reservation and execution costs for each supplier

Supplier Number	Execution Cost	Reservation Cost
1	0	42
2	10	33
3	20	25
4	30	19
5	50	10
6	65	5
7	80	2
8	100	0

TABLE 8.3 The reservation and execution price charged by each supplier

Supplier Number	Execution Price	Reservation Price
1	85	20
2	12	31.5
3	76	6.54
4	26	21.6
5	34	18
6	39	18
7	72	3.8
8	100	0

FIGURE 8.3 A convex hull showing active suppliers

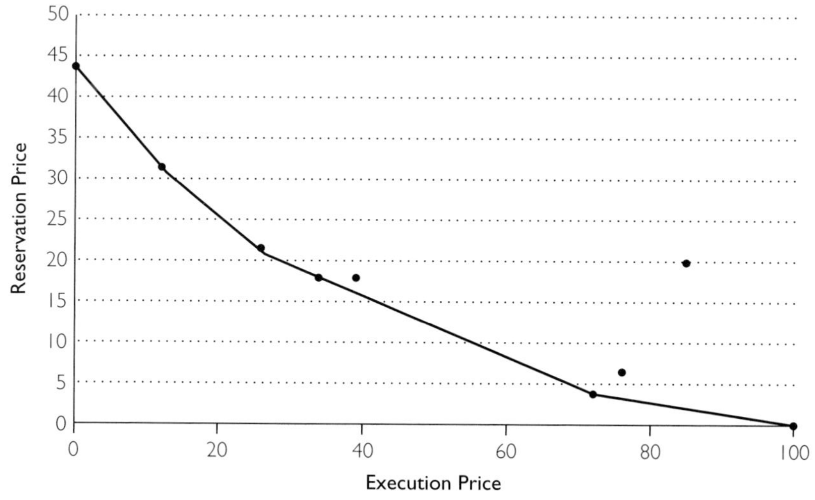

FIGURE 8.4 A convex hull showing equilibrium bids from suppliers

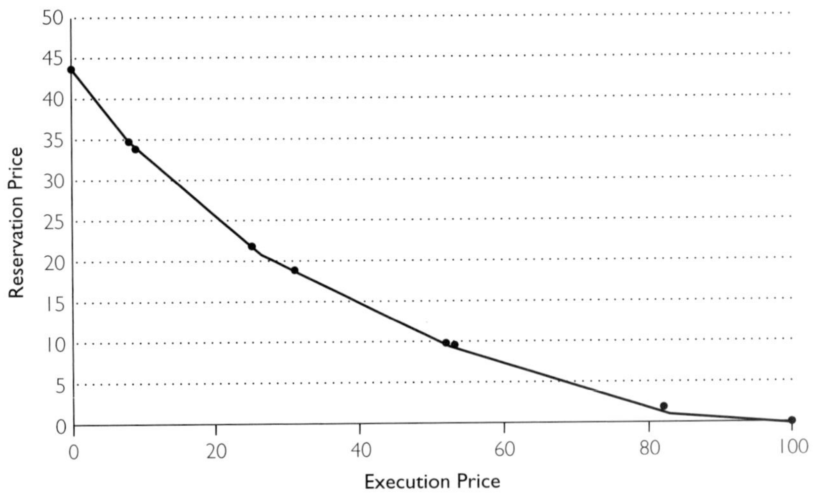

with these vendors. All the remaining suppliers that are not selected to reserve capacity are termed *inactive suppliers,* as described in [85]. To create a closed envelope, connect the active supplier with the lowest execution price with a point that is defined as having a 0 execution price as the x-axis value and the sum of this supplier's reservation and execution price as the y-axis value. In this example, this is the point (0,43.5) on the leftmost point of the connected set.

Note that the envelope described above suggests that once bids are obtained from all suppliers, each supplier has an incentive to react to change his bid to become active. As an example, if supplier 1 were to change his bid to offer an execution price of \$10 per unit and a reservation price of \$33.25 per unit, it would add a point (10,33.25) that would enable this supplier to become active and thus receive a portion of the buyer's capacity reservation. Thus, competition across the suppliers causes interaction among their bids due to their desire to win and thus impacts the buyer's price.

If the bids are revealed in each round and each supplier responds to adjust his bid, then supplier responses keep adjusting until everyone stops making changes, i.e., the system reaches an equilibrium. This means that the bidding process will conclude when each individual supplier's bid remains the same before and after all bids are revealed. For more details, see [85]. The corresponding set of bids obtained and the associated convex hull is shown in Figure 8.4. This section thus shows how a procurement manager can optimize across supplier bids to choose his cost-minimizing supply strategy.

8.18 CHAPTER SUMMARY

The procurement function focuses on managing order flows and consequent material flow from a supplier to a buyer. The purchasing decision requires choosing supply chain structure through the make–buy decision and the global location of manufacturing and distribution facilities. The capacity level chosen by suppliers is affected by buyer specifications and the extent of buyer coordination. An important issue to consider is the agency problem, which arises because of information asymmetry between the buyer and the supplier. In addition, buyer flexibility and cooperation can often affect supplier costs. Thus, it is important to get the buyer and supplier to commit the right level of resources to maximize joint performance. We focus on buyer approaches to work with suppliers to get the required product or component at a given price, quality, and capability. Purchasing coordination with suppliers can occur through contracts to resolve agency issues through appropriate choice of buyer involvement, use of auctions, and so on. Also, early supplier involvement and staggered model changes both serve as effective tools in managing suppliers. Competitiveness of the purchasing function involves measures such as cost, delivery performance, innovation, inventory levels, and so on. In the presence of supplier competition, buyers can use auctions as a filtering mechanism to improve performance. Solving the agency problem effectively is a key issue when managing suppliers.

The Adjustable Brake Pedal Procurement Case

ADJUSTABLE BRAKE PEDALS PURCHASING AT FORD MOTOR COMPANY

Disclaimer: The attached case was written by Jim Burrows (Ford Motor Company) and Professors Ananth Iyer and Leroy Schwarz (Krannert School of Management, Purdue University). It was written to facilitate class discussion and not to illustrate either effective or ineffective management practices.

FORD MOTOR COMPANY

THE INTRODUCTION OF ADJUSTABLE PEDALS AND PRICE/VOLUME ANALYSIS: A PURCHASING PROSPECTIVE

For many years, Ford has been improving vehicle design to extend its appeal to a cross section of society. This effort was particularly enhanced in recent years with the advent of the Women's Marketing Group. This select group of Ford engineers, designers, and marketers has come together to design concept vehicles with unique enhancements that target the vehicles to specific market segments. As a result of this effort, the concept of adjustable pedals was born. The basic concept of adjustable pedals is to make the vehicles more friendly to short-stature drivers. Through a toggle switch control, the pedals extend rearward in the vehicle some three additional inches. This adjustment in conjunction with seat adjustment has a significant effect. A few quotes from the focus group participants tell the tale:

- I'm in control of the vehicle.
- The brake is there for me.
- I feel safe.
- Finally a car company that cares about their customers.

As the pedals extend rearward, the driver moves away from the steering column and feels safer and more in control.

Adjustable pedals have met with considerable market acceptance. Dealers are increasing their orders and in some cases even ordering vehicles with adjustable pedals exclusively for vehicles displayed on their lots.

This market acceptance has generated welcome challenges for the manufacturing and purchasing side of Ford. Addressing these opportunities is the subject of this case.

PEDAL SUPPLY SITUATION

The pedal supply at Ford had been humming along with no real issues for a number of years. In the early 90s, no one had even heard of adjustable pedals. All pedals on all vehicles were of the fixed variety. Two main suppliers were included in the supply base. International Pedals had been the major supplier with approximately $65 million of business. This business had been stable for many years. Central Pedals also was in the supply base with an overall turnover of approximately $22 million of business.

International was an amiable supplier with a good reputation for quality and cooperation with Ford purchasing demands. However, when the concept of adjustable pedals was first brought forward, International did not believe that the idea would ever come to market. International along with their competitors had been presenting the concept to Ford engineers for a number of years with little result. Central Pedals on the other hand was very aggressive with the adjustable pedal concept. They continued to beat down the door. One day, along came the Ford Women's Marketing Group. Its key motivation was to differentiate the Ford product from competition. All the years of Central's efforts finally were fruitful. With a bit of help from the Women's Marketing Group and an upper management push, the concept was accepted. The first production was targeted for the Lincoln Navigator.

The Navigator was selected mostly due to its large, oversized interior. Although there are a number of benefits to this roomy layout, it generally was a bit more unfriendly to the small stature driver. The designers felt that adjustable pedals would broaden the market appeal for this large vehicle and increase sales. Initial production estimates were for 25,000 vehicles.

A cross-functional team including purchasing, engineering, and quality proceeded to conduct a design competition including both incumbent suppliers, Ace Pedals, and others. In the final analysis, Central Pedals was awarded the business.

ACQUISITION OF CENTRAL PEDALS

Central Pedals was a long-term supplier of pedals. They were very adept at producing automotive components and were knowledgeable of the procedures and methods of the industry. They proceeded with the engineering and began to gear up for production. This would be the first full-scale production of adjustable pedals. The Chrysler Viper had previously been in production, but only on a limited basis of

10,000 units per year. Ace Pedals was the supplier for the Viper. Central designed the adjustable pedal production line for the specified volume.

Enter Total Systems. Total Systems was a major $50 million-per-year supplier to Ford. They desired to broaden their product offering. With the advent of total system sourcing, many suppliers in the automotive industry are attempting to broaden their capabilities in an effort to obtain a larger part of the automotive pie. After considerable due diligence, Total acquired Central. Total is also a very capable supplier. However, they have a much greater revenue base, over a billion dollars, and they are diversified into five major segments: automotive, medical, aerospace, marine, and industrial. An income statement for Total Systems is provided in Table 1.

SOURCING OF ADDITIONAL PROGRAMS

Ford engineering has had considerable positive experience with Total in the past. When it was learned that Total had acquired Central, there was an immediate and strong acceptance within the engineering community. The final engineering of the Navigator program was a good example. It proceeded without a hitch due to the added resources of a billion-dollar supplier.

Subsequent to the award of the Navigator program, the Taurus, and Sable programs soon followed. The initial Taurus and Sable program volumes were 10,000 and 40,000 units respectively.

The negotiated purchase order piece price for all of the programs was only $85 each. Central and subsequently Total Systems were awarded all of the programs.

CENTRAL/TOTAL'S PRODUCTION LINE

Although Central had $22 million of Ford business, they were really a quite small supplier as far as automotive suppliers are concerned. Also, it would come to light later that they were generally undercapitalized. It may have been a fortunate turn of events for Ford that Central was purchased by such a well-positioned, billion-dollar, savvy supplier.

As Total began to further review the production line that Central had designed, they found that it was really not up to Total's standards. First it was located in the midst of a dirty, noisy stamping plant. As for the line itself, it was very labor intensive, with minimal poke yoke devices (error proofing), and inadequate end-of-the-line testing. Also, the welding equipment was antiquated.

They later determined that Ford had directed the sourcing of the pedal bracket assembly to International. International was the supplier of the fixed pedals. In an effort to reduce tooling expenses and to standardize the design, Ford Engineering preferred to stay with International. A peculiarity of the bracket was that a special stabilization ear was attached to the bracket to reduce pedal noise. An executive drive test had revealed the need for greater bracket rigidity.

DEMAND FOR THE ADJUSTABLE PEDALS GROWS

Soon after the launch of the Navigator, the demand for the adjustable pedals began to grow. The dealer take-rate increased markedly. Then adjustable pedals got a big endorsement. Marketing determined that the option should also be offered on the Expedition, a sister vehicle to the Navigator. The Expedition had the same vehicle platform and pedal design as the Navigator. So, the addition of the adjustable pedals was made possible with the simple addition of assembly line installation equipment at the Ford plant. Since Central was the Navigator supplier and the engineering and tooling had already been paid, Central became the Expedition supplier as well. The piece price was the same as the other programs. In a matter of months, the demand for the adjustable pedals increased by 300%. After six months, the demand increased even further. A chart showing the programs and their projected volumes is shown in Table 2. As shown, for the Navigator and Expedition, the required production of adjustable pedals increased to 100,000 units.

TABLE 1 Total Systems income statement

	1998	1997	1996
Revenues	$1,437,000	$1,145,000	$931,000
Cost of Goods Sold	$1,029,000	$794,000	$640,000
Selling and Administrative Expenses	$283,000	$244,000	$204,000
Total Expenses	$1,312,000	$1,038,000	$844,000
Income Before Taxes	$125,000	$107,000	$87,000

TABLE 2 Program volumes and launch dates

	Original Volume	Present Volume	Launch Date
Navigator	25,000	40,000	8 / 98
Expedition	Not Offered	60,000	12 / 98
Taurus	10,000	20,000	9 / 99
Sable	40,000	80,000	9 / 99
Fairlane	100,000	100,000	6 / 2000

Total Systems immediately found itself in a supply problem. Their production line had been designed for 25,000 units, and now they had to produce 100,000 just six months after launch. The main constraint to growth was the assembly line itself: the welding equipment, unbalanced assembly stations, slow end-of-the-line testing, and required quality inspections. Also, after production began, it was determined that the ear on the pedal bracket was leading to a 30% scrap rate for the bracket. Due to the extended length of the adjustable pedals, the tolerance between the ear and the remainder of the bracket needed to be controlled much more tightly. International was having extreme difficulty meeting the required production volumes. All of the above aspects ultimately came together to throw the launch of the adjustable pedals into jeopardy.

TEAM OF QUALITY ENGINEERS, LEAN ENGINEERS, AND PURCHASING SAVE THE DAY

Along with the mobilized resources of a very experienced Total Systems, a team of Ford quality engineers, lean engineers, and purchasing managers descended upon the unsuspecting Total and International plants. Total's assembly line and International's scrap problem were at issue. In a matter of a few weeks, the major constraints were identified and the fixes were being put in place. Production goals were met. In the midst of the effort, it was determined by the lean engineers that various improvements to the assembly line could be put into action. They determined that a 90% cumulative average experience curve was applicable to the operation. The curve is shown in Table 3.

TABLE 3 90% Cumulative average learning curve (log/log scale)

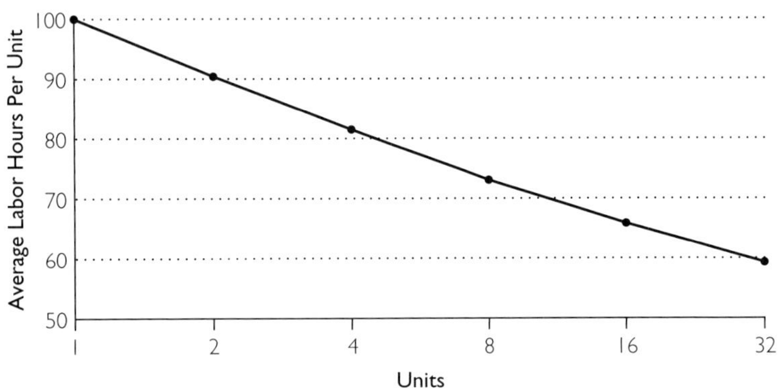

Units Produced	Labor Hours	Cumulative Labor Hours	Average Labor Hours
1st	100	100	100
2nd	80	180	90
4th	70	324	81

MANAGEMENT DEMANDS A PROTECTION OF FUTURE GROWTH

Although the swat team of engineers and purchasing management saved the day, the extreme effort that was necessary focused heavy attention on the issues and the capabilities of Total Systems. Ford marketing management was quick to point out to purchasing management that this new option was broadening the market appeal and selling additional vehicles. As everyone knew, this was in a segment of Ford's business with the highest returns for Ford shareholders. The point was made crystal clear to all concerned: "At all cost the growth of the adjustable pedal option must be supported, no excuses!!" The buyer may want to consider adding a supplier.

TAURUS AND SABLE VOLUMES INCREASED

In addition to the Navigator and Expedition launch, as shown in Table 2, the Taurus and Sable programs launched in September of 1999. Although originally projected at 10,000 and 40,000 units, the present level of production requested by these two programs has doubled to 20,000 and 80,000 units respectively.

As a result of all of the growing demand, in September of 1999, the total demand for adjustable pedals climbed to 200,000 units.

PURCHASING AND PROGRAM MANAGEMENT REQUIRE COST REDUCTION

As stated above, the original purchase orders to Central and Total Systems were cut at $85 per pedal assembly. This was for a combination accelerator and brake pedal assembly. As a result of the significant increase in volume, purchasing management and program management were quick to contact the buyer to request an immediately negotiated cost reduction.

DECISION MADE TO EXPAND THE OPTION TO THE FAIRLANE

With motives similar to Taurus and Sable of providing maximum driver comfort, Ford made the decision to offer the option on the new Fairlane as well. The Fairlane was launched in June of 2000. Instead of underestimating the requirement, the Fairlane launch team decided to target a volume of 100,000 units from the outset. So, a new program has become available requiring sourcing by the buyer at the very time that all of management is requesting cost reductions.

THE ASSIGNMENT

1. Predict the theoretically expected cost of the adjustable pedals for the Fairlane program using Price/Volume and Experience Curve analyses.
2. Suggest a strategy to be utilized with the supply base to best negotiate the desired price. (Respond simply with a list of bulleted points.)
3. Identify the best strategy to protect the growth of the adjustable pedal option. (Respond simply with a list of bulleted points.)

Hint: The proper utilization of price/volume and experience curves in a real live business situation is an art form. Do not get overly hung up on the exacting accuracy of the math.

INSERT: THE EVOLUTION OF AUTOMOTIVE PARTS SUPPLY

For a variety of investment, efficiency, and technology reasons, the automotive parts supply market continues to evolve. Although some would say that the movement is only related to the cost of labor, in reality there are many drivers much larger and probably more important than the cost of labor. To tap these macro drivers,

- Shift large asset investments to the supply base and reduce the fixed cost to protect from downturns.
- Migrate the engineering expense to the supply base and take advantage of supplier expertise.
- Increase JIT shipment efficiency to reduce inventory levels throughout the value chain.
- Reduce order to delivery timing to delight the customer.
- Delight the customer with the latest technology.

TIER 1 AND TIER 2

In the 80s, there were Tier 1 and Tier 2 suppliers. The Tier 1 suppliers worked with the OEMs on a direct basis to apply their parts to the vehicles. Engineering and prove-out was provided by the OEMs. In most cases the intricate details of the part were specified by the OEMs. The supplier was mainly charged with building parts to the print. Tier 2 suppliers were subsuppliers to the Tier 1.

TOTAL SYSTEM SUPPLIERS

The first evolution in the 90s was the migration to total system suppliers. With this alteration, the Tier 1 suppliers began to consolidate with other Tier 1 suppliers in order to provide an entire system. Pedals and cables are good examples. Originally there were two suppliers, one for pedals and one for cables. Since the OEM was attempting to shift engineering responsibility and move forward for all of the other macro reasons listed above, consolidation of the first-tier suppliers became necessary. In this case, the OEM desired only one supplier for the system from the pedal through the cable to the throttle, and it was determined that the pedal supplier would have the lead. The cable supplier either buys the pedal supplier and maintains Tier 1 status or is relegated to being a subsupplier. The subsupplier position is feared since it is more difficult to sell value. The commodity becomes more price based, purchasing only. Also, through consolidation, revenue and hopefully market capitalization grow, leading to the potential of further purchases. This is a powerful and sometimes frantic movement within today's automotive industry.

MODULE SUPPLIERS

The next evolution for 2000 and beyond appears to be toward modules, or chunks. *Chunks* is a good description, since that is exactly what is occurring. Large chunks of the car will be purchased from a megasupplier such as Visteon or Delphi. OEMs have identified from as few as three to as many as nineteen chunks of the car that will be purchased from one megasupplier. The large chunks will be shipped in separately from a close-in supplier plant and assembled just in time at the OEM's assembly plant. In the future world, this would occur just five days after the customer's order is placed on the internet. In our example, the pedals and cables become part of the cockpit module, including the steering wheel, steering column, pedals, cables, brake master cylinder, and even the dash panel.

As the supply base evolves, the challenges for the procurement process are also evolving. True supply management professionals will be needed in the next century.

APPENDIX

Adjustable pedal parts in assembly

Part Name	Supplier	Quantity per Assembly	Type Manufacturing Operation
Mounting Bracket	International	1	Metal Stamping
Electric Motor	Fasco	1	Motor Mfg
Brake Track Rod	Siler	1	Mach. Forging
Accel Track Rod	Siler	1	Mach. Forging
Drive Cable	Teleflex	2	Metal Rod
Brake Pedal Arm	Tower	1	Metal Stamping
Accel Pedal Arm	Tower	1	Metal Stamping
Brake Pedal Pad	Lapeer	1	Metal Stamping
Accel Pedal Pad	Lapeer	1	Metal Stamping
Brake Control Arm	Tower	1	Metal Stamping
Accel Control Arm	Tower	1	Metal Stamping
Brake Drive Gear	Acme	1	Metal Machining
Accel Drive Gear	Acme	1	Metal Machining
Brake Worm Gear	Acme	1	Metal Machining
Accel Worm Gear	Acme	1	Metal Machining
Brake Drive Nut	Superior	1	Metal Machining
Accel Drive Nut	Superior	1	Metal Machining
Fasteners	Fastech	4	Metal Machining

POTENTIAL ASSEMBLY IMPROVEMENT

As a part of the lean manufacturing review, the team identified various possible improvements to Total's operations. These improvements add credence to the applicability of the effects of the learning curve.

- New robotic welding equipment to replace the manually operated welders
- Modular assembly lines that allow added work station capacity at bottlenecks, thus reducing the cycle time
- Computer aided end-of-the-line test equipment to reduce cycle time and provide a permanent record of the test automatically
- Multiple error-proofing devices to be added throughout the line to reduce inspection requirements
- Relocation of the assembly operation to a facility that is clean and familiar with normal assembly operations
- Duplicate bracket inspection guides at Total and International to eliminate incoming inspections at Total
- Improvements to bracket ear welding fixture at International to reduce scrap rate

VALUE ANALYSIS/VALUE ENGINEERING AND VALUE CHAIN SUGGESTIONS

- Eliminate the bracket ear
- Utilize a formed metal track rod for the lower load accelerator pedal in lieu of a forging
- Begin manufacturing the stampings in-house at Total instead of outsourcing
- Manufacture the mounting bracket at Total in lieu of International
- Conduct lean manufacturing audits of tier 2 suppliers
- Conduct run-at-rate inspections at tier 2 suppliers
- Add additional tier 2 suppliers for critical components that are potential constraints
- Schedule a formal VA/VE session at the Ford Total Cost Management Center
- Utilize returnable dunnage with Ford assembly plants and Tier 2 suppliers

Central's Assembly Line Prior to Lean Mfg. Improvements

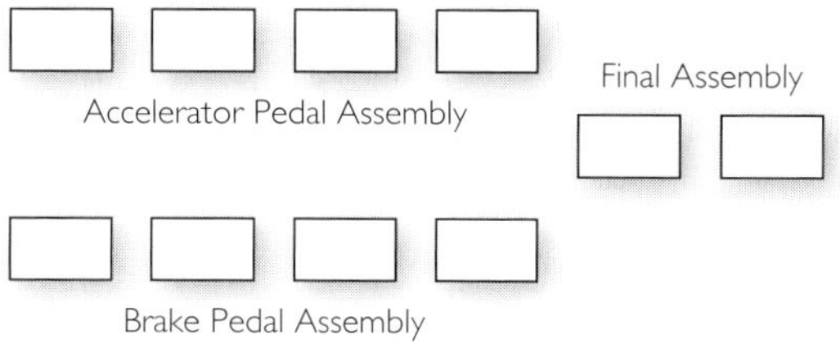

Layout Features

- Straight Flow Design
- Multiple Piece Flow
- Inventory Banks at Each Station
- Minimal Error Proofing
- Manual Test Station
- Line Not Balanced; Constraining Operations
- Welding and Stamping On-site
- Higher Cycle Time
- Limited Operator Work Instructions
- 100% Inspection

Total's Assembly Line After Lean Mfg. Improvements

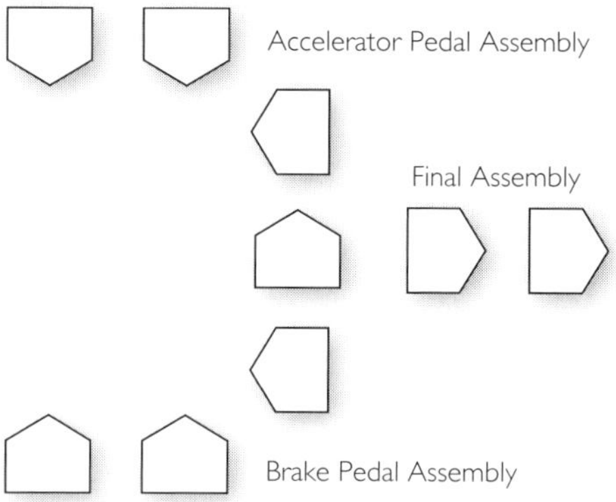

Layout Advantages

- Cellular Design
- Single Piece Flow
- No Inventory Banks
- Multiple Error Proofing
- Computerized Test Station
- Welding and Stamping Off-site
- Clean and Assembly Friendly
- Much Lower Cycle Time
- Excellent Operator Instructions
- Minimal Inspections

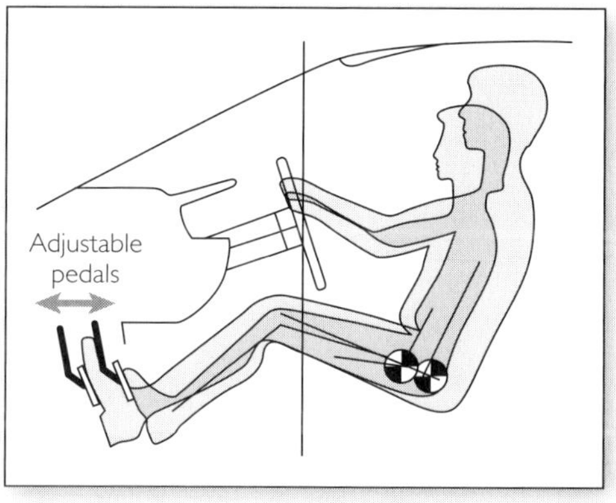

Customer Delight

- "I have always been so afraid of the steering wheel. I feel safe."
- "I feel secure. The brake is there for me."
- "Possibly the most amazing thing invented. I can stay comfortable."
- "I really feel big and in control. The company thought about me."
- "Company is listening to its customers, a company that cares."
- "Would love this feature on my next vehicle. The feature will definitely sell vehicles.

CASE QUESTIONS

1. Describe the process used to estimate the price that Ford thinks the supplier should charge for the additional volume. What data sources are used, and how precise is the associated number?
2. Assume that you are the current supplier of adjustable brake pedals. How would you react to the estimate generated in 1?
3. Comment on the use of the process described in the case as a mechanism to "manage suppliers."

Chapter 9

Grocery Supply Chains

The dollar value of US retail grocery sales was around $585 billion in 2010 ([42]), and food and its distribution play a vital role in an economy. The US grocery supply chain has some unique features. Retail chains control a significant portion of the overall market, with the top 20 retailers accounting for 58% of grocery retail sales in 2003 and sales to the top 20 customers by major food manufacturers reached 69% of total sales in 2003. But with the presence of several chains with stores in most markets, retail price competition is fierce, with net margins around 3.5% of sales. Retail price promotions are rampant, with customers expecting the Thursday inserts to provide details of the price promotions for the upcoming week. The industry introduced over 19,000 new products in the food and beverage category in 2009 ([119]).

9.1 GROCERY SUPPLY CHAIN CONSIDERATIONS

Manufacturers supply to retail chains through distributors or chain warehouses. Direct store delivery by the manufacturer is used for a few items, e.g., cookies, chips, ice cream, sodas, and so on. For most other products, manufacturers ship in bulk to distribution centers where products are combined with other items and shipped to the store. Capacity constraints to consider include store shelf space capacity, delivery truck capacity, store labor available to put products on the shelf, warehouse product handling capacity, and finally manufacturer plant capacity. There are coordination choices, such as increased frequency of store deliveries, that may increase transport costs but can decrease store inventories. Coordination schemes used in the grocery industry include vendor managed inventory at the warehouse, crossdocking, scanner-based promotions, slotting allowances, and category captains. These schemes aim to balance product availability without increasing retail inventories. Competitiveness metrics in this industry include freshness, variety of offerings, price competitiveness, and customized product assembled on site.

9.2 CHAIN

The supply chain in the dry grocery industry consists of the following:

1. **Customers:** These are people who shop primarily at the supermarkets. Their purchase quantities are influenced by store promotions, with the extent of impact of pricing depending on the mix of customers shopping at a store. Typically retail promotions may be accompanied by increased purchases as customers stockpile product to gain a low average price over time. The extent of this promotion activity is dictated by store customer characteristics.

2. **Store Inventories and Planograms:** Stores typically decide the amount of shelf space allocated to each item. This layout of products along aisles is called a *planogram.* Stores maintain similar planograms across locations to get customers to become familiar with their product locations. The store replenishes products subject to minimum order sizes (e.g., cases). Store reorders are filled by the distribution center operated by the store chain or by direct store delivery (DSD) by manufacturers (examples include Keebler for cookies, Frito Lay for chips, and Coke or Pepsi for beverages).
3. **Central Distribution Center (CDC):** The CDC receives orders for products from stores, picks orders, and delivers cases of products to stores. The CDC's goal is to minimize delivery costs and CDC inventories. The CDC chooses the timing of purchases from manufacturers in large quantities (truckloads or railcar loads) to manage inventory costs at the warehouse.
4. **Chain Buyers:** Chain buyers focus on managing purchases from manufacturers. Logistics efficiencies may be gained by coordinating purchases across manufacturers or by adjusting the quantities purchased to take advantage of quantity discounts. Further efficiencies may be gained by committing to steady order quantities from manufacturers. Yet other options include backhaul and picking up product from the manufacturer after delivering to stores to save transport costs.
5. **Manufacturers:** Manufacturers have to produce to supply the chain buyer purchases over time. But manufacturers often provide temporary price cuts or promotions to entice chain buyers to stock up. Their reason is the belief that once stock is pushed to the CDC, stock pressure will incent the retailer to promote the product at the retail store. Fluctuations in the quantities shipped to the CDC are covered either with manufacturer finished goods inventories or by adjusting the delivery lead time.

9.3 CAPACITY

A unique feature in grocery supply chains is the impact of retail prices and wholesale-price changes on associated order volumes. An example often quoted is that 40% of the annual sales for a chicken-noodle-soup manufacturer occurs over a two-week period in January when wholesale prices are dropped by 6%–8%. To accommodate this large increase in wholesale sales, the company has to manage details such as plant, warehouse, and transport capacities. Providing enough capacity to satisfy this demand requires planning to begin in September of the previous year, with the chicken futures markets reacting to this anticipated surge in demand.

Industry estimates suggest that these volume surges create added costs in the form of premium transport costs, increased plant and warehouse capacity, and associated inventory costs. A 1992 study by Information Resources, Inc. (IRI), an industry analysis company, suggests that these costs can be as high as about 5% of sales or an industry-wide cost of $18 billion ([84]).

9.4 COORDINATION

9.4.1 Vendor Managed Inventory

Grocery retailers have to carry store inventory to satisfy retail demand over the supplier lead time to ensure high in stock levels. Thus, retailers have to forecast demand at price levels offered. As discussed in the chapter on coordination, in an uncoordinated supply chain, double marginalization results in a lower retail service level than is optimal for the supply chain as a whole.

Vendor managed inventory (VMI) is a coordinating approach used in the grocery industry. Under VMI, the manufacturer chooses retailer inventory levels. A key feature of VMI is that ownership of the product transfers to the retailer, but decisions regarding replenishment are made by the manufacturer. This scheme, termed *channel alignment* in Lee, et al. ([80]), reduces the number of forecasting steps in the supply chain and thus improves performance and decreases costs. For example, Procter & Gamble (P&G) manages the inventory of its products at Walmart's distribution centers. However, the history of Walmart and P&G wasn't always smooth. In 1985 Sam Walton reportedly called the P&G CEO to inform him that P&G had been awarded their prestigious "Vendor of the Year" award. The call resulted in Sam Walton being transferred five to six times, never reaching the CEO. Since he never reached the P&G CEO, Mr Walton decided to give the award to another vendor ([49]). The follow-up conversations resulted in a transformed relationship, with more frequent data transfers and a VMI relationship between P&G and Walmart. The goods then flowed so quickly through the supply chain that items typically spent eight hours in a Walmart warehouse, were shipped to the retail store within four hours, and were usually sold within twenty-four hours. Other examples include Helene Curtis and Campbell's Soup managing inventories at the distribution center for Chicago retailer Dominick's.

As an example of the impact, analysis of shipment data from Campbell's Soup to a retail chain warehouse showed that after VMI, average lead time decreased from 10.8 days to 3.6 days, and standard deviation of lead time decreased from 3.5 to 2.8 days. Thus, after VMI, on-hand inventory at the warehouse dropped from 3.4 weeks to 1.8 weeks while service levels improved. The reasons for this improvement under VMI included smaller deliveries due to increased delivery frequency and a smaller supplier lead time.

But to make VMI economical, the manufacturer may have to pool deliveries across multiple retailers to optimize costs associated with frequent delivery. In addition, VMI may require the manufacturer to have access to detailed outbound retail shipment information in order to lower manufacturer forecast error and decrease safety stock at the retailer DC required to maintain the desired service level.

9.4.2 Scanner-Based Promotions

Another approach to coordination is scanner-based promotions. Under this approach, the manufacturer announces special discounts for all units sold at the retailer during specific periods. Iyer and Ye ([67]) study manufacturer costs with and without scanner-based promotions. They show that scanner-based promotions increase the predictability of retail sales for the manufacturer. This is because it becomes profitable for the retailer to schedule retail promotions at times when the manufacturer offers these deals. The associated lift in sales happens at predictable periods determined by the manufacturer, thus improving manufacturer forecasts and decreasing retail order forecast error. This retailer coordination permits manufacturer inventories to be better synchronized with projected retail sales, which decreases costs.

9.4.3 Markdown Money

Markdown money refers to payments by manufacturers to retailers to cover shortfalls in the planned increase in sales due to promotions. For example, some large retailers demand that observed sales be at least 85% of planned sales within 45 days of purchase order issued. For example, suppose a retailer purchased 100,000 units to cover anticipated sales, but only 60,000 pieces were sold. Under the 85% agreement, the vendor would need to provide funds to the retailer to get the 85% sell-through. This may happen, for example, by paying \$0.25 per unit for 85,000 – 60,000 = 25,000 units or \$6,250. For subsequent markdowns to clear product, it may be necessary to take an additional 25% of this markdown, i.e., \$6,250 × 25% = \$1,562. Note that markdown money holds the manufacturer responsible for reasonable forecasts by reducing the incentive to push stocks to the retailer.

9.4.4 Collaborative Planning, Forecasting, and Replenishment

Under collaborative planning, forecasting, and replenishment (CPFR), the retailer shares with the manufacturer the logic associated with the order, so as to permit store-level monitoring of stock availability and improved performance. Under CPFR, along with a retailer order, retailers submit both retail orders as well as logic for each order. This logic will explain to the manufacturer the reasons for the order placed. A local store may submit information regarding a promotion offered by a competitor in a particular week or a local store closing. Each of these two factors will cause a different effect on the order. In the first case, there may be a drop in store order, anticipating the demand drop due to the deep discounts offered by the competitor. In the second case, there may be an order increase to fill up the pipeline, i.e., to cover demand over the supplier lead time. Note that knowing this logic for the order enables the manufacturer to interpret the pipeline impact of the order.

Often the difficulty of forecasting demand during a retail promotion may mean that the retailer may order too much or too little. In addition, if the retail pricing information is not communicated to the manufacturer, then a forecasting rule that adjusts orders based on shipments will result in the manufacturer carrying high inventories between retail promotions. Sharing planned retail promotion information decreases these costs and thus improves supply chain profits.

9.4.5 Consignment Inventory

The main difference under consignment inventory is that the manufacturer continues to own the retail consignment inventory until the product is sold to the customer. Thus, consignment inventory is equivalent to the manufacturer purchasing store shelf space and choosing inventory levels to maximize his profits. Coordination is achieved because the supply chain decisions are made by one decision maker. Such an approach is common in the provision of spices; the spice racks in many retail stores are managed by the supplier.

9.4.6 Category Management

Under this approach, the retailer assigns a category manager, usually chosen from among one of the large suppliers, to play the role of a category captain. The category captain is provided access to all point-of-sale data for all of the SKUs in the category and assists the retailer in choosing prices, inventory levels, merchandising, and so on, to maximize profits for the entire category.

A study by Seidmann and Sundarajan ([109]) suggests that with an appropriately designed scheme, category management (CM) can deliver significant benefits to the retailer. Some of the cited benefits include, for example, suggestions by the manufacturer, based on systemwide data, that dropping some SKUs and replacing with others can improve category profits. For example, a study by P&G and Walmart suggested that if Walmart dropped fifty-six SKUs and replaced them with twenty-five others, the retailer and P&G would be better off. Such information regarding the potential benefits of product swapping would be difficult to measure without detailed consumer information of the available with the manufacturer.

There is however, a flip side to CM as described by Steiner ([115]). In many locations, the three leading manufacturers were category captains in over 50% of grocery retail stores and mass merchandiser sectors and in 67% of stores in the drug and convenience store sector. It is thus possible that as power shifts to a few large manufacturers, the benefits of CM efficiency may not be passed on to the consumer. It is this issue that has to be monitored, given the level of data sharing required by CM.

9.5 COMPETITIVENESS

Grocery retailers compete on many possible dimensions including price, freshness, in-stock levels, variety, organic products, and service. Walmart's everyday low price (EDLP) pricing policy is one such strategy. To optimize this metric, inventory and variety have to be chosen to guarantee that indeed the prices in every market are at the lowest level. The store-scanned data have to be tied to the inventory system so that replenishments can be triggered as demand is realized.

An alternate strategy is to compete on uniqueness, a strategy used by Trader Joe's. While other grocery stores carry 25,000 to 40,000 items, Trader Joe's stores carry 1,500 to 2,000 items. However the store also introduces about 50 items each week and carries 80% private-label products as well as products that are offered at lower prices than gourmet shops. The international sourcing of items such as cheeses, wines, and desserts enables the store to offer items that are not found at most other grocery stores. Trader Joe's buyers (which number about fifteen) tour the world and develop small suppliers with unique products. The company also has a unique personnel policy that encourages store employees to directly interact with customers, make recommendations, ask about choices, and so on. This interaction increases the perception of service received at the store. By offering nonstandard items that are not available at most other stores, the retailer avoids direct price comparison in establishing customer value. Historically store locations are in strip malls, and the company does virtually no advertising except for the descriptions in the in-store flyers.

Many stores use price promotions to attract customers. The associated hi-lo pricing strategy relies on the fact that store traffic may be influenced by deals on specific items. Customers who come in to the store to buy items on promotion may also pick up items at regular prices. Since most customers determine the reasonableness of store pricing based on monitoring prices for a subset of items, an important capability for the retailer is to identify that customer segment reference item list and thus price competitively for those products. Note that retail price variation creates associated order variance to the distribution center and thus might generate distribution center inventory increases. Synchronizing warehouse inventories with planned store promotions then becomes a key capability to manage the retail chain's profitability.

While grocery stores may compete on different dimensions, retail competition may also affect store pricing, variety, and inventory levels. Balachander and Farquhar ([3]) suggest that in an equilibrium environment, there may be situations where a store can earn more by stocking less. They show that when customers are willing to search, competing firms may have the incentive to lower product availability in order to lower the pricing pressures and thus increase their respective profits. In other words, firms are, as in Balachander and Farquhar's title, "Gaining More by Stocking Less."

The aggressiveness of private label and national brands in choosing their respective pricing plans can be affected by the nature of customer preferences across products. Banks and Moorthy ([4]) describe a model in which there are two customer segments: a brand-loyal segment with a search cost and a price-sensitive customer segment with no search costs. The branded product thus has to defend its brand by appropriate choice of price promotions. They show that as the search costs for the brand-loyal segment increase, the national brand becomes more aggressive in its promotions. The net effect is that the brand-loyal customers may in fact be paying a higher price on average because getting the lower price requires more search. In other words, competitiveness across products may affect their pricing and thus affect supply chain costs.

If competing stores are located close to each other, this may decrease the search costs for customers and thus increase the need for higher-than-normal service levels. Since any stockouts may well result in loss of the entire shopping basket, it may be optimal to carry higher service levels but at lower profit levels, in other words, a prisoner's dilemma outcome, in which all retailers see reduced profits even though they offer higher service levels.

9.6 GROCERY INDUSTRY STUDIES

A study by A. T. Kearney ([72]) tracked the days of finished goods inventory in the grocery supply chain. Imagine that a unit of product is sold at retail, and the lead time it takes for a fresh unit just manufactured at the plant to make its way to the store is recorded. This would require counting the time in inventory at the store, in transit from retail warehouse to store, at the retail warehouse, in transit between the manufacturer warehouse and the retail warehouse, and at the manufacturer warehouse. The estimated values of the days of inventory at each of these locations were twenty-four days at the store, eighteen days at the retail warehouse, six days in transit between the manufacturer and retail warehouse, and thirty-six days at the manufacturer warehouse. The total of days of inventory was thus estimated to be eighty-four days.

What is the industry supply chain cost associated with these days of finished goods inventory? One study suggested that the cost of this inventory is 5% of industry sales. This cost reflects additional investments in property plant and equipment, warehouse capacity and material handling, financing charges for inventories, and additional costs for premium transportation.

A Coca-Cola study entitled "New Ways to Take Costs out of the Retail Food Pipeline" ([21]) suggested using a supply chain perspective to reduce costs and improve performance. The efficient consumer response (ECR) movement was fostered by the Food Manufacturing Institute (FMI) and Grocery Manufacturers of America (GMA). It involved coordination between manufacturers, distributors, and retailers to increase in stock levels of product and product variety without increasing inventory levels. The approach focused on information sharing, joint forecasting, reduced price variation or at least synchronizing retail or wholesale pricing changes with associated inventory positioning, and so on. A corresponding movement in Europe has evolved an industry academic partnership and the *ECR Journal / International Commerce Review,* which features industry and academic articles focused on the grocery industry.

9.7 TRADE PROMOTIONS AND THEIR EFFECT

The grocery industry is famous for the use of temporary price cuts as a mechanism to stimulate sales. The price cuts, also called *trade promotions* or *deals,* encourage large-volume purchases by distributors and retailers and thus permit the manufacturer to push product downstream. Note that pushing product downstream creates "stock pressure" at the distributor or retailer, thus providing them the incentive to lower retail prices and "push" the product to the consumer. Inventory at the consumer's home increases the propensity to consume this item. In short, the grocery supply chain uses product inventory to stimulate product movement downstream and thus (potentially) product consumption.

To understand such pressures, consider the relationship between a retailer and a manufacturer in a supply chain. Assuming that the retailer's warehouse supplies many stores, the demand at the warehouse can be considered to be relatively stable, with a constant rate of D units per unit time. Given an ordering cost and a holding cost at the retailer, it is optimal for the retailer's order sizes to follow the economic order quantity to minimize retailer ordering and holding costs.

Consider the impact of the manufacturer offering a temporary price cut by decreasing the wholesale price by a factor of δ so that the offered price is δc. The retailer now has to decide the quantity Q_d to buy at this discounted price. The tradeoff is the lower cost of goods sold vs the increased inventory costs. Details of this section are from the model in [127].

List of Symbols
K = ordering cost for the retailer per order
c = wholesale price per unit (nonpromotion periods)
h_r = holding cost per day = ic (the product of the annual financing rate and product cost)
D = demand rate per day

In the absence of any trade promotion, the retailer would order the economic order quantity Q as follows:

$$Q = \sqrt{\frac{2KD}{h_r}}$$

Suppose the manufacturer offers a trade promotion, i.e., price reduction, of $(1 - \delta) \times 100\%$ every T periods (where $T > \frac{Q}{d}$). Thus, we have

δ = trade discount factor, i.e., cost during the deal = δc

If a trade deal is offered every T periods, how much should this retailer buy?

If Q_d is the amount the retailer buys during a promotion, then the retailer's inventory cost over T days is as follows:

Inventory and ordering costs are

$$K + \frac{\delta h_r Q_d^2}{2D} + \left\{\left(T - \frac{Q_d}{D}\right)\sqrt{2Kh_r D}\right\}$$

The total product cost during T periods is

$$\delta c Q_d + \{c(DT - Q_d)\}$$

Therefore the combined cost over the T periods is the sum of the inventory, ordering, and product costs. If this cost is minimized, the retailer purchases the following quantity:

$$Q_d = \frac{Q}{\delta} + \frac{(1-\delta)Dc}{\delta h_r}$$

Of course, if this quantity is greater than DT, the retailer will purchase DT.

What does this model suggest? First, if $\delta = 1$, then it is optimal to purchase the economic order quantity. In other words, increased purchases are only due to the manufacturer price discount. Next, the model suggests that the magnitude of the discount matters, i.e., Q_d increases as δ decreases, increasing proportional to $\frac{1}{\delta}$. This again is intuitive because as δ decreases, the reduced product cost justifies carrying more inventory to decrease overall retailer costs. The model also suggests that the retailer holding cost vs. product cost matters in determining the response to a given manufacturer price reduction. This reflects the trade-off in decreased product cost vs. increased inventory cost required to avail of the promotion.

The following example provides the details of the calculations and shows how some price cuts by the manufacturer can result in large orders by the retailer while decreasing retailer total costs. The purpose of this example is to show that since manufacturer price cuts and the corresponding inventory effects decrease retailer costs, any changes to this system will require more than just eliminating trade promotions. In addition, the example shows why high inventories might be common in the grocery supply chain as long as trade promotions continue to exist in the industry.

Example: Consider a retail warehouse that faces a weekly demand of $D = 100$ cases per week and is in operation 5 days per week. Assume that the retail holding cost is $h_r = 0.02$ per day per case, wholesale price is $c = \$20$ per case, and the retailer ordering cost is $K = \$80$ per order. The economic order quantity would be the order size and would be

$$Q = \sqrt{\frac{2 \times 80 \times 100/5}{0.02}}$$

$Q = 400$ cases

Now suppose the manufacturer were to offer a trade promotion of $\delta = 0.90$ (i.e., 10% off during the promotion), how much should the retailer buy? From the description earlier, we calculate the quantity Q_d purchased during the promotion as

$$Q_d = \frac{400}{0.9} + \frac{0.1 \times 20 \times 20}{0.9 \times 0.02}$$

$Q_d = 2{,}667$ cases

Thus, if the trade promotion is run every 26 weeks, the optimal retailer purchase quantity is 26 weeks of demand or 2,600 units. For this example, if the manufacturer promotes twice a year, the retailer will only buy during promotions. This will cause a sizeable inventory level increase for the retailer with the order quantity increasing from 4 weeks of inventory to 26 weeks of inventory and the average weeks of inventory increasing from 2 weeks to 13 weeks.

What is the difference in the retailer's total costs in the old system and during the promotion? Using the models presented earlier and the parameters for the example problem, we get the following results.

No Promotion System	*Promotion System*
Cost per unit time = \$408/day	Cost per unit time = \$384.01/day
Cost of product = \$400/day	Cost of product = \$360/day
Cost of ordering and holding = \$8/day	Cost of ordering and holding = \$24.01/day

Notice that the total cost per unit time, consisting of product cost and ordering and holding costs for the retailer, decreased from \$408 per day to \$394.01 per day. This reduced cost is a key driver to the retailer's preference for trade promotions. However, mere analysis of inventory levels will show an average of 13 weeks of inventory at the retailer rather than 2 weeks of inventory as suggested by an economic order quantity. A key takeaway is that in order to understand inventory levels it is necessary, in this industry, to understand manufacturer pricing. It also suggests that any attempts to decrease inventory have to be associated with pricing changes by the manufacturer.

How has the industry responded? There have been two types of industry responses. One approach, typified by Procter & Gamble's approach, is to switch to a lower price for all retailers but to use other means (other than price promotions) to stimulate sales. The other approach, typified by Campbell's Soup and Barilla, is to permit two pricing plans—the original trade promotions or a lower annual price in return for vendor managed inventory. The second approach lets the pace of adoption of manufacturer pricing reflect retailer market conditions. A Harvard case, Barilla Group, provides examples of the impact of a "customers choose" model. The case describes one distributor who chooses to move to VMI and the other who sticks to hi-lo. The impact is intense price competition during the period of trade promotions, increased stocking of competitor products, inability to forward buy in anticipation of price increases, and so on.

9.8 PROMOTIONS BY THE RETAILER

The retailer has to deal with various customer segments with different reactions to a promotion. Some customers may stockpile while others may not. The retailer can thus use a retail promotion to move product from retailer warehouse to the customer location depending on the customer segment's propensity to stockpile.

Assume that there are two customer segments with different holding costs that represent the retailer demand base. Customers with high holding costs continue to buy as needed and are unaffected by retail promotions. Customers with low holding costs h_L and stock up according to depth of the promotion. Suppose these customers constitute $\alpha\%$ of the total demand rate. Let total demand rate per day be D. Customers who are willing to carry the product will thus buy during a promotion and carry the product. The model described in this section is from [128].

How can the retailer characterize customer segments based on their propensity to stockpile? An empirical study by Iyer and Ye ([67]) takes data regarding retail sales of soup and provides results of a fitted model. Details of this model are provided in Section 9.9, but the key idea is that the characterization of customer segments, their size and propensity to stockpile, can come from a statistically fitted model to data.

Suppose the retailer were to buy from the manufacturer every k days. Dropping the retail price by \$$x$, will cause the low-holding-cost customers to do a break-even analysis and thus buy $\frac{\alpha x D}{h_L}$ units and stock up. This decreases the retailer's holding costs as long as $h_L < h_r$. Suppose we offer a discount so that the low-holding-cost customers buy for k days, i.e., $x = kh_L$. Then total retailer costs over k days will thus be

$$K + (x\alpha kD) + (x(1-\alpha)D) + \frac{h_r Dk^2(1-\alpha)}{2}$$

Any set of parameters that decrease retailer costs will provide an incentive for the retailer to promote at retail. Notice that this retail promotion model can permit the retailer to benefit from both customer segments. The low-holding-cost segment will assist in decreasing retailer costs by reducing retailer holding costs from h_r in return for a retail promotion, which will reflect customer holding costs of h_L. The high-holding-cost segment will be willing to pay regular price in return for the retailer holding the inventory. Thus the retailer has the potential to benefit from both customer segments.

Additional details that could be incorporated (and that are in the papers by Iyer and Ye [66],[67]) adjust for the reservation price differences between the two segments. The following example illustrates the calculations.

Example

Suppose the retailer has parameters K = \$80, α = 0.6, D = 100 cases per week, 5 days per week, h_r = \$0.02/case/day. Suppose the retailer buys once every 20 days. If the low-holding-cost customers have h_L = 0.009/case/day, then dropping the retailer price by x = \$0.18/case for 1 day would cause the retailer costs over 20 days to be

$$\begin{aligned} &80 + (0.18 \times 0.6 \times 20 \times 20) + (0.18 \times 0.4 \times 20) \\ &+ (0.02 \times 20 \times 20 \times 20 \times 0.4/2) \\ &= \$156.64 \end{aligned}$$

This is in contrast to the costs without this retail promotion:

$$\begin{aligned} &8 \times 20 \\ &= \$160 \end{aligned}$$

The impact of this promotion is to decrease retailer costs. Note that we showed that dropping the retail price to synchronize with purchases from the manufacturer permits the retailer to flow through part of the purchases so that inventory levels are decreased. In effect, inventory moves from the manufacturer and through the retailer to the low-holding-cost customer.

Why might customers have lower holding cost than retailers? One reason is that customers do not treat their extra space in the home (basements, cabinets, pantry space, and so on) as having commercial value and thus do not incorporate the opportunity cost of that space. Another reason is that customers may not be reflecting the cost of money correctly. Empirical data suggests that customers with low reservation prices do tend to have lower holding costs thus suggesting that they understand the need for the retailer to segment customers through pricing differences.

9.9 APPLYING THE STOCKPILING MODEL TO EMPIRICAL DATA

This section provides details from [67] that illustrate fitting the model described in the previous section to an empirical dataset from 60 stores. Consider a retail environment where customers arriving at a store belong to one of three possible segments, $s = 1, 2, 3$. The three segments have the following characteristics:

1. Segment 1 makes purchases every period to satisfy consumption of exactly one period.
2. Segment 2 does not purchase at the high price level.
3. Segment 3 does not purchase unless the retail price is low, i.e., lower than the average between the highest and the lowest price.

The model was applied to a data set consisting of sales of canned tomato soup over a two-year period for each of 60 stores. The average R^2 across the 60 stores was 76%, suggesting that the customer model was a reasonable representation of the observed sales. In addition, the forecast error (σ) associated with the fitted model parameters could be estimated and included in the description of customer demand. Furthermore, there was a very high positive correlation (around 0.99) between segment reservation prices and their holding costs. This suggested that customer segments willing to pay low prices also seem to be ready to stockpile, as evidenced by their low holding costs.

Table 9.1 provides the values of holding costs, reservation prices, and consumption rates for two stores with different characteristics.

TABLE 9.1 Fitted parameters for two sample stores

PARAMETER	STORE 1			STORE 2		
	Segment 1	Segment 2	Segment 3	Segment 1	Segment 2	Segment 3
r_s	1.511	0.5	0.35	1.511	0.5321	0.346
h_s	0.7555	0.05	0.0056	0.7555	0.0337	0.048
c_s	503.3	416.3	375.2	88.8	114.3	672.0

The parameter values for the two stores illustrate the different customer environments faced by these stores. While store 1 has a composition across segments of 39%, 32%, and 29%, store 2 has a composition across segments of 10%, 13%, and 77%. Thus we would expect a greater extent of promotions from store 2 than from store 1 due to the much larger size of segment 3 for store 2. Note that the holding cost of segment 3 customers for store 2 is larger than that for store 1. For example, a retail price of \$0.28 would generate a demand from segment 3 in store 1 of 4,690 units. This value is obtained as $\left[\frac{(0.346-0.28)}{0.048}\right]375.2 = 4{,}690$, following the definition in the earlier section. The same retail price of \$0.28 would generate a demand from segment 3 in store 2 of 924 units. This value is obtained as $\left[\frac{(0.346-0.28)}{0.048}\right]672 = 924$. Thus the size and depth of promotions that are profit maximizing depend on these customer characteristics. Finally, we note that the model forecast error for store 1 is $\sigma_1 = 0.24$. For store 2, the model forecast error is $\sigma_2 = 0.4$. This difference in model forecast error will affect the store inventory level required to provide the desired customer service level for a given store price. The holding cost associated with the safety stock at the stores impacts the choice of the optimal store prices.

As mentioned earlier, the R^2 values ranged from 53% to 87% with an average R^2 level of 76% across the 60 stores. It is clear that the product category (canned soup) affects these parameter levels. For example, we expect the values for customer holding cost to be larger for bulkier products (such as toilet paper) than for canned soup. Similarly we might expect the customer holding cost to be larger for expensive but small-volume products such as analgesics.

9.10 CHAPTER SUMMARY

A key driver of supply chain costs in grocery supply chains is the volatility in demand created by price promotions. However, price promotions enable multiple market segments to be served and do play an effective role in this industry. The chain structure of grocery supply chains offers multiple supply locations—from manufacturer plants, to field warehouses, to distributors and cooperatives, to direct store delivery. Capacity in this chain deals with store physical shelf capacity, truck capacity, warehouse capacity, and plant manufacturing capacity. Order lead time is impacted by the interaction between orders and capacity. Often, volatility of demand and lack of synchronization with production implies high levels of inventory across the supply chain. Coordination in grocery supply chains arises through vendor managed inventory initiatives, where manufacturers manage distributor inventory, better synchronization of promotions and production, collaborative forecasting, and so on. Competitive pressures in the grocery industry demand that retailers compete on attributes such as product variety, freshness, service level, promotions, and so on. Given such pressures, effective supply chain management generates a key source of competitive advantage.

With food being an important ingredient of most economies, grocery supply chains typically involve significant volumes of products flowing to match daily purchase and consumption. Grocery supply chains are typically fragmented and involve a large number of SKUs, relative to varied consumer tastes and price points. The competitive nature of the industry generates low net margins at retail and a tremendous focus on cost reduction. Supply chain coordination approaches such as vendor managed inventory, category management, scanner-based promotions, and the like are all focused on improving cost performance. Store shelf capacity and warehouse and delivery capacity coupled with manufacturer and retailer price promotions drive large levels of inventory in the supply chain. The industry has innovated with a tremendous focus on information-based coordination and use of radio frequency identification (RFID) devices, for example, to improve supply chain performance in this industry. National and store brands compete to capture the customer sales dollars and influence consumer inventory so as to influence consumption.

9.11 PROBLEMS

1. The Breeze grocery store sells canned organic peaches. Breeze purchases these peaches from Orgo, an organic fruit distributor, at a wholesale price of \$10 per case. This wholesale price includes delivery to Breeze's location. Breeze estimates an annual holding cost of 2% of product cost. Analysis of purchasing transactions suggests that Breeze incurs an ordering cost of \$100 per order placed with Orgo.

Breeze faces a retail demand of 100 cases per week. Assume 50 weeks per year.

1a. Provide the optimal order quantity that Breeze should order to minimize ordering and holding costs. Provide the associated ordering and holding cost per week and the product cost per week.

1b. Orgo has decided to offer a trade promotion of 4% off the wholesale price, once every 13 weeks. Given this trade promotion, Breeze wants to decide the quantity to order to minimize product costs, and ordering and holding costs.

Provide the optimal order quantity, the associated product, ordering, and holding cost per week under this system.

1c. Breeze's retail manager analyzes his retail customer base and finds that 70% of the customers can be estimated to have low holding costs, and 30% have the high holding costs. The low-holding-cost customers are estimated to have a holding cost of \$0.005 per case per week. The regular retail price is \$15 per case.

Suppose Breeze wants to run a retail promotion to get the low-holding-cost customers to buy all their requirements over the size of the wholesale promotion purchase immediately. How deeply should Breeze decrease the retail price? What will be the impact on Breeze's ordering and holding, and discount costs per week? Will Breeze benefit from running such a promotion? Explain.

1d. Orgo and Breeze are considering an alternate scheme whereby Orgo drops its price for the product by 4% throughout the year and runs no wholesale promotions. If such a choice were made, how would it affect Breeze's ordering and holding, and product cost per week? Will they be lower than the costs in 1b? Explain.

2. Fresh is a supermarket chain that offers low-cost organic foods. One of their top sellers is a line of canned organic fruit, supplied by Best fruit company. Weekly retail demand for the product is 100 cases. The holding cost incurred by Fresh is an annual rate of 25% of product cost. The regular cost per case from Best is $50 per case. Ordering cost is $1,250 per order.

2a. How many cases should Fresh order, and how frequently should the orders be placed to minimize Fresh's ordering and holding costs? What are the ordering and holding costs?

2b. Given that Fresh orders as per the decision in 2a, assume that the retail store has two customer segments. The low-holding-cost customer segment has a holding cost of $0.025 per unit per week. This segment comprises 70% of the overall weekly retail demand at Fresh. Suppose Fresh wanted to offer a retail promotion to sell the entire requirements of low-holding customers over the order interval. This promotion would be synchronized with purchases in 2a so that purchases from Best could be crossdocked to retail stores to support the promotion.

What should be the promotion price that should be offered at Fresh's retail stores? What would be the impact of this promotion on Fresh's costs? Do these promotions enable Fresh to benefit from both the low- and the high-holding-cost customers? Explain.

2c. Best has decided to offer a manufacturer promotion. This promotion involves reducing the wholesale price by 12.5% once every 50 weeks. Given this promotion by Best, how much should Fresh purchase at the promotion price? How much should Fresh purchase at the regular price during the 50 weeks? Provide Fresh's ordering and holding costs per week given this promotion.

2d. Given the purchases in 2c, under Best's promotion, suppose Fresh wanted to offer a retail promotion to sell the entire requirements of low holding customers over the order interval. This promotion would be synchronized with purchases in 2c so that purchases from Best could be crossdocked to retail stores to support the promotion. Note that if there are two purchases by Fresh (from Best), there would be two separate retail promotions.

What promotion should Fresh's retail stores offer over the 50 weeks? What would be the impact of this promotion on Fresh's costs? Do these promotions enable Fresh to benefit from both the low- and the high-holding-cost customers? Explain.

3. The Organic market is a chain with a buyer who get canned fruit from a supplier, Fruita. The canned fruit has a long shelf life (more than one year). Currently the ordering and delivery cost is $500. The 100-case demand per day is constant throughout the chain. Each case has a wholesale price, i.e., paid by the buyer to Fruita, of $182.50. Organic's buyer uses an annual holding cost rate of 20%. (Assume 312 days a year, i.e., 52 weeks and 6 days a week of operation).

3a. How much should Organic's buyer get each time he makes a purchase from Fruita? What is the associated daily cost of the product for Organic? What is the Organic's daily ordering and holding cost associated with this decision?

3b. The supplier, Fruita, has decided to run a trade promotion that occurs two times a year in equally spaced intervals i.e., this promotion runs once every 156 working days. During this promotion, Fruita drops the wholesale price by 3%.

The buyer at Organic always stocks up during the promotion and buys the entire 156 days of supply during this promotion. Given this decision, what is the associated daily cost of product and the associated daily ordering and holding costs that Organic experiences?

Is the total cost higher or lower than that in 3a? Explain.

3c. A consultant hired by Organic suggests that buying the entire 156 days of supply is not optimal for Organic given the 3% trade discount. How much do you think Organic should buy during a promotion? What are the associated average daily cost of the product and the associated daily ordering and holding cost of the product that Organic would experience?

Is the total cost higher or lower than that in 3a? Explain.

3d. Assume that the buyer makes the ordering decision that you suggest in 3c. The retail merchandiser at Organic has observed that his retail store has two market segments. One of these segments buys at a constant rate each day and constitutes 70% of the demand rate. The remaining segment has a daily holding cost of $0.05 per case per day.

If the merchandiser wanted to get the customers with lower holding costs to purchase their entire demand over the promotion period synchronized with the manufacturer promotion, how much should retail price be dropped for each case? What will be the associated retail ordering, holding, and price-cut related costs? Will this cost be lower than the associated costs in 3c? Explain.

4. The BestFoods market is a chain with a buyer who purchases canned fruit from a supplier, Fruita. The canned fruit has a long shelf life (more than one year). Currently the ordering and delivery cost is $200. The 200-case demand per day is constant throughout the chain. Each case has a wholesale price, i.e., paid by the buyer to Fruita, of $100. BestFoods's buyer uses an annual holding cost rate of 25%. (Assume 312 days a year, i.e., 52 weeks and 6 days a week of operation).

4a. How much should BestFoods's buyer purchase each time he places an order from Fruita? What is the associated daily cost of the product for BestFoods? What is the BestFoods daily ordering and holding cost associated with this decision?

4b. The supplier, Fruita, has decided to run a trade promotion that runs once every 156 working days. During this promotion, Fruita drops the wholesale price by 5%.

The buyer at BestFoods always purchases the entire 156 days of supply during this promotion. Given this decision, what is the associated daily cost of product and the associated daily ordering and holding costs that BestFoods experiences?

Is the total cost higher or lower than that in 4a? Explain.

4c. A consultant hired by BestFoods suggests that buying the entire 156 days of supply is not optimal for BestFoods given the 5% trade discount. How much should BestFoods buy during a promotion? What is the associated average daily cost of the product and the associated daily ordering and holding cost of the product that BestFoods would experience?

Is the total cost higher or lower than that in 4a? Explain.

4d. For this question, assume that the buyer makes the ordering decision that you suggest in 4c. The retail merchandiser at BestFoods has observed that his retail store has two market segments. One of these segments buys at a constant rate each day and constitutes 30% of the demand rate. The remaining segment has a daily holding cost of $0.05 per case per day.

If the merchandiser wanted to get this lower-holding-cost segment to buy some of their demand of the product purchased during the manufacturer promotion to synchronize with the promotion, how much should retail price be dropped for each case? What will be the associated retail ordering, holding, and price-cut related costs? Will this cost be lower than the associated costs in 4c? Explain.

5. Green is a grocery store that purchases canned fruit from Deal, a manufacturer. In the current system, ordering cost is $100, holding cost annually is 20% of cost, wholesale price is $20 per case, and annual demand is for 5,000 cases. (Assume 50 weeks per year and 5 days per week of operation.)

5a. What should be Green's optimal purchase quantity, and what is the associated cost of goods sold and holding and ordering cost per week for Green?

5b. Deal has decided to run a trade promotion once every 20 weeks. The promotion will offer product at 96.22% of the regular wholesale price of $20 per case, i.e., at a price of $19.25 per case. This promotion will be offered once every 20 weeks.

Given this promotion, how many units should Green buy? Provide the associated average cost of goods sold per week and the average ordering and holding cost per week associated with this policy.

5c. Given the purchases under 5b, Green would like to create a retail promotion so all low-holding-cost customers synchronize their purchase with Green's wholesale purchases. The low-holding-cost customers correspond to 40% of the market and have a holding cost of $0.01 per case per day. All other parameters are as provided earlier. Provide the retail prices Green should use and the associated average ordering and holding cost associated with this scheme.

5d. Deal has agreed to an everyday-low-price policy where Green gets to pay the weighted average price per case across the purchases in 5b. What will be that wholesale price that maintains cost of goods sold for Green? Given that price, what is Green's optimal order quantity? What are the associated average cost of goods sold, and the ordering and holding costs for Green?

6. Quick is a grocery store known for its ability to manage logistics effectively. One of the products Quick sells is a dry pasta produced by Barist. A case of pasta is sold by Barist to Quick for $30 per case. Quick estimates an annual holding cost that is 20% of wholesale price. Ordering cost by Quick is estimated to be $200 per order placed. Assume 300 days per year of operation, 50 weeks per year, and 6 days per week of operation.

Quick charges a retail price that is $40 per case. Retail demand at this price is 200 cases per day.

6a. Provide an economic order quantity that Quick should use to place orders, the associated ordering, holding, and product costs per day, and the associated average inventory carried by Quick and associated annual inventory turns.

6b. Barist offers a quantity discount to Quick: if order size exceeds 5,000 cases, then Quick can get the product at $25 per case. What should be the order size by Barist to minimize ordering, holding, and product costs per day? Provide the associated ordering, holding, and product costs per day, and the associated average inventory carried by Quick and associated annual inventory turns.

6c. Barist has identified that its retail customer base consists of 60% low-holding-cost customers, whose holding cost per day is $0.005 per case per day. The remaining 40% consists of high-holding-cost customers who do not stock up during a promotion. Assume that Barist has purchased the quantity in 6b and availed of a quantity discount.

Identify the retail promotion price cut that will get the low-holding-cost customers to purchase their entire requirements between successive purchases by Quick (from Barist). Identify Quick's costs per day under the retail promotion and compare it to the costs without a retail promotion.

Does the retail promotion increase profitability from both segments? Explain.

7. The RightFoods store normally buys cases of canned fruit from a local supplier A. Ordering cost from supplier A is $20. The cost per case is $100. The cases are sold for $125. The holding cost per year is 16% of product cost. Assume that annual demand is for 4,000 cases. Assume 50 weeks per year and 5 days per week of operation.

7a. Provide the optimal order size that RightFoods should place with supplier A. Provide the associated ordering and holding costs per year and the associated annual product cost.

7b. Another supplier, B, offers to supply RightFoods. Supplier B is located far away and thus causes an ordering (and transport) cost of $2,000. However supplier B offers a promotion of 10% off the usual cost of $100 per case every 26 weeks. Provide the optimal order size for RightFoods. Provide the associated ordering and holding costs per year and the associated annual product cost. Should RightFoods buy the product from supplier B instead of from supplier A? Explain.

7c. A consultant has analyzed customers who shop at RightFoods and estimates that 70% of the demand is from customers with a low daily holding cost of $0.02 per case per day. The remaining is from high holding cost customers who do not respond to price promotions. This consultant recommends buying from supplier B and running a retail promotion at the same time to sell all of the demand from the low-holding-cost customer over the promotion purchase. Provide the impact of this strategy on RightFoods's ordering, holding, and promotion cost. Does this retail promotion improve profitability for RightFoods? Explain why or why not.

8. Grocer is a store with an excellent buying staff at the warehouse. Grocer carries a unique canned tomato product, made with genuine Roma tomatoes and subject to a special processing operation. Demand for the canned tomato product is 50 cans per day, and the store is open seven days a week. The tomatoes are supplied by a producer who charges a wholesale price of $0.50 per can. Ordering cost is $50 per order but includes delivery to Grocer's warehouse.

Grocer is charged a cost of capital of 25% per year, and the goods incur a storage cost of 15% per year. Assume 364 days per year. The product is sold at retail at $0.60 per can.

8a. How many cans should Grocer order each time an order is placed? What are the associated average product, ordering, and holding costs per day for Grocer?

8b. The manufacturer offers products at a temporary price of $0.40 per can once every six months. Grocer's buyers currently buy three months of demand during this promotion. They would like your help in determining if they should buy all of their demand for six months during this trade promotion. Analyze the optimal purchase quantity during promotion and the associated product, ordering, and holding costs per day under this promotion purchase.

8c. Grocer's merchandising team has analyzed the customer base that shops at the store and concluded that 60% of the customers behave as if their daily holding cost is $0.0002 per unit per day. The remaining 40% purchase only what they need and do not stockpile. Should Grocer run a retail promotion to get the low-holding-cost customers to buy their entire demand over a promotion cycle? What should the retail promotion price be? What will be the impact on Grocer's total costs with the promotion? Do Grocer's costs decrease as a result of this promotion? If so, by how much?

8d. Grocer's management team is concerned about the high levels of inventories and worries about the customer getting used to low price points. What ideas might Grocer discuss with the manufacturer to lower supply chain costs?

9. A retail grocery store, Perfect, currently purchases canned soup from a supplier. The cost of a case of soup is $12. This soup is sold at retail for $15 per case. The carrying cost of inventory is assumed to be an annual rate of 30%. Demand at retail for soup is 250 cases per week (52 weeks per year).

EXHIBIT 1 The old system and data

Week #	Last Year/DC to Store	Last Year/CSC to DC
1	14851	11031
2	24620	16841
3	14297	19151
4	12961	16574
5	12504	8949
6	13280	34443
7	19242	10569
8	11735	13280
9	0	0
10	14895	14334
11	14409	18099
12	14139	12783
13	13927	15256
14	17108	17636
15	15549	18879
16	14843	23983
17	18959	26426
18	15047	38464
19	16310	57183
20	20345	36840
21	22996	21451
22	38454	32366
23	24164	27804
24	19991	21667
25	22117	42251
26	25221	38958
27	26694	13739
28	30221	29310
29	26771	24199
30	18632	23146
31	20764	7068
32	27812	38224
Mean	18839.3125	22840.75
Stdev	7041.21046	12203.69672
Coefficient of variation	0.373750924	0.534294921

EXHIBIT 2 The CPR system and data

Week #	This Year/DC to Store	This Year/CSC to DC	SKUs
1	17129	10366	209
2	16296	9225	209
3	17438	18129	211
4	21047	26632	214
5	22139	24035	214
6	13512	23146	213
7	14411	17744	210
8	16613	9775	210
9	14403	30343	210
10	15001	10755	209
11	16872	13106	209
12	15284	17065	219
13	21587	11622	219
14	24802	20905	219
15	21307	31526	219
16	22343	12224	226
17	23192	28706	230
18	31232	39258	231
19	21031	23671	230
20	22964	38127	231
21	39300	50493	226
22	29916	76487	226
23	29838	36723	225
24	27742	31372	225
25	31934	23399	225
26	16541	18429	222
27	24875	25913	225
28	23710	20305	222
29	30243	23051	224
30	15763	16421	224
31	18432	11722	224
32	38568	43679	224
Mean	22358.28125	24823.5625	
Stdev	6951.216947	14118.5371	

CASE QUESTIONS

1. From the data and the lead time in the old system, generate a base stock level for the warehouse and evaluate the average inventory in the warehouse.
2. From the data for the new system and the lead time under the new system, generate a base stock level for the warehouse and evaluate the average inventory in the warehouse.
3. How should Nick present his observations at the CSCMP conference?

Prince and Grocery Coordination

PRINCE FOODS

Bill Walker, VP of supply chain management at Prince Foods, was a veteran in the food distribution industry. His 20 years of experience included incorporating several best-practice ideas at Prince Foods. Core carrier programs, flexible delivery to stores, quick response reshipping—each of these resulted in Prince Foods playing a pioneering role in the industry. It was thus natural that he would be responsible for efficient consumer response (ECR) initiatives at Prince Foods.

ECR had been the result of several studies of the US grocery supply chains that recorded between 80 and 110 days of finished-goods inventory with a cost consequence that was estimated to be 5% of industry sales. For a $500 billion dollar industry with net margins between 0.5% and 1.5%, this potential inefficiency represented a tremendous opportunity. How could Prince Foods incorporate ECR ideas and generate measurable savings?

BACKGROUND

Prince Foods owned a single warehouse that supplied over 100 of its retail stores. The chain had a reputation for freshness and believed in the concept of rolling stock as a way to minimize logistics costs. But private label cookies were becoming a problem. National brands like Nabisco and Keebler had started offering increasingly more sophisticated ECR programs that had made them price competitive while providing superior perceived value to the customer.

Bill Walker was determined to decrease the supply chain cost of private label cookies for Prince. The Prince-label cookies were made by Best Cookies, a local manufacturer situated not far from the Prince warehouse. Best Cookies operated a make-to-order system in order to ship fresh product to retailers. Because private-label cookie prices have to be coordinated with national-brand products, demand faced by the warehouse fluctuates significantly. Bill had complained about lead times to Best Cookies, and in turn Best Cookies complained about the unpredictable order streams from Prince Foods. Past attempts at developing quid pro quo agreements had yielded no results. Bill was determined to understand the cause of the problem. His past experience suggested that use of actual data streams from the system often permitted managers to understand the true issues. Examination of transactional data was the way to focus on specific decisions and outcomes in the system.

TRANSACTIONAL DATA

Bill focused attention on the twenty-three SKUs that constituted most of the product line for private-label cookies. To permit efficient manufacturing and shipping and synchronize with existing equipment, orders to Best Cookies were restricted to full pallet loads. The twenty-three products ordered each had different pallet configurations based on the ingredients, cookie shape, and packaging. The first row of Table 9.2 provides the item number for each of the twenty-three SKUs. The actual SKU number is 530,000 plus the number in the first row.

In addition, to optimize transportation from Best Cookies to Prince, multiple SKUs were included in each purchase order to create order handling efficiency. Table 9.2 also provides the composition of purchase orders placed during a period. Each row provides the date the purchase order was sent to Best Cookies, the date the order was delivered back to Prince Foods, and the quantity of each SKU included in the order.

Table 9.3 provides the starting inventory for each SKU on December 1. This starting inventory provides the inventory level before demands and before any purchase orders were placed or received. Table 9.4 provides the weekly shipments of each SKU to the retail stores. While Prince Foods shipped daily to individual stores, the recorded data accumulated all shipments and captured weekly outflow to stores.

ANALYSIS

Bill wanted to come up with a stabilizing set of orders that would permit Best Cookies to plan for capacity and thus decrease lead time while at the same time allowing Prince Foods to decrease its warehouse inventory. He knew that he would have to pull together all the inflows of deliveries with the outflows of demand to generate an inventory picture at the SKU level. He was also curious about the ordering pattern used by the buyer and wanted to understand the logic associated with the order. Finally he was curious if the demands for SKUs had a pattern that could be planned for in advance.

He developed the following tasks to assist in the analysis:

(a) Understand the inventory level variation and the inventory turns by SKU

(b) Understand the ordering policy used at the SKU level and its link to pallet sizes and joint replenishment

(c) Understand the delivery lead times for purchase orders and potential links to order compositions in turns of volume ordered, SKUs ordered, etc.

(d) Understand if there is a base volume that can be ordered for each SKU

(e) Explore agreements that can be signed with Best Cookies that might permit lead-time reduction (either mean or variance or both) as well as inventory-level reduction

TABLE 9.2

PO #	ORDER DATE	Delivery Date	Total Cases	Item # (add 530000 to get actual number)																						
				519	493	501	97	311	279	261	782	667	634	808	89	170	295	303	329	360	444	204	6	212	238	220
477253	12/1/2011	12/16/11	767			112				40			105								240	112	50	72	36	
477680	12/2/2011	12/19/11	792		56		100					162	70								210		50		72	72
478331	12/5/2011	12/19/11	822					40	80	200					150								100	72	108	72
478332	12/5/2011	12/20/11	711	56	56			80					105	84							330					
479363	12/7/2011	12/22/11	771		56	112				40		108	35								240			108		72
480242	12/8/2011	12/11/11	804				150								100								50	252	72	180
480244	12/8/2011	12/23/11	849	112	112						108	162	175								180					
480243	12/8/2011	12/23/11	694					80	80	120											270				144	
481542	12/12/2011	12/28/11	742				100	120		120											150			108	72	72
481543	12/12/2011	12/28/11	791		56	168						108	105	84							270					
482685	12/14/2011	01/03/12	812	112	56					40	54		70		100						180	56		36	72	36
484313	12/16/2011	12/22/11	600																		600					
483849	12/16/2011	12/29/11	774						40	80		54	70	126		84					270					
484431	12/19/2011	01/05/12	891	112	56			120			54	216	105	168							60					
484430	12/19/2011	01/05/12	674					40	80	40					100	126								108	36	144
486137	12/22/2011	01/09/12	887	112	112			120		120		108	105	126		84										
486880	12/23/2011	12/29/11	800					800																		
487003	12/27/2011	01/10/12	861				200				108	162	35	42	50						120			144		
488072	12/29/2011	01/12/12	646										70	126							450					
488071	12/29/2011	01/13/12	742					120	120	280											150				72	
488070	12/29/2011	01/13/12	720																					288	144	288
488778	12/30/2011	01/18/12	769				100		80	80		108	35	42		42					210			36	36	
492232	1/6/2012	01/19/12	1050														250	300	250	250						
492233	1/6/2012	01/23/12	1050														250	300	250	250						
491753	1/6/2012	01/23/12	752							320														216	144	72
493310	1/11/2012	01/24/12	874	56	112	56	100	120	120	40			140		100						30					
495733	1/13/2012	01/27/12	898	56	112	112				120		108	70		100						120		100			
496260	1/16/2012	01/30/12	698							200	54										300				72	72
496848	1/17/2012	01/31/12	654				36		80	40											210			144	72	72
496849	1/17/2012	01/31/12	758		112	56					108	162	140								180					
498751	1/20/2012	02/03/12	891	56	112	112		120		40			105		150						60		100			36
499939	1/24/2012	02/06/12	884	112	112		100	160			54		70								120	56	100			
500898	1/26/2012	02/09/12	881		112	112	100	40				162	105								150		100			

TABLE 9.2 *continued*

PO #	ORDER DATE	Delivery Date	Total Cases	Item # (add 530000 to get actual number)																						
				519	493	501	97	311	279	261	782	667	634	808	89	170	295	303	329	360	444	204	6	212	238	220
501681	1/30/2012	02/10/12	966					80		80					150		200		200	150		56	50			
501682	1/30/2012	02/13/12	917	168	224	112						108	105							50	150					
502688	2/1/2012	02/14/12	1040														250	240	200	250			100			
503380	2/2/2012	02/16/12	959	112			100	80	80	40	108	108	35	84		42					120		50			
504324	2/6/2012	02/17/12	600																		600					
504323	2/6/2012	02/17/12	860				100	80	40	120	54		140	84	100	42							100			
504892	2/7/2012	02/21/12	877		56			40	40	80	54	162	105	84		84							50			72
506320	2/10/2012	02/22/12	902				150		80	240					150	126						56	100			
506321	2/10/2012	02/22/12	852					120			108	108	70	126			50		50	100	120					
519756	2/10/2012	03/24/12	928				50		120						100	42	100	180				56	100	36	72	72
507388	2/14/2012	02/27/12	730				100			280						84	100						100			66
507389	2/14/2012	02/28/12	772		112	56							140	84					100	100	180					
507759	2/15/2012	02/28/12	759							40		108	35		100		150		100	50	120	56				
508650	2/17/2012	03/02/12	652	112						200			70								270					
509139	2/20/2012	03/02/12	831								270	162	105	84							210					
509138	2/20/2012	03/03/12	848				150		120	200					100	168					60		50			
510009	2/22/2012	03/06/12	896	112	56				80	120				168				120			240					
514215	2/27/2012	03/10/12	834		56	112		80		80		108	140	84							120					
514214	2/27/2012	03/10/12	910				100		160	320					150			180								
516074	3/2/2012	03/09/12	926	112	80	112			80							126										216
516533	3/3/2012	03/15/12	704					120		40		108	140								240	56				
517233	3/6/2012	03/17/12	814	112	112	112					54		70	84							270					
517232	3/6/2012	03/17/12	794				150	160	80	120											90		50		72	72
517750	3/7/2012	03/17/12	885	56	56			40				108	35		350						60			72	36	72
519757	3/10/2012	03/24/12	887	112	56	112		120				108	105	84						100	90					
520850	3/14/2012	03/28/12	876		56		100	40			108					84	100	60	50	50	120			36	36	36
522561	3/16/2012	03/30/12	694	56	168	112						162	70	126												
522560	3/16/2012	03/30/12	844					120							100	84	50	60	50	50	8		100		30	72
523470	3/20/2012	03/31/12	834	168	112	56		40					140	168							150					
523469	3/20/2012	03/31/12	886				100	80	160	120						126							150			
524783	3/22/2012	04/05/12	917	56	56	56		120		120	54	108	35	42		84					30	56	100			
526223	3/23/2012	04/06/12	832				100	40		240						84	50				60		150			108
526224	3/23/2012	04/06/12	875	112	56	56					108	162	105	126							150					
528319	3/29/2012	04/12/12	852		56			40	80	120	108		70	84		84					60		50			

continued

TABLE 9.2 *continued*

				Item # (add 530000 to get actual number)																						
PO #	ORDER DATE	Delivery Date	Total Cases	519	493	501	97	311	279	261	782	667	634	808	89	170	295	303	329	360	444	204	6	212	238	220
528722	3/30/2012	04/13/12	800			56	50			80			70	126		126					120		100			72
528723	3/30/2012	04/14/12	829	56		56	50			120			35	168		168					90		50			36
530411	4/4/2012	04/18/12	844			56		40	40	80	54	54	70	84	50	84					90		50			36
530412	4/4/2012	04/18/12	808	56	56				40	80		54	70	126		84					120					72
531846	4/6/2012	04/19/12	855					40		40	54	54	35		50	84	100	60		50	90		50	36	36	36
531847	4/6/2012	04/19/12	897		56		50		40	80		54	35	42		42	100	60	50	50	60	56	50		36	36
531848	4/6/2012	04/20/12	877		56		50	40	40	40		54		42		42	100	60	50	50	60		50	36	36	36
531846	4/6/2012	04/21/12	867		56		50	40	40	40		54		42		42	100		50	50	60		50	36	36	36
534904	4/12/2012	04/25/12	861							160	54		105			42	150	60	100	100	90					
535210	4/13/2012	04/26/12	877				100		120	40	54		35				100	60	50	100	90	56		72		
535596	4/14/2012	04/27/12	867	56	56	56		40	40	80		54	35		50	42	50	60	50		90			36	36	36
535597	4/14/2012	04/27/12	885	56	56	56		80	40	80	54	54	35		50					50	60	56	50		72	36
535598	4/14/2012	04/28/12	869	56	56	56			40	80		54	35	42	50	42			50	50				36	36	36
537655	4/20/2012	05/03/12	933	56	112	112				40		108	35				50	60	50	50	60	56		108		
538197	4/21/2012	05/04/12	882	56	56	56	50	80	80	80	54		70		50		50	60		50						
538198	4/21/2012	05/05/12	898	56	112	56	50	40	80	40	54		70		100		100		50		90					
541619	4/27/2012	05/08/12	960														250	60	200	250		56				144
542447	4/28/2012	05/09/12	871	56	112	112			120	40		162	35			84					150					
543945	5/2/2012	05/12/12	777	56	112			80		80	54		35								180			72	36	72
543946	5/2/2012	05/12/12	765		56	56		40		80	108		35								210			36	72	72
544924	5/4/2012	05/16/12	777		56		50	40	40	94		54	35	42		42					180			72		72
544924	5/4/2012	05/16/12	777		56								35	42		42					180			72		72
544922	5/4/2012	05/16/12	1200																		1200					
546418	5/9/2012	05/18/12	848				100		80	80	54	54	70	42	50	42		60						72	72	72
546419	5/9/2012	05/19/12	842				50		40	120	54	108	70	42	100	42								72	36	108
547596	5/11/2012	05/23/12	876				50	80	80	80		54	70	42	50	42	50	120					50	36		
547597	5/11/2012	05/24/12	866				100	120	80	40		54	70	42	50	42	50	60					50		72	
551137	5/17/2012	05/30/12	791	40						80	54		35	84	50	42		60		50	210		50	36		
551138	5/17/2012	05/31/12	776						40	40	54		70	84	50	42	50				210		100			36
553504	5/18/2012	05/30/12	879	112	56	56	50	40	40		54		35	84		84			50		60		50	36		72
553505	5/18/2012	05/30/12	881	56	56	56	50	40	40	40	54	54	35	84		84				50	60		50	36		36
553506	5/18/2012	05/31/12	911	56	112	9	50	40		40	54	54	35	84		42	50				60	56	50	36		36
555405	5/23/2012	06/01/12	965	112	112	112	100			120	54		35	42	150	42							50	36		
555406	5/23/2012	06/02/12	970	112	168	112	50			40	54			84	150	42							50	36	72	

TABLE 9.2 *continued*

PO #	ORDER DATE	Delivery Date	Total Cases	Item # (add 530000 to get actual number)																						
				519	493	501	97	311	279	261	782	667	634	808	89	170	295	303	329	360	444	204	6	212	238	220
555803	5/24/2012	06/02/12	1092	224	392	280					160													36		
556205	5/24/2012	06/05/12	1120	336	448	336																				
556333	5/25/2012	06/06/12	842		56	56		80	21	80	54	54	70								30	56	50	72	72	
556332	5/25/2012	06/06/12	805		56	56		40	80	40		54	105			42					30		50	108	72	72
556334	5/25/2012	06/07/12	812	56	56			40	40	80		54	70	42		42					60	56		72	72	
556706	6/1/2012	05/26/12	600							400	200															
558485	6/2/2012	06/13/12	816				100	80	40	120	54	54		42	50	42					90			36	36	72
558486	6/2/2012	06/13/12	814	56			50	40	80	80		54		42	50	42					120	56		36	36	
558487	6/2/2012	06/14/12	792				50	80	40	80		108		42	50	42					120			36	72	72
562134	6/8/2012	06/20/12	674										210		50						270			144		
562134	6/9/2012	06/20/12	896										432		50						270			144		
564788	6/15/2012	06/26/12	887		56	56	50	80	40	80		108	105	42	100	84	50									36
564789	6/15/2012	06/27/12	868	56		56	100	80	80	40		54	140	84	50	42	50									36
572160	6/28/2012	06/29/12	348																		240					108
572854	6/30/2012	07/11/12	801				50	40	40	80		54	35	84	50	42							50	72	72	72
572855	6/30/2012	07/12/12	825				100	40	80	40	54	54	35	84	50	42								72	72	72

TABLE 9.3

#	SKU #	Starting Inventory
1	530519	544
2	530493	1567
3	530501	1016
4	530097	527
5	530311	656
6	530279	611
7	530261	1208
8	530782	1200
9	530667	735
10	530634	789
11	530808	557
12	530089	1005
13	530170	1218
14	530295	202
15	530303	172
16	530329	28
17	530360	65
18	530444	3380
19	530204	271
20	530006	747
21	530212	600
22	530238	693
23	530220	1295

Bill knew that the secret to effective inventory management involved diving into the detailed transactions to adjust supply chain strategies with product characteristics and manufacturing constraints. He needed help to get this executed in time to benefit the next financial reporting deadline within the company.

CASE QUESTIONS

1. Summarize the inventory level variation and the inventory turns by SKU.
2. Explain the ordering policy used at the SKU level and its link to pallet sizes and joint replenishment.
3. Describe the delivery lead times for purchase orders and potential links to order compositions in turns of volume ordered, SKUs ordered, and so on.
4. Explore if there is a base volume that can be ordered for each SKU.
5. Describe agreements that can be signed with Best Cookies that might permit lead-time reduction (either mean or variance or both) as well as inventory-level reduction.

TABLE 9.4

Date	Julian Date #	530519	530493	530501	530097	530311	530279	530261	530782	530667	530634	530808	530089
3-Dec	3	69	109	80	148	154	86	223	254	215	239	152	144
10-Dec	10	139	200	132	126	188	68	184	219	248	236	87	136
17-Dec	17	108	180	128	141	308	67	216	170	272	205	65	133
24-Dec	24	106	107	67	74	206	28	105	55	137	151	41	70
31-Dec	31	161	197	123	90	103	50	135	59	147	166	120	84
7-Jan	38	111	145	107	129	122	87	177	67	157	187	139	124
14-Jan	45	62	100	54	128	107	130	438	62	165	215	126	124
21-Jan	52	60	109	50	128	121	140	250	106	199	217	86	123
28-Jan	59	104	178	115	126	117	115	301	118	210	204	102	132
4-Feb	66	198	219	186	188	217	127	320	118	172	248	159	151
11-Feb	73	184	196	119	139	155	125	240	150	172	207	132	130
18-Feb	80	77	97	65	153	123	88	274	119	183	209	233	121
25-Feb	87	82	97	57	142	106	141	402	66	207	209	208	125
4-Mar	94	93	78	52	124	109	161	261	68	161	190	187	116
11-Mar	101	120	163	108	133	87	160	311	64	164	193	104	136
18-Mar	108	117	196	130	129	284	138	276	73	179	197	104	500
25-Mar	115	132	181	105	138	126	161	213	76	201	23	98	126
1-Apr	122	301	380	297	139	178	150	398	166	211	218	250	148
8-Apr	129	110	149	86	141	213	67	405	176	129	242	160	149
15-Apr	136	41	64	30	102	88	178	288	36	157	148	405	88
22-Apr	143	40	239	169	121	93	197	273	180	177	203	173	106
29-Apr	150	172	196	117	140	177	296	403	226	168	208	86	131
6-May	157	116	207	131	131	168	148	277	225	161	212	98	143
13-May	164	131	164	92	153	170	112	356	253	180	219	121	141
20-May	171	110	94	66	145	152	92	381	125	161	234	110	282
27-May	178	57	1130	814	126	126	168	359	166	169	200	245	142
3-Jun	185	851	279	227	137	105	164	161	181	167	210	210	138
10-Jun	192	186	207	139	153	221	182	218	278	161	198	177	139
17-Jun	199	138	163	118	138	171	119	312	227	156	311	108	144
24-Jun	206	114	179	125	146	177	88	403	107	167	238	94	127
1-Jul	213	102	114	65	119	104	159	262	70	155	195	80	130
TOTAL		4392	6117	4154	4127	4776	3992	8822	4260	5508	6332	4460	4483

TABLE 9.4 *continued*

Date	Julian Date #	530170	530295	530303	530329	530360	530444	530204	530006	530212	530238	530220	Total
3-Dec	3	107					1304	59	186	178	173	200	4080
10-Dec	10	74					1337	65	149	380	249	301	4518
17-Dec	17	47					979	45	44	366	208	245	3927
24-Dec	24	27					175	20	45	73	47	53	1587
31-Dec	31	64					253	23	89	39	35	61	1999
7-Jan	38	87					1088	23	84	297	304	307	3742
14-Jan	45	84					347	19	100	105	107	142	2615
21-Jan	52	75	183	182	181	184	314	17	120	25	48	91	3009
28-Jan	59	92	29	23	15	20	374	57	202	27	28	81	2770
4-Feb	66	133	75	70	58	64	932	78	178	27	32	68	4018
11-Feb	73	202	500	497	446	447	670	71	152	25	41	63	5063
18-Feb	80	221	78	71	38	59	548	52	141	37	33	89	3109
25-Feb	87	188	66	47	30	41	281	47	109	24	28	76	2779
4-Mar	94	104	43	63	16	31	319	34	96	75	115	152	2648
11-Mar	101	130	42	27	5	22	317	30	86	75	104	211	2792
18-Mar	108	240	54	26	8	25	374	24	93	82	86	196	3531
25-Mar	115	269	146	120	80	103	454	26	195	70	59	137	3239
1-Apr	122	177	212	141	95	137	303	40	191	71	52	137	4392
8-Apr	129	409	114	61	20	56	287	17	107	143	129	168	3538
15-Apr	136	158	50	25	12	25	274	75	149	117	155	192	2857
22-Apr	143	100	560	237	424	449	241	65	121	107	121	217	4613
29-Apr	150	100	62	25	4	15	1118	63	75	72	63	190	4107
6-May	157	124	80	30	4	28	651	39	87	142	110	209	3521
13-May	164	125	68	34	4	26	393	37	100	103	121	202	3305
20-May	171	253	142	64	22	58	269	10	127	65	51	89	3102
27-May	178	236	129	47	9	52	226	51	157	146	141	207	5103
3-Jun	185	182	87	34	3	31	272	70	128	92	93	178	4000
10-Jun	192	131	70	25	5	36	820	68	82	99	97	212	3904
17-Jun	199	126	53	24	9	34	381	45	71	62	79	142	3131
24-Jun	206	94	149	66	25	64	421	14	64	40	27	70	2999
1-Jul	213	120	112	44	21	51	283	15	64	194	163	239	2861
TOTAL		4479	3104	1983	1534	2058	16005	1299	3592	3358	3099	4925	

Chapter 10

Apparel Supply Chains

The US apparel industry generated over $199 billion in annual sales in 2011 [99]. Every season (there may be six to eight each year), manufacturers strive to get product to the retail market in time. Between 80% and 95% of new SKUs are introduced each season. Product that is left over at the end of the season is sold through store markdowns or at outlet stores. Retail gross margins for fashion apparel ranges from 200% to 250%. It is an extremely competitive industry with demand forecasts involving high margins for error, ranging from 100% to 300% of sales.

The *chain* of entities through which apparel flows is globally dispersed in order to be competitive. Effective management of these flows is subject to the long lead times associated with their global sojourn and requires integration of orders with demand information as events unfold. The *capacity* available to manufacture product during the short season is often not sufficient to meet a large surge of demand; thus buffer inventories become the main strategy to maintain service levels. In addition, the historic imposition of textile quotas (which have yet to disappear) necessitates longer order lead times. The choice of the mix of domestic and foreign supplier capacity can thus be a crucial determinant of competitiveness. In this industry, *coordination* agreements between retailers and manufacturers are often necessary to generate incentives to share demand information and provide faster deliveries. Finally, measures of *competitiveness* of this industry vary from being in fashion to being in stock to being value competitive.

10.1 APPAREL SUPPLY CHAIN CHALLENGES

Fashion products, like avant-garde, defy definition. While there is significant disagreement regarding what will be fashionable in a season, at the end of the season there is usually far more consensus regarding what was fashionable. This large shift in uncertainty over a short selling season, combined with very long supply lead times, makes managing fashion supply chains challenging. There are several reasons for the long lead times of supply chains, but the impact is just one or two deliveries per season for many products. Long lead times, high demand uncertainty, and the need for high service levels or the potential for lost sales justify large safety stock for fashion products.

The typical time from design to retail sales for apparel can vary from twelve to eighteen months. Data from the Harvard case "Sport Obermeyer" ([54]) provide an example of a fourteen-month lead time; the Liz Claiborne case ([41]) describes a twelve-month lead time; other examples ([55]) suggest a ten-month lead time. These long lead times reflect the large fraction (over 80%) of new products each season. Typically designers choose the fabric, components of the apparel, styling, and so on, to entice the customer to purchase new apparel every season. Each of these unique features creates lead time challenges, given that the industry has historically been fragmented, with globally dispersed outsourced entities forming the supply chain. In addition, since many of the orders from buyers end up coinciding, the associated congestion for supplier capacity creates lead times. Finally, regions such as the United States and the euro zone impose quotas on the amount of different kinds of fabric that may be imported from a given source country. These quotas create an incentive to order early in order to avoid running out of the country quota. All of these issues result in long lead times in the global apparel supply chain.

A consequence of long lead times is that the retailer has to place orders for the current season without access to data regarding sales of product in the adjacent season or even the same season the previous year. This means that it is difficult to adjust to trends that may arise closer to the start of the season, and that might cause significant demand shifts. How can such shifts affect forecast error? A study commissioned by the trade group Crafted with Pride in the USA ([23]) suggests that a movement from a two-month to an eight-month lead time can increase forecast error from 20% to 55% of the mean demand for fashion products. As an example, Iyer and Bergen ([60]) describe an example in which demand for a woman's blazer at a catalog retailer varied from 1 million units to 10,000 units between successive years.

Thus, fashion apparel products have far greater demand uncertainty during the planning stage, when what will be fashionable is not known, but far more agreement regarding fashion as trends unfold and customer choices become clearer. This trend-spotting feature or trend-following aspect of demand leads to SKUs becoming dogs (low-demand items) or runners (high-demand items) during a season. Notice also that such a broad definition of fashion products suggests that fashion need not refer to apparel alone; books, compact discs, toys, and electronic products all have such runner–dog demand evolution, with a winner-take-all demand structure. This also means that long lead times have consequences that are far larger than the safety stock effect that is usually anticipated. The long lead time also increases the demand variance and thus significantly increases safety stock.

10.2 CHAIN STRUCTURE

The apparel industry supply chain consists of material flow from fiber producers to fabric producers to apparel manufacturers to retailers who supply consumers ([55]). Fiber manufacturing involves large capital expense and research and is a concentrated industry with ten firms providing over 90% of the market. Fabric producers convert the fiber into a variety of fabrics. There are over 6,000 firms involved, and about twelve firms supply 25% of the fabric market. Apparel manufacturing is a fragmented industry, with 70% of the firms employing fewer than fifty people. Apparel manufacturing also involves factors of manufacturing in which the sewing machines might cost less than the annual labor costs to operate the machine. Thus apparel manufacturing has low barriers to entry and low economies of scale. Finally retailing takes place in many different formats: from department stores to branded stores to outlet malls to catalog stores to e-retailers.

Since apparel designers enjoy no intellectual property protection in the United States for the look and feel of their designs, many sell the apparel and not just the design; thus they are involved in coordinating the manufacturing and distribution. Most retailers are part of supply chains of dispersed entities that are spread throughout the world. The locations of supply chain entities are also affected by textile quotas imposed bilaterally by countries. For example, if the quota limit for China has been reached, there is incentive for Chinese manufacturers to produce in Mauritius and ship to the US market. This might involve sending Chinese employees to work in Mauritius in order to manufacture the product. The resulting supply chain thus adds lead time and costs to the end customer, but given the associated expertise and cost advantages, it may also determine supply chain structure.

10.3 CAPACITY

The capacity for apparel manufacturing is dispersed globally. In addition, apparel manufacturing takes place in smaller firms with little ability to take business risks. Textile quotas historically require early order placement and delivery to guarantee that the volumes shipped to the US market remain within the quota limits. The net effect of uncertain demands and limited capacity is the presence of long lead times.

The nature of capacity, i.e., the mix of automation and manual labor as factors of production, also varies across manufacturing locations. For example, orders accepted by factories in Hong Kong tend to involve more automation and thus higher costs per unit and lower order minimums than factories located in mainland China ([54]). These restrictions on order sizes, influenced by the nature of capacity, affect the particular products sourced in each of the locations. There is also the choice of domestic capacity vs. imported capacity. Studies by the apparel industry trade group Crafted with Pride suggest that for products with high forecast error, which have the potential to decrease closer to the start of the season, it is profitable to source domestic even with higher prices.

The distribution of work across employees in an apparel line can also add to the productivity of capacity. As an example, see the description of the bucket brigade production lines at Champion Industries reported in Bartholdi and Eisenstein ([6]). They summarize the impact of switching from a piece-goods, bundle system to a bucket-brigade system. The key change was to make the work zones flexible and responsive to production rates of individual workers and work content of individual pieces being produced. The system showed significant improvement in productivity (about 15%) over the original system. In addition, the system permitted self-managed work teams to completely handle the manufacturing of the product. This resulted in an observed improvement in quality and productivity.

Finally, as part of a coordination agreement with suppliers, capacity commitment is used to reserve capacity at suppliers in anticipation of demand. But capacity markets are also observed in certain areas of the industry. The Italian apparel manufacturing industry has the *impannatori* or capacity brokers, who mediate between the need for capacity and its availability across the small entrepreneurs in Prato, Italy ([69]). Studies of the Prato markets suggest that in return for the ability to sell capacity, sewing and printing machine manufacturers have increased the extent of investment in modern machinery to levels significantly higher than the rest of the world.

10.4 COORDINATION

The typical time line from design to retail sales for apparel can vary from twelve to eighteen months. Data from the Harvard case "Sport Obermeyer" ([54]) provides an example of a fourteen-month lead time, the Liz Claiborne case ([41]) describes a twelve-month lead time, and the example in [55] describes a ten-month lead time.

Surveys by major retailers suggest that service levels at various stores are around 70%. Thus one out of three customers does not find the item in stock at a store that carries it. Note that apparel SKUs refer to color, style, and size availability, which requires demand estimates of specific sizes at a location. From a supply perspective, if manufacturer deliveries are of a fixed assortment of product across sizes, then it is clear that any deviation from the average size mix can cause stockouts. Thus, stockout reductions may require coordination between a flexible manufacture of varying sizes (driven by observed store sales) and careful retailer monitoring of inventory levels by size level demand and availability. The additional complication is the impact of fit preferences across customers, ranging from slim fit to loose, baggy fit choices. Such trend effects may add additional complexity to the problem of forecasting demand at the SKU level.

Furthermore, mall traffic has shown modest growth (if any) thus making it critical to maximize each customer who walks through the door. However, studies show that despite the effort to attract consumers into the store, only around 33% of the customers leave the store having bought something. Surveys of the remaining 67% of the customers who leave the store without purchases show that many of them did not buy items because the specific color or size was out of stock. In such a context, maximizing consumer effectiveness implies managing out-of-stocks carefully.

But planning a high service level well in advance of the beginning of the season does not imply that the consumer will observe a high service level during the season. For example, consider the example where a product's demand is either high or low with probability 50%. Choosing a 90% service level may well imply a 100% service level for low-demand items and an 80% service level for high-demand items. Thus the consumers during the season may observe a high service level for products without much demand: these are the products that are subsequently marked down. However, for products with a high demand, stockouts may be observed. Industry estimates of forced markdowns are about 13% of net retail apparel sales. The corresponding inventory carrying costs are estimated to be 6% of sales. At the same time, stockout-related costs are estimated to be 5% of sales. Thus overall annual apparel pipeline costs estimated to be $24 billion ([55]).

How can coordination schemes improve supply chain performance? One such approach is quick response movement in the apparel industry. Quick response is defined as "a strategy for tying apparel and textile retailing operations to apparel and textile manufacturing operations in order to provide the flexibility needed to quickly respond to shifting markets" ([55], p. 3) Because assortments are planned close to the selling season, after consumer testing and limited introductions to pretest and fine-tune specific color, style, and size options, forecast error is decreased, in-stock products are consequently increased, and markdowns reduced. Such an approach could then provide both improved in stock and lower inventory levels.

In many contexts, there is a need for coordination agreements to implement quick response. Iyer and Bergen [60] provide a set of possible Pareto-improving coordination agreements. One agreement involves the manufacturer offering quick response in return for the retailer improving service level for the product. Another involves the retailer providing a volume commitment across a set of products in return for the flexibility to adjust specific SKU orders. A third describes a wholesale price agreement with a quantity discount as a mechanism to implement quick response. Each of these coordination agreements represent different risk-sharing agreements used in the industry.

10.5 COMPETITIVENESS

How do apparel supply chains compete? One approach is to compete on cost, an approach used by Walmart and other department stores. This strategy focuses on developing a cost-efficient supply chain that may require global sourcing with low costs but long lead times. Such supply chains then require large buffer stocks to compensate for demand uncertainty or a focus on predictable demand for basic products with low demand uncertainty. But there are many other dimensions of competition in the apparel industry.

The multibillion dollar Spanish retailer Zara focuses on being synchronized with trends by adapting, in real time, to consumer suggestions: the focus is on speed of supply and product availability over selected periods. The company has stores all over the world, owns large sections of the apparel supply chain, and manages the entire chain to speed innovation and product availability. One secret is the constant flow of customer requests and information from stores to the design studios as well as constant flow of product from plants to stores, with planned replenishment. Zara sources the fabric from all over the world (e.g., Italy, China, Japan, India). But it owns its own machines that cut the fabric in batches. The layout of templates is optimized within each roll of fabric to minimize scrap. Independent sewing shops in Europe and Morocco do most of the stitching. The apparel comes back to Zara where it is ironed, packaged, and grouped by store. Zara contracts with independent trucking companies to distribute the products to stores. The retail stores worldwide are solely owned by Zara. Customers expect fresh assortments every time they visit the store and do not expect products to be in stock for a long time. This creates an urgency to buy and consequent expectations of in-stock levels. By controlling most steps in the supply chain, Zara is able to respond faster to market trends.

Zara represents a mainly vertically integrated supply chain with intense coordination between levels. Store managers pass along customer requests to designers, who then incorporate customer suggestions into new designs that are manufactured and delivered frequently to stores. This coordination enables faster cycle times, under two weeks from start to finish. Capacity for cutting, packing, and delivery is managed directly by Zara. The sewing capacity is subcontracted but managed by Zara. Is the Zara supply chain competitive? The company has a market value that is significantly larger than most firms in the apparel industry. Success comes from significant control of assets as well as an intense coordination of information flows throughout the supply chain.

Another approach to compete is a focus on customized apparel. Such an approach is offered by Lands End with its custom direct pants. Such customization may create longer lead times and issues with handling returns of customized products, especially noteworthy in an industry where returns could run 30% of volume.

Another competitive offering is guaranteeing that if an item is not in stock, either the item or delivery (to the customer's home address) will be free. Under such a scheme, the retailer's product margins, anticipated customer demand (given such guarantees), or supplier delivery lead-time improvements are expected to cover the additional costs.

In addition, competition across stores gets stores to provide higher service levels than individually optimal, and thus they obtain lower profit levels in order to retain customers. Under competitive conditions, customer service level extends to offers of returns at full credit, thus increasing the forecast errors and inventory underage or overage levels. Competition across stores also forces higher levels of product variety and lower levels of customer loyalty as customers start following trends to determine shopping preferences rather than looking to the brand or designer to make apparel choices.

10.6 A CONCEPTUAL MODEL OF THE APPAREL INVENTORY DECISIONS

Consider the demand model faced by an apparel buyer. Suppose this demand becomes more predictable as the season approaches. A conceptual approach, using a specific example adapted from [35], may incorporate current information to improve demand forecasts. Suppose demand at the end of the season can be classified into two possible demand levels, dogs and runners. These groups of items have increasing average actual demand levels and associated mean and variance. Next, suppose probability distributions are fit to the ex post demand from each category as shown in Figure 10.1.

FIGURE 10.1 Demand distribution by ex post classification

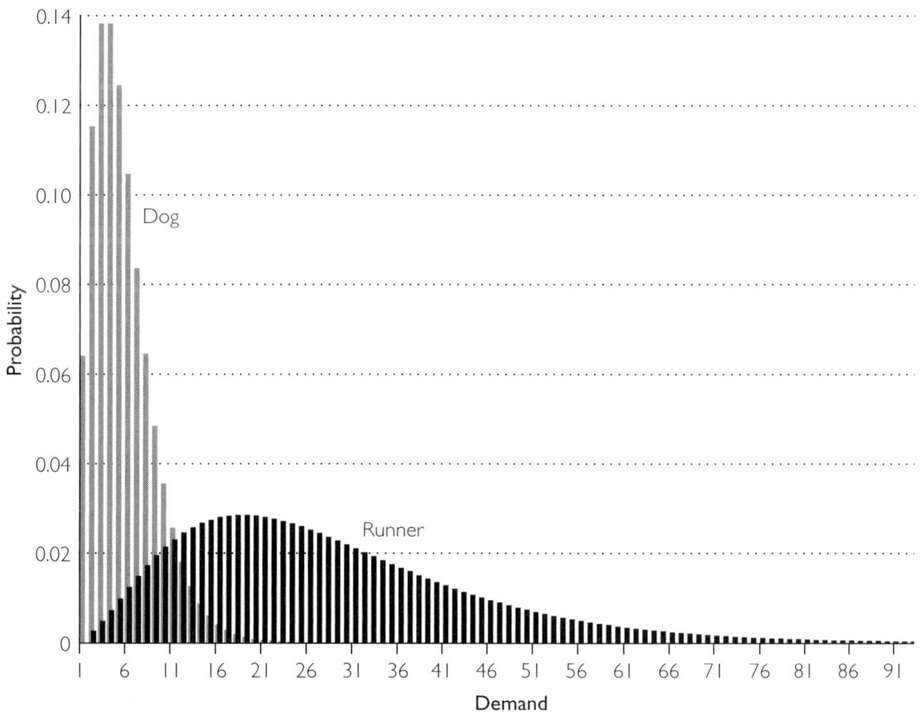

The associated mean and standard deviations for dogs are 4.5 and 3.35, and for runners, 27 and 16.43.

While the products can perhaps be classified accurately as dogs or runners at the end of the season, the buyer's classification of product category is often imperfect at the start of the season. Thus, for example, if a buyer classified a product as a dog at the start of the season, there may be an 80% probability that the item ended up being a dog and a 20% probability that the product ended up being a runner. Similarly, if a buyer classified an item as a runner at the start of the season, there may be a 65% probability that the item ended up as a runner and as a dog, 35%.

The demand distributions described for each planned classification are obtained by taking the probability that the product actually belongs to a segment and multiplying it by the probability of that demand being realized (from Figure 10.1). In other words the demand distribution for an item classified as a dog is a weighted mixture of the two possible distributions, as in Figure 10.2. Similarly, Figure 10.3 shows the distribution for items classified as runners.

FIGURE 10.2 Demand distribution for planned dogs

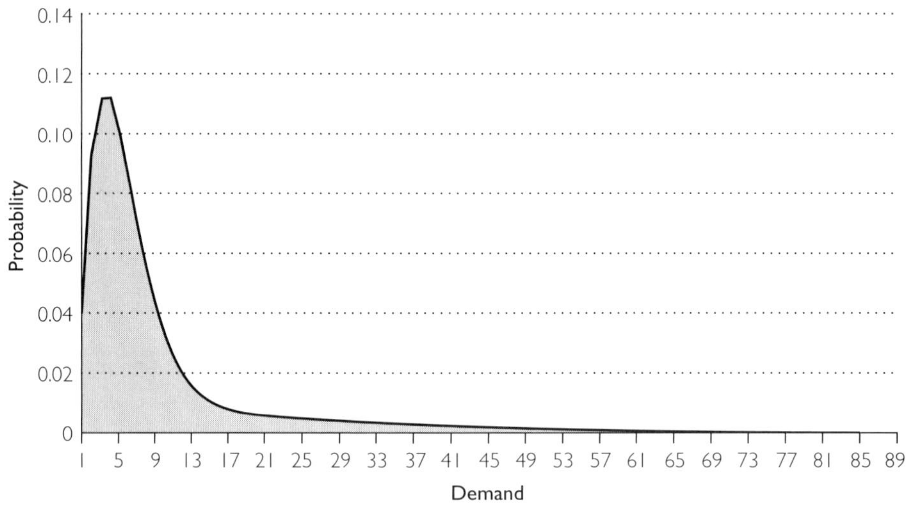

FIGURE 10.3 Demand distribution for planned runners

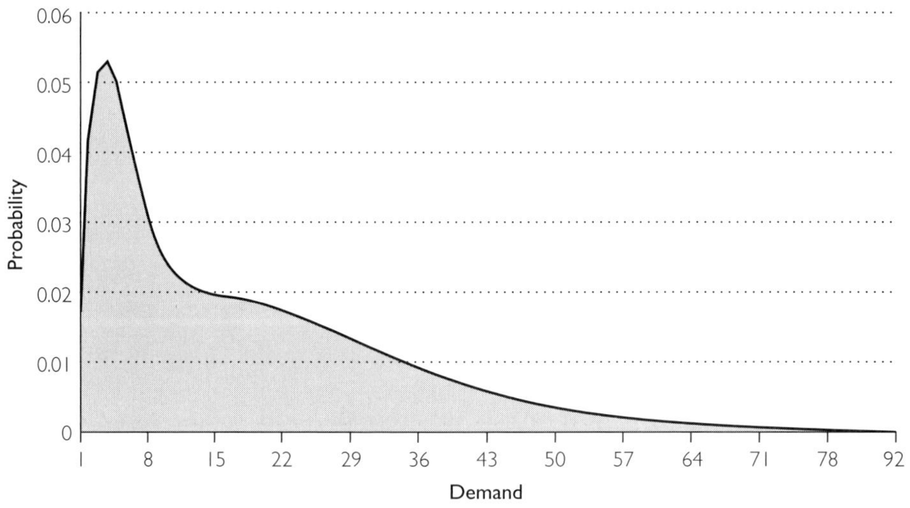

Thus the actual mean for a product classified as a dog is 9, and the associated standard deviation is 12. The corresponding means and standard deviations associated with items classified as runners are 19.13 and 17.14, respectively.

The preceding example shows that, given the buyer's inherent difficulty in classifying the product, the forecast error associated with classifications is large. For example, an accurate classification of a product as a dog would have a forecast error (standard deviation/mean) of 3.35/4.5, or 0.75. However in the presence of inaccurate classifications, the standard deviation of a product classified as a dog changes to 12/9, or 1.33. This greater ratio of standard deviation divided by the mean suggests the need of a larger level of safety stock and associated inventory costs. Of course, the major difficulty in accurately classifying a product is the lag between the forecast decision and actual demand data due to the long procurement lead time before the season.

10.7 USING RECENT OBSERVED DATA TO IMPROVE FORECASTS

How can the approaches described earlier be improved if there is access to more current data regarding season demands? One approach is to use Bayesian updating ([35]) to improve demand forecasts. To understand this approach, consider the classification of products and their associated actual demand distribution as in the example in the previous section. Before discussing details of the approach, consider how collected data can be used to project season demand for a product.

One of the features of the apparel industry is the existence of stable percent-done curves. The percent-done curve provides an estimate of the percent of total demand that is realized at different points during the season. An example is shown in Figure 10.4.

In Figure 10.4, the x-axis shows the time from the start of the season to the end of the season. The y-axis shows the percent of total season demand observed at different points in time. The y-axis thus varies from 0% to 100%. Thus a demand of five units, observed over two weeks, translates into 20% of the season demand and thus suggests a $\frac{5}{0.2}$ or a 25 unit

FIGURE 10.4 Percent-done curve

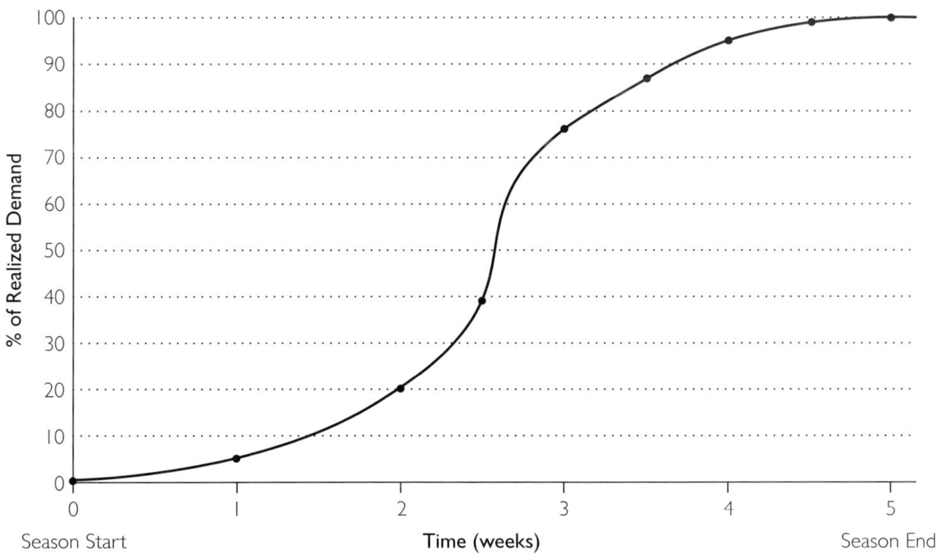

season demand projection. This ability to project season demand based on observed selling rate over shorter time periods permits early demand data to be used to improve demand forecasts. Given an observation of demand data, the buyer can revise the weights or probability that the product belongs to a segment.

As an example, suppose that a product had been classified as a runner, but the early demand projection suggested a demand level of 25 units. Then the Bayesian updated weights for that product are obtained as follows:

$$P\left(\frac{Runner}{Demand = 25}\right) = \frac{P\left(\frac{Demand = 25}{Runner}\right) P(Runner)}{P(Demand = 25)}$$

Using the data provided earlier, the calculations would be

$$P\left(\frac{Runner}{Demand = 25}\right) = \frac{0.0251 \times 0.65}{0.0164} = 0.998$$

Thus, given a revised demand estimate of 25 units, the revised weights for that product being a dog or a runner are 0.002 and 0.998. Note that the effect of the new data is to increase the probability that the item will be a runner. This change in estimates reflects the incorporation of observed data in the Bayesian updating procedure. Thus, as data are received during the season, the weights get updated, the associated demand distribution converges to the actual product classification, and forecast error decreases.

10.8 BUYER FORECASTING PROCESSES COMMONLY USED

What is the consequence of long procurement lead times? Note that the retailer has to place orders without access to data regarding sales of product in the adjacent season or even the same season of the previous year. This means that it is difficult to adjust to trends that may arise closer to the start of the season and that might cause significant demand shifts. How does a buyer in a fashion product environment make purchase decisions given the long lead times? There are numerous descriptions of the process; a typical one was described earlier in this chapter. Buyers are provided all historical background information regarding past products. Buyers then use the information to create a description of product demand if the product is a runner or a dog.

The buyers' meeting then makes a consensus determination regarding demand for the product. Usually the meeting results in buyers providing input regarding why they think demand will unfold at a particular level. Since the goal is to get the product demand right, the consensus decision often ends up close to the mean of all of the buyers estimates. This estimate from the buyers' meeting is then used to determine the amount to order for the upcoming season.

One key problem is that, when one examines the relationship between buyer estimates and observed season demand, the scatter plot is often skewed towards optimistic forecasts. One of the causes for such optimism by buyers is that they are often loathe to run out of product given the high product margins. Thus, rather than examining the process as one of demand forecasting, they end up trying to prevent inventory levels from being too low, thus denying themselves the upside benefits of higher sales levels.

In addition, many buyers are provided access to databases of customer purchases where each SKU is cataloged based on over 1,000 attributes. This permits the buyer to check sales of products with zippers, products with a particular color palette, products with particular fabric types, and so on. The goal of the buyer is to perform the appropriate data mining of product sales, identify opportunities by flagging upcoming trends and then get ahead of the curve by positioning inventory of the correct type, anticipating demand for products. For catalog stores and department stores facing long lead times, often the earliest season sales data may come from Miami or San Diego, where seasons begin earlier than in the rest of the country.

Given the processes used by buyers in practice, improving the apparel supply chain requires a healthy combination of statistical processes and buyer judgment. The approaches outlined in this chapter provide such a scheme.

10.9 A MODEL OF THE PROFIT IMPACT OF QUICK RESPONSE

If decisions regarding purchase quantity are made closer to the start of the season, then better demand information is available, resulting in lower forecast error. Figure 10.5 provides results obtained by the industry trade group called Crafted with Pride in the USA. Their study used fifty buyers across the industry and had them forecast demand for fashion products and basic products at different points in time before and during the season. The graph shows how the forecast error varied with time and across product type for a fashion product. As the season approaches, there are many entities that provide sources of information. Fashion shows all over the world showcase upcoming trends. Fashion consulting services provide their judgments regarding the upcoming season, while color consultants project popular colors for the upcoming season. Fashion magazines highlight specific features and designs. All of this information gradually defines the fashion trend for the season.

In order to illustrate the need for coordination agreements to implement quick response, consider the example of a retailer Assort that sells women's dresses. The first analysis will use a long lead time relationship between a manufacturer and Assort. In this relationship, the retailer has access to historical data and uses that data to project possible demand levels for products.

Assume that analysis of the historical demand data for reported products has indicated that demand through the season can be divided into two groups: low and high demand. The

FIGURE 10.5 Forecast error vs. time

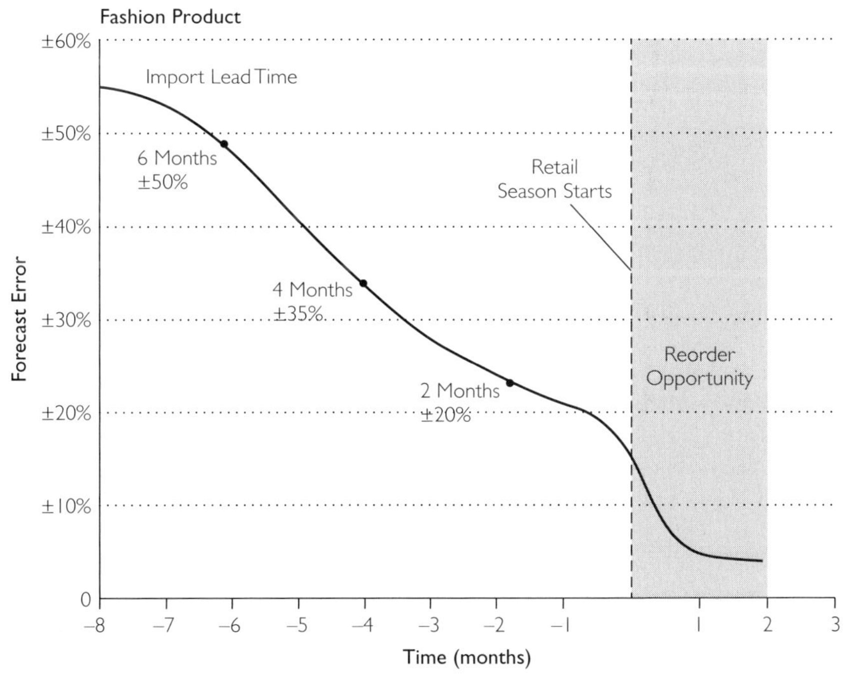

set of dresses in the low demand category is observed to have demands whose distribution is uniform between 1 and 5. The set of dresses in the high demand category is observed to have demands whose distribution is uniform between 4 and 8 units. Notice that there are some dresses whose categorization is not perfect. This reflects the uncertainty regarding whether they are high observed demands in the low category or low observed demands in the high category. Note that the best that the sales managers can do for the products is categorize them into these categories. (As an analogy that does not allow for overlap, in most classes, there is a range of performance scores that warrant the same final letter grade.)

The role of the buying team is to assess, about eight months in advance, when the order is placed, the probability that demand for a product is from each of the possible categories. For this example, assume that the best estimate is that demand for a particular dress will be either low or high with a 50% probability.

These dresses are bought for \$100 and sell for \$200. If Assort runs out of dresses, the future profit impact is estimated to be \$200. Dresses that are held through the fashion season incur a holding cost of \$20. Those dresses that do not sell during the season are sold off to an outlet store for \$40.

Under this system, what should be Assort's optimal order size and associated expected profit, if orders have to be placed eight months in advance?

Answer: Given these costs, note that Assort will estimate the optimal service level to be

$$\frac{r+g-c}{r+h+g-s}$$

where $r = 200$, $c = 100$, $h = 20$, $s = 40$, $g = 200$. Thus the optimal service level is 78.9%.

Note that we are provided the conditional demand distributions, i.e., demand realizations depending on whether the product is in the low or high demand category. The buyer's estimates have also assigned a 50% probability that the product being considered for the upcoming season falls in the low or high category. Thus, for example, the probability that the demand is for 1 unit is equal to

Probability (Demand = 1 unit) = (Probability (Demand = 1/Low Category)
× Probability (Low Category)) + (Probability (Demand = 1/High Category)
× Probability (High Category))
= (0.2 × 0.5) + (0 × 0.5)
= 0.1

Thus the forecasted demand distribution, eight months in advance, is

Demand	*Probability*
1	0.1
2	0.1
3	0.1
4	0.2
5	0.2
6	0.1
7	0.1
8	0.1

With this demand distribution, and to attain the optimal service level, the inventory of dresses purchased is 6 units. Associated with this inventory purchased, Assort's expected profit is as follows:

$$(-100 \times 6) + \text{(Purchase Costs)}$$

$$((0.1 \times 200 \times 1) + (0.1 \times 200 \times 2) + (0.1 \times 200 \times 3) + (0.2 \times 200 \times 4) + (0.2 \times 200 \times 5) +$$

$$(0.1 \times 200 \times 6) + (0.1 \times 200 \times 6) + (0.1 \times 200 \times 6)) + ((0.1 \times 20 \times 5) + (0.1 \times 20 \times 4) +$$

$(0.1 \times 20 \times 3)+$	(Expected Revenue)
$(0.2 \times 20 \times 2)+(0.2 \times 20 \times 1))+$	(Expected salvage – Holding Costs)
$((-0.1 \times 200 \times 1)+(-0.1 \times 200 \times 2))$	(Expected Penalty Costs)

$=216$

The associated manufacturer revenue is $100 \times 6 = \$600$.

10.9.1 Quick Response: Retailer Impact

Consider the quick response (QR) approach. Under this scheme, the manufacturer has to receive the order only four months in advance. The retailer can collect data regarding sales of similar products at points closer to the upcoming season before placing an order. Intuitively, the ability to order closer to the season increases the possibility that more recent trend information or economic conditions can be used to better forecast demand. For this example, assume that data regarding demand for similar product enables the retailer to further refine the demand distribution estimates. **What will be the impact of QR on the retailer?** (For now, assume manufacturer prices remain the same.)

Answer: Under QR, the retailer collects four more months of demand. Assume that the demand (d1) during these months follows the same distribution as demand during the upcoming season, i.e., the outcomes belong to the same demand category. What might cause such a relationship? Perhaps styles, color, or patterns link products from different seasons. Thus, assume that the retailer observes a draw from the demand distribution for the adjacent season. Depending on the value of this observed demand, Assort will adjust demand estimates as follows, using the Bayesian approach for updating weights (Section 10.7):

Demand	*Probability*
$1 \leq d1 \leq 3$	P(Low) = 1, P(High) = 0
$4 \leq d1 \leq 5$	P(Low) = 0.5, P(High) = 0.5
$6 \leq d1 \leq 8$	P(Low) = 0, P(High) = 1

Thus, the observed demand changes the conditional weights (last column above) placed on each of the two demand distributions. As before, we can then derive the optimal inventory policy and associated expected profit for the retailer as follows:

Demand (d1)	*Probability*	*Inventory*	*Expected Profit*
$1 \leq d1 \leq 3$	0.3	4	\$144
$4 \leq d1 \leq 5$	0.4	6	\$216
$6 \leq d1 \leq 8$	0.3	7	\$444
Total Expected Profit			\$262.80

Thus, the retailer's profit increases from \$216 to \$262.80, an increase of 22%.

What is the expected quantity purchased from the manufacturer under QR?

$$(0.3 \times 4) + (0.4 \times 6) + (0.3 \times 7) = 5.7 \text{ units}$$

Thus manufacturer revenues decreases to \$570, a drop of 5%.

It is clear that since the retailer-expected profits increase while the manufacturer revenues decrease, manufacturer profits decrease (if costs were to remain the same). Thus QR is not Pareto improving without coordination agreements. This suggests the need for agreements between the manufacturer and the retailer to implement QR.

10.9.2 Quick Response: Service Commitment

Since QR without any agreements does not benefit the manufacturer, coordination agreements may be necessary. One possible agreement is that the retailer commits to a higher service level, say 100% in this example, in return for the manufacturer providing QR.

What is the impact on the manufacturer and retailer under this scheme?

Answer: We will have to change the inventory purchased after observing demand to guarantee a 100% service level. We will thus get the following results:

Demand (d1)	*Probability*	*Inventory*	*Expected Profit*
$1 \leq d1 \leq 3$	0.3	5	\$140
$4 \leq d1 \leq 5$	0.4	8	\$170
$6 \leq d1 \leq 8$	0.3	8	\$440
Total Expected Profit			\$242.0

The associated manufacturer revenue is

$$100\ ((0.3 \times 5) + (0.4 \times 8) + (0.3 \times 8)) = 710.$$

Thus the manufacturer and the retailer are better off with this agreement than in the original system because it is Pareto improving.

How do we implement this increased service level?

Consider two different newspaper advertisements that can be interpreted as enabling monitoring of these agreements. In the advertisement for Enzo Angiolini shoes, the retailer told the public that if the shoes were not in stock at the store, then customers would be mailed a free pair (either from another store or from the manufacturer). Note that this guarantees a 100% service level. In the second advertisement for Dockers pants, the manufacturer guaranteed that the pants will be shipped within a fixed number of days or provided free to the customer. Again, the customer is assured a 100% service level. Clearly, in this case, the customers play the role of monitoring agents and guarantee compliance.

How does this higher service level help the manufacturer? In a retail store that carries products from hundreds or thousands of manufacturers, additional service can range from such commitments to store personnel getting the inventory for the customer or providing free product. This extra servicing of manufacturer products provides the incentive for the manufacturer to implement QR.

Where are the retailer's increases in expected profit coming from?

Answer: Consider the service level in the old system and the new QR system with a 100% service level.

Demand (d1)	*Probability*	*Old System Service Level*	*QR System 100% Service Level*
$1 \leq d1 \leq 3$	0.3	100%	100%
$4 \leq d1 \leq 5$	0.4	80%	100%
$6 \leq d1 \leq 8$	0.3	60%	100%

By choosing the assortment of dresses closer to the season, Assort faces a lower forecast error. This enables the retailer to have fewer stockouts, the manufacturer to have higher revenue, and the customer to have a higher service level. All of this is accomplished without a decrease in retailer profits. In addition, customers would see a higher in-stock level that is uniform across products and thus get better service.

Note that providing a 100% service level in the old system would have decreased retailer profits to \$170 because of the increased holding and salvage related costs.

Thus QR allows the customer service level to be increased without decreasing retailer profits.

This shows that improving lead times and enabling decisions under a lower demand forecast error may require coordination agreements between members of the apparel supply chain. Once such coordination agreements are established, the access to manufacturing capacity closer to demand enables improved competitiveness of the apparel supply chain. Notice that all four Cs played a role in improving the supply chain.

10.10 CHAPTER SUMMARY

The US apparel industry had $199 billion in sales in 2011. The industry has high gross margins (200%–250%), long lead times (ten to fourteen months), and six to eight fashion seasons each year. There is a large percent (80%–95%) of new products each season and large demand forecast errors due to the fickleness of fashion trends. Given demand volatility, the industry has seen a tremendous number of retail and manufacturer closures in the past decade.

The global apparel supply chain is dispersed, with production at cost-competitive locations. Regulations and expectations regarding production processes require continual rethinking of production locations to match supply locations with consumer price and ethical expectations. One approach, followed by competitive chains such as Zara, is to have a significant level of vertical integration. Other fashion manufacturers, such as Liz Claiborne, leverage a collection of independent suppliers with close coordination and long-term relationships.

Since manufacturing capacity is located far from the demand points and is often not sufficient to meet a large surge of demand, buffer inventories become the main strategy to maintain service levels. The quick response (QR) movement in the fashion industry focuses on coordination agreements between retailers and manufacturers, along with information sharing, to incentivize shared demand information and provide faster deliveries. Retailers and manufacturers use different measures of competitiveness, including being in fashion, in stock, and value competitive.

The retail environment continues to increase in competitiveness, offering new formats such as e-retailing and mass customization. As competition increase, pressures for increased in stock without the corresponding increased prices have created the need for careful integration of the supply chain operation with the marketing divisions.

10.11 PROBLEMS

1. The Fashion store has decided to use state-of-the-art statistical analysis to improve management of its inventory. Fashion buys bags with detailed inlays from InBags for $50 each and sells them at a retail price of $120 per bag. Any bags not sold during the regular season are sold to an outlet store at $20 per bag.

Analysis of previous year's data suggests that bags can be divided into two sets: dogs and runners. The dogs represent the low-demand items, and the runners represent the high-demand set. The distribution of dogs and runners is shown below:

Dog, Demand	*Probability*	*Runner, Demand*	*Probability*
100	0.4	300	0.4
200	0.4	400	0.3
300	0.2	500	0.3

Eight months before the start of the season, Fashion has to order the bags from InBags. Fashion's buyers have estimated that, for the upcoming season, the probability that a given bag is a runner or a dog is each 50%.

1a. Given this data, determine the optimal service level that Fashion should offer. Also, determine the optimal order quantity and the associated expected profit for Fashion. Finally, provide the expected revenue for InBags.

1b. Fashion is exploring a new approach in the industry called quick response (QR). Under this approach, orders would be placed four months before the start of the season. Fashion estimates that this will permit data to be gathered from a related product sold in during the four months available for data gathering.

Under QR, provide the orders that will be placed by Fashion as it observes different demand levels. Also provide the associated expected profit obtained by Fashion under QR. Finally, provide the expected revenue for InBags. Is this a Pareto-improving scheme? Explain.

1c. As an alternative, Fashion offers a 100% service level for InBags in return for InBags providing QR delivery. For this scheme, provide the orders that will be placed by Fashion as it observes different demand levels. Also provide the associated expected profit obtained by Fashion under QR. Finally, provide the expected revenue for InBags. Is this a Pareto-improving scheme? Explain.

2. Hip is a fashion retailer that sells formal apparel. Demand for a SKU sold by Hip can be classified at the end of the fashion season as either a dog (low demand) or a runner (high demand). The demand distributions for these two categories is given below:

Dog Demand Distribution	*Demand Probability*	*Runner Demand Distribution*	*Demand Probability*
10	0.2	30	0.3
15	0.3	35	0.5
20	0.4	40	0.2
25	0.1		

Hip's buyers have to place an order with the supplier, Trim, eight months in advance of the upcoming season. For a particular SKU, Hip's buyers have assigned the probability that it is a dog as 60% and the probability that it is a runner as 40%. Hip buys the SKU from Trim for $100 and sells it at retail for $175. The production cost per unit incurred by Trim is $50. Goods held through the season by Hip incur a holding cost of $25. These leftover goods are sold to an outlet store for $50. If Hip runs out of stock, it incurs a goodwill cost (future profit impact) of $100.

2a. How many units should Hip order eight months before the start of the season to maximize expected profit? Provide the associated expected profit to Hip. Also provide the expected profit for Trim, given this purchase by Hip.

2b. Hip has heard of a concept called quick response, whereby an order would be placed four months before the start of the season. At that time, based on information collected by Hip, buyers would know if the product is a dog or a runner.

Given the same parameters as in 2a, how many units should Hip order if the SKU is a dog, and what is Hip's associated expected profit? How many units should Hip order if the SKU is a runner, and what is Hip's associated expected profit? What is Hip's overall associated profit under quick response? What is Trim's expected profit under quick response? Is this a Pareto-improving system?

2c. Hip has decided to offer the following contract to Trim: Trim should provide QR delivery, and Hip will provide a 100% service level for Trim's SKU. What is Hip's expected profit under this contract? What is Trim's expected profit? Is this a Pareto-improving system?

2d. Hip is considering the option of buying out Trim and placing orders following a quick response system. What will be the optimal service level under this combined system? What will be the total expected profit for the combined system? Compare this total expected profit to the total expected profit under 2a, 2b, and 2c. Comment on the reason for the differences.

3. The Smart company sells educational toys. Their big season is the winter holiday season, and Smart prides itself on its customer service. Smart buys toys from a supplier, Precise. All purchases for the season have to be made one year in advance, with deliveries scheduled to occur at the start of the season.

Smart's buyers have determined that demand at the end of the season can be classified into runners and dogs. Demand for dogs has the following distribution:

Demand	*Probability*
1,000	0.3
3,000	0.5
5,000	0.2

Demand for runners has the following distribution:

Demand	*Probability*
10,000	0.5
20,000	0.3
30,000	0.2

Smart's buyers have estimated one year in advance that for the toy Brinko, the probability that it will be a dog is 40% and that it will be a runner is 60%. Precise charges Smart $40 per Brinko toy. Smart retails these toys for $100. To induce customers to come and shop, Smart has agreed to emergency order and ship product to a customer if the toy runs out of stock. This emergency order and shipping raises the cost to Smart from $40 to $150. However the customer now always gets demand satisfied. Toys left over at the end of the season can be sold to an outlet store for $5 each.

3a. What optimal service level should the buyers target for Brinko? What is the optimal inventory level of Brinkos that Smart should buy? What is the associated expected profit realized by Smart? What is the associated revenue for Precise?

3b. Smart's buyers have heard of quick response, whereby suppliers permit retailers to order six months before the start of the season. This would permit Smart to learn from its sales operation in overseas markets where demand for toys follows the same statistical distribution as that in the US markets. Thus the additional six months to delay placing orders permits Smart's buyers to observe demand from the same distribution as the US market and better categorize demand for Brinkos.

How many Brinkos should Smart purchase as it observes different demand levels from its overseas markets? What is the associated expected profit for Smart? What is the associated expected revenue for Precise? Is this a Pareto-improving system?

3c. Precise demands a 100% service level for toys in return for offering QR. If Smart agrees, what will be the associated expected profit for Smart? What will be the expected revenue for Precise? Is this Pareto improving over the values in 3a?

4. The Smart company sells toys. Their big season is the winter holiday season, and Smart prides itself in its customer service. Smart buys toys from a supplier, Best. All purchases for the season have to be made one year in advance with deliveries scheduled to occur at the start of the season.

Smart's buyers have determined that demand at the end of the season can be classified into runners and dogs. Demand for dogs has the following distribution:

Demand	*Probability*
10	0.3
20	0.6
30	0.1

Demand for runners has the following distribution:

Demand	*Probability*
40	0.4
50	0.5
60	0.1

Smart's buyers have estimated one year in advance that for the toy Monster, the probability that it will be a dog is 40% and that it will be a runner is 60%. Best charges Smart $25 per toy but requires a minimum order of 30 units. Smart retails these toys for $100. To induce customers to come and shop, Smart has agreed to emergency order and ship product to a customer if the toy runs out of stock. (The customer would pay $100 for the toy, but the toy would have to be procured and mailed to the customer's home.) This emergency order and shipping raises the cost to Smart from $25 to $125. However the customer now always gets demand satisfied. Toys left over at the end of the season can be sold to an outlet store for $10 each.

4a. What optimal service level should the buyers target for the Monster toy? What is the optimal inventory level of toys that Smart should buy? What is the associated expected profit realized by Smart? What is the associated revenue for Best?

4b. Smart's buyers have heard of quick response, whereby suppliers permit retailers to order six months before the start of the season. This would permit Smart to learn from its sales operation in overseas markets where demand for toys follows the same statistical distribution as that in the US markets. Thus the additional six months to delay placing orders permits Smart's buyers to observe demand from the same distribution as the US market and thus better categorize demand for Monsters. Best demands a 100% service level for toys in return for offering QR. If Smart agrees, what will be the associated expected profit for Smart? What will be the expected revenue for Best? Is this Pareto improving over the values in 4a?

4c. Suppose Smart could obtain perfect information regarding demand. What is the associated expected profit for Smart? What are the associated expected sales for Best?

4d. Smart's buyers have identified a new supplier Quick. Quick demands no service level commitment and offers to provide QR but has a pricing strategy that offers Monster toys for $25 per unit if the order size is over 40 units. Quick charges $30 per unit if the order size is below 40 units. Emergency shipment costs for Smart would continue to remain at $125. Should Smart switch to this new supplier instead of the contract with Best in 4b? Explain.

5. The Shirt store sells designer shirts by a renowned designer. Demand for these shirts is either low or high as classified by buyers at the end of the season. If demand is low, then the distribution is

Demand	*Probability*
100	0.3
200	0.5
300	0.2

If the demand is high, then the distribution is

Demand	*Probability*
400	0.7
500	0.2
600	0.1

Ten months before the start of the season, buyers have to choose inventory of a patterned shirt. The probability that the demand is low has been estimated at 60%, and the probability that demand is high is estimated as 40%. Shirt purchases shirts from a supplier Rapid at a wholesale price of $100. The shirts are sold at retail for $250. Leftover shirts can be salvaged at an outlet store for $50, but the holding cost for these shirts is assessed at $30. Goodwill cost for lost sales is estimated at $100.

5a. How many units should Shirt purchase to maximize expected profit? What will be the associated expected profit at that optimal purchase and the associated service level? Provide the expected revenue obtained by Rapid.

5b. Shirt wants Rapid to shift to a quick response mode of operation. Under such a scheme, Shirt will order five months in advance. But because Shirt will get data regarding its operations in other parts of the world, Shirt will be able to classify demand for the patterned shirt with certainty as high or low demand before choosing inventory.

What will be Shirt's order quantity under low demand? Under high demand? What will be Shirt's associated expected profit under QR? What will be the expected revenues received by Rapid?

5c. Rapid proposes that wholesale price be increased under QR to $125. How would this change Shirt's associated purchases under high and low demand and associated expected profit under QR with the new wholesale price? What will be the expected revenues received by Rapid? Is increasing wholesale price an approach to generate Pareto-improving profits?

5d. Rapid proposes that Shirt provide a 100% service level in return for QR. Will this generate a Pareto-improving agreement? Provide Shirt's expected profits and Rapid's expected revenues under this contract.

5e. Rapid wants Shirt to agree to the following deal in return for extremely rapid QR. Shirt has to guarantee a purchase of 300 units for $100 each. Any more units (i.e., more than the 300) can be ordered by Shirt after seeing actual demand at a wholesale price of $125 per shirt. Rapid will deliver quickly, and thus the customer demand will remain. Will this approach be Pareto improving for Rapid and Shirt over the original system? Provide the expected profit for Shirt and the expected revenue for Rapid under this scheme.

6. Blokus is a popular toy retailer in Indianapolis that is known for its savvy in forecasting the toy hit every season. For the upcoming season, Blokus has to decide eight months in advance the quantity to purchase of a new toy, TMX Blog. Past data suggest that demand can be low or high for this toy, and the demand distribution is given below for each category.

LOW DEMAND		*HIGH DEMAND*	
Demand (units)	*Probability*	*Demand (units)*	*Probability*
100	0.4	1,000	0.5
200	0.4	1,100	0.3
300	0.2	1,200	0.2

Blokus's buyers have estimated low demand with probability 60% and high with probability 40% eight months in advance of the season. The toy is purchased from the supplier at a wholesale price of $50 per unit and is sold at retail for $110 per unit. The toys not purchased during the season are sold to an outlet store for $10 per unit. Blokus plans a high service level and estimates a goodwill cost per unit of lost sales of $100 per unit.

6a. Identify the optimal service level that Blokus should offer its customers. Identify the associated optimal quantity that should be purchased from its supplier. What is the associated expected profit for Blokus? What is the expected revenue for the supplier?

6b. Assume that under quick response, if Blokus could place orders four months in advance of the season (instead of eight months), it would know if the toy is a low- or high-demand item. Using the same cost parameters as in 6a, provide the order quantity under low and high demand, the expected profit in each case, and the overall expected profit for Blokus. Provide the associated expected revenue for the supplier. Is the quick response system Pareto improving for both Blokus and its supplier? Explain.

6c. Blokus is considering an agreement under which the supplier provides QR and Blokus guarantees a 100% service level to retail customers. Using the same cost parameters as in 6a, provide the order quantity under low and high demand, the expected profit in each case, and the overall expected profit for Blokus. Provide the associated expected revenue for the supplier. Is the quick response system Pareto improving for both Blokus and its supplier? Explain.

6d. A consultant suggests that the supply chain consisting of Blokus and its supplier is not coordinated. The consultant suggests that coordinating agreements under quick response could further improve performance for the supply chain over the values in 6c. What would be the optimal service level for the supply chain as a whole? Using this information, explain if you agree or disagree with the consultant.

7. The Rapid store is an apparel retailer that sells fashion apparel. Rapid's products appeal to two market segments. Segment 1 represents teenagers between the ages of 14 and 18, and Segment 2 represents college students between the ages of 19 and 22. Demand for the two segments is shown below.

SEGMENT 1 DEMAND		*SEGMENT 2 DEMAND*	
Demand	*Probability*	*Demand*	*Probability*
100	0.6	200	0.5
200	0.4	300	0.5

Rapid buys a specific apparel for $200 per unit and retails it for $400 per unit. Leftover apparel is sold to an outlet store for $100 per unit. Currently Rapid has to purchase its apparel from a manufacturer Fast eight months in advance.

Segment 1 is a loyal demand group that always buys the apparel. However, eight months in advance, Rapid's buyers estimate that there is a 50% probability that segment 2 will buy the product (and therefore a 50% probability that they will not). Thus if both segment 1 and segment 2 buy the product, the total demand will be the sum of the demand from both segments. Otherwise, the demand will only come from segment 1.

7a. What is the optimal service level that Rapid should offer its customers? What is the corresponding optimal order quantity? What is the associated expected profit for Rapid? What is the revenue for Fast?

7b. A consultant suggests quick response as an approach whereby Rapid will get to order later, i.e., four months before the season. At this point, Rapid would know whether or not segment 2 would buy the product. For this system, what is the corresponding optimal order quantity if segment 2 were also to buy the product? What is the expected profit if only segment 1 were to buy the product? What is the associated expected profit for Rapid? What is the revenue for Fast? Is this a Pareto-improving scheme for Rapid and Fast?

7c. The consultant suggests that Fast offer quick response while Rapid offers a 100% service level for Fast's products. For this system, what is the corresponding expected optimal order quantity? What is the associated expected profit for Rapid? What is the revenue for Fast? Is this a Pareto-improving scheme for Rapid and Fast?

7d. What scheme would you suggest to make the system Pareto improving for Rapid and Fast? Explain.

8. Smart is a toy retailer that attempts to generate hits every Christmas season. However, analysis of Smart's products shows that they end up either as runners (and sell many units) or as dogs (and sell few units). The distribution of runners and dogs historically is as follows:

DOGS		*RUNNERS*	
Demand	*Probability*	*Demand*	*Probability*
100	0.3	400	0.4
200	0.4	500	0.3
300	0.3	600	0.3

Smart currently imports its toys from the Far East from a manufacturer, Quick, with a ten-month lead time. That far out, Smart's buyers cannot forecast if the toy will be a runner or a dog, so they put equal weights of 50% of the product being in either category.

Smart buys the toys for $25 a unit and sells them to customers for $40 per unit. Leftover toys are sent to an outlet store and are sold for $10 per unit. Given its price points, Smart incurs a future goodwill cost of $20 per unit of demand not satisfied. Assume that Quick's cost to produce in the Far East and supply Smart are $15 per unit.

8a. How many units should Smart buy ten months in advance to maximize its profits? What is the associated expected profit for Smart? What is Quick's associated profit?

8b. Quick has a facility in the United States that can make the toy closer to the start of the season and thus permit Smart to order two months in advance, per the quick response system. At that time, assume that Smart would be able to decide if the toy is a runner or a dog.

Smart would like to identify its expected profit if purchases were made from Quick's facility in the United States at the same prices as before.

But Quick's manufacturing cost increases from $15 per unit to $16 per unit. Provide Quick's expected profit under this quick response system.

Is it Pareto improving for Quick to supply Smart from the US plant at the same price points?

8c. Quick suggests that if Smart provided a 100% service level, then the US plant would be feasible as a supply location for Smart. Should Smart accept the quick response and a 100% service level? Is it Pareto improving compared to 8a?

9. The Style store is in the process of choosing an order size for its affordable sportcoats. Style orders from a supplier who charges a price of $50. Style retails the coats for $100. Coats left over at the end of the four-month season can be sold to an outlet store for $15 but incur a holding cost of $25. Despite being affordable, Style wants to provide good customer service, hence demand not satisfied from inventory is assessed a goodwill cost of $100.

Analysis of historical data has shown that sportcoats can be divided into two categories. The low demand category has demands as follows:

Demand	*Probability*
200	0.4
300	0.4
400	0.2

The high demand category has demands as follows:

Demand	*Probability*
400	0.2
500	0.4
600	0.4

Currently Style has to order eight months in advance. Style's buyers acesses the probability that the sportcoat being ordered is a low seller as 40% and the probability it is a high seller as 60%.

9a. Provide the optimal order quantity that Style should order, the associated service level, and the associated expected profit. Provide the expected revenue that the supplier receives.

9b. Style's managers have heard of a new technology called quick response (QR). Under QR, orders can be placed four months before the start of the season. Under QR, Style can observe sales of a related product and use that information to improve demand estimates for the sportcoat under consideration. What will be the impact of QR on Style's expected profit? What will be the impact on the supplier's expected revenue? Is this a Pareto-improving system?

9c. The supplier agrees to provide QR to Style in return for 100% service level. What will be the impact of such an agreement on Style's expected profit? What will be the corresponding supplier expected revenue? Is this a Pareto-improving system compared to 9a?

9d. Did the supplier revenue increase and retailer expected profits increase in 9c? Explain why or why not.

10. The Scoop Company prides itself on printing offbeat books that can sometimes generate great public enthusiasm. Within the company, books are classified as runners or dogs. Demand for dogs usually follows the following distribution:

Demand	*Probability*
2,000	0.4
3,000	0.4
5,000	0.2

Demand for runners usually follows the following distribution:

Demand	*Probability*
10,000	0.3
20,000	0.4
30,000	0.3

A new book is being offered by Scoop to the public. Scoop sells the books to distributors who then sell the book to the public through their channels. Scoop's printer Prompt has very long lead times. Given the long lead time, Scoop's marketing staff estimates that the book being offered will be a runner with a 60% probability and a dog with a 40% probability. The book costs Scoop $10 to print, plus royalties. Scoop sells the book for $20 to the distributors. Leftover unsold books are salvaged at $5 per book.

10a. Provide the optimal service level that Scoop should offer, the associated order size, and the expected profit to Scoop. Provide also the expected manufacturer revenues.

10b. Scoop has heard of a new technology called quick response and urges its printer Prompt to consider using it. Under this new technology, Scoop will get to order close to the start of the selling season and will know if the book will be a runner or a dog. (The probability of it being a runner would be 60% and a dog, 40%). Provide Scoop's order size and expected profit in this new system. Provide the impact on Prompt. Is this a Pareto-improving system?

10c. Scoop agrees to offer a 100% service level in return for Prompt offering quick response. Is this a Pareto-improving agreement? Provide the profit impact and revenue impact for Scoop and Prompt in this system.

Buying Fashion at Catco

ANANTH V. IYER

Maria DeFranco, senior buyer at Catco, pondered her decision for her order with Liz Claiborne for the upcoming fall line of blended wool blazers. Demand volatility had been severe the past few years, yet orders had to be placed eight months in advance. Despite healthy gross margins, net margins were razor thin, with demand forecast errors and high customer service levels eroding away any brand-name retail advantage. Maria wondered if there was some science to go with what was historically a "gut feel" decision in the end. Surely there should be some analysis that could assist her with the spend decision.

Spread on the desktop in front of her were spreadsheets summarizing past sales projections and observed demands for Liz Claiborne products that she considered the peer group for the products this upcoming season. Exhibit 1 provided information regarding twenty-four products—including the planned demand (or forecast) and the observed demand (at the end of the season) for each product. A scatter plot of the planned vs. actual demands was shown in Exhibit 2, suggesting large forecast error levels.

She also had demand projections for jackets for the upcoming season. The main questions concerned the order quantity for these jackets. Financials for most of these jackets were clear: Catco purchased the jackets for $62 and sold them for a standard markup so that the selling price was $138. Units not sold during the season were usually sent off to the Catco outlet store, which provided the buyer a credit for 53% of the purchase price. Any units short were recorded as providing a goodwill penalty per unit of 20% of the selling price.

EXHIBIT 1 Planned vs. actual volumes for twenty-four comparable blazers

Item #	Description	Planned	Actual
1	Hyacinth	537	100
2	Basketweave	672	112
3	Novelty Plaid	1298	115
4	Tweed	700	124
5	Cotton Clay	1005	145
6	Fuschia Flannel	504	156
7	Flannel	830	170
8	Houndstooth	362	174
9	Rose Linen	357	193
10	Plushombre	527	255
11	Black Flannel	199	310
12	Fuschia Denim	337	349
13	Purple Flannel	676	372
14	Chenille	406	381
15	Plaid	868	403
16	Wool Double Breasted	548	504
17	Wool Gabardine	597	586
18	Flax	587	686
19	Denim	994	1113
20	Olive Tweed	1629	1139
21	Silk Tweed	1422	1156
22	Donegal	1452	1197
23	Novelty	1385	1888
24	Military	1245	2332

THE OPEN-TO-BUY DOLLARS AND BUYER EVALUATION

Catco also had a process for releasing buying capability to buyers like Maria. Each season, a buyer was provided a fixed "open-to-buy" dollars budget. As a buyer purchased product, the open-to-buy budget was depleted. If the products were sold by the catalog, the budget was replenished by the purchase price of the units sold. At any point in time, the buyer had an opportunity to "declare" the product, handing it to the outlet store and for 20% of cost. However, the system also tracked customer demand not satisfied and calculated a dollar-weighted cancel rate. The dollar-weighted cancel rate was ratio of the total dollars of retail price lost due to stockouts divided by the total demand for the product. Catco required buyers to have no more than a 20% dollar-weighted cancel rate across products managed by the buyer.

HELP FROM A STATISTICIAN

Todd Gandalf was the resident statistical analyst at Catco. Maria shared the data in Exhibits 1 and 2 with Todd, and he was intrigued by the data he saw. His first reaction was to generate a plot as in Exhibit 3. The plot suggested that actual demand levels could vary from 99 units through 2,300 units, a large demand spread for the blazers. He wondered if there were any data that the buying committee had generated regarding demand for the upcoming season that could help separate the items.

However, before going down that path, he wondered what quantity would be optimal, given that costs were as provided earlier and that possible demands were generated by the distribution in Exhibit 3. He also wondered about the expected profit associated with this optimal inventory choice. Finally, he suggested that it may be useful to find the highest

EXHIBIT 2 Scatter plot of actual vs. planned demands from Exhibit 1

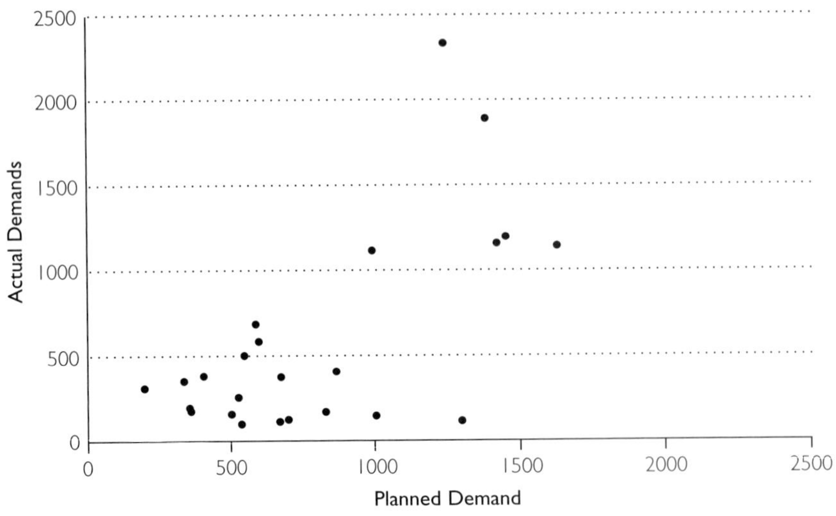

EXHIBIT 3 Histogram of Catco actual demands for the 24 blazers

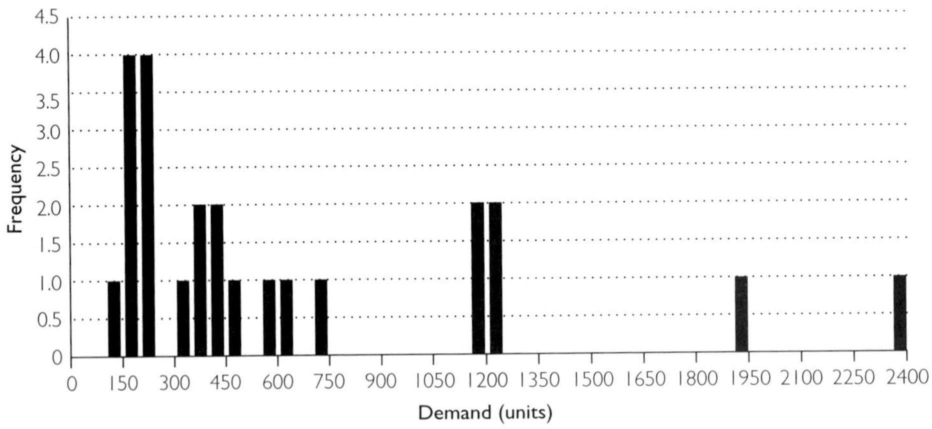

possible expected profit if Catco had advance knowledge of the demand that occurred so that purchased quantities exactly matched demand with no stockouts or no excess inventory. The difference would represent the penalty due to uncertain demand information.

LINKING FORECASTS TO ACTUAL DEMANDS

Despite accepting that forecasting was a difficult business, Maria felt that there was some content in the initial forecasted quantity. She used the following rule of thumb: If the actual demand during a season was more than 15% of what she planned, she classified the product as a good seller. If the actual demand was within 15% of what she planned, the product was a normal seller. A product whose demand was 15% below planned was classified as a poor seller. Her classification of products is thus shown in Exhibit 4. She wondered if this classification would provide a useful input to choosing order quantities for products.

She also had data, generated by the buying committee, regarding the current demand forecasts for ten products. She was not sure if the data should be used as is or if there was a way to tie this estimate with the past performance of the buyers at Catco.

A BAYESIAN APPROACH

Todd suggested a Bayesian approach to the data. He first suggested dividing up the actual demand data into groups based on buyer classification. For each category, the actual demands would be used to define a "pure demand distribu-

EXHIBIT 4 Maria's classification of the items based on the quality of forecasts

Item #	Description	Maria's Classification
1	Hyacinth	poor
2	Basketweave	poor
3	Novelty Plaid	poor
4	Tweed	poor
5	Cotton Clay	poor
6	Fuschia Flannel	poor
7	Flannel	poor
8	Houndstooth	poor
9	Rose Linen	poor
10	Plushombre	poor
11	Black Flannel	good
12	Fuschia Denim	medium
13	Purple Flannel	poor
14	Chenille	medium
15	Plaid	poor
16	Wool Double Breasted	medium
17	Wool Gabardine	medium
18	Flax	good
19	Denim	medium
20	Olive Tweed	poor
21	Silk Tweed	poor
22	Donegal	poor
23	Novelty	good
24	Military	good

tion." Based on the distribution of observed demand data in Exhibit 3, he created four demand categories and characterized them, from lowest demand to highest, as dogs, crawlers, walkers, and runners. His suggestion was categorize demands based on each of the ranges in Exhibit 5.

Once demands were categorized, he suggested using the demand data to generate a mean and standard deviation and then fit a negative binomial distribution. He suggested fixing a value of n and defining each of the pure distributions by varying p. The negative binomial distribution had two parameters, n and p, and the mean was defined as $n(1-p)/p$. The logic for choice of a negative binomial was based on the required properties from the inventory parameters and had been explored in an academic paper by Eppen and Iyer ([35]). Maria chose the parameters to define the distributions and generated the four distributions and associated p values by setting $n = 30$.

EXHIBIT 5 Classification of items based on actual demands

Classification	Demand Range
Dogs	< 260
Crawlers	260–690
Walkers	690–1200
Runners	1200–

USING BUYER JUDGMENT

As an example, a set of four distributions is shown in Exhibit 6. How could buyer estimation of the demand for a product be combined with the statistical descriptions developed? One suggestion was to take the classifications of products into the four categories from the ranges in Exhibit 5 and then consider where the products ended up based on the actual demands. Thus the data in Exhibit 1 generated the matrix in Exhibit 7. This matrix could then be used to identify a prior distribution based on the demand classification by the buyer. Thus, if the buyer selected a planned demand level below 260, then the following probabilities can be generated from Exhibit 7: dog, 0.67; crawler, 0.33.

The demand for the product would then be described as a weighted combination of the four descriptions with weights defined as Exhibit 7. Thus the composite distribution for items classified as dogs or as crawlers would be as shown in Exhibit 8, using the weights in Exhibit 7 and the distributions in Exhibit 6.

THE PURCHASE QUANTITY

Given that buyers classified a product as a dog, crawler, walker, or runner, what should be the optimal inventory decision? Maria used the cost data, the pure demand distributions, and the probabilities implied by the classification of demand to generate the order quantities for each product classification.

Starting with a spreadsheet that generated the expected profit for any specified mixture of negative binomial demands, the associated expected profit was then generated using a spreadsheet that simulated the demand for these distributions.

THE ROLE OF THE BUYER

Dorothy Masters, COO of Catco, examined the analysis but wondered aloud whether there was any value to buyer's classifications. In other words, would Catco be better off eliminating all buyers and instead using a historical frequency of occurrence of products as weights for all products? Such an analysis would suggest use of the weights based on the fraction of the twenty-four products in each of the categories.

Maria generated an inventory decision based on the binomial probabilities from Exhibit 6 and weights from Exhibit 7 and calculated the associated expected profit.

EXHIBIT 6 Plot of a sample of four distributions associated with each classification (scaled plot to show the distributions)

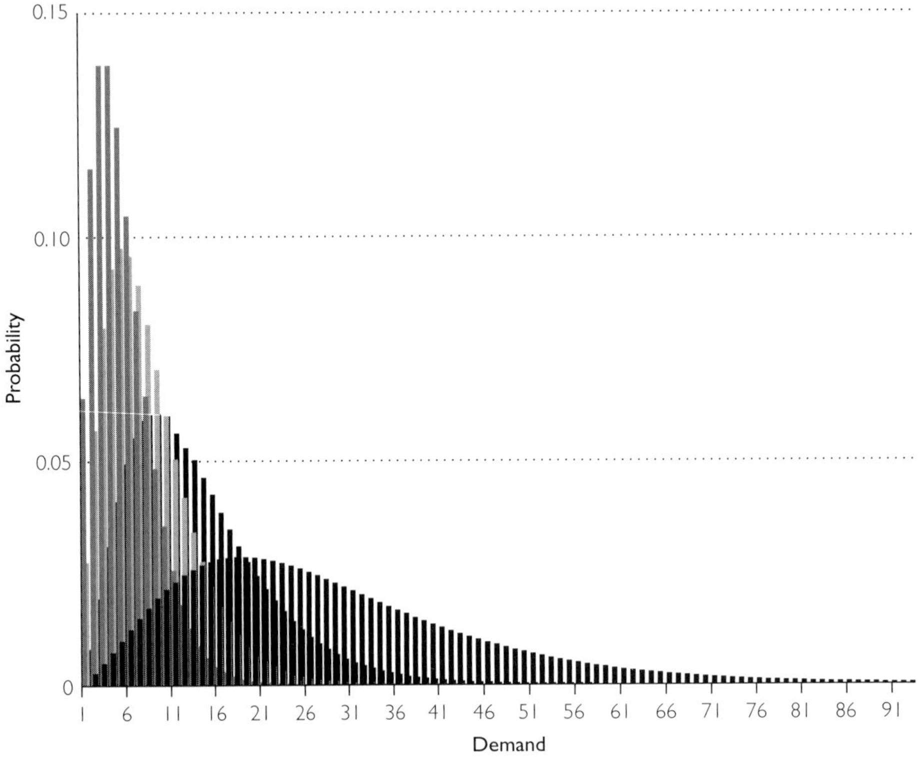

EXHIBIT 7 Matrix of planned classification vs. actual realized classification. The bottom table provides prior probabilities for each planned classification.

FREQUENCY OF OCCURRENCE OF PLANNED AND ACTUAL CLASSIFICATIONS

Actual/ Planned	Dog	Crawler	Walker	Runner
Dog	2	5	2	1
Crawler	1	6	1	0
Walker	0	0	1	3
Runner	0	0	0	2
Total	**3**	**11**	**4**	**6**

Actual/ Planned	Dog	Crawler	Walker	Runner
Dog	0.67	0.45	0.50	0.17
Crawler	0.33	0.55	0.25	0.00
Walker	0.00	0.00	0.25	0.50
Runner	0.00	0.00	0.00	0.33

IDEAL CLASSIFICATIONS

Maria then considered the best possible outcome, which was to flawlessly classify the products in their actual category. That would imply prior probabilities which had a probability of 1 for the correct classification. The implied inventory, expected profit, and total expected profit could be calculated. The gap between the observed profits and the ideal profit levels could provide an estimate of the cost of the forecast errors.

SELLING THE CONCEPT TO MANAGEMENT

How should buyer judgment and archived data be combined to improve decision making at Catco? Dorothy Masters had asked Maria to present the Liz Claiborne blazer test case to David Sun, VP of procurement at Catco. David emphasized that fashion buying was all about "gut feel." "No statistical model could replace buyer judgment," he had proclaimed.

How could the presentation to the executive be successful? Maria realized that all of the models had used data for the all years except last year. Could she use the model to show how much better Catco may have done if they had used the model the previous year? Could a model using

EXHIBIT 8 Distributions of items classified as dogs or crawlers by buyers

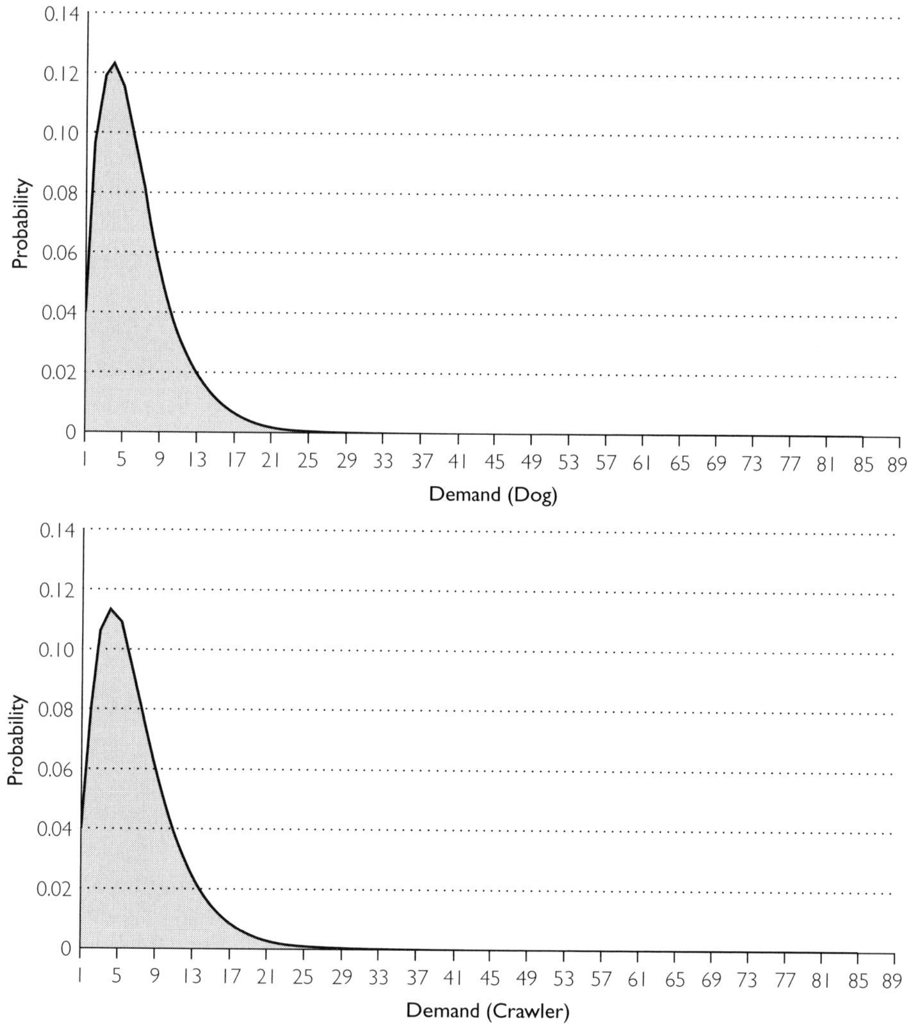

expected profits outperform for a realization of twenty-four products in any given year?

She started to put together her summary presentation as the sun was descending, ushering in an inky darkness outside her window.

EXHIBIT 9 Mean and standard deviation for each of the four classifications

Classification	Mean	Standard Deviation
Dog	154.31	46.63
Crawler	448.97	131.00
Walker	1151.37	34.92
Runner	2110.35	314.08

CASE QUESTIONS

1. Given the past performance of buyer classifications and the buying committee's classification of products into each of the four categories, provide the quantity that should be purchased by Catco to maximize expected profits. Provide the associated expected profit in each case.
2. Assume that the buying committee could perfectly identify product demands, what would be the expected profit? What is the value of perfect information in this case?
3. Consider Dorothy Masters's suggestion to eliminate buyers and identify associated expected profits. What is the value of buyers at Catco?
4. Put yourself in the role of David Sun, presented with the approach defined in the case. What considerations will influence your decision regarding adoption of this approach at Catco?

FIGURE 2 Original demand vs. actual demand

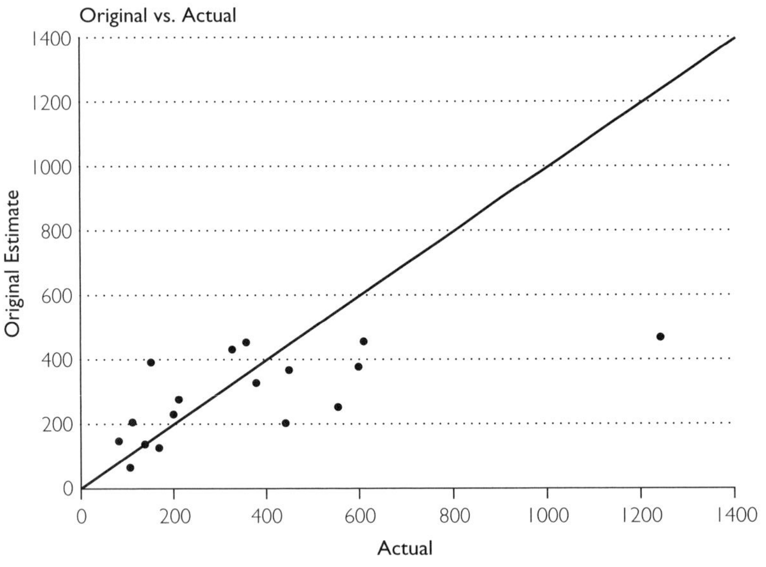

FIGURE 3 Original demand vs. actual demand after observing 2.14% of actual demand

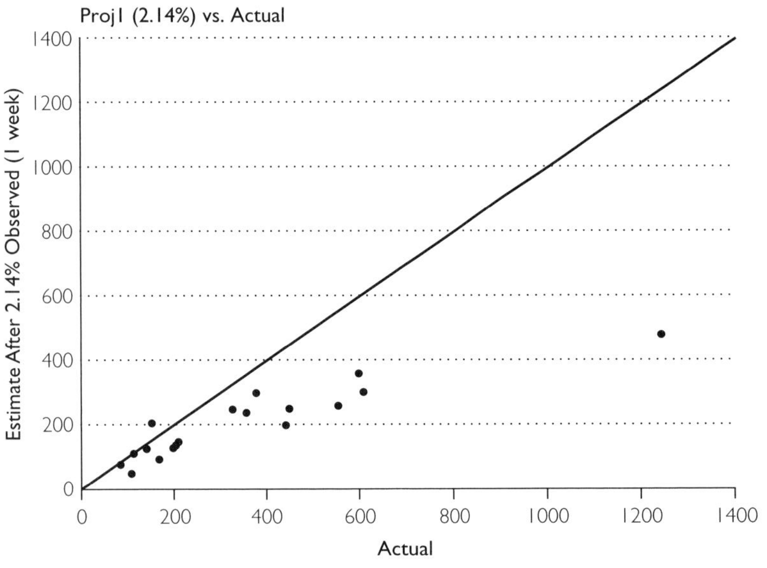

FIGURE 4 Original demand vs. actual demand after observing 7.07% of actual demand

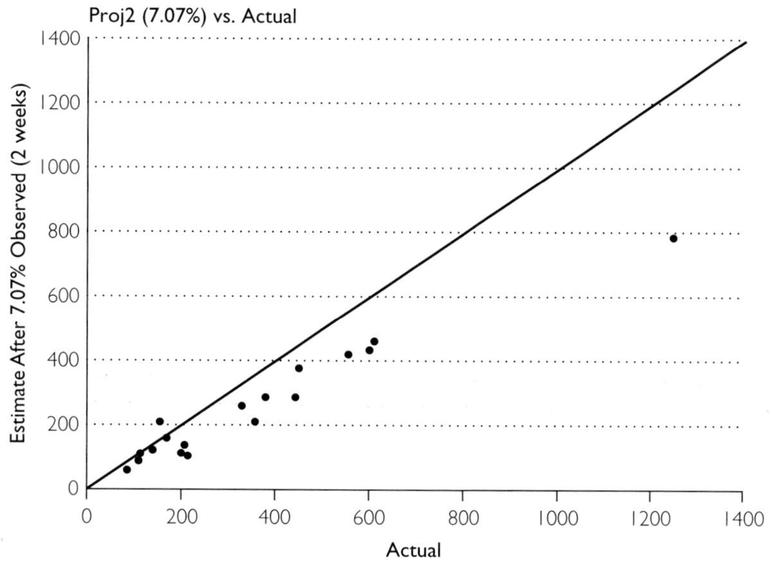

FIGURE 5 Original demand vs. actual demand after observing 13.37% of actual demand

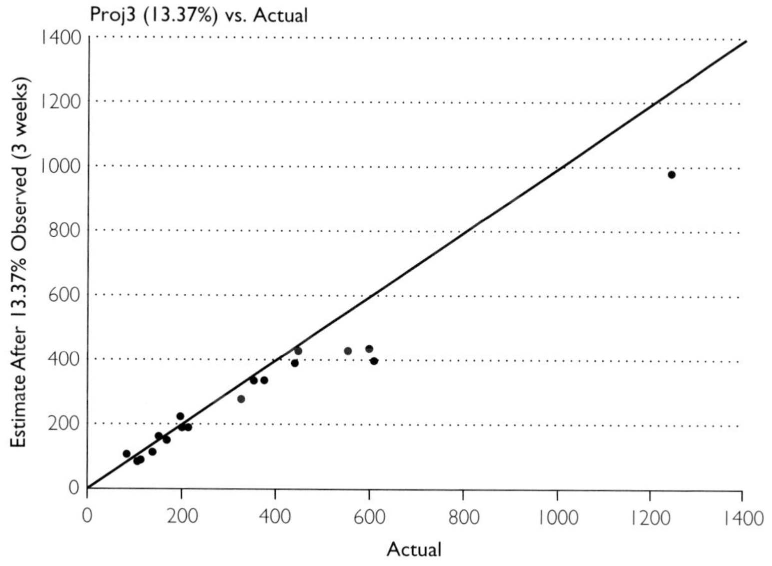

FIGURE 6 Original demand vs. actual demand after observing 21.17% of actual demand

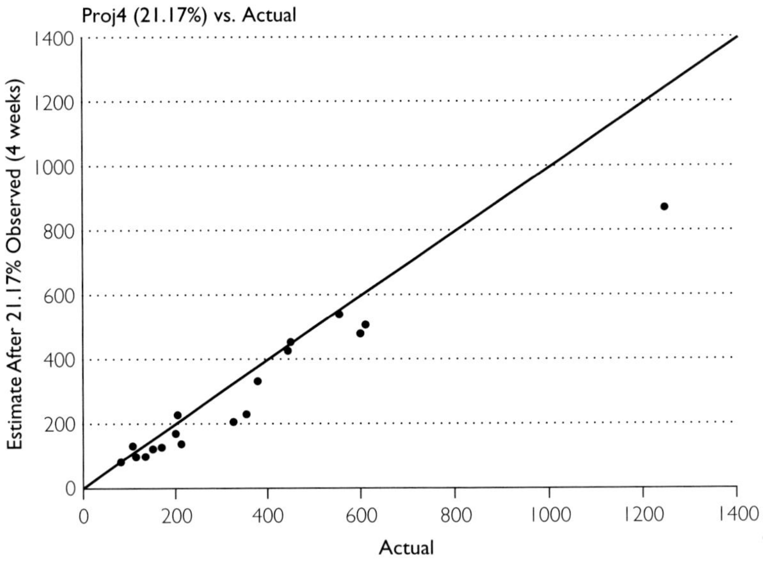

FIGURE 7 Original demand vs. actual demand after observing 54.96% of actual demand

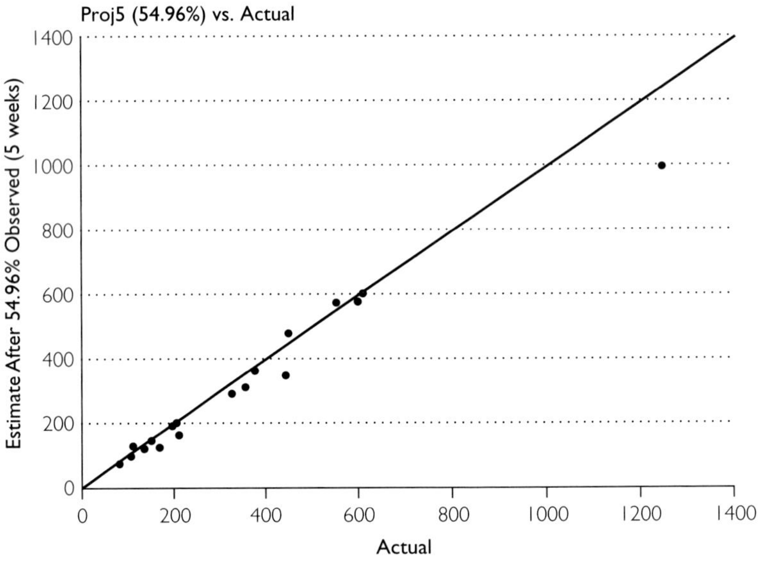

Chapter 11

Spare Parts

In many industries, the provision of spare parts and associated services represents a significant component of supply chain profits. Some studies ([20]) estimate US sales of spare parts and after-sales services to be 8% of the annual gross domestic product (GDP) or $1 trillion. Others ([25]) suggest, for example, that in 2001, General Motors earned relatively more profits from its $9 billion in after-sales revenues than it did from $150 billion in car sales. Another estimate ([124]) suggests that the total cost of ownership of a product may far exceed the amount spent on the initial product purchase and may vary between five and twenty times the original product cost. The main conclusion from these studies is that managing spare parts supply chains and related services after a product is sold may have a significant impact on both primary demand as well as on profits.

11.1 SPARE PARTS AND THE 4CS OF SUPPLY CHAIN MANAGEMENT

Consider the architecture of the spare parts supply chain. Demand flows from specific customer locations, where breakdowns and thus demands for specific spare parts and service occur, to dealers, regional distribution centers, central distribution centers, and manufacturing plants. Parts flow in response to these demands, with lead times decreased by forward positioning inventories. The capacity to service demand requests depends on the availability of parts at each of the levels of the supply chain as well as on the availability of associated servicing capacity. Design of the product can assist in increasing this capacity by permitting replacement of entire modules, thus decoupling product repair from the lead time for diagnosis and repair of the module. Coordination of maintenance information and product design updates with product usage data and management of the associated spare parts inventory can improve supply chain performance. In addition, coordinating the pricing and service guarantees with adjustment of the associated service capacity enables service guarantees to be met with high probability. Competitiveness metrics in aftermarket can range from speed of response to minimizing the cost of response to an offer of ironclad performance guarantees to offer of product on a pay-as-you-use basis, which moves the responsibility for product availability to the manufacturer.

The next sections provide a set of specific problem contexts along with a description of an adjustment of the supply chain architecture that improved performance of the supply chain.

11.2 MANAGING SPARE PARTS AT THE US COAST GUARD

Chapter 5 on coordination provides a description of the spare parts inventory supply chain at the US Coast Guard (USCG) ([27]). We summarize the specific features of the spare parts system and the changes made to improve performance. The main supply chain support for air assets for the Coast Guard is the Aircraft Repair and Supply Center (ARSC) located in Elizabeth City, NC. Aircraft failures in the airstations are often tracked to part failures. Those parts are replaced with working parts from field inventory at the air station and the salvageable broken components are shipped to ARSC for repair. In turn, ARSC replenishes field inventory.

Figure 11.1 shows a supply-chain view of the aircraft service activities. Data are tracked in two separate databases: Aviation Computerized Maintenance System (ACMS) and Aviation Maintenance Management System (AMMIS). The ACMS database stores individual part-level serial number tracking and history of repairs and planned maintenance. The AMMIS database tracks flow of the broken part as it is repaired. In the original system, these two databases did not communicate ([27]).

Item managers (IMs) at USCG were responsible provision of spare parts, with each IM responsible for a group of parts. Typically, IMs used a part's demand history and treated demand for a part as an independent event. They chose a sufficient inventory level to satisfy demand, using ad hoc rules, developed through years of experience, to run the system.

FIGURE 11.1 A supply-chain view of spare parts flows at US Coast Guard

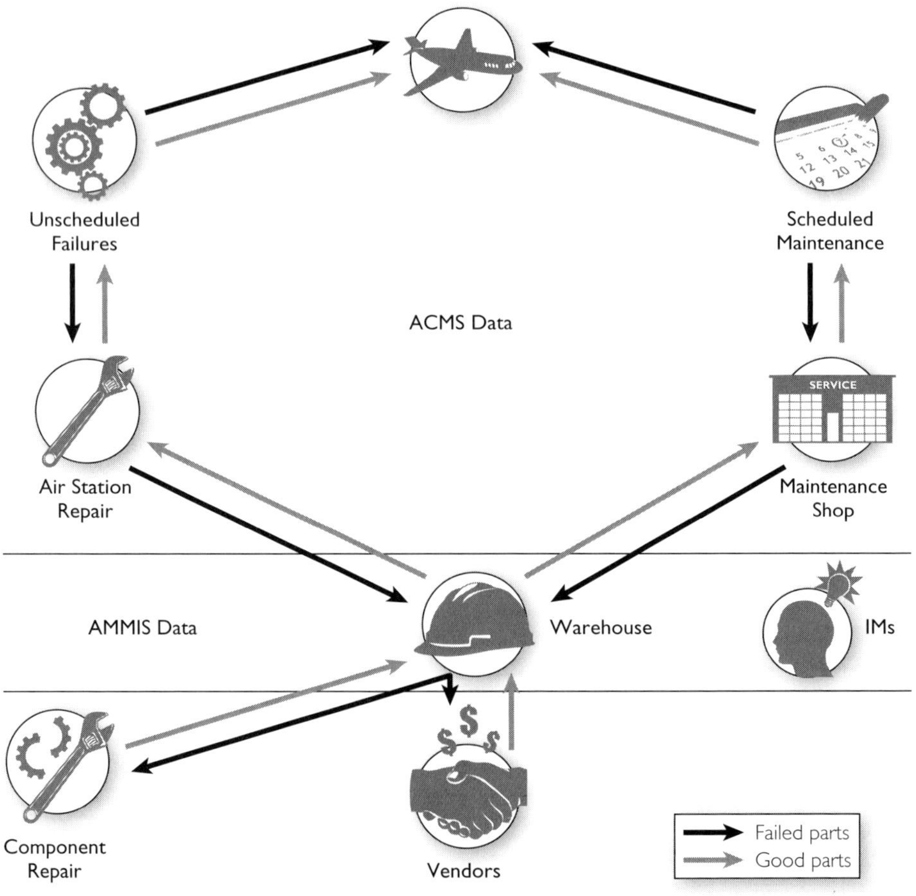

FIGURE 11.2 An integrated supply-chain view based on analysis at US Coast Guard

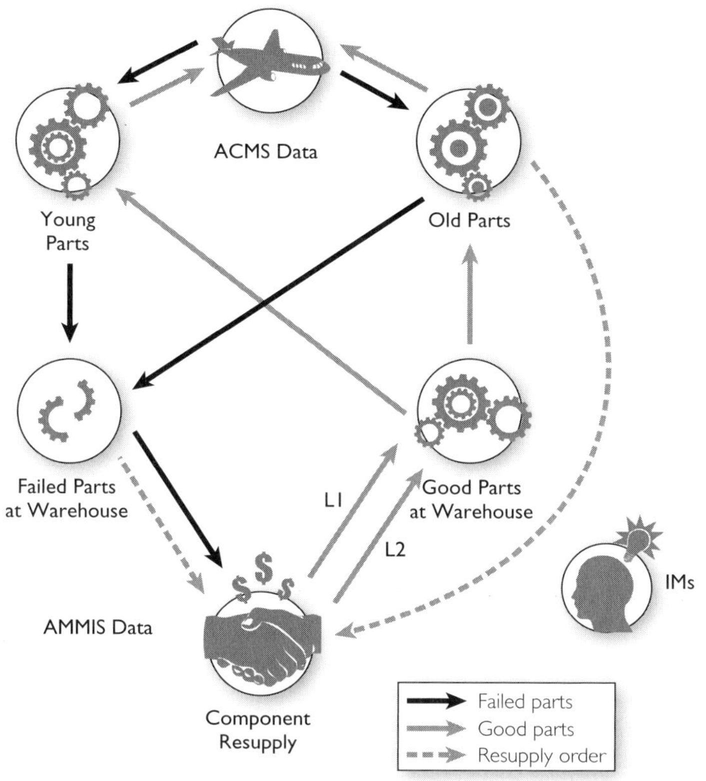

Officers at the USCG wanted to devise a scheme to use ACMS maintenance information to improve performance.

Figure 11.2 summarizes the approach described in [27]. While several details are skipped, the key step is to incorporate part age information in the replenishment policy used by the IMs. This was implemented using an age-trigger mechanism that would signal when a part's age crossed a certain threshold. The idea was to use the number of parts whose age exceeds a certain threshold as a signal to forecast impending demand and thus adjust the level of inventory. The approach synchronized inventory with forecasted upcoming demands, thus decreasing costs while improving service.

The inventory policy tracks the number of old and new parts in the system, and the age threshold is optimized to account for marginal costs of shortage and holding and repair lead time. As Figure 11.2 shows, we anticipate the demand for old parts and trigger advance orders for these parts directly with the suppliers. For failures of young parts, we wait for failure to generate a replenishment order. If failures of old parts are more predictable, then triggering advance orders for these parts has the potential to decrease expected residence time for parts in the system and thus decrease overall inventory costs.

An outline of the specific adjustment of the inventory is as follows. Suppose the observed demand is correlated with the advance signals regarding the number of old parts. The observed correlation for different age thresholds is shown in Figure 11.3. Consider a model where the part age signal and the observed demand over supply lead time follow a joint bivariate normal distribution. Each period, once the part age signal is observed, the conditional distribution of actual demand during lead time can be generated. For any given service level, the associated inventory level is obtained.

The paper [27] provides details of the application using data from USCG. The projected benefits from using this approach were an increase in service for the same budget and a decrease in costs to provide the current level of service. The key idea—coordinating part use and thus

FIGURE 11.3 Correlation between signal and demand for different thresholds

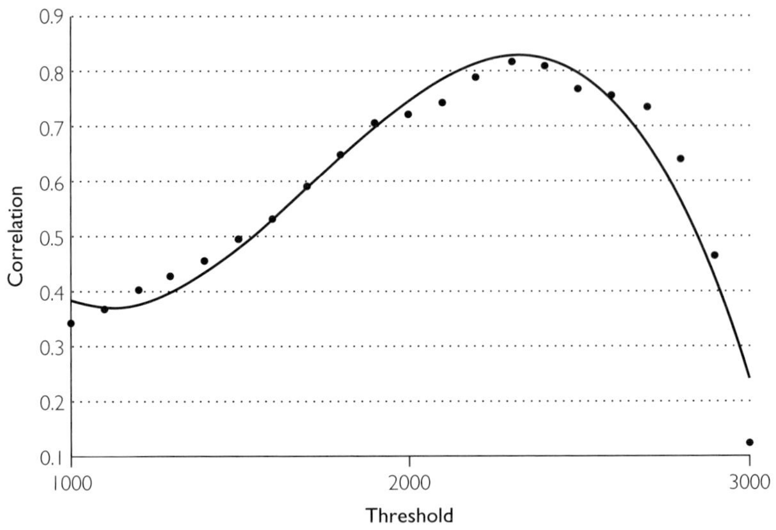

part age with the associated demand forecast—can permit part inventory to be adjusted proactively, thus improving performance. In contrast, a purely replenishment approach would have decreased part inventory if demands are not observed for a while. Note that this is the opposite of the idea that was implemented, because low observed demands suggests that the parts being used on aircraft were getting old, thus increasing the likelihood of high demands soon. This difference in perspective generated improvement in supply chain performance.

11.3 SPARE PARTS AT SATURN

Cohen et al. ([18]) describe the management of the after-sales parts availability at Saturn, a division of General Motors. They report that, in 2000, Saturn had the highest off-the-shelf parts availability across all brands. As a result, customers of Saturn return for repairs and scheduled maintenance for many more years than other automobile owners.

Demands for automobile parts can be triggered by a car crash or other repair incident, routine maintenance, a do-it-yourself project, or the needs of a non-Saturn repair-service provider. Repairs can occur at scheduled times (due to planned maintenance) or at random. The parts required for a repair would not be known until the car was diagnosed at the shop. Customers, however, prefer to wait for no more than one day to receive their repaired car back.

The usual part-procurement process for Saturn is as follows ([18]): If the part was out of stock at the retailer, the order would go to a "pooling group," consisting of nearby retailers who may be able to supply the part from their inventory. If the pooling group could not supply the part, it would be ordered from the DC or from the supplier. Inventory at stocking locations would be visible in real time to all entities to determine part availability with all costs of part transfers borne by Saturn. The stocking and replenishment decisions at locations would be revised based on daily sales data by location.

Two key issues were managed to ensure high in-stock levels ([18]). (1) Product criticality: There may be differences in necessity of the parts for function of the car. For example, a failure of an engine part might be serious, while a failure of a radio part is less serious. Thus it may be important to determine the cost to the customer associated with product failure and thereby the value of the component's uptime. (2) Decisions regarding a centralized or distributed service strategy: Under a centralized strategy, the goal is to achieve the highest turnover at lowest cost, with point-of-sale data used to forecast sales and thus choose inventory levels. Under a distributed service system, the goal is to determine customer need and obtain the part. In such a case, forecasting may depend on estimates of part reliability and the local installed base of cars. Coordination across locations to obtain parts plays an important role in managing performance.

As described in [18], the main challenges in the auto parts supply chain are (1) intermittent parts consumption with very low turns, (2) enormous disparity across part costs, (3) great variety across models, with hundreds and thousands of SKUs worth billions of dollars in inventory across the supply chain, (4) variable value of delivered service based on the severity of the failure, (5) lack of dealer interest in becoming efficient inventory managers, and (6) failure to see the connection between providing good service and selling cars.

11.4 SUPPLYING PRODUCT IN THE CHICAGO SCHOOL SYSTEM

Eisenstein and Iyer ([33]) provide a description of a project to improve supply availability in the Chicago Public Schools system. The supply chain consisted of a warehouse that supplied products to 600 public schools. The products included engineering and educational supplies. Engineering supplies, also called Class A, included toilet paper, paper towels, rock salt, and so on, and accounted for about 50% of dollar value of the warehouse shipments but 1% of the items and 70% of the shipment volume. Educational supplies, also called Class B, accounted for 99% of the items, 50% of the dollar volume, and 30% of the physical volume. In the original system, all items shared a common truck capacity to minimize waste shipment space. Each school had a scheduled delivery once every two weeks.

At the start of the project, schools had observed poor on-time delivery of products. The planned delivery lead time of two weeks was often replaced by an observed lead time of three weeks and a maximum of up to eight weeks. Figure 11.4 shows the original distribution of delivery lead times. Figure 11.5 shows the fluctuation in volume of loads across days as a line

FIGURE 11.4 Lead times originally observed by schools

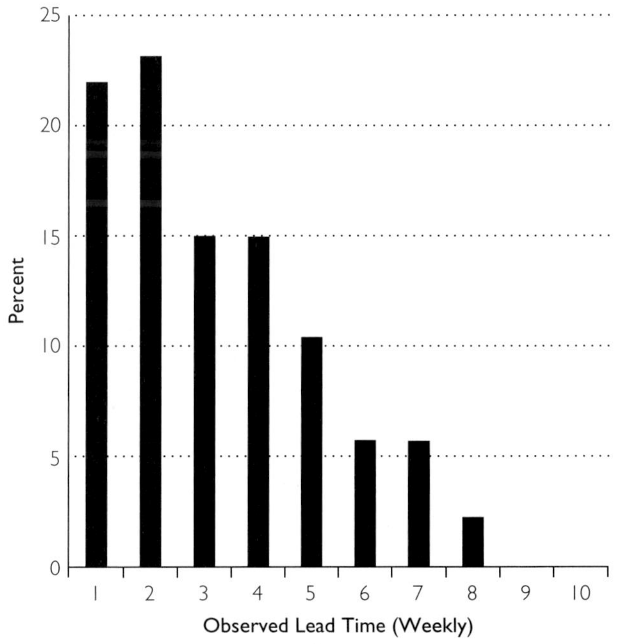

FIGURE 11.5 Demand volume fluctuations over time

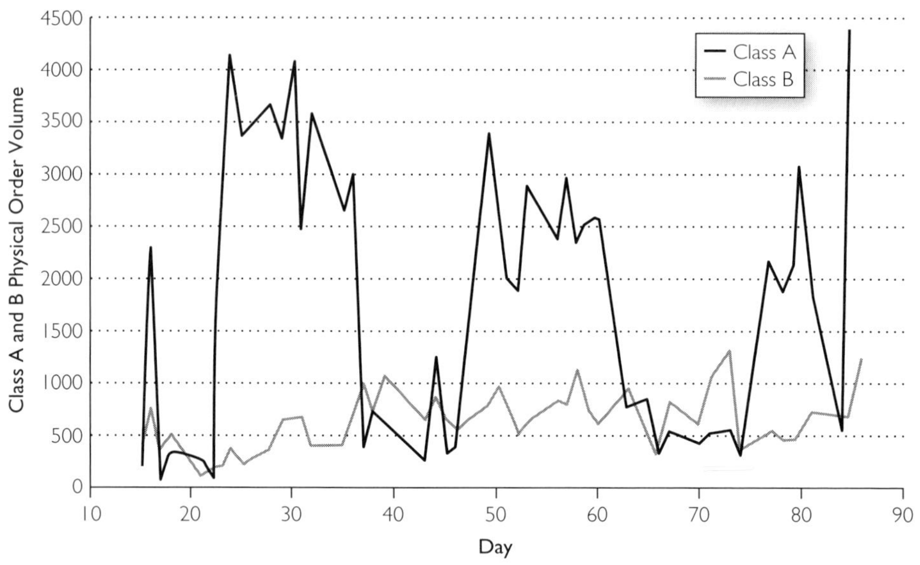

FIGURE 11.6 Capacity in pallet loads compared to trucking capacity

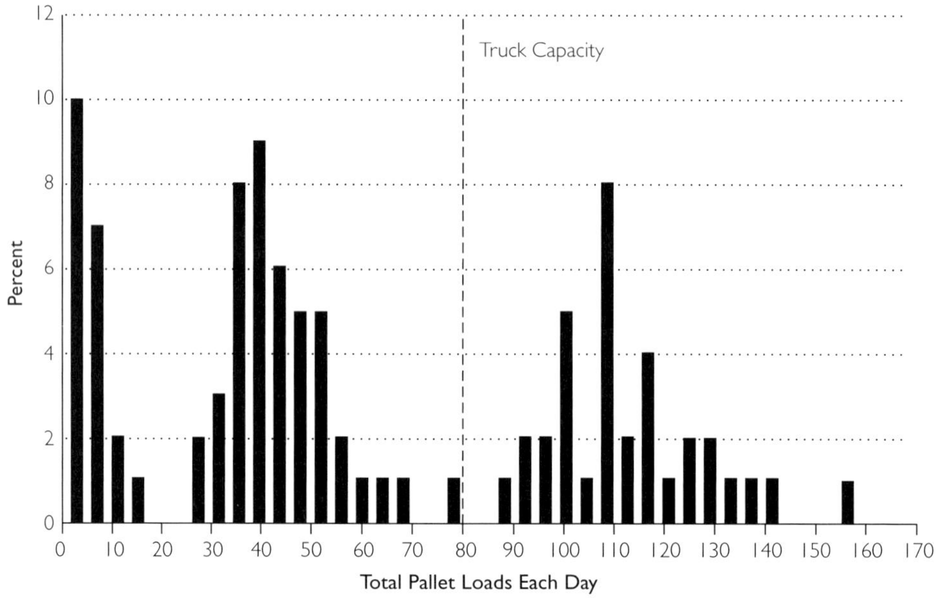

graph and as a histogram with the truck capacity indicated. Figure 11.6 shows the same volume each day relative to the available trucking capacity. It is clear that there are many periods when the loads exceed truck capacity and thus result in the lead times observed in Figure 11.4.

The project ([33]) describes a new system in which truck capacity was split so that deliveries of engineering goods, whose demands were predictable, were done once every two weeks. However, delivery of hard-to-predict educational supplies was done overnight, via the schools' internal mail system. This synchronization of delivery lead times to part demand characteristics improved system performance. The reorganized system observed faster delivery without any increase in truck capacity and reduced costs by over $150,000 per year.

Notice that the new system replaced the single supply chain with two separate supply chains, each with its own product and delivery characteristics. In Chapter 4 on capacity, we described conditions when splitting capacity may improve the system (Section 4.5). In the same chapter, we also discussed how offering different lead times for different products may improve system performance (Section 4.8). The application at the Chicago Public Schools system is such an implementation.

11.5 LOCATING SAFETY STOCKS AT EASTMAN KODAK

Graves and Willems ([48]) provide an example of a network model to determine safety stocks in a supply chain at Eastman Kodak. The supply chain involves a high-end digital camera, procured from an outside vendor, that came with lens, shutter, and focus functions. The imager, circuit board assembly, and many other parts were assembled and tested. The final product was then moved to a distribution center and shipped against demands. The parts in the camera were classified into two groups, one with a lead time of under 60 days and the other with a lead time of over 60 days.

The model (described in Section 11.18) determined the optimal safety stock levels at each location to minimize the overall holding costs. In this example, individual functional areas added constraints. Marketing determined that the service time for the customer should be five days. The assembly group required safety stock of the imagers to be held at the assembly plant, thus setting the lead time for imager to zero. The effect of these constraints was to increase the safety stock by 8.7%. The optimal solution held no inventory at the distribution center and generated a cost of holding safety stock of $78,000. The product flow team also used the model to evaluate the effect of adding other constraints such as both manufacturing and distribution holding safety stock and quoting zero service times. This increased costs to $89,000. Another policy examined was only the distribution center holding safety stock. This changed the cost to $81,000 and was used as the solution acceptable to management. The authors state that the model use coincided with an improvement in delivery performance from 80% to 97%, while worldwide finished goods inventory decreased from $6.7 million to $3.6 million, and worldwide raw material inventory and work in process inventory decreased from $5.7 million to $2.9 million between 1995 and 1997 at one assembly site ([48]).

11.6 VOLVO GM HEAVY TRUCK CORPORATION

Narus and Anderson ([90]) describe a study of Volvo GM Heavy Truck Corporation and its dealers. An important source of revenue for Volvo GM is its sales of repair parts for its commercial trucks. However, in the mid 1990s, dealers reported high stockout rates even though inventory levels of spare parts were rising. Dealers complained that lack of consistent service was causing lost business as customers replaced Volvo parts with generics.

Analysis of the demands faced by dealers showed that customers placed orders for two reasons: scheduled maintenance and emergency roadside repairs. Since scheduled maintenance was predictable, the necessary parts could be ordered ahead of schedule and managed. But demands for emergency repairs were not predictable and required a different supply process. Volvo GM, working with FedEx Logistics Services, set up a warehouse in Memphis, TN, and stocked it with truck parts. All emergency repair requests were shipped out by FedEx, for delivery either overnight or the same day. Parts are picked up at the airport or are delivered to the roadside repair site with delivery charges paid for by customers. This dual delivery approach for the supply chain enabled Volvo GM to eliminate three warehouses and decrease total inventory by about 15% while increasing service level and substantially decreasing stockouts.

(3) replenishment requirements to restock lower echelon locations. Developing demand from these building blocks enabled insights into demands that were from a combination of replenishment orders and emergency orders. The implemented model enabled the system to adjust inventory levels to synchronize with impending demand, service guarantees, and product architecture, thus permitting either lower costs or increased service levels at the same cost.

11.13 ESTIMATING THE IMPACT OF ECHELON STOCK

The goal of this section is to develop intuition regarding the optimal inventory location point in a supply chain. The concepts will be illustrated with a numerical example.

Consider a supply chain with two spare-parts demand stations that face a daily demand for a part that follows a normal distribution with a mean (μ) of 50 and a standard deviation (σ) of 25. Assume that the parts stations face a replenishment cost (K) of \$125, a holding cost (h) of \$0.2/day/part, a backorder cost (b) of \$5/day/part. Also, suppose each station faces a supply lead time (L) of 3 days to be replenished by the central warehouse. The corresponding service level *ser* $\dfrac{b}{h+b} = 0.96$ and the associated $Z_{ser} = 1.75$.

If each parts station were to operate a (Q, r) policy, they would each maintain a reorder level r as follows:

$$r = (\mu \times L) + \left(Z_{ser} \times \sigma \times \sqrt{L}\right)$$

$$= (50 \times 3) + \left(1.75 \times 25 \times \sqrt{3}\right) = 225.8$$

Also, the order quantity Q would be calculated as

$$Q = \left(\sqrt{\frac{2 \times K \times \mu}{h}}\right)$$

$$= \left(\sqrt{\frac{2 \times 125 \times 50}{0.2}}\right) = 250$$

The central warehouse processes orders received from the parts stations. Suppose the costs for the central warehouse are also K = 125, h = 0.2, b = 5, and L = 3. The central warehouse is replenished by vendors and serves as a consolidation point.

Using an Excel worksheet, simulation of the orders received at the central warehouse generates an average demand across 100 periods of $\mu_C = 101.07$ and the standard deviation, $\sigma_C = 141.57$. With this mean and standard deviation, and using the same formulas as before, the corresponding values of reorder level and order quantity at the central warehouse are as follows:

$$r_C = (\mu_C \times L) + \left(Z_{ser} \times \sigma_C \times \sqrt{L}\right)$$

$$= (101.07 \times 3) + \left(1.75 \times 141.57 \times \sqrt{3}\right) = 732.32$$

$$Q_C = \left(\sqrt{\frac{2 \times K \times \mu_C}{h}}\right)$$

$$= \left(\sqrt{\frac{2 \times 125 \times 101.07}{0.2}}\right) = 355.43$$

Again, using an Excel spreadsheet, simulation of the expected costs across 100 iterations and 100 periods yields an expected cost per day at the central warehouse of \$166.26, an expected inventory level each day of \$658.99.

Note, however, that the orders received by the central warehouse follow a "lumpy" pattern with demands bunched up with erratic intervals in between. This lumpiness reflects the batch sizes of orders placed by parts stations. But orders received by the central warehouse display a negative serial correlation across time, i.e., if we receive an order from a parts station at time t, there is a much smaller probability of receiving another order from that same station in period $t + 1$.

Suppose we maintain the value of Q_C as equal to the economic order quantity at the warehouse, i.e., we set

$$Q_C = \left(\sqrt{\frac{2 \times K \times \mu_C}{h}}\right)$$

$$= \left(\sqrt{\frac{2 \times 125 \times 101.07}{0.2}}\right) = 355.44$$

Modeling of the demand stream at the central warehouse shows that it is possible to decrease the inventory (in this case by 34% in simulations) and associated costs (by about 26% in this example) by taking into account the demand structure. This example illustrates the need for careful analysis of the inventory policies at an echelon of a distribution system that faces a demand that reacts to the costs and demands experienced by the lower levels of the distribution system.

11.14 VARIANCE OF ORDERS FACED BY AN ECHELON

In this section, we discuss a simple model that shows the variance of order sizes arriving at an echelon of a logistics system. Suppose we have N inventory locations, each facing a demand rate of D_i units per day and a batch size of Q_i. These locations place orders that arrive at an echelon. The goal is to obtain the mean and variance of orders arriving at the echelon.

Note that location i places orders once every $\frac{Q_i}{D_i}$ units of time. Thus the probability that the echelon observes an order from location i on any given day (p_i) is $\frac{D_i}{Q_i}$ We assume that $Q_i \geq D_i$. Thus, from location i, the echelon receives an order of size Q_i with probability p_i and an order of 0 with probability $1 - p_i$. The associated mean and variance across the N locations are as follows:

$$\text{Mean demand at the echelon/day} = \Sigma_{i=1}^{N} Q_i p_i.$$

$$\text{Variance of demand at the echelon/day} = \Sigma_{i=1}^{N} Q_i^2 p_i (1 - p_i).$$

11.14.1 Numerical Example

For the model described in Section 11.13, with $N = 2$, daily demand for a part that follows a normal distribution with a mean (μ) of 50 and a standard deviation (σ) of 25. Assume that the parts stations face a replenishment cost (K) of \$125, a holding cost (h) of \$0.2/day/part, a backorder cost (b) of \$5/day/part. Also, suppose each station faces a supply lead time (L) of 3 days to be replenished by the central warehouse. The corresponding service level $ser = \frac{b}{h+b} = 0.96$ and the associated $Z_{ser} = 1.77$.

The corresponding values of $Q_1 = Q_2 = 250$ and $p_1 = p_2 = \frac{50}{250} = 0.2$. This yields the values

$$\mu_C = (250 \times 0.2) + (250 \times 0.2) = 100$$

$$\sigma_C = \sqrt{(250^2 \times 0.2 \times (1 - 0.2)) + (250^2 \times 0.2 \times (1 - 0.2))}$$

$$= 141.42.$$

Thus the echelon faces a demand with a mean of 100 units and a standard deviation of 141.42 units. Notice that the increased standard deviation of demand at the echelon reflects both order uncertainty as well as the lumpiness caused by the batched ordering from locations.

11.15 INVENTORY LEVELS ACCOUNTING FOR THE IMPACT OF PART SUBSTITUTION

This section provides a numerical example to illustrate the inventory impact of part substitution on inventory levels and costs. Consider a retail location that sells two products. Product 1 costs $5, and product 2 costs $10. Product 2 can perform all the functions of product 1 and more. The retail selling price for product 1 is $10, and the retail selling price of product 2 is $13. Demand for each product is normally distributed each period with a mean of 50 units and a standard deviation of 25 units. Holding cost per unit per period is $0.20 per unit per period, and the backorder cost is $5 per unit per period. Each period the retailer places reorders from a supplier and faces a lead time of 4 periods for delivery. These data are captured in Table 11.1.

Table 11.2 shows the effect of decreasing the inventory of the first product (by x) and increasing the inventory of the second product by the corresponding quantity (i.e., by x), in other words changing the inventory mix. Note that increasing product 2 inventory allows the retailer to increase expected profit from $435.52 (under substitution) to $452.35 when x is 40 (Table 11.2), when the standard deviation is 25. This happens because of the flexibility of product 2 to satisfy its own demand as well as product 1's demand.

Consider the impact of the following retailer scheme: *If the location were to run out of product 1, offer the customer product 2 for the price of product 1.* Note that when the demand standard deviation is 25 units, the effect of substitution is to increase expected profit from $420.69 to $435.52. This increase in expected profit is realized because of the opportunity to get both revenue for product that could be potentially backordered as well as associated savings on the backorder costs in the presence of the alternate to substitute product demand.

Thus permitting substitution may help both decrease inventories and increase service levels in a supply chain.

11.16 PRIORITIZING DEMANDS TO IMPROVE INVENTORY LEVELS

Consider the school system example provided at the start of the chapter and the example from Volvo truck division. In Section 11.4, the more variable demand products were offered a shorter lead time while the less variable orders were offered a longer lead time.

TABLE 11.1 Impact of substitution on expected profits

Standard Deviation	Expected Profit (No Substitution)	Expected Profit (Substitution)
10	496.44	500.57
15	468.82	476.25
25	420.69	435.52
35	370.72	389.48
40	340.44	360.92

TABLE 11.2 Impact of substitution on adjusted inventory

x	Expected Profit (substitution)
0	435.52
10	441.29
20	447.73
30	451.98
40	452.35
50	450.69

Such an approach can decrease overall inventory levels because the safety stock associated with a lead time depends on both the demand variability and the lead time. But how can such a matching of demand variability to lead time be accomplished?

It is clear that the cost associated with inventory depends on the variance of demand during lead time. In such a case, the larger the demand variance, the greater the effect of lead time on safety stock. Now suppose orders to a facility came from two sources that differ in their demand variability. Suppose we provide priority to the higher demand variance orders and low priority to the low demand variance order; what is the impact? Note that, as shown analytically and illustrated with a numerical example in Chapter 4 on capacity management, if one set of orders receives a priority, the lead time for those orders will decrease. But, since the capacity level is unchanged, the lead time for the lower priority orders will increase. Thus, priorities are one mechanism to offer differentiated lead times across order streams and thus improve supply chain performance for spare parts.

The following example appears in Section 4.8, and is reproduced here for convenience. A manufacturer services two products sold by retailers, with demand for each of the two products being $m_1 = 140$ units per day and $m_2 = 60$ units per day, and demand standard deviations of $\sigma_1 = 125$ units and $\sigma_2 = 25$ units. The batch size for both products is 100 units. Thus, the order batch rate from each product would be $\lambda_1 = 1.4$ orders per day and $\lambda_2 = 0.6$ orders per day, respectively, for a total arrival rate of 2 orders per day across both products. Given the batch size, suppose the set-up time for an order is 0.1 days and the processing time per unit is 0.003 days. The corresponding service rate for any order batch of 100 units is 2.5 orders per day or $\left(\frac{1}{0.1+(0.003\times 100)}\right)$.

Notice that if both products were accessing capacity in order of arrival, they would both face the same lead time of 2 days. The corresponding impact on their safety stock would be 363.05 units for the first product and 72.61 units for the second product (obtained using the equation $Z\sigma\sqrt{L}$). Thus the total inventory across both products would be 435.66 units.

However, suppose product 1, which has a higher variability, is given priority over product 2. Then the new lead times, using the formulas provided in Section 4.8, would be $L_1 = 1.12$ and $L_2 = 4.03$ days. With these lead times, notice that the corresponding safety stock for the first product would be 272.55 units, which decreases from the earlier case, while the safety stock for the second product would be 103.15 units, which increases from the earlier case. Note that the total inventory across both products is now 375.72 units. This decrease in inventory reflects the benefit of tailoring access to the supply chain based on product demand characteristics. Notice that giving priority to the more variable product permits its lead time to decrease, thus decreasing the safety stock for that product. But clearly this comes at a cost to the less variable product, whose lead time increases but at a slower rate.

In other words, it may be worth reconsidering how products or orders get access to capacity. Tailoring the access to capacity based on product characteristics can improve the overall supply chain performance.

11.17 THE BENEFIT OF GEOGRAPHIC POSTPONEMENT OF CRITICAL PARTS

Express delivery companies, such as FedEx, offer services such as critical parts supply. This service stores critical parts for OEMs at one of FedEx's hubs. As soon as there is demand for a part, FedEx will schedule to get it delivered to the desired location based on the promised guarantee. The transportation mode used may vary from a next flight out from a regular airport to a FedEx same-day shipment to a next-day shipment. While premium transport is an expense, such services permit geographic postponement and thus an opportunity to pool demand risk across locations.

To estimate the benefit, let Δ be the additional cost per unit for premium transport. The benefit of a centralized location with express shipping is justified if we have $hZ\sigma\left(N-\sqrt{N}\right)>\Delta\mu$. As the premium paid for express shipments declines and the value of such service guarantees increases, geographic postponement increases in value to the OEM. Typical products that use such services include expensive but light parts, pharmaceutical products that are time sensitive, repair facilities for critical equipment, and so on.

11.18 STRATEGIC SAFETY STOCK POSITIONING

Graves and Willems ([48]) describe an approach to set safety stocks in a supply chain in order to provide the desired customer lead time. Their approach provides a conceptual basis to consider location of service parts inventory across a supply chain to optimize overall performance. The data for a sample five-stage serial supply chain is shown in Figure 11.7, with the supply chain details in the stage description row.

The supply chain is described along with production times, maximum demands over time, and costs. If for a location i, the inbound service level is S_{i-1}, the production time is T_i, and the outbound service level is S_i, then the net replenishment interval is $S_{i-1} + T_i - S_i$. In order to guarantee that demands up to a certain service level (ser) will be satisfied, the safety stock level that has to be maintained is $Z_{ser}\sigma\sqrt{S_{i-1}+T_i-S_i}$. A key result is that at each location i, it is optimal to have either $S_i^* = 0$ or $S_i^* = S_{i-1}^* + T_i$. This result implies that each location either carries no safety stock and is a pass-through location or that it decouples that stage from the result of the network upstream by providing a zero service time.

Next consider the possible locations of the zero service time across the five nodes in the network. This generates 32 possible service-time combinations involving the positioning of the zero service-time locations. Given these zero service-time nodes, in order to determine the requires safety stock, start from the first node (on the left) and set the service time equal to 0 (if specified) or to $S_{i-1} + T_i$ otherwise. Assume that $S_0 = 0$. Thus, for example, if all service times were set to 0, the required safety stock would be the sum of the safety stocks required to provide 0 service time, which is the sum of the safety stock values in Figure 11.7, as can be seen in the last column of the first row with service time values in Figure 11.8. On the other hand, if the service times for all nodes are nonzero except for node 5, then the service times will be set as 20, 25, 28, 29, and 0 respectively. The associated lead time to be covered by safety stock is 29 + 3, which includes the preceding stages' lead

FIGURE 11.7 Data for a sample supply chain

STAGE	1		2		3		4		5
	Purchase Parts	→	Build Subassembly	→	Produce Assembly	→	Ship to DC	→	Ship to Retailer
Holding cost %	15.00		15.00		15.00		15.00		15.00
Production Time	20.00		5.00		3.00		1.00		3.00
Stage Incremental Cost	20.00		25.00		45.00		10.00		10.00
Cumulative Cost	20.00		45.00		90.00		100.00		110.00
Z (service level)	1.64		1.64		1.64		1.64		1.64
Sigma	20.00		20.00		20.00		20.00		20.00
Service Time	0.00		0.00		0.00		0.00		0.00
Safety Stock	441.36		496.53		769.22		493.46		940.16

times as well as stage 5's production time of 3 periods. Thus the holding cost of safety stock is $0.15 \times 110 \times 1.64 \times \sqrt{29+3}$ or 3070.55, which is the holding cost (15% of cumulative cost through stage 5) times safety stock required to provide a zero lead time to the end customer. Figure 11.8 provides the holding cost of the safety stock for the 32 different possible settings of service levels across the five nodes in the network.

FIGURE 11.8 Data for a sample supply chain

SERVICE TIME					SAFETY STOCK COST
1	2	3	4	5	
Purchase Parts	Build Subassembly	Produce Assembly	Ship to DC	Ship to Retailer	
0	0	0	0	0	3140.73
0	0	0	1	0	2792.72
0	0	3	0	0	2864.96
0	0	3	4	0	2374.01
0	5	0	0	0	3131.11
0	5	0	1	0	2783.10
0	5	8	0	0	2861.89
0	5	8	9	0	2321.68
20	0	0	0	0	3313.11
20	0	0	1	0	2965.10
20	0	3	0	0	3037.35
20	0	3	4	0	2546.39
20	25	0	0	0	3783.63
20	25	0	1	0	3435.61
20	25	28	0	0	3597.50
20	25	28	29	0	3070.55
0	0	0	0	3	2200.57
0	0	0	1	4	1707.11
0	0	3	0	3	1924.80
0	0	3	4	7	937.89
0	5	0	0	3	2190.95
0	5	0	1	4	1697.49
0	5	8	0	3	1921.73
0	5	8	9	12	441.36
20	0	0	0	3	2372.95
20	0	0	1	4	1879.50
20	0	3	0	3	2097.19
20	0	3	4	7	1110.28
20	25	0	0	3	2843.47
20	25	0	1	4	2350.01
20	25	28	0	3	2657.34
20	25	28	29	32	0.00

From the data in Figure 11.8, notice that the optimal configuration of safety stocks can be identified for each possible lead time constraint by identifying the lowest cost safety stock cost (last column) for a given commitment of retailer lead time (in stage 5). Figure 11.9 provides the safety-stock-related cost associated with positioning inventory across the supply chain for different retailer lead time commitments. As expected, longer retailer lead times enables significant safety stock reductions. If the retailer can wait for the entire supply chain lead time of 32 days, notice that no safety stock need to be held anywhere in the supply chain, thus driving the safety stock holding cost to zero.

FIGURE 11.9 Optimal safety stock vs. retailer lead time

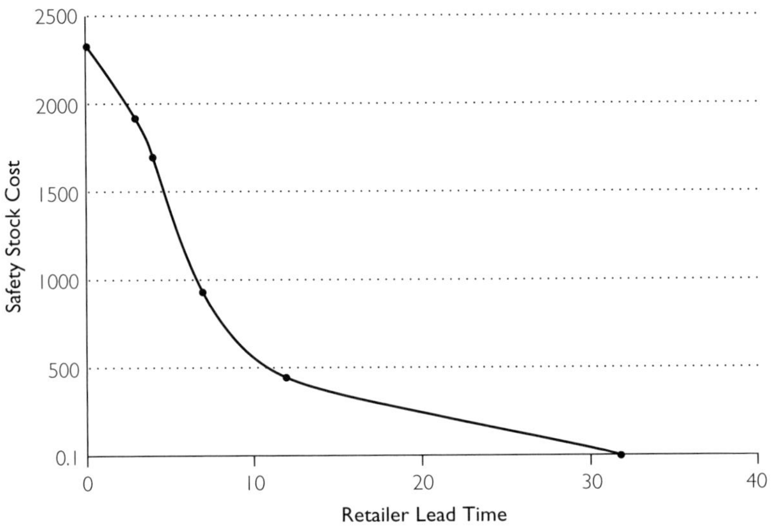

11.19 CHAPTER SUMMARY

Managing the supply chain for spare parts requires choosing an inventory location to satisfy demand where the primary product is being used and carrying sufficient inventory to ensure the required service level. Capacity of the intermediate warehouses, dealer capacity, and plant manufacturing capacity interact with demand and inventory to determine supply lead times, a key competitive metric for the aftermarket. Segmentation of the nature of the aftermarket demands from stable maintenance related demands or orders to replenish inventory to unpredictable breakdowns, and customizing the delivery mode and lead time to demand characteristics can improve supply chain performance. Coordinating maintenance information with inventory and repair decisions can enable reduction in inventory levels and costs and an increase in service levels. Competitive metrics include guaranteed delivery lead times, guaranteed product uptime, and improved life cycle costs.

Improving Supply Chains in the Chicago Public Schools System—A Case

It all began with an innocuous phone call. A member of a group sponsored by the Chicago Chamber of Commerce, Financial Resource and Advisory Council (FRAC), wanted to know if there were professors interested in working pro bono to assist the Chicago school system. The intended project would focus on the central warehouse and associated supply chain management issues. Given the possibility of using transactional data as part of research, a meeting was set for the following week.

The Chicago Public Schools (CPS) system consisted of about 600 schools that were supplied product from inventory at a central warehouse in Pershing Road, on the south side of the city. The central warehouse handled about 1,800 different SKUs and $100 million of product. Manny Ortiz, the senior manager at the Chicago Public Schools warehouse, was responsible for both procurement as well as delivery management of all product flowing through the warehouse. When the faculty team arrived to start the project, the warehouse faced a six-month ultimatum. As an interim step, schools had already been offered the flexibility to order products directly from vendors. Given delivery delays and associated frustration from schools, CPS was considering shutting down the warehouse and permitting direct delivery from vendors to individual schools. The six-month deadline suggested that any changes had to yield quick results, while adjusting the system towards long-term effectiveness.

FIGURE 1 Histogram of observed delivery lead times for a sample of 30 schools for the original system

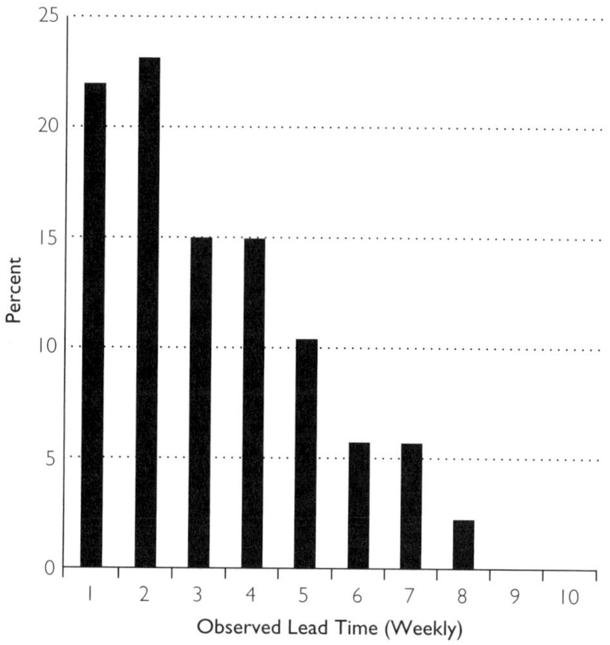

THE CPS SUPPLY CHAIN

Orders for product were placed by individual schools. The products ordered consisted of two groups of items: a set of twenty items (called Class A items) that accounted for 70% of the physical volume but 50% of the dollar volume and the remaining set of about 1,780 SKUs (called Class B items), accounted for about 30% of the physical volume and 50% of the dollar volume. The set of twenty items were mainly engineering supplies and consisted of paper towels, rock salt, copier paper, and so on. The remaining set of items consisted of educational supplies whose orders were driven by individual teacher needs. Orders were processed at the central warehouse and the entire order was delivered to the individual school. Trucks contracted and managed by CPS managed all deliveries, followed planned truck routes, and visited every school once every two weeks.

Despite the planned lead time of two weeks, the observed lead time at schools varied considerably. The team took the order and delivery dates for products offered and generated a lead time distribution as shown in Figure 1.

As soon as the team saw Figure 1, the question arose as to why such lead time variation was generated.

DELIVERY VOLUMES

The team presumed that the total delivery volume would vary across time. They thus generated the graph in Figure 2, which showed how the delivery volume varied across time. The team immediately concluded that the periodic changes in capacity interacted with the fixed delivery capacity and the planned delivery of all outstanding items, to generate the lead times in Figure 1. How could they demonstrate this, using a simple presentation?

One approach was to look at the variation in volume in Figure 2 as a frequency distribution and generate Figure 3.

Figure 3 shows the total volume and the interaction with available truck capacity. Any time the volume exceeds truck capacity, the delivery is scheduled for the next time the trucks run that route, which is two weeks later. This interaction between truck capacity and order volume suggested a reason for the observed lead time at schools.

It was clear to the team that there were several possible choices that could be made to improve the system. These included adding truck capacity, forcing schools to order in

FIGURE 2 Physical volume (cubic feet) of Class A and Class B items ordered over time. Note that the volumes of Class A items are significantly larger than Class B items.

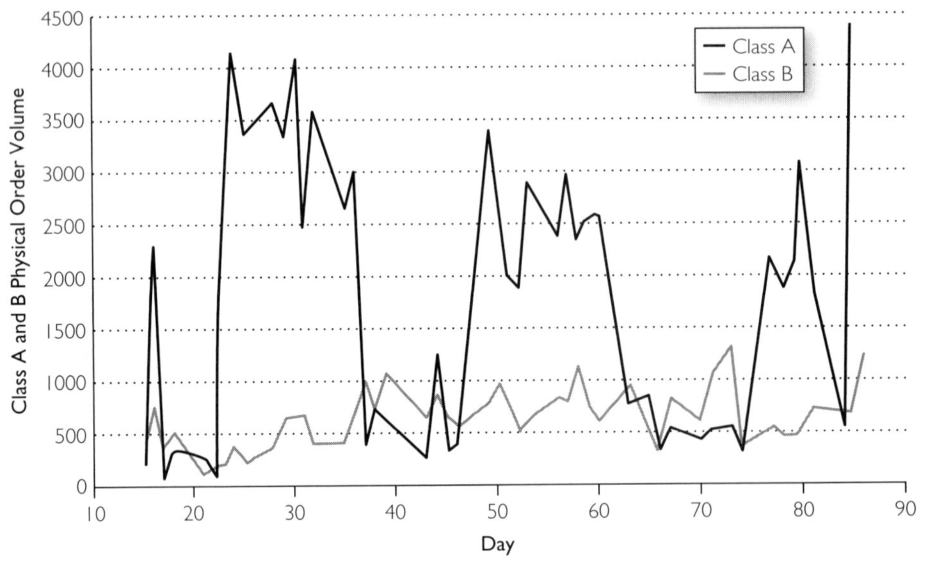

FIGURE 3 Histogram of the total volume ordered each day. The daily capacity is 3,500 ft^3.

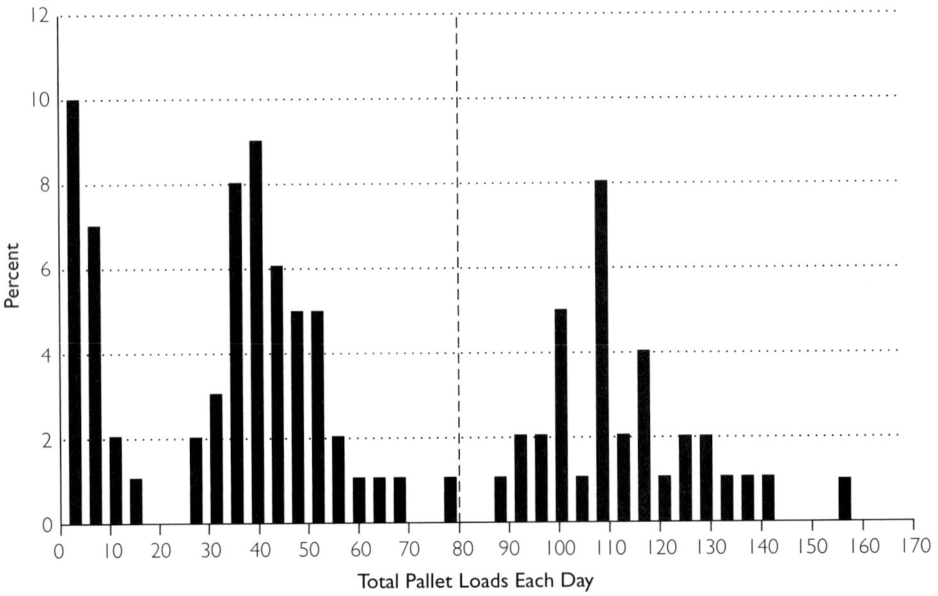

smaller lots, attempting to split deliveries, and moving to vendor delivery to schools. But Manny Ortiz wanted to save the warehouse and its supply chain if possible. His contention was that the warehouse and its delivery capability in a geographically concentrated region enabled lower overall supply chain costs than an outsourced entity that would have to generate profits from the running of the transport system. But he realized that some new ideas were needed quickly.

AN EXAMPLE AND A THEORY

To understand the possible impact of changes, the team pulled data for a sample of sixteen schools served by two trucks on Mondays. In the original two-week delivery cycle, two trucks traveled to different sets of schools on alternating Mondays. On the first Monday, schools 1, 2, 3, and 4 received deliveries from truck 1; and schools 5, 6, 7, and 8 received deliveries from truck 2. On the second Monday, schools 9, 10, 11, and 12 received deliveries from truck 1; and schools 13, 14, 15, and 16 received deliveries from truck 2. The logic for this delivery schedule was based on school spatial location (see Figure 4). However, when the delivery volumes for Class A items were recorded (Figure 5)—the team found that volumes frequently exceeded truck capacity, thus delaying deliveries. Schools preferred all outstanding orders to be delivered at one time, hence delays propagated. In addition, schools placed orders when deliveries were received, thus adding to demand volatility. The team took the planned routes in Figure 4 and, the actual volumes for each route in Figure 5, to estimate the variability in lead time observed by the system.

The next idea that the team came up with was the link between deliveries and observed variability of Class B items. Demand volume for Class B items could be represented as a normal distribution with a mean of 5 cubic feet and a standard deviation of 2 cubic feet. In the current system, if deliveries were received on time, then orders would be placed once every two weeks. Typical orders for Class B items were placed only four days each week. However, delayed deliveries generated additional order variability. In other words, the capacity and volume interactions through routes for Class A items generated variability in observed demand for Class B items, too. The team concluded that observed lead times were the result of these interactions. A simple spreadsheet-based analysis was used to demonstrate these interactions.

SPLITTING THE SUPPLY CHAIN

Could splitting deliveries of Class A and Class B items improve performance by disentangling links between the items? One reason the team considered this option was that the planned quantities of engineering supplies (Class A items) remained more or less stable throughout the year. Thus, the volumes in Figure 5 could be used to create routes for deliveries of Class A items by sacrificing miles driven for reliable two-week delivery. The first step was to check if the same two trucks could be assigned different routes that would maintain reliable two-week delivery of all planned Class A items.

The next step was to consider daily delivery of all Class B items—an aggregation of the total demand of Class B items across all sixteen schools showed a fairly stable demand that could easily be accommodated by sending them via the daily internal mail service to all schools. If all orders placed by the end of day on one day were picked and sent via internal mail the next day, then the one-day lead time for Class B items would make most of the teachers happy. A plan was devised to implement this system for a set of pilot schools.

REDUCING SCHOOL INVENTORIES

Manny Ortiz launched a pilot project with the sixteen schools. A new route structure guaranteed deliveries of all Class A items within the two-week interval. The extra thirty minutes of driving distance was easily accommodated within the course of the day, as deliveries now took less time. In addition,

FIGURE 4 Location of sixteen schools and delivery routes

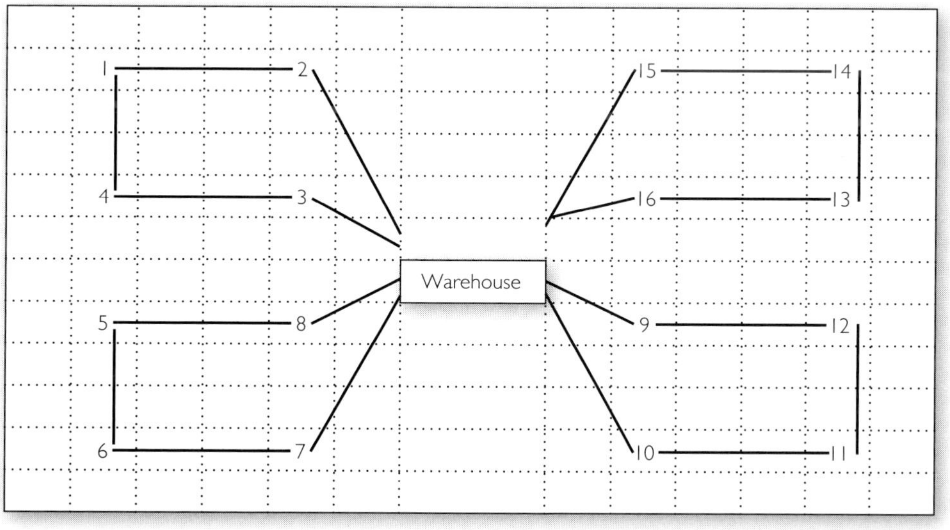

FIGURE 5 Volumes of Class A items demanded by the sixteen schools weekly

Week/ School	1	2	3	4	5	6	7	8	9	10	11	12	13	14	15	16
1	199	287	161	78	125	298	128	75	99	85	237	197	76	30	174	222
2	270	149	198	255	29	68	129	24	285	210	189	107	10	200	184	48
3	202	217	60	287	196	157	12	213	281	145	9	170	21	181	155	30
4	10	7	159	119	191	138	133	189	261	174	104	280	34	23	197	112
5	26	177	19	188	44	109	298	29	74	205	55	116	56	135	151	102
6	177	248	173	61	19	3	43	28	18	191	46	122	183	137	159	270
7	235	72	134	234	159	57	250	51	222	240	18	273	84	164	176	142
8	56	292	124	15	125	128	111	21	88	116	236	51	122	47	23	154
9	225	90	18	100	100	47	108	220	239	210	70	197	136	22	75	54
10	131	267	216	214	192	93	33	109	251	130	62	80	126	210	142	71
11	197	88	169	225	231	59	265	87	25	198	210	145	29	244	50	232
12	258	66	90	175	176	294	14	92	162	265	234	288	79	75	41	39
13	103	216	95	209	267	137	63	239	148	155	227	210	167	123	205	40
14	45	242	138	77	84	213	171	169	65	92	32	198	49	153	16	116

the reliable deliveries of Class A items meant that demand could be planned as per the original volume estimates.

Since Class B items were sent via internal mail and overnight, schools realized that they could order as needed and thus not have to carry much inventory. This was a welcome relief to school principals who had to contend with missing inventory as things got misplaced or lost in the classrooms. With teachers and personnel ordering and using products as needed, schools found it much easier to keep their personnel happy while decreasing supply costs. For the first time in many years, principals started rooting for the central-warehouse-based supply chain and opposing any plans to eliminate the services they had now come to expect.

EXPANSION TO THE ENTIRE SUPPLY CHAIN

With careful nurturing, the warehouse expanded the pilot to cover all schools. The new system split the warehouse into two separate entities, one for the twenty Class A items with a two-week lead time and another for the Class B items with a one-day lead time. Manny Ortiz estimated that systemwide costs had decreased at least $150,000 each year. The new supply chain had increased the confidence of the central warehouse and enabled consideration of alternate contracts with vendors that could increase the variety of choices for teachers.

CONCEPTUAL WINS

What could the CPS supply chain learn from this project? How could the ideas from this project be applied more broadly across the CPS system? What insights could be used by the professors in their classrooms? The two professors pondered these issues as they got ready for a practitioner-oriented conference on supply chain applications.

CASE QUESTIONS

1. Map the original supply chain and the timing of decisions.
2. Why did the original supply chain generate the lead times shown in Figure 1?
3. Explain the logic for the order variation observed in Figure 2.
4. Is there an alternate delivery of Class A items that can provide reliable delivery within a two-week lead time? Demonstrate that idea by applying it to the information in Figures 4 and 5.
5. What was the impact of stabilizing deliveries on orders of Class B items? Explain.
6. How did separating supply chains improve performance at the Chicago Public Schools system? What is the general concept?

Supply Chain Management at HANSA Airlines—A Case

"HANSA—A Commuter Airline That Cares" Chris Henkel read the new sign that had been installed at the entrance as he arrived. A supply chain specialist with HANSA, a commuter airline for short-distance travel (less than 750 miles), Chris was pensive as he parked his bike and entered the Boulder, CO, office building. Chris had joined HANSA fresh out of a supply chain master's program and had gained a reputation as a fierce cost cutter who understood that safety came first but that there were ways to maintain safe aircraft while reducing costs through the use of information and appropriate repair outsourcing.

He had just returned from a conference of the Supply Chain Society, a gathering of academics and industry representatives and was eager to try out one of the ideas he heard. The paper "Efficient Supply Chain Management at the U.S. Coast Guard Using Part-Age Dependent Supply Replenishment Policies" by Deshpande, Iyer, and Cho ([27]) described their efforts at the US Coast Guard (USCG). He was encouraged by the estimated savings and discussions with the faculty regarding implementation of the ideas at USCG. Having just downloaded the paper on to his iPad, he rushed up to his cubicle, pausing to look out at the snow-capped mountains before he settled down to read.

His goal today was to take data from HANSA's operation and estimate the potential benefit from implementing a system similar to that used for the Coast Guard. Any savings that could be attained without significant IT hardware outlays would be a welcome story in an airline industry facing a stark future.

THE PILOTLESS PILOT PROJECT

Any planning to avoid unnecessary repair costs without increasing aircraft downtime would save money and enable the repair budget to be more appropriately utilized over time. Chris decided to start by pulling some part repair data. He selected the widget, a component used by all aircraft that faced long repair lead times and significant repair cost and whose repair was outsourced to a vendor. Ideally, he wanted to evolve a system that would repair widgets whenever needed. In the process, if he could collaborate with the vendor to increase demand visibility and thus save costs, that would be great. Repairing widgets closer to their demand would permit repair budget use to be tailored to part demands over time. He had read that such synchronized approaches enabled repair budgets to be used to increase service levels or repair budgets to be trimmed for the same service level.

A quick analysis showed that widgets aged as they accumulated flight hours while installed on their aircraft. Since the specific aircraft usage varied by route and other factors, he first examined monthly widget failure data for the past two years. Each time a widget failed, it was swapped for a good widget, and the broken part was returned to the warehouse. Widgets also had a fixed life before they needed a complete overhaul. As a starting point, he created a supply chain map showing all the participants, ownership, and associated information and material flows—the first *C* of a 4C supply chain audit.

Since each widget failure represented "demand" from the warehouse, he created Table 1 to show the demand data. He noticed that aircraft usage varied based on the route

TABLE 1 Widget failures and warehouse demand data by month. Data are provided beyond twenty-four months to enable computation of demand over the supply lead time.

Month	Demand
1	46
2	51
3	68
4	88
5	71
6	63
7	70
8	60
9	68
10	63
11	43
12	43
13	42
14	51
15	49
16	38
17	49
18	50
19	63
20	44
21	52
22	47
23	57
24	52
25	38
26	37
27	60

TABLE 2 Costs for the HANSA supply chain

Costs	Value
Holding cost/unit/month	10
Backorder cost/unit/month	50
Repair cost/unit	2000

structure, adjustments to accommodate special events at cities HANSA served, fare promotions, and so on. The current inventory management system framed the problem as an open-loop "base stock" replenishment system. Thus, given the stream of demands, the inventory manager at the warehouse chose an inventory position of repaired widgets to cover the demand over the supply lead time of four months. Using the specific stream of data, such a level, as well as associated inventories, could be generated. Further, using sample data regarding repair costs, and holding and expediting costs in Table 2, he generated a total cost associated with the current mode of operation.

One point of discussion was the role of the holding and backlog costs listed in Table 2. All costs for repair were charged to the maintenance budget until the part went on the aircraft, after which time, the repair cost was paid to maintenance. That meant that repaired parts remained on the maintenance budget and implied a "borrowing" cost charged to maintenance by HANSA's corporate finance group. Similarly, if parts were not available, then aircraft operations were affected. This backlog cost represented a charge by operations that the maintenance group had to cover: missing parts required scrambling (by aircraft operations) to use other aircraft to maintain schedules or borrowing parts from other airlines while operations waited for a working widget to be delivered.

COLLECTING PART AGE INFORMATION

Chris decided to consider adding an indicator to aircrafts to signal if the age accumulated flight hours of the widget exceeded a threshold level. Thus, for example, if the threshold was set at 2,000 hours, then all widgets that had seen 2,000 hours of use on aircraft, regardless of whether or not they failed, would trigger a signal for replacement at the start of a given period. He was aware that repair lead time for the component was four weeks; thus any inventory policy had to adjust inventory position to cover demand over the repair lead time. A first question was how these signals could be used to adjust the level of working parts in inventory at the warehouse. He realized that when the parts came in for repair, the age of the repaired part was reset to zero. Thus, parts were continually circulated through the system, getting repaired, being used on aircraft, entering broken status, reverting back to zero age, and so on.

Chris realized that any proposed policy needed to look at past data to make decisions. Each period, once the signal was received, a possible policy was to adjust inventory position to be the *St* + *Basestock*, where *St* represented the signal of old operating parts (with age greater than a given threshold) and *Basestock* would be a level that would minimize costs across the 24 months. Looking at data in Table 3, for a threshold of 2,000 hours, and the cost data in Table 2, he generated the Basestock level to minimize total costs. In Table 3, for a given month, the signal for a lower threshold is never lower than the signal for a higher threshold, because a lower threshold would include all parts whose age is greater. But, for a given threshold (a column), as we move across months, if the signal decreases, the difference is the minimum number of components that failed. For example, for an age threshold of 400, since the signal decreased from 67 to 66 from month 1 to month 2, it implies that at least one component failed in month 2. The initial inventory position was using demand information only, rather than part age information.

How did the signal enable cost reduction? To illustrate the idea, Chris created a graph showing the duration of time a repaired widget spent in inventory before it was used. He created such a graph for the original system (without signals) and the new system (with signals). A shorter time between widget repair completion and usage implied a more synchronized system. Intuitively, setting a part age threshold that had improved ability to forecast impending demand would improve cost performance.

The goal of the pilot project was to provide both a recommended threshold for the component as well as an estimate of the savings, using the data from the field. For each possible threshold setting, he determined a planned repair policy and evaluated its impact when applied to the data over 24 months. A plot of this total cost vs. threshold provided an insight into a possible optimal setting of the threshold as well as the associated policy.

DEMAND AND SIGNAL LINKAGE

One question concerned whether it was optimal to respond to part age signals directly or if the system should model the "demand over supply lead time" distribution. Such a scheme required a statistical model of the relationship between demand over the four months and the signals for each threshold. He was also told by his team that a joint distribution of part age signals and the demand over lead time could be modeled as a bivariate normal distribution. Given the data in Table 3, his team first generated the correlation between signals and demand for different threshold levels. If a bivariate normal distribution was generated, it meant that, depending on the threshold data being used, the possible demand outcome could also be described as a normal distribution with an adjusted mean and standard deviation. In other words,

TABLE 3 Signals each month for different age thresholds

Month/ Age Threshold	400	450	500	550	600	650	700	750	800	850	900	950	1000	1050
1	67	67	67	67	67	67	67	67	67	67	67	67	10	10
2	66	66	66	63	63	63	62	62	62	47	47	47	47	47
3	120	120	120	120	120	120	59	59	59	59	59	59	31	0
4	74	74	74	74	74	71	71	71	49	49	49	49	17	17
5	74	74	74	74	74	60	60	60	60	60	60	22	22	22
6	87	87	74	74	74	74	74	74	74	74	74	74	44	44
7	52	52	52	38	38	38	38	38	38	37	37	20	20	0
8	84	84	84	84	84	84	84	84	66	66	66	12	12	0
9	76	76	76	76	76	76	76	76	76	24	24	24	21	0
10	80	80	61	61	61	61	61	61	61	61	0	0	0	0
11	77	62	62	62	62	62	56	56	32	32	32	9	9	0
12	64	64	64	64	64	64	64	64	64	47	47	47	47	36
13	132	78	78	78	69	69	67	40	40	40	8	8	8	8
14	83	83	60	60	60	60	60	60	60	60	60	60	60	21
15	76	76	76	76	76	76	76	76	76	66	66	62	62	62
16	80	80	65	53	53	53	53	53	53	53	51	51	51	4
17	65	65	65	65	51	51	51	51	51	51	51	51	27	13
18	83	83	83	83	60	60	60	60	60	60	60	60	41	0
19	102	69	69	69	69	55	55	55	55	55	55	55	55	55
20	109	109	109	109	95	95	95	65	27	27	27	25	25	25
21	85	85	85	85	85	85	48	48	34	32	32	15	15	0
22	100	100	100	100	71	71	71	71	71	47	47	35	15	10
23	91	79	79	79	79	79	74	41	41	28	28	28	28	28
24	83	83	83	83	51	51	51	50	50	49	49	49	49	49

suppose the observed part signal was dl and the correlation between the demand and signals was ρ. Then the associated conditional distribution of the demand during lead time could be generated. The associated forecasted benefit of using signal information could thus be linked to the value of ρ ([27]). Chris wanted to know if a quick analysis of the value of signal information could be used to estimate the benefit of part age information.

REAPING BENEFITS

What would be the value of developing a system that could use this data to improve inventory management? Chris resolved to develop a simple spreadsheet to demonstrate the value and to enable his managers to really understand the idea. However, he needed help to build such a system quickly.

Once the benefits were estimated, his thoughts turned to leveraging this information in negotiations with the vendor. Could data regarding part age signals be shared with the vendor to improve supply chain profits? Could the data collected regarding part age be shared with the outsourced repair company? If so, how could the information be used to decrease costs for HANSA and for the vendor?

His enthusiasm grew as he pondered how he could summarize the benefits and, better yet, create a prototype pilot run to demonstrate the benefits. The team that wrote the paper had become finalists for the 2007 Edelman Prize, and Chris wondered if the HANSA project could realize similar levels of success.

CASE QUESTIONS

1. Perform a 4C audit of the supply chain at HANSA. Identify opportunities to improve performance.
2. Given data in the case and no part age information, provide the optimal inventory position of widgets and associated cost.
3. Given the data for different part age thresholds, generate the optimal inventory position and associated costs. Suggest an optimal age threshold.
4. Can the correlation between demand during supply lead time and part age based signals provide insights into how to choose part age signals to improve the supply chain? Discuss.
5. How can collaboration between HANSA and the vendor improve the management of widgets?

Chapter 12

Reverse Logistics

The total value of products returned by US consumers is estimated at $100 billion annually. The management of reverse supply chain, i.e., flows from the consumer back to the manufacturer, is also increasingly important as producers are held responsible for the cradle-to-grave impact of their products on the environment. Increased emphasis on building sustainable products that minimize their impact on greenhouse gases, landfills, and water usage implies that production and destruction costs have to be considered beyond their flow from the manufacturer to the consumer. Some products can be reused in other markets (refurbished engines or used clothing), others can be reshipped (products returned to stores or catalog companies), and other products may require breakdown and remanufacturing (printers). In each of these cases, anticipating the reuse of the product suggests a new set of possible product design and assembly choices.

The reverse supply chain is inherently more complicated and involves less control than the primary movement of product out to the customers. Collecting product back from consumers requires intermediaries to play a key role. These could include the consumers themselves, city garbage pickup, collection centers, and so on. The capacity of collection is distributed across many intermediaries and thus impacts stability of supply. Coordination between participants has to include issues of regulatory compliance, e.g., new regulations regarding use of recycled content require companies to ensure availability of recycled material to produce primary product. Coordination across manufacturers to standardize the composition of packaged product or designs can increase the success of reverse supply chains by simplifying aggregation of returns. In some industries (such as batteries), effective recycling is key to ensuring availability of minerals such as lithium, given their restricted supply relative to projected demand. Finally, competitive metrics such as zero waste, reduced greenhouse gases, and 100% recycling are used by companies as part of product attributes to attract demand.

In reverse supply chains, each individual product has to be assessed, separated, treated, and then reused as is, salvaged, or recycled. Consider the typical flow of products back to the manufacturer. Some fraction of the products sold are returned. Of the returned product, some are in perfect, unused condition and so can be resold as soon as they are available for the market. Of the remaining products, some can be remanufactured and put back into the market. However, if these return steps are delayed, the product moves closer to the end of its life cycle, when its demand will run out. Blackburn et al. ([8]) suggest that products whose value loss over time is low should be matched with an efficient reverse supply chain, while products with a rapid falloff in value require a speedy product recovery, which may be achieved by being matched with a responsive value chain. An efficient supply chain can use a centralized approach to process returns, thus reducing costs to manage the reverse supply chain while potentially increasing the time to get the returned product ready for resale. However, a decentralized supply chain can adjust the speed of product pickup and thus permit trade-offs between speed of product recovery and marginal value of product.

The next few sections will describe interesting and effective reverse product supply chains.

12.1 RECYCLING USED DISPOSABLE KODAK CAMERAS

The single-use FunSaver camera by Kodak has between 77% and 86% of recyclable components by weight ([14], [29]). The product was designed and manufactured so that the customer could not reload the camera. This ensures that only Kodak film will be used in the camera. The components of the camera include an alkaline mercury-free battery and electronics showing the number of times the circuit boards had been recycled. All parts are color coded for recyclability.

The reverse chain starts with the consumer, who purchases the camera from a retail store and uses it to take pictures. Given the camera design, unexposed film remains in the camera, and the consumer takes the camera with the completed roll inside to a store to be developed. The store removes the film cartridge, develops the pictures, and delivers them to the customer. The retail store is paid $0.05 per unit core fee to send the camera to the recycling center. The battery is reused by some other supply chain.

At the recycling centers, Kodak removes the lenses from the returned cameras, regrinds them, and reuses them in a new camera. At OutSource, a state-sponsored organization in New York that employs handicapped people, covers and lenses are removed. The polymer covers are ground up into pellets, and the paper and cardboard are recycled. The chassis, camera mechanism, and electronic flash are tested, inspected, and reused. Those components that do not pass inspection are ground up and used as raw material. By using parts that snap together as opposed to being welded, Kodak can resell its FunSaver 35 camera components up to ten times, thus lowering the component costs and retail prices.

The disposable camera supply chain requires a careful design to incentivize the customer to take the finished camera to a retail store, coordination agreements to incent the retail store to return the product to the manufacturer, a counter to track use of the components, simple snap design to separate components, sufficient capacity of subsidized labor to break apart the camera, and a competitive pricing model to recover component cost over multiple product generations. In short, all the 4Cs of supply chain management had to be planned carefully to ensure an effective reverse supply chain for the FunSaver cameras.

12.2 USED CLOTHING SUPPLY CHAIN

The flow of used clothing from the United States to the rest of the world is described in ([101]). The United States accounts for 40% of the world trade in used clothing, representing 7 billion pounds of clothing exported between 1990 and 2003. Used clothing is donated by consumers throughout the United States as an act of charity (with associated federal tax benefits), thus the input costs for the used clothing supply chain are zero. Since the volume of donated clothing is far greater than US demand, this clothing now enters a reverse global supply chain, traveling from the United States to primarily Africa. The clothing is sorted into different sets with associated price points in order to appeal to potential global market segments. Notice that even if the final retail price is lower than original product cost, this reverse chain can be profitable, since it only has to cover transportation and margin requirements from supply chain participants.

The chain of flows starts with clothing collected by nonprofit charitable groups such as Goodwill and the Salvation Army. Usable clothing is selected and makes its way to the Goodwill or Salvation Army stores. The remaining product gets sold, by weight, to a secondary layer of the supply chain, involving companies such as Trans-Americas Trading Company. These companies identify valuable apparel that has significant market value. Used clothing brought in by trucks is emptied onto a conveyor belt where workers sort it by type: apparel made of cotton, skirts, men's pants, household materials, and jeans. Some products such as T-shirts are sent to a group of people called "miners and graders," who separate the clothing based on potential value. Vintage clothing such as band T-shirts (e.g., the Grateful Dead's New York tour) may have a high value, so they are separated. On the other hand, 30% of the clothing is sold at $0.05 a pound and is used as wiping rags. For such a purpose, the plain white T-shirt carries a lot more value than a colored T-shirt. If the T-shirt is too covered with paints or prints, it may only fetch $0.01–0.02 per pound and is classified as "shoddy." Shredded shoddy is used in automobile doors, carpet pads, cushions, and so on. Another group is T-shirts that are sold by weight at $0.60–0.80 per pound, where each pound consists of about three T-shirts.

The bulk of the T-shirts are shipped to traders in Africa who then create paths to consumers. Tanzania is the largest importer of used clothing from the United States. The exported T-shirts are separated into over thirty different groupings and sold in bulk at prices that are between $0.60 and $0.80 a pound ([101]). The implied wholesale price of a T-shirt is thus $0.25, which is less than the price of the raw material used to make the T-shirt. Retailers buy these T-shirts in bulk and separate them into single items that can sell for retail prices between $0.50 and $1.50. The author ([101]) estimates that 90% of the value of a bale would come from 10% of the items in it. However, at retail, dynamic pricing may be needed based on time of day, market volumes, time of month, and so on to adjust the retail prices to willingness to pay.

But what is the impact of all of this used clothing? It is very difficult for the local African textile industry to compete with the economics of this supply chain. As a result, the local apparel industries in many African countries have been devastated. What started off as a noble gesture of charity is transformed by the global supply chain to have the opposite impact in another part of the world.

12.3 DUPONT FILM RECOVERY PROGRAM

Dupont's film recovery program targets three markets: offset printing, medical services, and electronics ([73]). Dupont's focus on film recovery from the hospital X-ray film market was a result of the Environmental Protection Agency's Superfund liability standard, which makes site owners as well as parties involved in generating, managing, or arranging delivery liable for environmental impact.

Dupont authorizes 350 independent local collectors to pick up and consolidate used film from hospitals, clinics, and print shops and ship them to its reclamation centers. In addition to picking up used film, these collectors recover silver.

Dupont guarantees a 25-day cycle, which is a key parameter. Collectors are also offered the option of Dupont purchasing the silver and reselling it or simply using the reclamation services for a fee. Similarly the generators of the recycled material can work directly with Dupont or go through a third-party collector. The reverse supply chain thus aims to recover the silver, reimburse the customers within a promised lead time, and permit customers to decide a convenient alternative to collect the associated funds.

12.4 HOME DEPOT

At Home Depot stores, old pallets are backhauled by trucking companies to Advanced Pallet Recyclers (APR) ([73]). APR collects, shreds, and composts the pallets, creating two products—Enviro Mulch 2000 and Root Mulch. These brands are sold in Home Depot stores in bags marked with the environmentally friendly label.

Home Depot and Mindis Recycling have also created the Recycling Depot. This depot provides small contractors with a convenient alternative to disposing of materials from renovation jobs, such as aluminum window frames, water heaters, and electrical wires. Customers receive cash for the items they bring, based on current market prices. Mindis hopes that the plumbers and electricians who shop at the Home Depot will bring valuable scrap metal, such as copper wire and pipes, to the Recycling Depot.

12.5 RETURNS OF CLOTHING AT A CATALOG RETAILER AND THEIR IMPACT

For catalog companies, returns of clothing by consumers can be significant. In many cases, returned unopened product volumes may be significant enough that they have to be taken into account in the initial inventory purchase in order to manage profitability. Eppen and Iyer ([35]) describe returns and reuse in the context of a catalog company that purchased inventory at the start of the season but had opportunities to receive, process, and reship returned items.

Consider a context where products are shipped out against demand, but $v\%$ of the product is returned. Of this $v\%$, a fraction u return quickly enough to be reshipped, while $(1 - u)\%$ return too late to be reshipped or are damaged and cannot be reshipped. Thus out of each round of outbound shipped product, uv represent the returns that can be reshipped. Thus, if the system starts with initial inventory y, it can really be used to ship out $\frac{y}{1-uv}$ demands. Similarly if a demand x is shipped, then the realized demand is $x(1 - v)$. Typical rates quoted in the example in [35] are a 36% return rate (v) and a 30% reusable return rate (u).

If the per-unit costs are as follows, (1) end of season salvage value of s per unit ($s < c$), (2) holding cost of h, (3) revenue of r, (4) goodwill loss of π, and (5) product cost of c, then the optimal decision y is obtained as

$$\Phi\left(\frac{y}{1-uv}\right)=\frac{\left(r(1-v)+\pi-(h-s)v(1-u)\right)-c(1-vu)}{\left(r(1-v)+\pi+\left((h-s)(1-v)\right)\right)}$$

Note that the ability to reuse returned items permits a lower initial inventory because of multiple opportunities to sell the product. Of course, this suggests that schemes that enable items to be returned quickly, i.e., increasing u, can improve system profitability.

12.6 SURPLUS INVENTORY MATCHING IN THE PROCESS INDUSTRY

A typical problem in the steel industry concerns the allocation of orders to leftover surplus stock ([71]). The problem of matching unique customer requirements to existing inventory is termed the *surplus inventory matching problem.* The surplus stock arises because orders may be canceled after units are produced, because produced units are below acceptable quality levels, or because surplus units had been intentionally created to reduce customer lead times. While this problem is described from the context of steel mills and paper mills, the problem can be framed in a more general form, e.g., as dealing with leftover trucking capacity or production capacity.

The two key issues to consider are the assignment restrictions when an order is allocated to a surplus inventory item, i.e., geometric considerations and quality attributes and processing constraints when a set of orders is earmarked for an inventory item. While orders are allocated to surplus inventory, a goal is to do this allocation while minimizing the wasted product in order to avoid leftover product that has low possible value. One approach is to require that all orders be satisfied while minimizing the leftovers for the chosen slabs from inventory. Kalagnanam, et al., ([71]) report on solution of real-life problems in a steel plant. The deployed solution was used daily in the mill operations and generated savings on the order of $3 million per year.

12.7 CHAPTER SUMMARY

As sustainability becomes an important supply chain attribute, manufacturers are being forced to find mechanisms to reuse or recycle used products. We have considered examples of reuse (Kodak cameras, returned clothing, and donated T-shirts) and recycling (Dupont's silver and Home Depot's pallets). The supply chain and product design have to be organized to manage the 4Cs of the return flows effectively. The return flows impact choices of participants in the supply chain (retailers or the customer returning product), coordination of incentives for intermediaries, provision of sufficient capacity to process returned product in a timely manner so that its value is repatriated, and effective use of the competitive benefit of operating in a sustainable manner.

Reverse Supply Chains at a Bottle Manufacturer

SUSTAINABLE MANUFACTURING—MESSAGE IN A BOTTLE*

Hank Bilders, president of SGS Glassworks had cleared his schedule for Friday and the rest of the weekend. He had committed to a deadline of January 18 for a proposal to SGS's board, which, in turn, meant that his recommendation was due imminently. Spread before him were summaries and detailed analyses from several independent consultants, each espousing a novel strategy for SGS to position itself as an industry leader in sustainable manufacturing. It was up to Hank to select one of these strategies.

About SGS

SGS was a market leader in the manufacture of bottles and other glass-based products. With several decades of manufacturing experience, the company was regarded as a thought leader in the industry. SGS management pushed the industry to adopt innovative manufacturing approaches, identify ways to minimize environmental impact, and reduce breakage through standardized pallets and handling methods. Over the years, the plastics industry had made significant strides in shifting beverage manufacturers from using glass to using plastic; however, times were changing, and the tide was set to turn once more.

SGS Plant Network

The SGS manufacturing network consisted of five plants spread throughout the United States. These plants were located in Madera, CA; Waxahachie, TX; Dunkirk, IN; Henderson, NC; and Milford, MA. The spatial locations of these plants are shown in Figure 1. Some of these states had a bottle bill, which mandated that producers collect a fee from consumers which would then be refunded upon recycling. The current production region for each plant is shown in Figure 2.

Figure 2 shows the US population divided into five zones with their associated population levels.

Figure 3 shows the consumption of beverage glass material (bottles) in metric tons in each of the five regions.

The average recycling rates by state are estimated based on whether or not the state has a bottle bill. Figure 1 lists the next set of expected states that plan to adopt the bottle bill.

Hank expected these recycling rates to increase as the number of states with bottle bills increased in each region. Also, assuming that bottle usage rates per capita were constant, he realized that he could compute available recycled content for each state based on its population.

Each plant had different furnace technological constraints, energy availability, level of automation, labor skills, and so on. However, the current approach distributed the available

*This case was written by Professor Ananth Iyer at the Krannert School of Management, Purdue University. It is meant solely as a vehicle for teaching, learning, and class discussion. The data and details provided in the case are completely fictitious. Thanks to Thomas McDuffee and Peter Walters, senior managers at Saint-Gobain Containers for helping to provide a context for the case. The case is fictitious and is provided solely for pedagogical purposes.

FIGURE 1 Proposed bottle bill legislation plus existing states (2010)

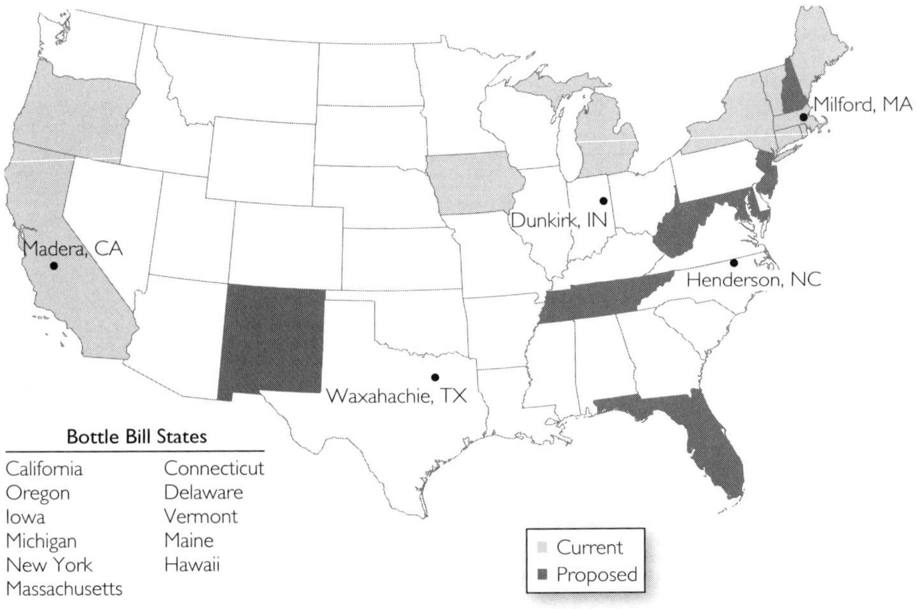

Bottle Bill States	
California	Connecticut
Oregon	Delaware
Iowa	Vermont
Michigan	Maine
New York	Hawaii
Massachusetts	

FIGURE 2 US population by region (2010)

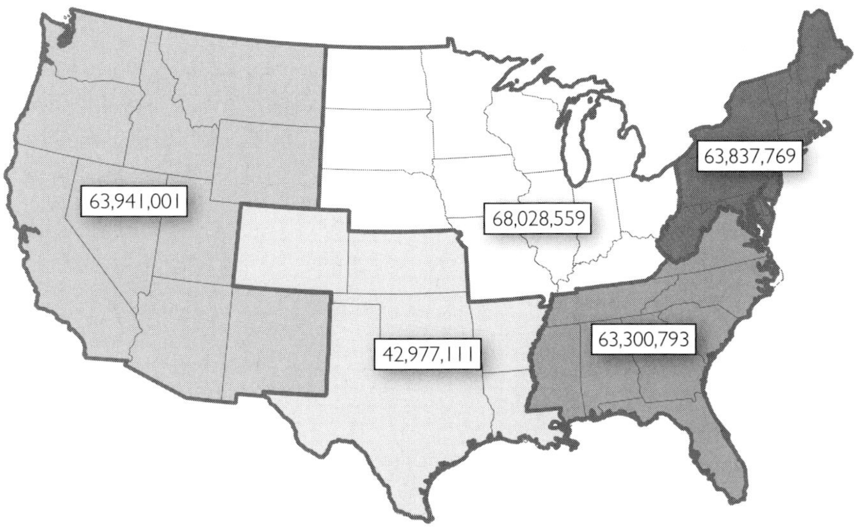

US population estimate of 302,085,233 for 48 contiguous states

FIGURE 3 Potential beverage glass material by region (based on population in 2010)

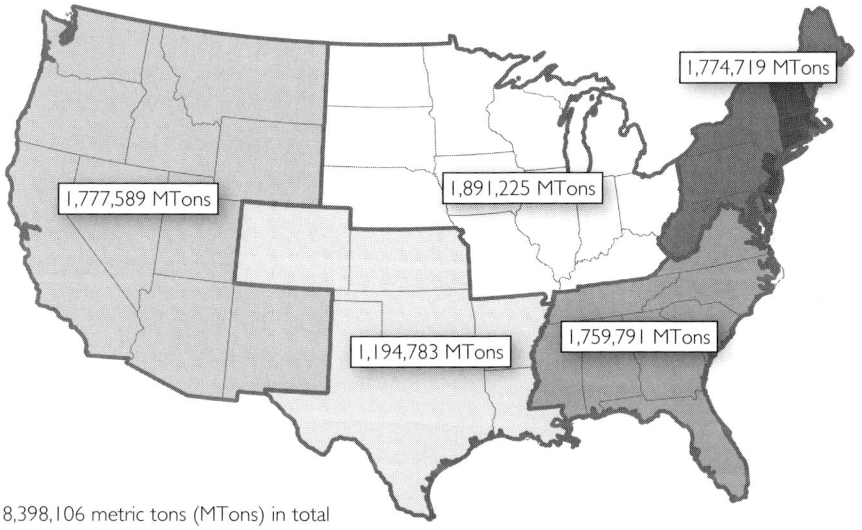

8,398,106 metric tons (MTons) in total

recycled glass to maintain the same input raw material mix across all plants. The current production at each plant covered the demand in its region. Assuming an average market share of 35% for SGS in all regions, the associated production could be estimated. Finally, the distance traveled to SGS's customer destinations was estimated as the median distance in the production region.

The manufacturing capacity of each plant could be expanded to cover the demand of at least two of the five regions in Figure 2 if required. But what if some of the input variables were changed at each of the plants? How would that affect the associated average manufacturing cost and optimal production?

The Impact of Cullet Use on Costs

Cullet, also known as recycled glass, is used as input to make new glass bottles. As a starting point, one of Hank's accountants had created the following list of potential ways that use of cullet could impact the cost structure of the supply chain.

- **Saves energy:** Using cullet allows us to reduce energy costs by 2%–3% for every 10% of cullet used in the manufacturing process.
- **Decreases by-products:** Using recycled glass is a closed-loop process, creating no additional waste or by-products and is indefinite.
- **Saves raw material and the carbon requirements to produce:** For every ton of glass recycled, over a ton of raw materials is saved, including 1,300 pounds of sand, 410 pounds of soda ash, and 380 pounds of limestone.
- **Reduces landfill dependence:** Avoids costs associated with disposal; however, this cost varies by the location of the waste bottles.
- **Lessens greenhouse gas emissions:** Using 10% recycled glass results in a 6% decrease in nitrous oxide and a 9.5% reduction in raw materials used.
- **Increases furnace life:** Cullet requires less heat to produce glass, and the life of a furnace is directly related to the heat applied to melt raw materials; even if the cost of cullet is high, the downstream effect of a negative initial cost element is positive, considering all factors. The company can produce the same tonnage with less energy and maximize capital by extending the furnace life.
- **Fulfills customer requirement and acts as marketing tool:** Customers want to know carbon usage to meet their requirements, and recycling provides a marketing tool: The organization can sell the product, perhaps at a premium.
- **Reduces use of soda ash:** The price of soda ash has doubled in last five years. Cullet is an offset; its inflation lags raw batch inflation.

Note: There is no effect on machine life due to cullet. The positive primary impact is in energy, environment, batch cost, and furnace life.

Recycling Options

Hank reminisced that in the past, it was common to recycle beer bottles: The recycle rate was over 80%. In fact, bottles were reused over 50 times, and recycling was the norm. Hank listed several possible options to increase the supply of recycled bottles. These included

1) **One-source recycling:** This refers to increasing the recycle rate by collecting all the waste as one bag from citizens and using centralized facilities to do the separation. Several studies indicate that the economics of such garbage collection schemes would increase the recycle rate by simplifying the process for households. One of the issues that was still unresolved was whether the quality of the recycled glass material would be acceptable for glass manufacturing plants.
2) **Technology to simplify the process of getting refunds:** Tomra (http://www.tomra.com/default.asp?V_ITEM_ID=380) was one company that had developed a unique approach to separating plastic or glass. Their technology would separate the inputs provided by customers using laser detection. This detection would allow instant determination of the recycled material and issue refunds to the customer.
3) **Grassroots movements to increase recycling rates:** There were several grassroots movements aimed at increasing the recycle rates. For example, Indiana has started a "Sustainindy" movement to encourage citizens to care about the environment. The approach galvanized students in schools and citizens in general and successfully generated recycled material.

   There were education initiatives being generated by glass manufacturing companies such as Saint-Gobain Containers. One such initiative created characters such as "Captain Cullet" and "Little Gob." These movies were distributed to schools and the general public as a way to encourage recycling among the population. Should SGS push for similar education initiatives to increase consumer awareness?
4) **Bottle bills:** There was tremendous variation in the recycle rate across states. The rate in California was close to 80%, while the average rate was 27%. While the majority of states had bottle bills in the 1980s, there had been a significant drop off and currently only eleven states had bottle bills.

   However, there were also differences in recycling across container usage. For example, wine-bottle recycling stood at an average of 15%. Recycling by pubs and other establishments was also significantly lower than the national average. The bottle bills also listed the specific products that were covered by the bill and did not include juices and water—these were emerging users. There was push back from manufacturers who worried that increased prices would drive down demand for their products.
5) **Reuse of bottles after washing:** Some environmental groups suggested that it was a lot better to wash and reuse bottles than to break them down as cullet. One company, Wine Bottle Recycling LLC, planned to supply wine manufacturers using a state-of-the-art technology to collect, sort, delabel, wash, sterilize, and repackage wine bottles at a rate of 72,000 bottles per hour from a single facility. Given that the green wine bottles were historically difficult to recycle, they had to be separated before use. Such processes focused on a particular

industry. The CEO of Wine Bottle Recycling LLC claimed that the energy use was 4.23% of the energy required to produce a new bottle. Hank was aware that such disruptive approaches would cannibalize sales for SGS, but he had to either join in or find an effective alternative.

6) **Easier recycling:** One company that announced a new technology was Green Mountain Glass LLC. The company aimed to permit mixed cullet from green and clear bottles to produce new glass. The technology would enable an easier recycling loop whereby all bottles could be mixed and used to form cullet. Given that in many countries, such as the United Kingdom, it was not feasible to use the green glass for local glass production, the company claimed that such technologies would significantly impact recycling rates and increase useable cullet supply to glass manufacturing plants.
7) **Penalties for those who do not recycle:** Current ordinances planned in San Francisco would penalize residents of the region who do not recycle material such as glass, plastic, and newspapers. The planned penalties were around $500. San Francisco hoped to increase recycling rates from the current levels of 70% to over 75%.

Hank had access to the detailed reports and/or URLs that contained reports for each of these options. He was also aware that he had to choose which of the options made the most sense for SGS to support (with human capital and funding) and was consistent with the company's goals. He was also aware that unless SGS provided leadership, the industry would not be able to claim significant advances in sustainable manufacturing. While influencing recycling rates and increasing sustainable manufacturing was important, Hank was reluctant to wade into a political minefield that put business growth of downstream customers at odds with cost savings by upstream producers.

Avoiding Future Tax Liabilities

One of the studies completed for SGS by S. Ash and Associates provided a life cycle cost analysis of changing to cullet. Their analysis suggested that the cost of acquiring cullet and the ability to raise usage of bottles by downstream customers were critical elements of a successful transition to use of cullet. The production rates for each of the five plants were already set, based on demand in the region supplied by the plant (Figure 2). But Hank also knew that public sentiment for sustainable manufacturing suggested that manufacturers would be hit with tax penalties for producing products that were not easily recyclable. Under that model, the impact of a manufacturer's product on landfill costs would be reflected on the manufacturer's tax bill. Anticipating such effects was part of Hank's strategic approach to decision making.

Choices, Choices, Choices

There were thus two significant changes that needed to be considered: increasing the supply of cullet and adjusting manufacturing at each plant based on supply. Increasing cullet availability at reasonable price points again required many of the ideas discussed earlier to be analyzed. Hank was well aware that wading into a political battle, particularly given the current economic environment, was a risky proposition. Retailers were not interested in raising retail prices, even if it meant that customers could get their money back by recycling. Also, political representatives were aware that they had to consider which products would be subject to the influence of the bottle bill. As an example, several states had chosen specific products and not others, while all used glass bottles. Beverage manufacturers were aware that the increased cost at retail, despite it being a deposit, could affect their demand. Thus, any scheme that let them benefit from the recycling without any costs would give them a competitive edge while keeping the customer oblivious. All this jockeying for coverage had created customer confusion when recycling bottles.

Finally, while schools were quite happy to talk about recycling, there were worries about whether the class discussions about relative packaging choices would reflect the sophisticated analysis that was necessary to make the right decision. Was it as simple of shifting from plastics or aluminum cans to bottles? Were the breakage rates the same across these different packages? In addition, there were some who were skeptical of the entire recycling movement in general. All of these voices would compete for airtime if a bottle bill discussion were happen. Some states had just postponed making any specific decisions.

What would be the best approach for SGS that put them on a path to increased sustainability? How could the company demonstrate leadership in the industry and regain the bottle demand lost to plastics? Could approaches to become sustainable enable local job creation and thus be economically sustainable? Could incentives be created across supply chain members to help the overall supply chain to be ecofriendly? Was there a need for government intervention to push the supply chain members on to a new manufacturing plateau that is more ecofriendly?

Hank pondered all of these issues as he started outlining his presentation. He was convinced that he needed persuasive arguments, quantitative estimates, and implementable approaches to succeed within SGS. He wanted help in a hurry.

Downstream Demand

There were several specific downstream customers who were focused on sustainable products and packaging. The organics industry had customers who appreciated the use of recycled material. Websites that pushed such material had manufacturers who offered a premium price for bottles with high recycled content. The product Love Water focused on use of glass bottles to carry water and promoted the recyclable nature of glass. The company website showed use of 30% recycled glass—the company was working with bottle manufacturers to identify sources that could be certified to have high recycled glass content). But the location of these producers was different from the plants that had access to high recycled bottle sources.

Should SGS transport the cullet to the plant closest to these downstream demand sources? Should the finished product be transported to the customer? Or, should the company use these sales opportunities to drive recycling as a local job creation device? Alternately, the company could choose to expand in the region where recycled content decreased input costs and cut production in other locations.

Adjusting the Production Network

The current approach at SGS was to provide a uniform raw material cost, which meant that all plants shared the recycled glass collected. This also meant that often cullet was transported from regions where large quantities were available (high-cullet regions) to plants in regions (primarily in the Midwest and East) where recycling rates were low (low-cullet regions).

One approach, suggested by the network planning group within SGS, was to adjust manufacturing to maximize the use of recycled glass closest to the source. Such an approach would change the production costs across plants. However, it would decrease raw material acquisition cost for some plants. But those plants, with a higher recycled content, could be used to showcase the benefits of recycling and its consequent impact on plant competitiveness. Should SGS switch to such an approach?

A second approach was to choose plant product mix, taking into account downstream demand sources for bottles based on the extent of recycled glass used in production. Such an approach would use the recycled glass in plants that could effectively supply to downstream manufacturers who preferred recycled glass (such as Love Water and the organic products discussed earlier).

A third approach was to include the commitments made to labor groups at each plant so that plant competitiveness would be balanced with labor capacity utilization guarantees.

But there was another school of thought that suggested that plant operational decisions should be decentralized and plants operated as individual profit centers. Such a scheme would permit plants to compete for customers, raw material, and operations so as to be profitable.

A Strategic Approach

Hank had picked up a copy of the book by Andrew Winston titled *Green Recovery—Get Lean, Get Smart, and Emerge from the Downturn at the Top* at the airport bookstore during one of his frequent trips. The book outlined ways that companies can look across their supply chain for opportunities to be sustainable as well as for opportunities to grow and survive amidst economic downturns (see the URL http://www.andrewwinston.com/blog/archives.php for examples). It outlined approaches for companies to view themselves as "solution providers" by adjusting their supply chain, their products, and their services. He also suggested using thought experiments (questions such as "Can a plane fly without jet fuel?" and "Can we send no waste to a landfill?") as a way to stimulate strategy formation. He wondered if any of the ideas in the book could be used as a theme for all of the decisions across SGS.

COMMUNICATING THE MESSAGE IN A BOTTLE

(A continuation of the case entitled "Message in a Bottle")

Hank Bilders had used an innovative approach to get ideas from his team. He had developed a case that summarized choices faced by SGS Glassworks and had permitted teams of employees to suggest solutions that would enable SGS to demonstrate industry leadership. They had all read a recent report by the Carbon Disclosure Project titled "CDP Supply Chain Report 2010" (at https://www.cdproject.net/CDPResults/CDP-Supply-Chain-Report_2010.pdf). The report highlighted that "Today, 60% of companies have elected a board committee member or other top-level executive who has overall responsibility for climate change and carbon reduction activities" (p. 5). The six winning teams from the first round (which had twenty-three competing teams) faced him now, eager to contribute their ideas towards a final single proposal to the board.

Hank identified a key question that needed to be decided and synchronized with the earlier analysis: Walmart had demanded that all products be identified with a sustainability index. *What could SGS Glassworks do to assist the OEMs (who used glass bottles or other containers) to increase their market share by declaring themselves to be more sustainable than the competition?*

The Sustainability Index

Ever since Walmart announced that it planned to provide a sustainability index for all products sold in its stores, there had been several groups examining this question. Walmart planned to develop a sustainability index that would evaluate suppliers, perform a lifecycle analysis of products, and develop a tool for consumers to use to choose between products based on their impact on the environment (see http://walmartstores.com/Sustainability/9292.aspx).

In calculating and declaring specific details of the product, SGS was aware that the Federal Trade Commission had already created guidelines for disclosure, listed as guidelines

Case Support Reference Table

Note: Check the text website for updates to this table.

Reference Name	URL
Tomra	http://www.tomra.com/default.asp?V_ITEM_ID=380
Green Recovery Book	http://www.andrewwinston.com/blog/archives.php
US Dept. of Energy	http://www.energy.gov
Saint-Gobain Containers	http://www.saint-gobain-northamerica.com/
Waste Age	http://wasteage.com/mag/waste_profiles_garbage_glass_2/index.html
Kids recycling video	http://www.youtube.com/watch?v=xTW9xqcb2Uw
Events to create a buzz about recycling glass	http://www.gpi.org/news/2009/oct/mail.htm
Focused segments for glass packaging	http://keepitorganic.org/about/
Sustainindy events	http://www.gpi.org/recycle-glass-week/gallery/indiana/
Recycling Facts	http://www.pacebutler.com/blog/recycling-facts/
Single-stream programs	http://www.container-recycling.org/assets/pdfs/reports/2009-SingleStream.pdf
Treehugger	http://www.treehugger.com/files/2009/05/calling-all-americans-we-need-to-recycle-more-glass.php
The Daily Green	http://www.thedailygreen.com/green-homes/latest/recycle-glass-47112004
Packworld dot com	http://www.packworld.com/news-26975
Dr. Vino	http://www.drvino.com
American Association of Wine Economists	http://www.wine-economics.org/workingpapers/AAWE_WP09.pdf
Sustainability Times	http://www.tricorbraun.com/sustainability.aspx
A report on FMCG World Resources Institute	http://www.wri.org/publication/rattling-supply-chains http://pdf.wri.org/rattling_supply_chains_technical_document.pdf
Japan Recycling	http://www.uwstout.edu/rs/2007/Recycling.pdf
Undergrad student compares Japanese and US recycling	http://www.cleanup.org.au/PDF/au/cua_glass_recycling_factsheet_final.pdf
Fact Sheet on glass recycling	http://www.cokecce.com/crs-reports/2009/s_index.html
Coca-Cola reports focused on recycling	http://www.cokecce.com/crs-reports/2009/s_index.html
Article addressing efforts to avoid burning in landfills	http://www.no-burn.org/article.php?id=569
Information about the impact of bottle bills	http://www.bottlebill.org/about.htm
Resources provided by the glass packaging institute	http://gpi.org/glassresources/education/
Glass recycling wiki	http://en.wikipedia.org/wiki/Glass_recycling
Inform	http://www.informinc.org/pages/research/waste-prevention/fact-sheets/case-reopened-reassessing-refillable-bottles-executive-summary.html
Life Cycle Analysis	http://www.gpi.org/lca/
Wine Business dot com	http://www.winebusiness.com/wbm/?go=getArticle&dataId=67379
Ask Leo and Lucy	http://www.guardian.co.uk/environment/2007/jan/14/ethicalliving.lifeandhealth
The Moseley Forum	http://www.moseleyforum.org.uk/?q=node/220
Telegraph newspaper	www.telegraph.co.uk/earth/main.jhtml?xml=/earth/2008/05/31/earecyc131.xm
Further information about recycling glass	www.wasteonline.org.uk www.recycle-more.co.uk

for environmental marketing claims (http://www.ftc.gov/bcp/grnrule/guides980427.htm). A quick read of these guidelines suggested that it was not sufficient to claim that a container was recyclable; there needed to be a reasonable process a customer could follow to actually get the container recycled near the location where it would be consumed. In addition, any claims of a closed loop, i.e., the same material is recycled or reused, for specific aspects of the recycling process needed to ensure that the customer clearly understood, within reason, what was specified and how much of the claims were feasible.

Educating the Consumer

A key question that faced the group was whether packaging suppliers such as SGS, who had to communicate to customers about recycling, should also educate customers about the benefit of bottles as containers (over plastics, or aluminum or paper cartons). Such an approach would create a dialog directly between a supplier like SGS and the OEMs customers, bypassing traditional serial supply chain flows.

An advertising agency had already prepared a proposal, and there were many other groups eager to tackle this issue. But was it money well spent? Would a communication initiative to the customer make sense, given that the bottles had to be purchased by an OEM, sold to a retailer, and then to the customer?

An alternative was to work on retailer councils to influence the sustainability index computation. Did the fact that the glass was recyclable mean that the carbon impact for the initial production should be split across the many times that the same material is used in bottles?

Hank wondered if successful recycling of bottles was a precursor to successful justification of the sustainability index improvement provided by glass bottles. If so, how aggressively should SGS Glassworks work to increase recycling rates?

The Bottom Line

Could SGS take steps to change the declining trend of bottle container use among beverage companies and milk, baby food, and other manufacturers who sold product to retail consumers? Was the sustainability index a powerful tool, which if harnessed effectively, could contribute a 2%–5% increase in the market share for glass bottles in the product packaging industry? Or, would these efforts be opening up Pandora's box as aluminum and paper carton manufacturers attacked bottle manufacturers for breakage, weight, slippage, and so on? How could bottles be marketed for kids products (milk, juices, etc.) as safe and sustainable alternatives? In short, was there a credible way to make the supply chain the highlight of the product? What Hank needed was a way to translate all of the details of the supply chain into an easy-to-understand message and an index to highlight its superiority.

Hank looked around the table for answers. The new time line for the teams to return with their solutions was just 24 hours.

CASE QUESTIONS

1. Do a 4C audit of the reverse supply chain for SGS.
2. Act as a procurement manager for SGS, analyze the possible options to benefit SGS, and provide a recommendation.
3. Explain how the demand benefit of recycled content can be used to understand profitable supply chain solutions for SGS.
4. Explain how coordination with municipalities enables Pareto-improving supply chain outcomes.
5. What should Hank Bilders do?

Chapter 13

Humanitarian Logistics

Humanitarian logistics deals with delivering aid and thus relief to people in situations caused by natural or manmade disasters. Over 35 million people in the world depend on emergency relief to survive in any given year. To envision the supply chain management challenge, imagine the television or newspaper coverage of a hurricane, tsunami, earthquake, civil war, forced migration, drought, or postwar reconstruction activity. In all of these cases, the goal of the supply chain effort is to focus on the management processes involving planning, ramp-up, sustainment and ramp-down to rapidly deal with the contingency ([95]). Many of these efforts are temporary and last only as long as it takes to stabilize the system and turn it over to local government or development agencies.

Every year, \$6–\$8 billion is spent on relief efforts. During the past 30–40 years, the number of nongovernmental organizations (NGOs) involved in relief efforts has gone from 938 in 1972 to over 26,000 in 1999. Though the distribution of funds is concentrated, with twenty NGOs receiving 75% of the funds, many smaller NGOs are involved in the distribution of aid to actual people, the "last mile" of aid provision. NGOs have started to depend on public funding, and public funds often focus on specific projects and places that are of interest to the donating country. In addition, the public's attention is focused on emergencies that attract a lot of television coverage; thus, for example, it was easy to generate \$225 per person in need in Kosovo but only \$18 per head was generated for Sierra Leone or Somalia.

In many complex emergencies, the humanitarian relief problem evolves quickly and unpredictably. There are usually significant life-and-death consequences associated with inadequate relief supplies. The associated locations may have poor infrastructure and poor telecommunications, as well as political constraints. In such environments, effective supply chains can significantly increase the odds of success. The overall goal of the humanitarian logistics activity is to restore the capability of the system, at least to the level prior to the catastrophe, and leave development to other entities.

13.1 CHAIN STRUCTURE

Humanitarian supply chains involve many separate entities, both governmental and nongovernmental, that ensure flow of product to the disaster victim. As described earlier, the last-mile service is provided by hundreds of NGOs and other entities. Funding for such relief may be provided in the form of in-kind or cash donations. The role of the supply chain is to match the supplies with demands and get the products to the destination location as effectively as possible.

In some cases, even establishing a chain of entities may be complicated by the need for permission from the sovereign government. There is also the need to sometimes work with local defense forces. Finally, as will be discussed in Section 13.5, these chains have to be created while respecting the humanitarian space expectations of the specific event.

13.2 CAPACITY

Often, at the location where the disaster has occurred, the infrastructure and leadership may be temporarily destroyed or significantly affected. For example, during the earthquake in Haiti, a significant portion of the United Nations leadership as well as several government entities were destroyed or diminished. In addition, there may be a shortage of trucks, ships, airplanes, and landing and docking facilities. Neighboring countries may not have adequate agreements to permit an adjustment in the mode or paths of flow.

In situations where the capacity is depleted, prices may increase significantly in the absence of coordination. Temporary difficulties with adding to the capacity add to pressure to the supply chain. Finally, the capacity and security of warehousing facilities end up being a key concern.

Another capacity constraint is the information technology capability. Efforts by Telecoms San Frontiers (in Sri Lanka for example) suggests that adding to wireless or telecommunications capability may boost an important weak link in the supply chain and act as an externality for everyone involved.

13.3 COORDINATION

Coordination in the humanitarian supply chain involves working with political enemies, military forces, local authorities, and NGOs. Given shortage of logistics assets, there is a need to prioritize and allocate tasks, deploy personnel, attract donor funds, indulge the mass media, and deliver relief. Another aspect of humanitarian logistics is that, in addition to bilateral aid provided directly by donor countries, frequently there are several NGOs such as the Red Cross, Doctors without Borders, World Vision, in addition to the United Nations (UN)–related entities such as the World Food Program, the World Health Organization, and the United Nations Humanitarian relief. As all these organizations rush in to provide relief, there are several basic steps to be managed, which include permissions from the host country to let individuals arrive, managing congestion, and managing the coordination with the military or security groups. How should this coordination be accomplished?

The United Nations Joint Logistics Committee (UNJLC) is a coordination body within the UN system whose goal is to coordinate logistics across independent agencies, UN, governmental, and nongovernmental. The mission of the UNJLC is summarized as "coordinate but not implement" i.e., facilitate the performance of other mission specific entities but allow them to do their own work. Over the years the UNJLC has played a key role in resolving conflicts and bottlenecks in several contexts, as the following examples illustrate. These examples are available as cases published by Professor Luk Van Wassenhove and colleagues ([102], [81], [103]).

When relief organizations were rushing in to provide aid in Afghanistan, a landlocked country, many organizations attempted to enter the country through Uzbekistan and send supplies on barges down the river ([81]). The hundreds of relief organizations, each operating independently, created such chaos that the Uzbek government shut down access to Afghanistan. The UNJLC played the role of "traffic cop," debottlenecking the situation by establishing a regular barge schedule and smoothing the flow of aid through the Uzbek entry point. This role of scheduling across independent relief organizations actually increased capacity available and decreased lead time for everyone. Such a coordination role can be considered as coordination by command, i.e., a centralized scheduler who plays the role of an externality that delivers value to all parties, coordinating the system and improving performance for everyone.

When relief organizations were pouring into Rwanda, the World Food Program (WFP) was shipping in food for hungry Rwandans while the UNJLC was shipping Rwandan refugees out from the war stricken area ([103]). Given the floods, the main mode of transport was air. WFP was flying in food and flying out empty; UNHCR was flying in empty and flying out full. The UNJLC coordinated the schedules across the two agencies so that WFP aircraft flew back with refugees while UNHCR aircraft flew in food supplies. The adjustments in flight schedules had to take into account loading issues at both ends, food and refugee arrival at each end, safety and security, and so on. But coordination enabled improved utilization and higher capacity at about the same cost. Such coordination is coordination by consensus across the relief organizations.

In Afghanistan, the UNJLC website provides security and weather updates, logistics shipment needs (similar to a college campus ride board), road conditions, and so on ([102]). The ensuing coordination is left to individual agencies who use this information to seek out interested parties to share resources. Such coordination is minimal, left to individual agencies, and thus is coordination by default.

The previous examples show three forms of coordination: coordination by command, i.e., a centralized approach; coordination by consensus, i.e., cooperative, Pareto-improving solutions; and coordination by default or no coordination except perhaps information sharing. In Section 13.7 we discuss possible reasons for each form of coordination. A complete theory that matches optimal coordination type to situation context remains a research topic at this point.

13.4 COMPETITIVENESS

There are several separate performance measures, almost a different one used by each donor. Some donors focus on the bottom line of getting the job done, others focus on specific efficiency measures (e.g., percent truck utilization, inventory turns, fraction of women and children receiving assistance). Often the recipient country has to spend an inordinate amount of time generating reports for each separate donor. While competing performance measures may be part of receiving aid, it does constrain funds usage effectively at the recipient location.

While there are several possible measures of performance of a humanitarian relief supply chain, one approach, suggested by Fearon ([37]), is to compare an actual outcome with the counterfactual outcome. In such an approach, the question is whether the humanitarian intervention did in fact improve the system in terms of lives saved, diseases avoided, crop failure averted, market functionality maintained, and so on. But other suggestions focus on the success of the appeal coverage, lead time between donation and delivery of aid, financial efficiency and assessment accuracy. Each of these metrics focuses on the process of forecasting the aid required and garnering the resources and then efficiently delivering the aid while respecting the planned humanitarian space.

But the issues are substantial, and the following list provides examples that suggest that choosing metrics can have an impact on solutions, some innovative and some that have unintended consequences:

1. In the past, plastic jerry cans were air dropped to regions where refugees accumulated to permit them to collect water and transport it to their camp site. In an effort to efficiently transport a large number, collapsible plastic containers were used. However, these collapsible containers required careful cleaning to prevent bacteria from accumulating at the folds of the cans. Cleaning required the use of chemicals such as potassium permanganate that changed the water's color to a purple hue. As refugees avoided this cleaning step, the food and water shortage evolved to a severe medical crisis for the population. Clearly the supply chain solved one problem while generating another.

2. In the past, severe malnutrition required delivery of milk powder or other enriching powdered nutrition that had to be mixed with water. Contamination of the water supply made disease a problem and thus prevented effective treatment of the malnutrition. An innovative entrepreneur in France came up with Plumpy-Nut, a paste made of peanuts and milk powder that could be squeezed into a child's mouth without addition of water. This innovation enabled a substantial reduction in the malnutrition soon after use. ([117])

3. Often, aid delivered is focused more on what donors have to offer rather than what is required. Soon after the 2004 tsunami in Asia, several loads of ski parkas and sweaters were shipped to Sri Lanka, a country where the weather seldom gets significantly cold. The ski parkas were often used as diapers and the donated clothing used as play things by children, rather than providing relief. One may argue that, by clogging up the delivery system with such ineffective aid, these donors compounded the problem ([5]).

4. Often effective delivery of purified water involves setting up large purification plants in the field. But this effective approach also requires aggregation of large numbers of frail and disease-ridden people in close quarters. This increases the prospect of spreading disease and thus hampers possibility of providing effective relief.

5. In El Salvador, most of the poor population felt that aid was being diverted to the richer sections of society and abetted by the people in power at the time. There was the need to create a new entity that would permit coordination between the different groups. Despite efforts to keep the process neutral, the opposition managed to convince voters that their party played a key role in aid distribution and thus won the elections held soon after. The ex post analysis may as well have concluded that some of the humanitarian principles were violated, even though aid delivery itself was acceptable.

6. In Indonesia, the government troops were battling local guerillas in Banda Aceh. When aid arrived to this badly devastated region after the 2004 tsunami, the government troops were affected far more than the guerillas in the mountainside. But the government did not want the international media and US Marines to appear on their soil and interact with these guerillas. The denial of permission to international military to offer assistance clearly complicated the efficiency of the associated relief supply chain.

7. In Ethiopia, aid groups brought in cooking oil as part of a food program. This oil competed directly with local producers and drove them out of business. The long-term consequence was a prolonging of the disaster.

13.5 THE HUMANITARIAN SPACE

What distinguishes the humanitarian supply chain management problem is that the deployment of the supply chain is the need to operate within a humanitarian space also referred to as the *humanitarian triangle*. The humanitarian triangle consists of three issues ([118]): (1) "The first principle, humanity, implies that human suffering should be relieved wherever it is found" (p. 12); (2) "the second principle, neutrality, implies that relief should be provided without bias or affiliation to a party in the conflict" (p. 13); and (3) "the third principle, impartiality, indicates that assistance should be provided without discrimination and with priority given to the most urgent needs" (p. 13). Each of these issues has to be weighed against its impact on the relief supply chain. The principle of humanity focuses on maximizing the number of people who benefit from the relief effort. But the principle of impartiality focuses on a weighted benefit, i.e., that of impacting those most in need of relief. Clearly each of these metrics might result in very different choices and deployment strategies. As an example, in the relief efforts following the floods in Rwanda, only after the relief organizations arrived at the scene did they realize the location of people most in need, which was in the border areas. From an evaluation perspective, the relief supply chain may have failed the impartiality test. Similarly, when relief efforts started following the hurricane in El Salvador, the ruling party was supported by the wealthy segments of society, while the guerilla army was supported by the poorer segments of society. Providing relief required coordination across both segments. The principle of neutrality required preventing any perceptions, apparent or real, that would benefit one or the other political parties.

13.6 AN ILLUSTRATIVE MODEL

The following is an attempt to translate the impact of these principles on the running of the logistics system. The model is simple, but it could be made to reflect more realistic situations.

Consider a situation in which a logistics manager has an inventory level of food (I) that has to be distributed at a port. We are planning on how to distribute the food over a planning period T. (Think of T as the replenishment interval if we want to imagine this as a rolling horizon problem.) There are two population groups P_1 (in location L_1) and P_2 (in location L_2). L_1 is located at a distance (time) of T_1 from the port, and L_2 is located at a distance (time) of T_2. Assume that $L_1 < L_2$. Now suppose that the demands in each location over the period T are greater than the inventory available. Also, the benefit per unit delivered in P_1 is b_1, while the benefit per unit delivered in P_2 is b_2, where $b_2 > b_1$. Assume that given the transport assets available, the food can be moved at a constant rate to either location. Finally assume that the existing political situation has two powerful parties, each representing P_1 and P_2. However, whoever is successful in delivering the food will gain the upper hand politically.

Suppose the goal is to distribute the food as quickly as possible. If the food is distributed at a constant rate, since L_1 is closer, less will be in the pipeline and thus more food will be distributed over a fixed time period. Thus a plan to assist the largest number in a fixed time (humanity) will deliver all of the food to L_1.

Now suppose the goal is to distribute food so as to generate the greatest benefit. The focus is less on the quantity delivered and more on the benefits realized. This tips the focus to L_2. If all of the food is shipped to L_2, then we will deliver less food (as food will be stuck in the longer pipeline) but realize greater benefits from the food distributed. This will give us the principle of impartiality as being maximized by delivering all of the food to L_2.

Now focus on the principle of neutrality. Under the delivery to L_1, we tip the political power to the P_1 party. Under the delivery to L_2, we tip the political power to P_2. If we want to do neither, but preserve the existing political climate, it is best to divide up the food and distribute (perhaps) half to P_1 and half to P_2. Note that given the differences in transport time, we will have to deliver $\frac{I - T_1 - T_2}{2}$ to each location. We will ship $T_1 + \frac{I - T_1 - T_2}{2}$ along the path to location L_1 and $T_2 + \frac{I - T_1 - T_2}{2}$ along the path to location L_2 in order to deliver equal amounts to each of the population centers P_1 and P_2. This will maintain the principle of neutrality.

13.7 DECISIONS

Coordination in the context of humanitarian supply chain management involves the delivery of relief in a cohesive and effective manner and involves (1) strategic planning, (2) gathering and managing information, (3) mobilizing resources and assuring accountability, (4) orchestrating a functional division of labor, (5) negotiating and maintaining a serviceable framework (6) providing leadership by injecting discipline without unduly constraining action ([65]).

Strategic coordination (SC) deals primarily with (1) negotiating access to affected populations, advocating respect for humanitarian principles and law and liaising with international political and military actors (including the UN system); and (2) setting the overall directions and goals of the UN humanitarian program, allocating tasks and responsibilities, ensuring correspondence between resource mobilizations and priorities, monitoring and evaluating the system-wide implementation. Tactical coordination (TC) tasks include managing (1) administration providing common services, communications, security and common logistics and (2) substantive decisions regarding deployment to specific sectors, geographical areas, choosing and prioritizing delivery to beneficiary groups, etc.

The three classic steps in any contingency are ramp-up, sustain, and ramp-down. During each of these phases, coordination activities can be described as consisting of reducing conflicts and bottlenecks and prioritization/scheduling. As discussed earlier, the varying nature of the scope activities suggests different management strategies over the life cycle. It is clear that there will be multiple agencies with individual missions, capabilities and metrics, separate donors, and so on. Furthermore, the choices made by the owners of the system (governments, ministries, other countries, etc.) create the humanitarian space in which the relief efforts have to operate. In addition, information may be local and decentralized (e.g., local security, truck rates, contracts, quality of service) or centralized (e.g., weather conditions, road network, satellite images). The resources may be available centrally or donated by agencies and operated by private agents, the military, or individual relief agencies.

13.8 THE LIFE CYCLE OF A CONTINGENCY PLAN

During ramp-up, the humanitarian space is not clear. The deployment requirements are urgent, and some donors make use of speed of deployment to determine who gets resources (i.e., the early bird gets the worm). Sometimes the CNN effect results—few agencies are there early, and information is fragmented. However, starting the process requires several one-time tasks to be completed with respect to permissions to operate, taxes on imports, licenses for operating vehicles, rules regarding ownership of goods, clarifications regarding laws, visas, landing rights, customs and religious observances, and so on. There may also be infrastructural needs such as air traffic control (ATC) requirements, bridges, and port clearance from neighbors. The region may be suited for centralized coordination because of the small number of entities involved and the critical nature of the congestion-related issues.

During the sustainment phase, the individual agencies need to operate efficiently but may still require assistance such as security info, weather information, sharing of resources, help with breaking up cartels, assistance with persistent problems involving interpretation of laws, and coordination with military. Since many parallel efforts may be in operation, with each agency having its own supply chain processes, it may be appropriate to coordinate by consensus.

Coordination between agencies is helpful during ramp-down, when there is a need to identify local groups to continue operations, coordinate with the military for exit, decide how much development activity will continue, take actions to prevent mission creep, and so on. Since many entities may be involved, and each may be planning a hand-off to an appropriate local entity, it may be best to permit independent coordination with just information exchange.

13.9 CHAPTER SUMMARY

The chain structure in a humanitarian logistics context is complex and consists of donors, collection groups (often NGOs), transport companies, aid groups at the destination, warehouses, relief camps, and recipients. The number of possible NGOs involved may be several hundreds, and the aid may be flowing in both through a pipeline as well as through bilateral efforts. Often the "last mile" of delivery requires coordination with local NGOs. The capacity of the local affected population to receive airplanes or ships, store products, and transport them to affected areas, and the level of skill of personnel are often key sources of complexity. Large demands on transport by several independently acting NGOs may create congestion and price increases and compound delivery problems. In addition, security concerns may add to the difficulty as well as the coordination problems with the military. The coordination choices made may include centralized coordination, coordination by consensus, and coordination by default. The nature of the coordination may depend on the stage of the contingency. Finally the metrics of performance vary greatly, including output measures of delivery effectiveness, truck utilization, and distribution of aid by population segments (e.g., women and children). In some contexts, significant portions of the aid are offered to the NGO who is first on the scene. Such metrics create a focus on speed at the cost of coordination or effectiveness. Given the increasing number of catastrophes, as well as the significant numbers of people depending on such aid, effective humanitarian supply chain management may well offer both intellectual challenges as well as personal satisfaction.

Chapter 14

Information Systems to Track, Report, and Adapt Supply Chains

The frequency and level of detail of information regarding product flows in a global supply chain can impact the chain's cost and performance. Technologies such as smartphones and radio frequency identification (RFID) tags, as well as new software that can be delivered as a service and reconfigured as needed, have changed customer expectations. This chapter provides a summary of a few emerging information-driven changes to supply chains, but the real objective for a supply chain is to leverage all possible information to impact performance.

The chain structure of the supply chain suggests the number of different entities that have to share data to enable detection of contamination or enable end-to-end visibility. When real-time information can be used to adjust to current events, firms such as the chemical company BASF claim success in adjusting capacity in response to data regarding current hurricane paths. But information from product tags also enables coordination between manufacturers and retailers, as described by Gillette and its retailers ([93]). Data collected regarding individual products enable Walmart to drive sustainability targets while simultaneously decreasing costs and enhancing its competitiveness. Retailers such as Metro and manufacturers such as Gillette claim success in better synchronizing promotion to current conditions using electronic product identification, thus enhancing their competitiveness. Information and its use impact the 4Cs of the supply chain.

14.1 UBIQUITOUS DATA FROM RFID TAGS

New technologies incorporated into products enable even more information to be leveraged by the supply chain. Radio frequency identification (RFID) tags represent one approach that could, theoretically, enable even a single unit of a product to be tracked. An RFID system "transmits the identity (in the form of a unique serial number) of an object or person wirelessly, using radio waves" ([2]).

The system consists of "a tag which contains information regarding the unit it is attached to, an antenna which send signals to the tag to activate it, a reader that emits radio waves, decodes the data received and sends it to a computer for processing" ([2]). There are different types of RFID tags—passive, semiactive, and active. Passive RFID tags have no power supply and depend on the signal sent to the tag for energy. Semiactive tags have power for the tag but not to broadcast. Active tags contain power for the device and can transmit. The prices for these tags vary from \$0.10 to \$0.20 for passive tags to as much as \$100 for an active tag. An electronic product code (EPC) enables tracking of individual product units using a unique serial number.

In 2003, the Metro retail chain in Germany opened a store equipped with RFID tags for many of its items. Over time, this "store of the future" has used the technology to adjust promotions and develop a smart scale that automatically detects items, such as fruit, providing easier checkout and tracking, and so on. Since RFID readers can track items as they are loaded on to a customer's cart, it saves customers the need to wait at checkout. Such tracking at the warehouse level would enable pallet loads to be distributed anywhere in the warehouse and still enable quick identification and shipping. The main challenge is to have RFID readers at a close enough proximity, 10 to 20 feet, to enable accuracy while preventing signal confusion from multiple reads.

Once a pallet of product or a single item can be tracked, the associated information regarding product status in the supply chain is immediately available. Sensors can transmit product location, temperature, and quantity, as well as whether there were any changes in the status of the container or product over time. Such information can assure the customer that the product sold was not tampered with and was not counterfeit.

The shaving products company Gillette, owned by P&G, claimed a 25% return over a ten-year period, using RFID tags on its products ([24]). Product tracking showed that the time from production to store was six days and ten hours, which included about three days to move product from the manufacturer to the retailer distribution center, and a significant portion of the remaining time (three days) was spent reaching the store. Data showed that many promotional items remained at the back of the store and generated out-of-stocks at the retail store. This information enabled the manufacturer and retailer to work on a smoother flow of product to decrease stockouts, increasing sales by 28% during promotions at test locations.

Military convoys with smart tags (RFIDs with independent power sources) have been used to facilitate information gathering in the field as deployment changes and conditions unfold. Continuous monitoring of engine conditions or blades in aircraft enable proactive maintenance, thus enabling quick aircraft turnaround.

But similar changes are occurring as smartphones enable the detection of potential customers, using global positioning systems (GPS) tracking. A customer whose location is known to a retailer can be offered service commensurate with their importance to the firm, using shopping assistance, prioritized service, and special coupons sent to the cellphone.

As the need to pair individual product units with the appropriate customers increases, the role of the supply chain in enabling such a union offers fascinating challenges.

14.2 RATING A PRODUCT BASED ON SUPPLY CHAIN CHOICES

The availability of smartphones that can run apps, read barcodes using the phone's camera, and pull information from the web means that data regarding the suppply chain's choices may well impact a consumer's purchase decision and thus demand. Goodguide is such a company, whose website contains an index summarizing information regarding over 100,000 products (in July 2012) ([45]). A consumer with a smartphone can install an app, direct the camera to the barcode of a product, and immediately receive a product rating that also provides details regarding all supply chain choices made by the company.

As an example, in July 2012, I downloaded information regarding a specific kind of Crest toothpaste—the Crest ProHealth Multiprotection rinse, Clean Mint, 16.9 oz., made by Procter & Gamble. This product was shown as having a rating of 7.4 out of a maximum of 10. The rating combined three scores for this product—Health (10), Environment (6.2), and Society (6.0). Each of these criteria has several specific measures that are directly impacted by the supply chain. Under the Environment metric, the section on governance includes the supply chain, the role of suppliers, waste management, emissions tracking, and so on. For each of these criteria, data are gathered about reports filed and whether specific targets were set, with scores set higher if specific steps were taken to improve on each dimension. For example, under the reporting criteria, specific initiatives to reduce product transport, disclose the identity of top suppliers, and reduce waste and emissions are measured. Each of these initiatives ends with a judgment regarding the appropriate measurement and mitigation plans. Under the impact on society, the metric records whether specific steps have been taken to protect worker rights and whether suppliers are evaluated based on their sustainability performance. The site provides a measure for each product, but also computes the data across all products to reflect the company's commitment to sustainability initiatives. For example, P&G has its own aggregate rating of 6.1, measured as an aggregate over its processes and products. Similarly, across all Crest products, the site provides an average rating of 5.9. This information enables customers to assess their view of the company as well as the brand sold by the company.

How does the supply chain impact a product's score? Notice that several of the decisions we discussed in previous chapters have a direct impact on a product and a company's score: supplier management, transportation, emissions, waste, recycling, packaging, and so on. As more customers start comparing products and making purchase decisions reflecting their individual preferences, the supply chain will impact the top line revenues, in addition to the costs.

14.3 TRACING AND TRACKING PRODUCTS

In this section, we will discuss a challenge associated with tracing food supply. As food moves through the supply chain, there is potential for contamination at each step in the process. For example, a pathogen like *E. coli* could enter the food system at any number of stages, such as production, transport, processing, distribution, or retail sales points.

There are many stages that livestock products go through to reach the consumer, and, given the large market, there is a lot of product volume involved. For example, in 2011, 34.1 million head of cattle were slaughtered ([120]) and the average weight of each animal was on the order of 1,277 pounds. Assuming a dressing percentage of 50% to account for the skin, bones, and offal, and assuming an average retail package size of three pounds, the number of packages of beef to be tracked annually is on the order of 8.1 billion. This tracking represents an interesting challenge: if a slice of beef purchased at a retail outlet is contaminated, how can the other potentially affected products be traced to protect the food supply?

Of course a large fraction of beef that is ultimately consumed does not go through retail outlets but rather is delivered to consumers via the restaurant and food service industries. Thus, given the scale of US food production, automated systems will be required to identify the source of the contamination, take effective and remedial measures to identify and isolate the contaminated food, and inform the public of the possible risks. One example of such a system is available to consumers of Japanese Wagyu beef, who can key in the product code associated with a unit sold and obtain all information regarding the animal, its feed and treatment, and its pedigree ([17]).

But if sensors were used throughout the life of the animal to track position and health indicators (e.g., body temperature, heart rate, respiration rate), the data from a herd of beef cattle could be used to gauge herd health and spread of disease. In addition, knowledge of disease incubation periods coupled with animal health information can provide useful information on the potential for hazardous infection in animals that have already been harvested for food production.

Another detail is that there are many participants in the supply chain from the farm to the consumer. At the farm level, genetics and feed are combined to produce livestock products. Beyond the farm, the livestock product is transported, processed, and packaged for retail distribution, typically passing through the hands of several agents who are receiving nearly identical inputs from a large number of sources. In addition, animals move about, interacting with their cohorts and the environment. A further complication is that at various points along the supply chain, one animal may be divided into several products and distributed through different channels. Because of this branching in the supply chain, it is important to identify the path of livestock products both backward and forward through the supply chain.

Imagine that contamination is detected and there is the need to trace the origin of the animal. The necessary data are spread across the private databases of the various enterprises that make up the supply chain, from farms to grocery stores. The technical challenge for data management thus comes from the need to integrate data from numerous independent databases while preserving privacy. Due to the significant risk of losing competitive advantage, most of these entities are unwilling to freely share this information. Thus an acceptable solution must provide privacy guarantees for the large number of entities involved.

14.4 GREEN REPORTS

In 2005, Walmart CEO Lee Scott declared specific sustainability goals ([107]), driven by the principles that the company would work towards zero waste, use 100% renewable energy, and sell products that were sustainable in their use of resources and the impact on the environment. These broad goals were converted into specific goals that included (1) increasing their transportation fleet's efficiency by 25% in three years and doubling it in the next ten years, (2) eliminating 30% of the energy used in stores and, (3) reducing greenhouse gas emissions by 20% in seven years. The goals were all attained with the help of the supply chain, but they also created a model of creating savings while being sustainable.

In a milestone meeting in April 2012 ([31]), the company highlighted specific product changes that impact sustainability. An initiative to replace the metal wires used in packaging toys with natural fibers was estimated to have saved 1.6 billion feet of wire from 2010 through 2012. A focus on reducing waste had managed to decrease the waste down to 20% at all stores, thus preventing material from going to the landfill. The packaging-focused recycling efforts at stores saved the company $231 million in 2012. Driving 41 million fewer miles and better packing of products saved $75 million in fuel costs. Each of these specific savings for Walmart can be tracked to alternate supply chain decisions.

One example involving a focus on wheat production described exploration of backhaul movement of manure from poultry farms to wheat farms to decrease use of fertilizer while improving soil performance. In another context, Pepsico worked to decrease the need to grow rice saplings but instead grew from seeds. The savings in water from adoption of such farming techniques compared to water used for the soft-drink manufacturing enabled the firm to claim to be a negative water footprint company in India. Product specification changes, supplier innovation, better movement, all generated sustainable solutions that also decreased costs, lowered prices, and improved quality.

Companies like Walmart provide annual global responsibility reports that summarize the overall impact of the supply chain on the environment ([30]) along with progress towards the goals stated earlier. A review of this report suggests that the choices in the global supply chain of this company will directly impact this external reporting of the company's performance and thus increases the scrutiny of the supply chain. There are many companies that have significant efforts to increase their product and supply chain's sustainability, including Starbucks, Nike, Samsung, Unilever, and Subaru. In other words, the supply chain is now in a glass box: its choices are more transparent and of greater consequence to the performance of the company.

In addition to companies themselves, there are nongovernmental organizations (NGOs) like Greenpeace that also focus on the global supply chain. The Greenpeace report on apparel ([50]) tracks the input of hazardous chemicals used in apparel manufacturing. In particular, the report focuses on nonylphenol ethoxylates, their use in manufacturing, and their subsequent release into the water supply, which impacts the food supply. Such reports put pressure on apparel manufacturers to take responsibility for manufacturing choices across the supply chain. In the electronics industry, specific laws such as the Conflict Materials Trade Act also impact the sourcing of materials used and hold companies responsible for guaranteeing that their products do not contain any minerals mined in conflict regions.

14.5 SOURCEMAP

In addition to summary reports regarding the supply chain, there are efforts to track the specific details for individual companies' sourcing of their products. An open source software application called Sourcemap ([113]) maps supply chains linked to a dictionary of details such as their carbon footprint, greenhouse gas emissions, lead time, and more. The open source nature of the software enables crowdsourcing of supply chain maps and enables tracking down to the raw material source. The site contains source maps for electronic products, apparel, food, and many others. The software permits any user to create such maps based on the data they possess and then pass the data along to others to edit and develop.

But individual firms can use these maps to work with their suppliers to ensure that the associated supply chains conform to regulations or the company's ethical constraints, inform the customer regarding the environmental impact of the product sourcing, and so on. For example, the site shows the sourcing of chocolate across the world ([15]), along with specific supplier-related issues that are causes for concern. The data in these supply chain maps, similar to the NGO reports, potentially impact consumer choices and put pressure on companies to make changes.

14.6 INFORMATION SYSTEMS TO ADAPT TO CONTINGENCIES

Consider supply chains that face significant short-term changes: events that require rapid adjustment and adaptation of flows. In a book titled *Orchestrating Supply Chain Opportunities,* Iyer and Zelikovsky ([63]) focus on the information system as one tool to manage events that include weather-related disruptions (like Hurricane Katrina), product failures that require rapid redesign (like the Kryptonite bicycle lock), demand surges (such as those faced by Amazon.com), among others.

One example focuses on BASF, a global chemical company, and how it used its event-based enterprise system to manage the impact of hurricanes Katrina and Rita using SAP's event management software ([104]). When the hurricanes hit, several of the shipments to the United States were in transit on ships. The choreography of the changes to the supply chain had to synchronize with information regarding the path of the hurricane and its landfall. The company had to account for safety of personnel, potential product vulnerability, security issues, requirements by customs rules, and specific requirements of critical components. The specific needs were confirmed just one day before Hurricane Katrina hit. "BASF knew which consignments were still in port, which ones were in transit, and which ones had already reached their destination port in Houston or New Orleans. BASF could therefore take the necessary steps to ensure that its customers suffered as little as possible," explains European project team member Peter Nikolaus ([104], p. 4).

BASF claims that its enterprise event management software helped orchestrate the reconfiguration of its supply chain while the events were happening. Ships were dynamically rerouted to safe harbors, in some cases several times, as the situation changed. BASF's customers were kept informed as the company adjusted its supply chain to maintain its level of service. Enterprise systems, of which SAP is one example, provide event management, detection of changes, and response opportunities all the way to the batch level. The software tracks serial numbers beginning with manufacturing, thus possessing a complete picture of everything that goes on in the supply chain from manufacturing to distribution to supply logistics and finally to point of sale. Moreover, this visibility extends beyond a single client into global movement of goods and services. Putting these product tiers in one cohesive solution set gives clients the visibility and reconfiguration capability to manage stretch goals.

The ability to track product at the unit level across the supply chain provides the ability to adapt to events, thus providing the flexibility required to face volatile demand environments with significant short-term shifts.

14.7 CHAPTER SUMMARY

Information systems provide supply chains the opportunity to both capitalize on opportunities and react to shifts. As ownership of supply chains becomes more fragmented, technologies such as RFID and enterprise software such as SAP enable firms to react efficiently, minimizing costs to maintain performance. Threats such as food contamination, hurricanes, and product failures, as well as opportunities such as new designs that improve product sustainability and monitor global supply chain performance to guarantee ethical practices, all rely on an effective information system.

Chapter 15

Tools for Supply Chain Management

This chapter provides a review of tools used in analyzing supply chains, focusing on (a) linear programming models, (b) simulation models using Excel, and (c) inventory models. We use models to understand and improve supply chains. All of the associated spreadsheets will be available on the website for this book.

15.1 LINEAR PROGRAMMING TO SOLVE THE NETWORK FLOWS PROBLEM

In this section, we use a linear programming approach to optimize the flows in the supply chain. The model takes a global look at the problem and incorporates the path of flows, the capacity impact, and the benefit to taking multiple paths of flows to balance use of capacity and demand satisfaction.

The approach is illustrated for the sample problem in Chapter 2 on chain structure. The same concept can be extended to larger or different problem structures by adjusting the decision variables, constraints, or objective. Consider the example network shown in Figure 15.1.[1] The supply chain consists of two plants, P1 and P2, that can each supply the

FIGURE 15.1 An example network with data

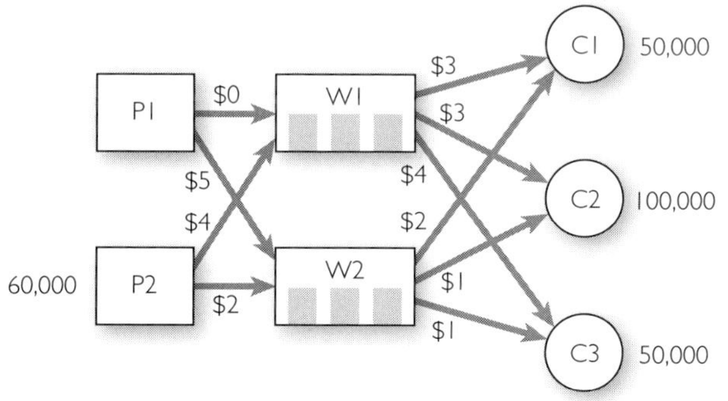

[1]This example is from the presentation by Jeffrey Karrenbauer from Insight Consulting in a class I taught several years ago.

demands at warehouses W1 and W2, which in turn can supply each of three customer zones C1, C2, and C3. Demands at C1, C2, and C3 are 50,000, 100,000, and 50,000, respectively. Warehouses W1 and W2 are intermediate points with no capacity constraint. The capacity at plant P2 is 60,000 units. The costs per unit are provided for each link between plants and warehouses and between warehouses and customer zones.

In order to structure the optimal shipment problem, we need to define the following decision variables:

$$x(\text{P1,W1}) = \text{amount of goods sent from plant P1 to warehouse W1}$$

$$x(\text{P1,W2}) = \text{amount of goods sent from plant P1 to warehouse W2}$$

$$x(\text{P2,W1}) = \text{amount of goods sent from plant P2 to warehouse W1}$$

$$x(\text{P2,W2}) = \text{amount of goods sent from plant P2 to warehouse W2}$$

Similarly let

$$x(\text{W1,C1}) = \text{amount of goods sent from warehouse W1 to customer zone 1}$$

$$x(\text{W1,C2}) = \text{amount of goods sent from warehouse W1 to customer zone 2}$$

$$x(\text{W1,C3}) = \text{amount of goods sent from warehouse W1 to customer zone 3}$$

$$x(\text{W2,C1}) = \text{amount of goods sent from warehouse W2 to customer zone 1}$$

$$x(\text{W2,C2}) = \text{amount of goods sent from warehouse W2 to customer zone 2}$$

$$x(\text{W2,C3}) = \text{amount of goods sent from warehouse W2 to customer zone 3}$$

The goal is to choose values for these variables that are relevant for the context defined by the problem. In order for the decisions to be implementable or feasible, the flows between the warehouse and the customer zone should satisfy the specified demand at each customer zone. (Note that we assume that we have committed to satisfy the demands; thus maximizing profits reduces to minimizing the costs associated with satisfying the demands). The associated constraints are defined as follows:

$$x(\text{W1,C1}) + x(\text{W2,C1}) = 50{,}000$$

$$x(\text{W1,C2}) + x(\text{W2,C2}) = 100{,}000$$

$$x(\text{W1,C3}) + x(\text{W2,C3}) = 50{,}000$$

Next, the constraints should ensure that the supplies received from plants by the warehouses are sufficient to cover the required deliveries to the customer zones. The following constraints ensure that requirement:

$$x(\text{W1,C1}) + x(\text{W1,C2}) + x(\text{W1,C3}) = x(\text{P1,W1}) + x(\text{P2,W1})$$

$$x(\text{W2,C1}) + x(\text{W2,C2}) + x(\text{W2,C3}) = x(\text{P1,W2}) + x(\text{P2,W2})$$

Finally, the capacity constraint of plant P2 requires that no more than its capacity is planned to be shipped from P2 to the warehouses:

$$x(\text{P2,W1}) + x(\text{P2,W2}) \leq 60{,}000$$

All variables are ≥ 0.

In order to minimize costs, the goal is to set values for these material movements i.e.,

$$\textbf{Minimize } (0 \times x(\text{P1,W1})) + (5 \times x(\text{P1,W2})) + (4 \times x(\text{P2,W1}) + (2 \times x(\text{P2,W2})) + (3 \times x(\text{W1,C1})) + (3 \times x(\text{W1,C2})) + (4 \times x(\text{W1,C3})) + (2 \times x(\text{W2,C1})) + (1 \times x(\text{W2,C2})) + (1 \times x(\text{W2,C3}))$$

Notice that we have framed the problem to simultaneously consider costs of flows, capacity, and feasible paths. Such a supply chain view often uncovers interesting alternatives.

15.2 SOLVING THE PROBLEM USING MICROSOFT EXCEL

Create a worksheet with cells B3:C4 for flows from the plants to the warehouses and cells B7:C9 for flows from the warehouses to customer zones. Record the costs in cells E3:F4 and E7:F9. This spreadsheet is provided on the website. The constraints are as follows:

$$\text{B4} + \text{C4} \le 60{,}000$$

$$\text{B3} + \text{B4} = \text{B7} + \text{B8} + \text{B9}$$

$$\text{C3} + \text{C4} = \text{C7} + \text{C8} + \text{C9}$$

$$\text{B7} + \text{C7} = 50{,}000$$

$$\text{B8} + \text{C8} = 100{,}000$$

$$\text{B9} + \text{C9} = 50{,}000$$

$$\text{H3} = (\text{E3} \times \text{B3}) + (\text{F3} \times \text{C3})$$

$$\text{H4} = (\text{E4} \times \text{B4}) + (\text{F4} \times \text{C4})$$

$$\text{H7} = (\text{B7} \times \text{E7}) + (\text{C7} \times \text{F7})$$

$$\text{H8} = (\text{B8} \times \text{E8}) + (\text{C8} \times \text{F8})$$

$$\text{H9} = (\text{B9} \times \text{E9}) + (\text{C9} \times \text{F9})$$

$$\text{G10} = \text{H3} + \text{H4} + \text{H7} + \text{H8} + \text{H9}$$

The active cells are B3:C4 and B7:C9, and the set cell is G10. We want to minimize the set cell.

How would we evaluate the effect of potentially closing plants or warehouses and the impact on flexibility to respond to changing circumstances?

For the formulation provided earlier, define the following additional variables: $y(\text{P1}) = 0$ referring to plant P1 closed and $y(\text{P1}) = 1$ as referring to plant P1 open. Similarly $y(\text{P2}) = 0$ if plant P2 is closed, 1 otherwise. $y(\text{W1}) = 0$ if plant W1 is closed, 1 otherwise. $y(\text{W2}) = 0$ if warehouse W2 is closed, 1 otherwise. Then make the following changes to the constraints:

$$x(\text{P1,W1}) \le 250{,}000y\ (\text{P1})$$

$$x(\text{P1,W1}) \le 250{,}000y\ (\text{W1})$$

$$x(\text{P1,W2}) \le 250{,}000y\ (\text{P1})$$

$$x(\text{P1,W2}) \le 200{,}000y\ (\text{W2})$$

$$x(\text{P2,W1}) \le 220{,}000y\ (\text{P2})$$

$$x(\text{P2,W1}) \le 250{,}000y\ (\text{W1})$$

$$x(\text{P2,W2}) \le 220{,}000y\ (\text{P2})$$

$$x(\text{P2,W2}) \le 200{,}000y\ (\text{W2})$$

To implement these changes to the formulation in the spreadsheet, create new cells J3:J6, which refer to whether facilities P1, P2, W1 and W2 are open or closed.

Let cells J3 to J6 refer to the four variables $y(\text{P1})$, $y(\text{P2})$, $y(\text{W1})$, and $y(\text{W2})$. Also let cells K3 to K6 refer to the fixed costs from Table 2.1 in Chapter 2, i.e., 300,000, 280,000, 100,000, and 90,000 respectively associated with each facility. Let cells D3 and D4 contain the capacities of plant P1 and P2. Also let cells B5 and C5 contain the capacities of warehouses W1 and W2.

$$B3 + C3 \leq D3 \times J3$$

$$B4 + C4 \leq D4 \times J4$$

$$B3 + B4 \leq B5 \times J5$$

$$C3 + C4 \leq C6 \times J6$$

$$B3 + B4 = B7 + B8 + B9$$

$$C3 + C4 = C7 + C8 + C9$$

$$B7 + C7 = 50{,}000$$

$$B8 + C8 = 100{,}000$$

$$B9 + C9 = 50{,}000$$

$$H3 = (E3 \times B3) + (F3 \times C3)$$

$$H4 = (E4 \times B4) + (F4 \times C4)$$

$$H7 = (B7 \times E7) + (C7 \times F7)$$

$$H8 = (B8 \times E8) + (C8 \times F8)$$

$$H9 = (B9 \times E9) + (C9 \times F9)$$

$$L3 = J3 \times K3$$

$$L4 = J4 \times K4$$

$$L5 = J5 \times K5$$

$$L6 = J6 \times K6$$

$$L7 = L3 + L4 + L5 + L6$$

$$G10 = H3 + H4 + H7 + H8 + H9 + L7$$

The active cells are B3:C4 and B7:C9, the set cell is G10, and the solver window is set to minimize the set cell. To close or open each facility, change the constraint and solve again. This provides an estimate of the cost changes as the facility configuration changes. Verify by running Solver that you get the results described in Section 2.8.

15.3 SIMULATION MODELS

Excel can be used to build simulation models of logistics systems. There are many large-scale models available, but our objective is to use simple models to develop insight.

Simulation models examine systems in which some aspect of the system is a *random variable,* e.g., demand or lead time. The information regarding a random variable is usually summarized as a *probability distribution.* The probability distribution, e.g., normal distribution or uniform distribution, provide the probability associated with the occurrence of different values for the random variable. The spreadsheets associated with this section are available in the website for this book.

For example:

Create the following cells in Excel:

A2: 1
A3: + A2 + 1
A4:A101 (Copy from cell A2)
B2: =NORMINV(RAND(),100,25)
B2:B101 (Copy from cell A2)

The entries in the spreadsheet show us a simulated set of values for a random variable that follows a normal distribution with a mean of 100 units and a standard deviation of 25 units.

This is a sample of 100 demands whose population mean and standard deviation are 100 and 25 respectively.

Now develop a histogram of these 100 values.

15.4 HISTOGRAM

To develop a histogram, use the Tools Data Analysis Histogram command. (If you do not see the Data Analysis option, please follow commands to add in the option.)

15.5 DESCRIPTIVE STATISTICS

We can get statistical information regarding this set of 100 values using the command Tools Data Analysis Descriptive Statistics.

What is the difference between the probability distribution and the histogram we have generated?

How do we use these simulated demands?

Example Problem

Consider the problem faced by Steco, a retailer of titanium rods. Weekly demand for these rods follows a normal distribution with a mean of 100 units and a standard deviation of 25 units. These rods cost $5 each, and the cost of holding a rod in inventory for a year is 20% of its cost. The cost to Steco to place an order for replenishment is $25 per order. Delivery lead time is 2 weeks. Management wants a less than 6% probability of stocking out, corresponding to a backorder cost per unit per day of $1.50. Assume 50 weeks per year.

Develop a (Q,r) policy for Steco. Use an Excel simulation model to provide the optimal r value.

Answer

First create a worksheet and name it **Inventory**.

The first thirteen rows provide us the data regarding the problem (see the Steco worksheet in the CD attached to this book). Each row shows time (t) increasing. The entries in the columns are as follows:

Physical Inventory (t) = Physical Inventory ($t-1$) – Demand ($t-1$) + Orders Received ($t-1$)

Pipeline Inventory (t) = Pipeline Inventory ($t-1$) – Demand ($t-1$) + Orders Placed ($t-1$)

Demand (t) = Maximum (0, NORMINV(RAND(),D7,D8),0) i.e, the demand follows a normal distribution with parameters shown in cells D7 (mean) and D8 (standard deviation) with a nonzero value.

Ending Pipeline Inventory (t) = Beginning Pipeline Inventory (t) – Demand (t)

Order (t) = 0 if Ending Pipeline Inventory is $> r$

= Q if Ending Pipeline Inventory is $\leq r$

Order Cost = s if order is placed, 0 otherwise

Holding Cost = $h \times$ Max (0, Physical Inventory (t) – Demand (t))

Backorder Cost = $b \times$ Max (0, Demand (t) – Physical Inventory (t))

Cost = Order Cost + Holding Cost + Backorder Cost

The Lead Time of L means that order placed at t arrives at $t + L$

Columns N through T show the scheduled number of days to receive the order, i.e., Order 1 is received the following period, Order 2 is received two periods later, and so on.

Column U shows the total outstanding orders, i.e., the sum of columns N through T.

The Service Level Column records = 0 if the entire order is filled, 1 otherwise.

The Fill Rate column shows the fraction of the order that is filled.

Finally the overall statistics concerning average costs, service levels, fill rates, and so on are recorded in cells A121:D130.

15.6 SIMULATING THE EFFECT OF DIFFERENT REORDER LEVELS

If we want to simulate the effect of different reorder levels, we do the following:

Create new worksheet (Insert Worksheet). Name the worksheet **Reorder**.

For the worksheet Inventory, enter the reorder level *r* in cell D12 as Reorder!B12.

Go back to the worksheet **Reorder**. Starting with row 14,

A14: = Inventory!D122

(This means that we want to record the average expected costs in that worksheet.)

Create the values you want to try along B14:J14. Insert values 1:25 for A15:A39. Select the range A14:J39. Click the Data menu. Click Table.

In the Table Dialog Box, enter cell B12 for row input cell (i.e., replace the row input cell with values B14:J14) and the value A1 in the column cell.

The effect is that each value in the range B14:J14 is substituted for cell B12 (i.e., the reorder level). Each value in the range B11:B114 is then substituted in cell A1, the workbook is recalculated, and the resulting value in cell Inventory!D122 is then entered in the appropriate cell in the matrix. Average across the 100 simulation sets to get the average service level.

The figure in the worksheet page shows a plot of the effect of r on service level. Note that the service level improves with r.

We can also similarly record the expected cost per unit time vs r. Note the effect of r on system costs.

15.7 RANDOM LEAD TIME

Suppose the lead time were a random variable. Data have indicated that the lead time has the following distribution:

TABLE 15.1 Lead time and associated possibilities

Lead Time	Probability
1	0.33
2	0.33
3	0.34

Create a new worksheet. Name it **InvLead**. Copy the contents of the Inventory worksheet to this new worksheet. Other than a few changes that we discuss below, the Invlead worksheet is the same as the Inventory worksheet.

The *only* change is that the InvLead worksheet permits lead times to be a random variable.

Create a new worksheet (using the File New Worksheet command). Name the worksheet **Parameters**. This worksheet will contain the lead time distribution.

Then enter the values as follows (in the worksheet Parameters), starting with the cell A1, at the top left of the worksheet:

0.33	0	0.33	1
0.33	0.33	0.66	2
0.34	0.66	1.00	3

In the worksheet InvLead do the following:

In the rows for the lead time enter

=VLOOKUP(RAND(),Parameters!*B*2:*D*4,3)

Copy this to all cells in the column M17:M116

Now run the spreadsheet again and create the new graphs. You will have to use the Data Table command to run the spreadsheet for different values of *r*. Discuss the values obtained and recorded in the worksheet.

15.8 THE FASHION STORE

The Fashion Store sells fashion items, which it has to order many months in advance of the fashion season in order to get a good price on the items. Each unit costs Fashion $100. These units are sold to customers at a price of $160 per unit. Items not sold during the season can be sold to the outlet store at $75 per unit. If the store runs out of an item during the season, it has to obtain the item from alternative sources, and the cost including air freight to Fashion is $190 per unit.

Analysis of past historical data indicates that the demand follows a normal distribution with a mean of 85 units, and the standard deviation is 25 units.

Fashion wants help in choosing the initial order quantity to maximize store profits. Use an Excel simulation model to choose this optimal initial order quantity.

Examine the worksheet FASHION.XLS in the CD attached to this book. Run the worksheet to generate the graph of inventory vs. expected profit shown in Figure 15.2. Read off

FIGURE 15.2 Inventory vs. expected profit

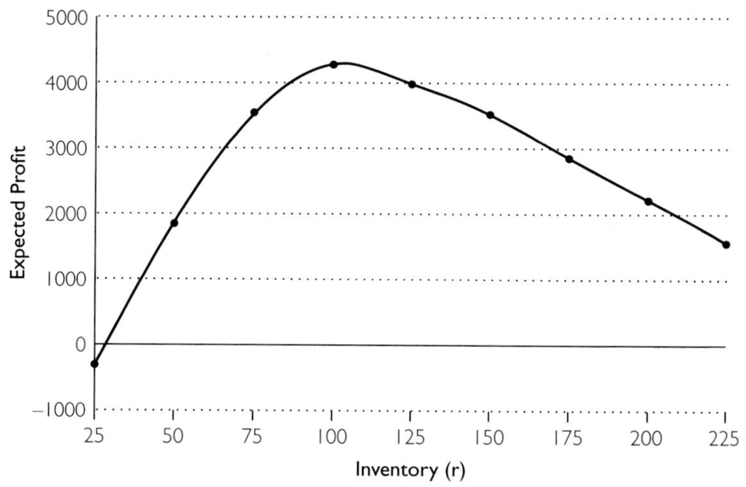

the optimal order quantity. Simulate the service level implied by this order quantity. Run the two example problems FASHION.XLS and STECO.XLS to familiarize yourself with the software.

15.9 INVENTORY CONTROL FOR STABLE DEMAND ENVIRONMENTS: THE ECONOMIC ORDER QUANTITY MODEL

In this section, we focus on systems with predictable demand, i.e., low forecast error. In such contexts, we will focus on the impact of set-up costs and their interaction with holding costs. We will develop a model of optimal batch sizes, study the impact of problem parameters, and then focus on the managerial implications of such a model.

The costs considered are (1) holding or carrying costs, (2) production or procurement costs, and (3) variable costs. Holding or carrying costs are per unit per unit time and include costs of storage facilities, handling, insurance, pilferage, obsolescence, opportunity cost of capital, and so on. Production or procurement costs are fixed costs per batch: ordering or set-up costs and costs to prepare the purchase or production order, equipment setups, moving out previous stock, and transportation (a single delivery truck). Variable costs include per-unit charges associated with shortage costs, loss, delay, or sale.

15.9.1 An Inventory Policy

An inventory policy consists of two parameters—the quantity ordered and frequency of orders. Each inventory policy has an associated cost to the organization.

Exercise: Choosing an Inventory Policy

You manage the warehouse of the Chicago Public Schools, and you are considering the purchase of copier paper, one of your largest-selling items. Although an individual school may fluctuate a bit in its demand, your aggregate demand for the item (from the 600 schools) is fairly constant at 100,000 cases for the year. Due to your volume, your supplier has agreed to provide you an everyday low price of \$55.00 a case. The board of education, tired of what they consider "wasted" use of the warehouse, is considering renting out excess space to a local business and charging you the same market value for the space you use. You calculate that it will cost about \$4.00 per case per year to hold each case. The cost of red tape each time an order is placed and the supplier's delivery charges yield a fixed ordering cost of \$75.00.

Consider the following inventory policy:

1. Place an order for Q units.
2. When inventory reaches zero, place another order for Q units and repeat.
3. Assume lead time is zero.

   Which of these inventory policies do you recommend?

   1) Review daily, resulting in daily shipments of about 385 cases each

   2) Review weekly, resulting in order sizes of about 1,923 cases each

   3) Place an order each month of about 8,333 cases each

   4) Place only two orders per year at about 50,000 cases each

4. If the lead time were to increase to three weeks, would your order quantity change? Explain.

Exercise: Evaluating the Cost of an Inventory Policy

To calculate the costs of each policy, let:

d = yearly demand in units

h = holding costs in dollars per unit per year

s = setup or ordering costs in dollars

Q = quantity of each order

Q uniquely defines this simple inventory policy.

Total Cost (AHO) = Annual Carrying Costs + Annual Ordering Costs

$$AHO = \frac{Q}{2}h + \frac{d}{Q}s$$

So

d = 100,000 units/year

h = \$4/unit/year

s = \$75

1) $Q = 385,\ AHO = \left(\frac{385}{2}\right)4 + \left(\frac{100{,}000}{385}\right)75 = 20{,}250$

2) $Q = 1{,}923,\ AHO = \left(\frac{1{,}923}{2}\right)4 + \left(\frac{100{,}000}{1{,}923}\right)75 = 7{,}746$

3) $Q = 8{,}333,\ AHO = \left(\frac{8{,}333}{2}\right)4 + \left(\frac{100{,}000}{8{,}333}\right)75 = 17{,}566$

4) $Q = 50{,}000,\ AHO = \left(\frac{50{,}000}{2}\right)4 + \left(\frac{100{,}000}{50{,}000}\right)75 = 100{,}150$

From these policies, the lowest cost is to order weekly with Q = 1,923.

Economic Order Quantity (EOQ) Model

Consider the following inventory model:

Place an order for Q units. When inventory reaches zero, place another order for Q units and repeat.

d = yearly demand in units

h = carrying or holding costs in dollars per unit per year

s = setup or ordering costs in dollars

Q^* = Economic Order Quantity (EOQ)

$Q^* = EOQ = \sqrt{\frac{2ds}{h}}$ minimizes the total cost function:

$$AHO = \frac{Q^*}{2}h + \frac{d}{Q^*}s$$

For

d = 100,000 units/year

h = \$4/unit/year

s = \$75

$$Q^* = \sqrt{\frac{2(100{,}000)(75)}{4}} = 1{,}936$$

$$AHO = \left(\frac{1{,}936}{2}\right)4 + \left(\frac{100{,}000}{1{,}936}\right)75 = 7{,}746$$

Assumptions Underlying the Basic EOQ Model

- It is a single-product model.
- Demand is known and reasonably constant.
- Lead time is constant.
- Each order is received in a single delivery.
- There are no quantity discounts.

15.9.2 A Service Application: Training Airline Flight Attendants

You manage the training department for airline attendants for a major airline, and you have to organize and plan the training sessions for all new hires. Each week personnel sends you a list of the new hires that you must schedule into the next available training session—they are on the payroll and basically idle until they can be trained and put into service. The yearly demand for new attendants is fairly constant at 1,200; personnel is always interviewing and hiring to keep up with the demand. The new hires, on average, cost the company about $40,000 per year in salary and benefits.

You wonder if there is a better way to think about the costs in the system and manage them. First you realize that personnel and training should coordinate better. Why should personnel put someone on the payroll before they can be scheduled for training? After all, a new hire won't argue about a week here or there on a start date. This seems like an easy thing to accomplish, but it certainly puts the burden on you to schedule the sessions and keep personnel abreast of your plans. Next you wonder how to best plan the training sessions: **How often should you hold sessions, and how many trainees should you put in each class?** The combined costs of the teachers, the conference rooms, and so on result in a fixed cost of $10,000 per training session.

How should you plan the sessions to minimize total cost?

Notice that if we set $K = 10{,}000$, $h = 40{,}000$, and $d = 1{,}200$, we get an economic order quantity that is close to 25, which corresponds to training sessions every week to cover the new hires that week. The associated total cost is $980,000. Note that if training sessions were held once a month, the corresponding cost would be $2.12 million.

15.9.3 The Benefits of Part Commonality

Consider a decision by a company to replace two separate parts with a single common part. For example, suppose General Motors were to replace the separate batteries in car models produced at a plant with a single common battery. How might such a decision decrease inventory costs? We will use the EOQ model to get such an estimate.

Old system:

$$Q_1 = \sqrt{\frac{2d_1 s}{h}} = \sqrt{\frac{2s}{h}}\sqrt{d_1}$$

$$Q_2 = \sqrt{\frac{2d_2 s}{h}} = \sqrt{\frac{2s}{h}}\sqrt{d_2}$$

$$\text{Average inventory} = I = \frac{Q_1 + Q_2}{2} = \frac{1}{2}\sqrt{\frac{2s}{h}}\left(\sqrt{d_1} + \sqrt{d_2}\right)$$

Combined new system:

$$Q_{new} = \sqrt{\frac{2(d_1 + d_2)s}{h}} = \sqrt{\frac{2s}{h}}\sqrt{d_1 + d_2}$$

$$\text{New average inventory } = I_{new} = \frac{1}{2}\sqrt{\frac{2s}{h}}\sqrt{d_1 + d_2}$$

$$\text{Let } d = d_1 = d_2, \text{ then } \frac{I_{new}}{I} = \frac{1}{\sqrt{2}} \approx 70\%$$

The inventory is reduced by 30% when parts are combined.

15.10 INVENTORY CONTROL UNDER UNCERTAIN DEMAND ENVIRONMENTS: SINGLE-PERIOD NEWSVENDOR MODEL

Our focus is on problems where decisions regarding inventory are made once for an entire season when demand is uncertain. Examples of products that might require inventory decisions that cover demand over a single period include

- newspapers/magazines,
- fruits/flowers,
- baked goods,
- fashion products,
- hotel room reservations, and
- airline reservations.

15.10.1 An Example: The Fashion Store

The Fashion Store sells fashion items. These items have to be ordered in advance of the season and produced in Asia in order to get products at a low price point. Suppose that each unit costs the Fashion Store \$100 but can be sold at retail for \$160. Assume that items not sold during the season can be salvaged, i.e., sold to an outlet store for \$75 per unit. In order to guarantee excellent customer service, assume that if the store runs out of an item during the season, it commits to air ship the item to the customer at a cost to the store of \$190 per unit, while continuing to charge the customer \$160 per unit. How should the Fashion Store choose its initial order quantity to maximize overall expected profits?

15.10.2 Historical Demand Data

What should we do?

Look at historical demand data.

Historical data from comparable items over the last few years include 100 demand observations as follows:

86	94	90	86	82	84	91	76	85	83	92	82	89	88	79	83	83	85	89	90
73	84	86	90	90	92	83	91	85	85	82	81	81	76	81	81	78	85	84	82
88	86	85	88	86	89	87	84	83	79	90	87	83	87	82	81	85	84	87	89
82	80	92	85	88	85	83	87	84	84	86	80	87	80	89	79	83	80	86	87
81	93	91	89	80	86	87	86	88	84	81	84	84	82	77	93	94	97	87	75

A frequency table of these points and the corresponding cumulative probabilities for each demand value are as follows:

Demand (D)	*Frequency*	*P(demand) P(D)*	*Cum. Prob. P(Demand ≤ D)*
73	1	0.01	0.01
75	1	0.01	0.02
76	2	0.02	0.04
77	1	0.01	0.05
78	1	0.01	0.06
79	3	0.03	0.09
80	5	0.05	0.14
81	7	0.07	0.21
82	7	0.07	0.28
83	8	0.08	0.36
84	10	0.10	0.46
85	10	0.10	0.56
86	9	0.09	0.65
87	8	0.08	0.73
88	5	0.05	0.78
89	6	0.06	0.84
90	5	0.05	0.89
91	3	0.03	0.92
92	3	0.03	0.95
93	2	0.02	0.97
94	2	0.02	0.99
97	1	0.01	1.00
	100	1.0	

The sample mean is 85 units, and the standard deviation is 4.43 units.

15.10.3 Marginal Cost Analysis

Suppose we are trying to decide whether to order an inventory of 85 units for the start of the season or increase the inventory ordered to 86 units.

We will do a marginal analysis of moving from 85 to 86 units of inventory.

We increase our initial inventory from 85 to 86.

If the extra item is not sold, we incur a marginal cost of 100 – 75 = 25.

If the extra item is sold, we save the cost of procuring the product from an alternate source and thus gain a marginal profit of 190 – 100 = 90

We have the following probabilities:

- p(The extra item is not sold) = p(Demand ≤ 85)
- p(The extra item is sold) = p(Demand > 85)

Thus we would increase the order from 85 to 86 if:

- p(Demand ≤ 85) × 25 < p(Demand > 85) × 90
- 0.56(25) < 0.44(90)
- 14 < 39.6

In general we increase our inventory I while

p(Demand ≤ I) × (Cost of excess item) < p(Demand > I) × (Cost of item shortage)

We would stop increasing I when

p(Demand ≤ I) × (Cost of excess item) = p(Demand > I) × (Cost of item shortage)

If we allow

$$C_e = \text{Cost of an excess item}$$

$$C_s = \text{Cost of an item short}$$

Then rewriting the relationship above, we get:

$$p(D \le I)C_e = p(D > I)C_s$$

$$p(D \le I)C_e = (1 - p(D \le I))C_s$$

$$0 = C_s - p(D \le I)(C_s + C_e)$$

or we find the inventory level r so that,

$$P(D \le r) = \frac{C_s}{C_s + C_e}$$

15.10.4 The Newsvendor Model Summary

Consider an inventory decision maker who has to choose inventory before demand is realized. Suppose that C_e = is the cost per unit of an excess item at the end of the period. If the purchase or production cost is less than the salvage value, then we will have $C_e > 0$. Next, suppose that C_s = is the cost per unit of an item short. This cost will include the cost to satisfy demand from alternate source and the associated opportunity cost or goodwill cost. Given these parameters, the optimal probability of being in stock should be set as

$$ser^* = \frac{C_s}{C_s + C_e}$$

ser = probability that all demand in a period is satisfied immediately from primary stock

From our example, we have

$$C_e = 25$$

$$C_s = 90$$

So,

$$= \frac{C_s}{C_s + C_e} = \frac{90}{90 + 25} = 0.782$$

From frequency distribution in Section 15.11.2, for an in-stock probability of 0.782 we get

$$r^* \approx 89$$

When Demand Follows a Normal Distribution

Example 1. Fashion Store: Approximate by normal with $m = 85$ and $\sigma = 4.43$.

$$ser^* = \frac{C_s}{C_s + C_e} = \frac{90}{90 + 25} = 0.782$$

so

$$r^* = 85 + Z_{.782}(4.43) = 85 + 0.78(4.43) = 88.45 \approx 89$$

Example 2. Fashion Store: Approximate by normal with $m = 85$ and $\sigma = 4.43$

Suppose the Fashion Store wants to provide a service level of 90%. What level of inventory is required?

$$r_{.90} = 85 + Z_{.90}(4.43) = 85 + 1.29(4.43) = 90.7 \approx 91$$

Therefore, if Fashion has an inventory of 91 items, then with probability 0.90, all the demand in a period is satisfied from primary stock.

If a service level of 90% is used, then Fashion is either losing money, or their estimates of C_e and C_s were incorrect.

15.11 UNCERTAIN DEMAND AND ORDERING COSTS

In this section we will consider the impact of demand uncertainty on the inventory policy. This will enable us to explore many more reasons for the existence of inventory in systems. The basic idea is that in the presence of uncertainty and lead time for delivery, orders have to be placed well in advance of inventory depletion in order to guarantee a high level of availability.

15.11.1 Impact of Lead Time

If we consider the problem in Section 14.10.1, with constant demand and just add in a lead time L between order placement and delivery, when should orders be placed?

Orders should be placed when the inventory level hits dL. This level is called the *reorder level.* The order size remains Q (as calculated in the EOQ model).

15.11.2 Lead Time and Demand Uncertainty

In the presence of lead time and demand uncertainty, the reorder level requires us to decide how much of the demand should be satisfied from stock. This factor can be expressed as *service level* or as a *probability.*

Probability Level

When expressed as a *probability,* the goal of the inventory is to satisfy demand from stock with a certain likelihood. The probability level is a number that the customers (generating the demand) can use to do their own planning. This probability will depend (intuitively) on the industry and on the extent of competition faced by the company.

If demand follows a normal distribution, merely generate a z value that corresponds to the desired cumulative probability. Then set the reorder level as

$$r = (dL) + (z\sigma L)$$

where σ refers to the standard deviation of demand per unit time and d is the mean demand per unit time.

15.11.3 A (*Q*,*r*) Policy

We now formalize our multiperiod inventory system. By convention, some parameters are usually given in annual terms (the EOQ parameters), while other parameters are stated in smaller period terms (the lead time parameters).

s = ordering cost

d = average annual demand

h = annual holding cost per item

L = fixed lead time in periods

ser = planned in stock probability

Z_{ser} = the z value that generates the required in stock probability

m = mean demand during a period

σ = standard deviation of demand during a period

First we calculate

$$Q = \sqrt{\frac{2ds}{h}}$$

And then the reorder point:

$$r = (mL) + \left(Z_{ser}\sigma\sqrt{L}\right)$$

$$\text{Average physical inventory level} = \frac{Q}{2} + r - (mL)$$

15.11.4 An Example Problem

Consider the inventory decision-making problem faced by Steco, a retailer of bolts. Steco experiences a weekly demand for these bolts that can be modeled as a normal distribution with a mean of 100 units and a standard deviation of 5 units. Suppose it costs Steco $5 per unit to procure these bolts, and the product has a holding cost per bolt per year of 20% of its procurement cost. Assume that the ordering cost associated with replenishment is $25 per order and that the delivery lead time for an order is 1 week. Suppose Steco would like to choose its inventory in order to ensure a less than 6% probability of stocking out. Assume 50 weeks per year.

Develop a (Q, r) policy for Steco.

Answer

Ordering cost = s = $25/order

Holding cost = h = $1/unit/year

Annual Demand = $d = 100 \times 50 = 5{,}000$ units/year

$$Q = \sqrt{\frac{2sd}{h}} = 500$$

$m = 100$, $\sigma = 5$, $L = 1$, $ser = 0.94$, and $Z_{0.94} = 1.56$ (from any standard normal table)

$r = 107.8$

Thus Steco should reorder Q units whenever the pipeline inventory level falls to below r units.

Steco's average inventory level = $\frac{Q}{2} + r - (mL) = 257.8$.

15.12 CHAPTER SUMMARY

This chapter provided a summary of tools used throughout the book. The main tools we focused on were linear and mixed integer programming, simulation, and calculus-based inventory models. The goal of these models is to enable optimal responses to problem parameters, thus improving supply chain performance.

Bibliography

[1] Arntzen, B., Brown, G.G., Harrison, T.P., Trafton, L.L. Global Supply Chain Management at Digital Equipment Corporation. *Interfaces,* 25(1):69–93, January–February 1995.

[2] Association for Automatic Identification and Mobility. What is RFID? http://www.aimglobal.org/technologies/rfid/what_is_rfid.asp, downloaded July 2012.

[3] Balachander, S., and Farquhar, P. Gaining More by Stocking Less: A Competitive Analysis of Product Availability. *Marketing Science,* 13(1):3–22, Winter 1994.

[4] Banks, J., and Moorthy, S. A Model of Price Promotions with Consumer Search. *International Journal of Industrial Organization,* 17(3):371–398, April 1999.

[5] Barta, P., and Bellman, E. Sri Lanka Is Grateful, But What to Do With the Ski Parkas? *Wall Street Journal,* February 3, 2005. http://online.wsj.com/article/0,,SB110736905464843808,00.html, downloaded September 27, 2012.

[6] Bartholdi, J.J., and Eisenstein, D.D. Bucket Brigade Assembly Lines. Georgia Tech College of Engineering, H. Milton Stewart School of Industrial and Systems Engineering. http://www.bucketbrigades.com, downloaded 2006.

[7] Blackburn, J.D. *Time-Based Competition: The Next Battleground in American Manufacturing.* Homewood, IL: McGraw-Hill Professional Series, 1990.

[8] Blackburn, J.D., Guide, D.R., Jr., Souza, G.C., Van Wassenhove, L.N. Reverse Supply Chains for Commercial Returns. *California Management Review,* 46(2):4–22, Winter 2004.

[9] Blumenfeld, D., Burns, L.D., Daganzo, C.F., Frick, M.C., and Hall, R.W. Reducing Logistics Costs at General Motors. *Interfaces,* 17(1):26–47, January–February 1987.

[10] Bovet, D., and Martha, J. Value Proposition: Crafting the Offer. *Value Nets: Breaking the Supply Chain to Unlock Hidden Profits.* New York: John Wiley & Sons, 2000.

[11] Boyaci, T., and Ray, S. Product Differentiation and Capacity Cost Interaction in Time and Price Sensitive Markets. *Manufacturing and Service Operations Management,* 5(1):18–36, Winter 2003.

[12] Burnson, P. 22nd Annual State of the Logistics Report: A Bumpy Ride. *Logistics Management,* 26–38, July 2011.

[13] Byrnes, J.L.S., and Shapiro, R.D. Unlocking Inter-Company Operating Ties. Working paper, Harvard Business School, 92-058,1991.

[14] Chengalur, S. Kodak and Wastewise: Beyond Recycling. May 2005. http://www.epa.gov/climateleadership/documents/events/may2005/chengalur0505.pdf, downloaded June 2012.

[15] Chocolate Sourcemap. *Sourcemap.* http://sourcemap.com/view/2176, downloaded July 2012.

[16] Clark, K.C. Project Scope and Project Performance: The Effect of Parts Strategy and Supplier Involvement on Product Development. *Management Science,* 35(10):1247–1263, 1989.

[17] Clemens, R. Meat Traceability and Consumer Assurance in Japan. MATRIC Briefing Paper 03-MBP 5, Ames, IA: Iowa State University, September 2003.

[18] Cohen, M., Cull, C., Lee, H.L., Willen, D. Saturn's Supply-Chain Innovation: High Value in After-Sales Service. *Sloan Management Review* Reprint 4147, 41(4):93–101, Summer 2000.

[19] Cohen, M., Kamesan, P.V, Kleindorfer, P., Lee, H.L., Tekerian, A. Optimizer: IBM's Multi-Echelon Inventory System for Managing Service Logistics. *Interfaces,* 20(1):65–82, January–February 1990.

[20] Cohen, M.A., Agarwal, N., and Agarwal, V. Winning in the Aftermarket. Harvard Business School, Case R0605H, Cambridge, MA, May 1, 2006.

[21] Coke.net. New Ways to Take Costs Out of the Grocery Retail Food Pipeline. https://www.ccrrc.org/studies/new-ways-to-take-costs-out-of-the-retail-food-pipeline/, downloaded November 2012.

[22] Council of Supply Chain Management Professionals. CSCMP Supply Chain Management Definitions. http://cscmp.org/aboutcscmp/definitions.asp, downloaded June 2012.

[23] Crafted with Pride, Inc. Domestic Sourcing. Report provided to author, 1990.

[24] DC Velocity Staff. Gillette Shaves Costs with RFID. http://www.dcvelocity.com/articles/20051101newsworthy_gillette_shaves_costs_with_rfid/, downloaded July 2012.

[25] Dennis, M.J., and Kambil, A. Service Management: Building Profits After the Sale. *Supply Chain Management Review,* 7(1):42–48, 2003.

[26] Deshpande, V., Cohen, M., and Donohue, K. An Empirical Study of Service Differentiation for Weapon System Service Parts. *Operations Research,* 51(4):518–530, July–August 2003.

[27] Deshpande, V, Iyer, A.V., and Cho, R. Efficient Supply Chain Management at U.S. Coast Guard Using Part-Age Dependent Supply Replenishment Policies. *Operations Research,* 54(6):1028–1040, November–December 2006.

[28] Dixon, L., and Porter, A.M. JIT II: Revolution in Buying and Selling. Dallas, TX: Cahners Publishing Company, 1994.

[29] Doppelt, B., and Nelson, H. Extended Producer Responsibility and Product Take-Back: Applications for the Pacific Northwest. The Center for Watershed and Community Health, Portland: Portland State University, March 2001.

[30] Duke, M.T. 2012 Walmart Global Responsibility Report. http://www.walmartstores.com/sites/responsibility-report/2012, downloaded July 2012.

[31] Duke, M.T. Milestone Meeting 2012. April 18, 2012. http://news.walmart.com/media-library/youtube/walmart-2012-milestone-meeting-highlights-nkneqjdggas, downloaded September 2012.

[32] Eisenstein, D.D., and Iyer, A.V. Garbage Collection in Chicago: A Dynamic Scheduling Model. *Management Science,* 43(7):922–933, July 1997.

[33] Eisenstein, D.D., and Iyer, A.V. Separating Logistics Flows to Improve Distribution at the Chicago Public School System. *Operations Research,* 44(2):265–273, November–December 1996.

[34] Elmaghraby, W., and Keskinocak, P. Technology for Transportation Bidding at the Home Depot. Case study, Atlanta: School of Industrial and Systems Engineering, Georgia Institute of Technology, November 2000.

[35] Eppen, G.D., and Iyer, A.V. Backup Agreements in Fashion Buying: The Value of Upstream Flexibility. *Management Science,* 43(11):1469–1484, November 1997.

[36] Eppen, G.D., Martin, R.K., and Schrage, L.E. A Scenario-Based Approach to Capacity Planning. *Operations Research,* 37(4):517–527, July–August 1989.

[37] Fearon, J.D. Measuring Humanitarian Impact. Discussion Issues, Center for International Security and Cooperation, Stanford University, August 24, 2002.

[38] Feder, B. Moving the Pampers Faster Cuts Everyone's Costs. *New York Times,* July 14, 1991. http://www.nytimes.com/1991/07/14/business/moving-the-pampers-faster-cuts-everyone-s-costs.html?pagewanted=all&src=pm, downloaded September 2012.

[39] Fetzinger, E., and Lee, H.L. Mass Customization at Hewlett-Packard: The Power of Postponement. *Harvard Business Review,* Reprint 97101:115–122, January–February 1996.

[40] Fine, C. *Clockspeed: Winning Industry Control in the Age of Temporary Advantage.* New York: Perseus Books, 1998.

[41] Flaherty, M-T and Dalby, J.S. Liz Claiborne, Inc., and Ruentex Industries, Ltd. Harvard Business School, Case 9-690-048, Cambridge, MA, March 6, 1990.

[42] Food Manufacturing Institute. Supermarket Facts: Industry Overview 2010. http://www.fmi.org/research-resources/supermarket-facts, downloaded July 2012.
[43] Fuller, J.B., O'Connor, J., and Rawlinson, R. Tailored Logistics: The Next Advantage. *Harvard Business Review,* Reprint 97101:87–98, May–June 1993.
[44] Fuller, T. China Trade Unbalances Shipping. *New York Times,* January 29, 2006. http://www.nytimes.com/2006/01/29/business/worldbusiness/29iht-ships.html?pagewanted=all&_moc.semityn.www, downloaded September 2012.
[45] Goodguide. http://www.goodguide.com, downloaded July 2012.
[46] GoodmanSparks. Revenue Share Services (Route Agreements). http://www.goodmansparks.co.uk/article.php/29, downloaded June 2012.
[47] Gorham, J. The Player. (Blockbuster May end rental revenue-sharing programs). *Forbes,* September 3, 2001. http://business.highbeam.com/392705/article-1G1-77353205/player, downloaded September 2012.
[48] Graves, S.C., and Willems, S.P. Optimizing Strategic Safety Stock Placement in Supply Chains. Working paper, Sloan School of Management, Massachusetts Institute of Technology, January 1998.
[49] Green, M., and Shaw, M.J. Supply Chain Integration Through Information Sharing: Channel Partnership between Walmart and Procter & Gamble. Working paper, Department of Business Administration, University of Illinois at Urbana Champaign, March 2000.
[50] Greenpeace. Dirty Laundry 2: Hung Out to Dry. 2011. http://www.greenpeace.org/international/en/publications/reports/Dirty-Laundry-2, downloaded July 2012.
[51] Gue, K. CrossDocking: Just-In-Time for Distribution. Working paper, Naval Postgraduate School, May 8, 2001.
[52] Gue, K., and Meller, R.D. Aisle Configurations for Unit Load Warehouses. Working paper, Auburn University, 2006.
[53] Gue, K. Warehouse Tours. http://gallery.mac.com/krgue, downloaded September 2011.
[54] Hammond, J., and Raman, A. Sport Obermeyer. Harvard Business School, 695022-HCB-ENG, Cambridge, MA, October 13, 1994.
[55] Hammond, J.H. Quick Response in the Apparel Industry. Harvard Business School, Case N9-690-038, February 1990.
[56] Hammond, J.H., and Kelly, M. Merloni Elettrodomesticii SpA: The Transit Point Experiment. Harvard Business School, Case 9-690-003, 1992.
[57] Hart, C.W. The Power of Unconditional Service Guarantees. *Harvard Business Review,* Reprint 88405, 54–62, July 1988.
[58] Henke, J. OEM Purchasing Summit: Tier 1 Supplier Working Relations Study. May 23, 2011. http://www.oesa.org/Doc-Vault/Presentations/2011/052311-SAA-Henke/Henke-Planning-Perspectives-for-posting.pdf, downloaded July 2012.
[59] Heskett, J. Logistics: Essential to Strategy. *Harvard Business Review,* Reprint R0605H, 85–96, 1977.
[60] Iyer, A.V. and M.E. Bergen. Quick Response in Manufacturer-Retailer Channels. *Management Science,* 43(4):559–570, April 1997.
[61] Iyer, A., and Seshadri, S. Transforming an Indian Manufacturing Company: The Rane Brake Linings Case. In *Building Supply Chain Excellence in Emerging Economies,* Eds. H. Lee and C-Y Lee, New York: Springer Verlag, 441–454, 2006.
[62] Iyer, A., and Sommer, S. The Furniture Supply Chain in Dubois County: An INDOT Report. Joint Transportation Research Program, 2008. http://www.researchgate.net/publication/27230308_Indiana_Furniture_Supply_Chain, downloaded September 2012.
[63] Iyer, A., and Zelikovsky, A. *Orchestrating Supply Chain Opportunities.* New York: Business Expert Press, 2011.
[64] Iyer, A., Seshadri, S., Vasher, R. *Toyota Supply Chain Management.* New York: McGraw Hill Trade Press, 2009.

[65] Iyer, A.V., and Van Wassenhove, L.N. A Framework for Humanitarian Logistics Coordination. Working paper, Krannert School of Management, Purdue University, July 2003.

[66] Iyer, A.V., and Ye, J. Assessing the Value of Information Sharing in a Promotional Retail Environment. *Manufacturing and Service Operations Management,* 2(2):128–143, Spring 2000.

[67] Iyer, A.V., and Ye, J. A Network Model of a Promotion-Sensitive Grocery Retail Environment. *Networks,* 38(4):169–180, 2001.

[68] Iyer, A.V., Schwarz, J.E., and Zenios, S. A Principal Agent Model for Product Specification and Production. *Management Science,* 51(1), January–February 2005.

[69] Jaikumar, R., and Upton, D.M. The Coordination of Global Manufacturing. In *Globalization, Technology and Competition: The Fusion of Computers and Telecommunications,* Eds. Stephen P. Bradley, Jerry A. Hausman, and Richard L. Nolan. Boston, MA: Harvard Business School Press, 1993.

[70] Jejurikar, R., and Nakra, V. Project Scorpio: A Tale of Category Creation. *India Times,* April 2004. http://www.etstrategicmarketing.com/Smmarch-april04/art7-1.html, downloaded July 2012

[71] Kalagnanam, J., Dawande, M., Trumbo, M., and Lee, H. The Surplus Inventory Matching Problem in the Process Industry. *Operations Research,* 48(4):505–516, July 2000.

[72] Kearney, A.T. Grocery Information Flow. Presentation at Council of Supply Chain Management Professionals conference, San Antonio, TX, October 11–14, 1992.

[73] Kopicki, R., Berg, M.J., Legg, L., Dasappa, V., and Maggioni, C. Reuse and Recycling: Reverse Logistics Opportunities. Council of Logistics Management, 1993.

[74] Kumar, N., and Linguri, S. Fashion Sense. *Business Strategy Review,* London Business School, London, Summer 2006. http://bsr.london.edu/lbs-article/247/index.html, downloaded June 2012

[75] Lalonde, B.J., Cooper, M.C., and Noordeweier, T.G. *Customer Service: A Management Perspective.* Chicago: Council of Logistics Management, 1988.

[76] Laseter, T.M., Houston, P.W., Wright, J.L., and Park, J.Y. Amazon Your Industry: Extracting the Value from the Value Chain. *Strategy & Business,* January 2000. http://www.strategy-business.com/article/10479?gko=7b809, downloaded September 2012

[77] Ledyard, J.O., Olson, M., Porter, D., Swanson, J.A., and Torma, D.P. The First Use of a Combinatorial Value Auction for Transportation Services. *Interfaces,* 32(5): 4–12, 2002.

[78] Lee, H.L. The Triple-A Supply Chain. *Harvard Business Review,* Reprint R0410F, October 2004.

[79] Lee, H.L., and Kopczak, L. Hewlett-Packard DeskJet Printer Supply Chain (A). *Harvard Business Review,* Reprint GS3A, 2001.

[80] Lee, H.L., Padmanabhan, V., and Whang, S. The Bullwhip Effect in Supply Chains. *Sloan Management Review,* Reprint 3837, 38(3):93–102, Spring 1997.

[81] Levins, J., Samii, R., and Van Wassenhove, L.N. Fuels: A Humanitarian Necessity in 2003 Post-Conflict Iraq, The Role of UNJLC. INSEAD Case Study, (04/2005-5290), 2005.

[82] Magretta, J. Fast, Global, and Entrepreneurial: Supply Chain Management, Hong Kong Style. Harvard Business School, Case R0605H, 1998.

[83] Manufacturing and Material Handling website. Sears New Shoe DC. Manufacturing and Material Handling, 1999. http://www.manufacturing.net/magazine/mmh/archives/1999/mmh0501.99/05wom.htm, downloaded June 2002

[84] Martin, A. Potential Costs of Promotions. Presentation at CSCMP conference, 1992.

[85] Martinez-de-Albeniz, V., and Simchi-Levi, D. Competition in the Supply Option Market. Working paper 189, Center for eBusiness, Massachusetts Institute of Technology, April 2003.

[86] McCardle, K., Rajaram, K., and Tang, C.S. Advance Booking Order Programs under Retail Competition. *Management Science,* 50(5):701–708, May 2004.

[87] McDonough, W., and Braungart, M. *Cradle to Cradle.* New York: North Point Press, 2002.

[88] Moore, E.W., Warmke, J.M., and Gorban, L.R. The Indispensable Role of Management Science in Centralizing Freight Operations at Reynolds Metal Company. *Interfaces,* 21(1): 107–129, January 1991.

[89] Moore, J.D. Team on Trent Engines. *Aviation Week and Space Technology,* 148(3):48, January 19, 1998.

[90] Narus, J.A., and Anderson, J.C. Rethinking Distribution: Adaptive Channels. *Harvard Business Review,* July–August: 112–120, 1996.

[91] Neary, L. Publishers push for new rules on unsold books. *NPR.* June 2008, http://www.npr.org/templates/story/story.php?storyId=91461568, downloaded June 2012.

[92] Nishiguchi, T. Competing Systems of Automotive Components Supply: An Examination of the Japanese 'Clustered Control' Model and the 'Alps' Structure. Policy Paper, International Motor Vehicle Program, Massachusetts Institute of Technology, 1987.

[93] O'Connor, M.C. Gillette Fuses RFID With Product Launch. *RFID Journal,* March 2006. http://www.rfidjournal.com/article/articleprint/2222/-1/1, downloaded September 2012

[94] O'Laughlin, K.A., Cooper, J., and Cabocel, E. European Transportation Infrastructure. In *Reconfiguring European Logistics Systems.* Chicago: Council of Logistics Management, 31–49, 1988.

[95] Oppenheim, J.M., Richardson, B., and Stendevad, C. A Standard for Relief. *McKinsey Quarterly,* July: 91–99, 2001.

[96] Oxford Dictionary. *Oxford Dictionaries,* "coordinate." http://oxforddictionaries.com/definition/english/coordinate, downloaded June 2012.

[97] Ozer, O., and Wei, W. Strategic Commitments for an Optimal Capacity Decision under Asymmetric Forecast Information. *Management Science,* 52(8):1238–1257, August 2006.

[98] Prahalad, C.K., and Hart, S. *Fortune at the Bottom of the Pyramid.* Upper Saddle River, NJ: Wharton School Publishing, 2006.

[99] PRWeb. NPD Reports on the U.S. Apparel Market 2011. *PRWeb.* March 29, 2012. http://www.prweb.com/releases/2012/3/prweb9343091.htm, downloaded May 2012.

[100] Ragsdale, C.T. Modeling and Solving LP Problems in a Spreadsheet. In *Spreadsheet Modeling and Decision Analysis,* Mason, OH: South-Western Cengage Learning, 43–114, 1995.

[101] Rivoli, P. *The Travels of a T-shirt in the Global Economy.* Hoboken, NJ: John Wiley & Sons, 2005.

[102] Samii, R., and Van Wassenhove, L.N. The United Nations Joint Logistical Center: The Afghanistan Crisis. INSEAD Case Study, No. 052003-5092, May 2003.

[103] Samii, R., and Van Wassenhove, L.N. UNJLC: The Genesis of a Humanitarian Coordination Platform. INSEAD Case Study, (04/2003-5093), 2003.

[104] SAP Customer Success Story: Chemicals. BASF Achieves Transparency in Its Ocean-Freight Supply Chain to Manage the Unexpected with SAP Event Management. http://www.sap.com/portugal/solutions/pdfs/BASF.pdf, downloaded July 2012.

[105] Schmidt, M., and Aschkenase, S. The Building Blocks of Service Excellence. *Supply Chain Management Review,* July–August: 34–40, 2004.

[106] SCOR-version 9. Supply Chain Operations Reference Model, 2008. http://www.supply-chain.org/scor, downloaded June 2012

[107] Scott, L. 21st Century Leadership. October 24, 2005. http://walmartwatch.com/wp-content/blogs.dir/2/files/pdf/21st_Century_Leadership.pdf, downloaded September 2012.

[108] Segel, A., Chu, M., and Herrero, G. Patrimonio Hoy. Harvard Business School, Case 9-805-064, 1–18, July 2006.

[109] Seidmann, A., and Sundarajan, A. Sharing Logistics Information Across Organizations: Technology, *Competition and Contracting,* 1–31, May 2003. http://oz.stern.nyu.edu/papers/slog.pdf, downloaded September 2012.

[110] Shapiro, S., Rangan, V.K., and Svoikla, J. Staple Yourself to an Order. *Harvard Business Review,* Reprint 92411, July–August 1992.

[111] Sheffi, Y. Combinatorial Auctions in the Procurement of Transportation Services. *Interfaces,* 34(4):245–252, 2004.

[112] Sheffi, Y. *The Resilient Enterprise: Overcoming Vulnerability for Competitive Advantage.* Cambridge, MA: The MIT Press, 2007.

[113] Sourcemap. Instructions for Sourcemap. http://sourcemap.com/info/instructions, downloaded July 2012.

[114] Stalk, G. Time: The Next Source of Competitive Advantage. *Harvard Business Review,* 41–51, July–August 1988.

[115] Steiner, R.L. Category Management: A Pervasive, New Vertical/Horizontal Format. *AntiTrust,* 77–81, Spring 2001.

[116] Stock J.R., and Lambert, D.M. Channels of Distribution. *Strategic Logistics Management,* 70–109, 1993.

[117] Thurow, R. In Battling Hunger, A New Advance: Peanut Butter Paste. *Wall Street Journal,* April 12, 2005.

[118] Tomasini, R.M., and Van Wassenhove, L.N. A Framework to Unravel, Prioritize, and Coordinate Vulnerability and Complexity Factors Affecting a Humanitarian Response Operation. Working paper, INSEAD Fontainbleu, February 2005.

[119] United States Department of Agriculture. New Products. 2009. http://www.ers.usda.gov/topics/food-markets-prices/processing-marketing/new-products.aspx, downloaded July 2012.

[120] United States Department of Agriculture. Livestock Slaughter 2011 Summary. April 2012. http://usda01.library.cornell.edu/usda/current/LiveSlauSu/LiveSlauSu-04-23-2012.pdf, downloaded April 2012.

[121] Venkatesan, R. Strategic Sourcing: To Make or Not to Make. *Harvard Business Review,* Reprint 92610, November–December 1992.

[122] Wendel, K. Lorain County Joins Revenue-Sharing Agreement for Wind Power. May 2011. http://www.wkyc.com/news/story.aspx?storyid=191333, downloaded June 2012.

[123] Wielgat, A. Manufacturing the Mahindra Way: India's Largest SUV Maker Turns Design and Development to Suppliers. *Automotive Industries,* October 1, 2002.

[124] Wise, R., and Baumgartner, P. Go Downstream: The New Profit Imperative in Manufacturing. *Harvard Business Review,* 99512, 134–141, September–October 1999.

[125] Zsidisin, G.A., and Smith, M.E. Managing Supply Risk with Early Supplier Involvement: A Case Study and Research Propositions. *Journal of Supply Chain Management,* 41(4):44, November 2005.

[126] Jin, M., and Wu, D. Coordinating Supplier Competition via Auctions, Working paper, Lehigh University, 2004. http://www.lehigh.edu/~sdw1/jin1.pdf, downloaded July 2012.

[127] Cachon, G., and Fisher, M. Campbell Soup's Continuous Product Replenishment Program: Evaluation and Enhanced Decision Rules. *Production and Operations Management,* 6:266–276, 1997.

[128] Blattberg, R.C., Eppen, G.D., and Lieberman, J. A Theoretical and Empirical Evaluation of Price Deals for Consumer Nondurables. *Journal of Marketing,* 45(1):116–129, Winter 1981.

[129] Walmart. Walmart U.S. Logistics. http://corporate.walmart.com/our-story/our-stores/logistics, downloaded December 4, 2012.

[130] Lecavalier, J. All Those Numbers: Logistics, Territory and Walmart. May 24, 2010. http://places.designobserver.com/feature/walmart-logistics/13598/, downloaded December 4, 2012.

Index

A

B

C

D

E

F

G

M

N

O

P

Q

R

S

T

U

V

W

Y

Z